"Rarely have I read a collection of such stimulating and suggestive theoretical and clinical essays by a range of scholars and practitioners of contemporary psychoanalytical psychotherapy for various mental illnesses understood in the context of 'dis-eases'. Drawing on the work of several traditional and modern schools of thought, these authors consider the constraints and restraints of body, mind, and society in the context of what group analysts call the 'tripartite matrix', with its emphasis on interpersonal relations, values and norms, and perhaps above all patterns of communication, both verbal and non-verbal. I was profoundly moved to realise the extent of the growth and development of a European federation of organisations, colleagues, languages and ideas, which augurs well for our continuing cooperation in the service of the well-being of our patients and clients, even in adverse political and economic conditions."

—*Earl Hopper*, *PhD, Mem.Inst.GA. DFAGPA, psychoanalyst, group analyst and organisational consultant in private practice in London*

"The special strength of this innovative book arises exactly from the connection between its topic and its intrinsic creativity: open to an international vision, this text shows a combination of curiosity in exploration and freedom from any official academic attitude, while going to depth into unusual psychoanalytic and widely cultural areas. I recommend *A Psychoanalytic Exploration on Sameness and Otherness* both as a fascinating read and as a potential educational instrument for psychologists, psychotherapists and psychoanalysts."

—*Stefano Bolognini*, *IPA Past President*

A PSYCHOANALYTIC EXPLORATION ON SAMENESS AND OTHERNESS

In dialogue with the most famous myth for the origin of different languages – The Tower of Babel – *A Psychoanalytic Exploration on Sameness and Otherness: Beyond Babel?* provides a series of timely reflections on the themes of sameness and otherness from a contemporary psychoanalytic perspective. How are we dealing with communication and its difficulties, the confusion of tongues and loss of common ground within a European context today? Can we move beyond Babel?

Confusion and feared loss of shared values and identity are a major part of the daily work of psychoanalytic psychotherapists. Bringing together an international range psychoanalytic practitioners and researchers, the book is divided into six parts and covers an array of resonant topics, including: language and translation; cultural identity; families and children; the cyber world; the psychotherapeutic process; and migration. Whereas the quest for unity, which underpins the myth of Babel, leads to mystification, simplification, and the exclusion of people or things, multilingual communities necessitate mutual understanding through dialogue. This book examines those factors that further or threaten communication, aiming not to reduce, but to gain complexity. It suggests that diversification enriches communication and that, by relating to others, we can create something new.

As opposed to cultural and linguistic homogeneity, Babel is not only a metaphor for mangled communication, alienation, and distraction, it is also about the acceptance or rejection of differences between self and other. This book will be of great interest to psychoanalytic psychotherapists and researchers from a wide variety of backgrounds.

Anne-Marie Schlösser is a psychologist and training and supervising analyst with the IPA, DPG, and DGPT, working in private practice after many years at the Department of Medical Psychology at the University of Goettingen. She is a member of German committees for the development of psychotherapy, an expert for psychoanalytic treatment in the German Health Services, past president of the DGPT and EFPP, and has offered training in psychoanalytic psychotherapy in Shanghai. She is Editor-in-Chief of the EFPP Book Series published by Routledge.

The EFPP Monograph Series
Anne-Marie Schlösser (Series Editor)

A series of Monographs produced in conjunction with the European Federation for Psychoanalytic Psychotherapy (EFPP). Each volume brings together writings on a particular topic by authors from several European countries. The EFPP promotes communication and discussion between psychotherapists across national boundaries in the child and adolescent, adult, family and group sections of the organisation, through its conferences and seminars on topics of interest in contemporary psychoanalytic psychotherapy. The organisation represents some 13,000 psychoanalytic psychotherapists in twenty-two countries in Western, Central and Eastern Europe and is concerned with many matters which are relevant to the profession, such as training and registration.

Recent titles in the series include:

Countertransference in Psychoanalytic Psychotherapy with Children and Adolescents
Edited by John Tsiantis, Dimitris Anastasopoulos, Anne-Marie Sandler & Brian Martindale

Invisible Boundaries
Psychosis and Autism in Children and Adolescents
Edited by Didier Houzel & Maria Rhode

Psychoanalytic Psychotherapy of the Severely Disturbed Adolescent
Edited by Dimitris Anastasopoulos, Margot Waddell & Effie Lignos

Families in Transformation
A Psychoanalytic Approach
Edited by Anna Maria Nicolo, Pierre Benghozi & Daniela Lucarelli

For further information about this series please visit
https://www.routledge.com/The-EFPP-Monograph-Series/book-series/KARNACEFPPPM

A PSYCHOANALYTIC EXPLORATION ON SAMENESS AND OTHERNESS

Beyond Babel?

Edited by Anne-Marie Schlösser

LONDON AND NEW YORK

First published 2020
by Routledge
2 Park Square, Milton Park, Abingdon, Oxon OX14 4RN

and by Routledge
52 Vanderbilt Avenue, New York, NY 10017

Routledge is an imprint of the Taylor & Francis Group, an informa business

© 2020 selection and editorial matter, Anne-Marie Schlösser; individual chapters, the contributors

The right of Anne-Marie Schlösser to be identified as the author of the editorial material, and of the authors for their individual chapters, has been asserted in accordance with sections 77 and 78 of the Copyright, Designs and Patents Act 1988.

All rights reserved. No part of this book may be reprinted or reproduced or utilised in any form or by any electronic, mechanical, or other means, now known or hereafter invented, including photocopying and recording, or in any information storage or retrieval system, without permission in writing from the publishers.

Trademark notice: Product or corporate names may be trademarks or registered trademarks, and are used only for identification and explanation without intent to infringe.

British Library Cataloguing-in-Publication Data
A catalogue record for this book is available from the British Library

Library of Congress Cataloging-in-Publication Data
Names: Schlösser, Anne-Marie, 1945– editor.
Title: A psychoanalytic exploration on sameness and otherness / edited by Anne-Marie Schlosser.
Description: New York : Routledge, 2019. |
Series: The efpp monograph series | Includes bibliographical references and index.
Identifiers: LCCN 2019033708 (print) | LCCN 2019033709 (ebook) | ISBN 9780367374075 (hardback) | ISBN 9780367374082 (paperback) | ISBN 9780429353635 (ebook)
Subjects: LCSH: Other (Philosophy) | Social psychology. | Communication.
Classification: LCC BD460.O74 P88 2019 (print) | LCC BD460.O74 (ebook) | DDC 302.5/44—dc23
LC record available at https://lccn.loc.gov/2019033708
LC ebook record available at https://lccn.loc.gov/2019033709

ISBN: 978-0-367-37407-5 (hbk)
ISBN: 978-0-367-37408-2 (pbk)
ISBN: 978-0-429-35363-5 (ebk)

Typeset in Bembo
by codeMantra

CONTENTS

About the editor and contributors   x
Copyrights and original publications   xvii
Preface   xviii

PART I
Translating, understanding and language confusion   1

1 Inside Babel   3
   Anna Ursula Dreher

2 The gift of Babel   20
   Jan Philipp Reemtsma

3 Longing for connection   33
   Antje von Boetticher

PART II
Cultural identity and accepting otherness   43

4 What Arab and Jewish school counsellors remember from within-group diversity in academia and how it affects their work   45
   Lori Greenberger and Ariela Bairey Ben Ishay

5 Women today: when equality turns into a trap   57
   Daniela Lucarelli and Gabriela Tavazza

PART III
Families and children at risk — 69

6 Psychodynamic family therapy of anorexia nervosa — 71
Günter Reich, Antje von Boetticher and Manfred Cierpka+

7 Hello/goodbye new families! Groupwork with looked after siblings — 81
Heather Lee Messner and Elizabeth Stevenson

8 The creation of identity: the way to gender distinction and identity in the family — 95
Anne Loncan

9 Misunderstanding and confusion: educational and psychotherapeutic work in a kindergarten — 103
Christiane Ludwig-Körner

PART IV
Cyber: new forms of communication — 111

10 Zoom, Skype, the uncanny third ones and psychotherapy — 113
Irmgard Dettbarn

11 Like or dislike: questions and challenges in the consulting room of a 'Society 2.0' — 127
Angelo Bonaminio, Domenico Scaringi and Giusy Daniela Spagna

PART V
Babel in psychotherapy — 139

12 Is there such a thing as 'psychoanalytic identity'? — 141
Michael B. Buchholz

13 Is psychoanalysis in a state of 'Babylonian confusion'? — 160
Heinrich Deserno

14 Linguistic confusion in the psychoanalytic process: about understanding and communication — 170
Anne Laimboeck

15 'To hear significance is to translate' (George Steiner).
   Psychoanalytic considerations about capabilities and
   limitations of translation processes in literary and clinical work   177
   Angela Mauss-Hanke

16 Sameness and otherness in a group supervision experience   197
   *Annarita D'Uva, Loreta Negro, Maria Carmela Schiavone,
   Alessia Serra and Ludovica Grassi*

17 Psychic deadness in the consulting room: the role of
   vitalizing supervision   205
   Effie Layou-Lignos and Vassiliki Vassilopoulou

18 Lost and gained in translation: language choice,
   triangulation and transference with bilingual patients   214
   Annette Byford

PART VI
Migration   **231**

19 "So they walked behind their words": language and sense
   of self in the process of migration   233
   Gisela Zeller-Steinbrich

20 Quest for identity: borderland adolescents with migration
   backgrounds   247
   Annette Streeck-Fischer

21 An unequal matrix: Western Germans, Eastern Germans,
   migrants   261
   Jens Preil

22 Accepting otherness to find sameness: when a Jewish child
   realizes that the therapist is an Arab   272
   Caesar Hakim

Thank you   *281*
Index   *283*

ABOUT THE EDITOR AND CONTRIBUTORS

The editor

Anne-Marie Schlösser is a psychologist and training and supervising psychoanalyst of DPG, DGPT, IPA and, after many years at the Department for Psychological Medicine at the University of Göttingen, in private practice. She was president of the DGPT (1995–2005) and of the EFPP (2011–2019) and Consulting Expert at the Federal Board for Medical Services (Psychotherapy). She also was a member of the German group of psychoanalysts teaching in Shanghai, China, on which she published. She is Editor-in-Chief of the EFPP book series.

The contributors

Ariela Bairey Ben Ishay, has an EdD in Human Development and Psychology from Harvard University and is a certified group facilitator, private consultant and director of the Program for Group Facilitation in Diverse Societies, co-founder and co-director of the Institute of Advanced Studies at Beit Berit Academic College, Israel, where she lectures and also in the departments of Informal Education and Masters' degree in Educational Counselling. She also conducts groupwork and has special expertise in identity groupwork and Palestinian–Jewish intergroup encounters.

Angelo Bonaminio is a psychoanalytic psychotherapist of the "Associazione Romana per la Psicoterapia dell'Adolescenza". He works in private practice and at Nostos, Psychological Services for Children, Adolescents and Families.

Michael B. Buchholz, is a psychologist, psychoanalyst and social scientist, Professor of Social Psychology at the International Psychoanalytic University (IPU),

Berlin (Germany), and affiliative professor at Hermann-Paul-School of Linguistics, Freiburg/Basel (Germany). His research interests lie in psychoanalysis and conversation analysis, and he has more than 200 publications to his name.

Annette Byford gained an MA in History and German, and taught at a secondary school in Germany before going on to study psychology and to train as a psychodynamic psychotherapist in the UK. For the past 25 years, she has worked as a psychologist and psychotherapist in private practice and as a supervisor and lecturer in a variety of settings (NHS, university and the voluntary sector). She is a senior practitioner on the Register of Psychologists specializing in Psychotherapy (BPS). Her publications include *A Wedding in the Family*, published by Free Association Books in 2019.

Manfred Cierpka+, MD, was a psychiatrist and psychoanalyst (DPV, IPA). Until summer 2015, he was professor and director of the Institute for Psychosomatic Cooperation Research and Family Therapy, at the Medical Faculty, University of Heidelberg. Until his death in December 2017, he was a Senior Researcher. He published widely on psychotherapy, couple and family therapy, prevention programmes for families with babies and young children, and psychotherapy for parents, babies and toddlers.

Heinrich Deserno, MD, is Professor emeritus at the International Psychoanalytic University (IPU), Berlin. He also worked at the Sigmund-Freud-Institute, Frankfurt (1981–2010), and from 2009 to 2016 at the International Psychoanalytic University (IPU), Berlin. He specialized in clinical psychology and psychotherapy. He is head of ambulatory services and co-head of the Berlin APS-centre. He is a psychoanalyst (IPA, GPV), and scientific topics of interest to him are: psychotherapy process research, anxiety disorders, depression, and conceptual publications on dreaming and symbolization.

Irmgard Dettbarn, PhD, is a psychologist and a private practitioner in psychoanalysis in Berlin, Germany. She is a member of the German Psychoanalytical Association. Since 2004, she has been a trainer in psychodynamic psychotherapy in Zhongdeban Chinese–German Academy of Psychotherapy, in Shanghai, Mental Health Hospital, and an IPA training analyst in Beijing since 2007. She is a lecturer at the Karl-Abraham-Institut-Berlin and a child and adult psychoanalyst in Zürich, Switzerland. Her special interest lies in ethnopsychoanalysis and she conducted a field-stay in a nomad society, the Himba Tribe, in Kaokoland, Namibia.

Anna Ursula Dreher, MD, psychologist, is a psychoanalyst in private practice in Frankfurt am Main, Germany (DPV/IPA); co-editor of the *Forum der Psychoanalyse*; member of research committees of the IPA: 2001–2009 on conceptual research, since 2009 on clinical research; member of the European task force of the

IPA's Encyclopedic Dictionary. She has published on the basics of psychoanalytic research, on clinical and conceptual research, and on central clinical concepts (e.g., psychic trauma, transference, interpretation).

Annarita D'Uva is a psychologist and psychotherapist working in private practice with children, adolescents and families. Her interests are psychoanalysis with children, adolescents and family psychotherapy, and work with multi-problematic families.

Ludovica Grassi, MD, is a child and adolescent neuropsychiatrist and psychoanalyst (member of IPA, EFPP, AIPCF). She is a psychoanalytic trainer and supervisor in private practice with adults, children, adolescents, couples and families. Areas of interest: couple and family psychoanalysis, infant psychoanalysis, ethnopsychoanalysis, and the role of music in psychic development.

Lori Greenberger has a PhD in Developmental Psychology from San Jose University, USA. She is a psychotherapist, family and couples' therapist and educational counsellor. She is also Senior Lecturer and Full Faculty member at Beit Berl Academic College, Israel, and a teacher in the Masters' degree in Educational Counselling and the Department of Educational Evaluation and Research there.

Caesar Hakim, PhD (Haifa University, Israel), is a clinical psychologist. Since 2009, he has been working in private practice in Haifa. Currently, he is clinical director of the Guidance and Training Centre for families and children in Bethlehem, Palestine, Assistant Professor at An Najah National University, Nablus, and honorary lecturer at the College of Medical and Life Sciences, Glasgow University, UK.

Joachim Küchenhoff, MD, is a psychoanalyst and member of the IPA and of the Swiss and German psychoanalytic societies. He is also a specialist in psychiatry/psychotherapy and in psychosomatic medicine and Professor emeritus at Basel University. He worked as the medical director of the department of adult psychiatry in the canton Baselland, Switzerland, from 2007 to 2018. He is editor-in-chief of the SANP (Swiss Archives of Neurology, Psychiatry and Psychotherapy). He is president of the supervisory board and visiting Professor at IPU (International Psychoanalytic University) Berlin. The list of his publications can be found via his homepage (www.praxis-kuechenhoff.ch). His last book publications are (2019) *Verständigung und Selbstfindung. Psychoanalytisch-philosophische Gedankengänge. Schwabe Basel*, and (2019) *Sich verstehen im Anderen. Erkenntniswege der Psychoanalyse: Vandenhoeck&Ruprecht*.

Annemarie Laimböck was born in 1951, studied of psychology at the J. W. G. University Frankfurt (Dipl.-Psych.), and has a PhD in Philosophy, especially

Psychoanalysis. She undertook psychoanalytic training at the Sigmund Freud Institut in Frankfurt, is a Member of the IPA and a teaching analyst at the Innsbrucker Arbeitskreis für Psychoanalyse (IAP) and in Shanghai. She is also the Founder and Chair of the psychoanalytic ambulance of the IAP. She is the author of several publications, especially on the subject of the psychoanalytic method, including a recent book: *Die Szene verstehen. Die psychoanalytische Methode in verschiedenen Settings*, published by Brandes & Apsel Verlag, Frankfurt, 2015.

Effie Layiou-Lignos BSc, ACSW, MPsych, is a child and adolescent psychotherapist, President of the Hellenic Association of Child and Adolescent Psychoanalytic Psychotherapy, clinical supervisor at the Department of Child Psychiatry, Athens University Medical School, Aghia Sophia Children's Hospital Athens, Greece. She is a member of ACP (UK), the Tavistock Society of Psychotherapists, Greek delegate to the EFPP founding societies (1991), member of the organizing committee of the EFPP Infant Observation Workshop (2005–today) and the Syros Summer Workshop (1998–today). She teaches and supervises in Greece, Cyprus, Turkey and Poland, mostly on infant observation and early therapeutic intervention, with relevant publications and film production.

Heather Lee-Messner is a child and adolescent psychotherapist and started her work in the USA before moving to the UK. She trained at the Independent School of Psychoanalytic Child & Adolescent Psychotherapy Training (IPCAPA) at the British Psychotherapy Foundation in the UK and also teaches there. Other places of work include NHS CAMHS teams, hospital based paediatric liaison team, Lead for Parent–Infant Mental Health Services, and she worked together with E. Stevenson in the Fast Track Service for Looked After Children, and as Consultant Child Psychotherapist in Essex in CAMHS. She now works exclusively with children, adolescents and their families in private practice.

Anne Loncan, PhD, is a child psychiatrist, couple and family psychoanalyst, former President of the Société Française de Thérapie Familiale Psychanalytique (French Society of Psychoanalytic Family Therapy). She is a former General Secretary of the International Association of Couple and Family Psychoanalysis and Editor-in-Chief of *Le Divan familial*, a review of psychoanalytic family therapy.

Daniela Lucarelli, PhD, is a psychologist, psychoanalyst, full member of the IPA/SPI and IPA recognised expert on children and adolescents. She is Editor-in-Chief of the IACFP Review (International Review of Couple and Family Psychoanalysis), and member of the board and Chair of the Couple and Family Section of EFPP (European Federation for Psychoanalytic Psychotherapy). She works as a teacher and supervisor at Istituto Winnicott, Rome, and is a founding member of SIPsIA (Società di Psicoterapia Psicoanalitica dell'Infanzia e dell'Adolescenza), Rome. She is also a teacher and supervisor at PCF (Corso Postspecialistico di

Psicoanalisi della Coppia e della Famiglia), Rome, a member of the editorial board of *Interazioni* (Franco Angeli, Milan, Italy), and author and co-author of publications on children, adolescents and couple and family psychoanalysis.

Christiane Ludwig-Körner, PhD, is a professor at the International Psychoanalytic University, Berlin, a psychologist, training analyst and supervisor of the IPA, DPG and DGPT. She has constructed and leads the training programme Parent–Infant Psychotherapy ESKP in Germany, and is Head of the Parent–Infant Working Group at IPA. Her work and research focuses on primary prevention, parent–infant therapy, psychotherapy approaches, and biography research of female psychoanalysts.

Angela Mauss-Hanke is a psychoanalyst for adults, children and groups and a training and supervising analyst for adults (DPV, DGPT, IPA) and groups (D3G). She works in private practice in Wolfratshausen and Munich and is a member of the Editorial Board of the *International Journal of Psychoanalysis* (IJP). From 2008 to 2016, she was Editor of *Internationale Psychoanalyse* (the German annual of IJP) and Editor-in-Chief of the European Annuals of IJP from 2014 to 2016. She is also a member of the IPA Website Editorial Board, responsible for the IPA blog (www.ipa.world). She has numerous psychoanalytical publications and presentations to her name, mostly on topics relevant to society, for example: 'The killing of the so-called handicapped in Germany and the Nuremberg medics trial 1946/47' (2000); on September 11th ('The low voice of sanity', 2004); on 'Fluidity and fundamentalism – two sides of one coin' (2016); 'Revenge knows no measure: psychoanalytic considerations about an all-too-human impulse' (2018).

Loreta Negro is a psychologist and psychoanalytical psychotherapist working in private practice with children, teenagers and adults. She collaborates with the local Juvenile Court in child custody litigations, and cooperates with the main territorial agencies. Her interests lie in child and adolescent psychotherapy and school problems.

Jens Preil, MD, PhD, is a psychoanalyst (DGPT, DGAP) and group analyst (SGAZ). He studied Medicine in Goettingen and trained at the Max Planck Institute for Psychiatry, Munich and at the Institute for Psychotherapy, Berlin. He works in private practice for psychoanalysis and psychotherapy in Berlin, Germany, as well as psychodynamic organizational consulting, and is a senior manager in Clinical Research and Development of a global pharmaceutical company.

Jan Philipp Reemtsma, Prof. PhD, is the founder and managing director of the Hamburg Foundation for the Advancement of Research and Culture; founder and, until March 2015, leader of the Hamburg Institute for Social Research. His working priorities are: literature of the 18th and 19th centuries, theory of civilisation, and the history of human destructiveness. He has numerous publications in these areas.

Günter Reich, PhD, is a psychological psychotherapist, psychoanalyst (DGPT, DPG), couple and family therapist (BVPPF), and psychotherapist for children and adolescents. He is a professor at the Clinic for Psychosomatic Medicine and Psychotherapy, University Goettingen and also works in private practice. He has published widely on psychotherapy, couple and family therapy, psychodynamics, family dynamics and therapy of eating disorders.

Domenico Scaringi is a psychoanalytic psychotherapist of the Associazione Romana per la Psicoterapia dell'Adolescenza. He works in private practice and at Nostos, Psychological Services for Children, Adolescents and Families, in Rome, Italy.

Maria Carmela Schiavone, is a psychologist and psychotherapist working in private practice with children, adolescents and couples. She is also a psychotherapist at the Paediatric Division, University Hospital Umberto I, Rome. Her interest focuses on rare diseases and gender identity.

Alessia Serra is a psychologist, psychotherapist, a member of the Italian Society of Child, Adolescent and Couple Psychoanalytic Psychotherapy (SIPSIA), and of EFPP. She works in private practice with children and adolescents.

Giusy Daniela Spagna is a neuropsychiatrist in the Associazione Romana per la Psicoterapia dell'Adolescenza. She works in private practice and at Nostos, Psychological Services for Children, Adolescents and Families in Rome, Italy.

Elizabeth Stevenson is a psychologist and trained as a child psychotherapist at the Tavistock Clinic. She worked in the Fast Track Service for Looked After Children for nine years as team lead and has long experience of working in social care as a social worker prior to training as a child psychotherapist. She is now retired from the NHS.

Annette Streeck-Fischer, MD, PhD, was, from 1993–2013, director of the department Clinical Psychotherapy of Children and Adolescents at Asklepios Fachklinikum Tiefenbrunn, Göttingen. Since 2009 she has been Professor of Developmental Psychology and Diagnostic at the International Psychoanalytic University (IPU) in Berlin, and also a training and supervising analyst at the Lou-Andreas-Salomé-Institute, Göttingen, and a member of the DPG. She was Editor of the journal *Praxis der Kinderpsychologie und Kinderpsychiatrie*, and, from 2011 to 2015, President of the International Society of Adolescent Psychiatry and Psychotherapy (ISAPP). Her interests centre around adolescence, violence and maltreatment.

Gabriela Tavazza is a psychologist, psychoanalyst, full member of the IPA/SPI (Italian Psychoanalytical Society and International Psychoanalytical Association), supervisor and lecturer in the Couple and Family Psychoanalytical Society (PCF), Rome. She is head of the task force for the prevention of mental disorders and education in mental health at the Mental Health Department ASL RM D, Rome, and Professor of Social Psychology in the Master's degree programme 'Theory and technique of the parent couple'. She is also Editor-in-Chief of *Interazioni*, the Italian review of psychoanalytical research on individuals, couples and family and author and co-author of a number of articles on couple and family psychoanalysis.

Antje von Boetticher, psychologist, is a psychoanalyst and family therapist in private practice, and a lecturer. Her areas of interest are: concepts of psychoanalysis and psychoanalytic family therapy, young adulthood, and eating disorders.

Vassiliki Vassilopoulou, MSc., is a psychologist, child and adolescent psychotherapist, and member of the Hellenic Association of Child and Adolescent Psychoanalytic Psychotherapy. He works in private practice with a special interest in early therapeutic intervention.

Gisela Zeller-Steinbrich is a psychologist, psychoanalyst, lecturer, supervising and training psychoanalyst at the Training Centre for Psychoanalytic Psychotherapy Basel, Switzerland and at the Institut for Psychoanalysis and Psychotherapy, Freiburg, Germany. She is a former lecturer at Cologne University and President of the EFPP Child and Adolescent Section, Switzerland.

COPYRIGHTS AND ORIGINAL PUBLICATIONS

Chapter 1, by A. U. Dreher, is a translation from the original German version, first published in *Forum der Psychoanalyse*.

Chapter 3, by A. von Boetticher was previously published in *Revista de psicoterapia y salud mental del nino y del adolescente*.

Chapter 6, by G. V. Reich, A. Boetticher, and M. Cierpka was previously published in *Revista de psicoterapia y salud mental del nino y del adolescente*.

Chapter 18, by A. Byford. Copyright 2015 by BPF and Wiley & Sons Ltd, London.

Chapter 20, by A. Streeck-Fischer was previously published in the *American Journal of Psychoanalysis*. It can be found on the PEP website (1941 to date): www.pep-web.org/toc.php?journal=ajp

PREFACE
Joachim Küchenhoff

How should we interpret the subtitle of this remarkable book? What does the formula 'Beyond Babel?' indicate? Does it address our present situation, asking whether we are still in Babel or whether we have left behind the Babylonian confusion of tongues? Does it imply a search for a future perspective: the possibility to go beyond Babel? Or the alternative of always being forced to stay within Babel? Does it ask for an ethical reflection in which we have to take sides: should we leave Babel and go beyond, or should we accept Babel as the right place to be?

In the title, the formula is preceded by the two words 'sameness' and 'otherness'. These words serve as a specification of what Babel is meant to be and what the myth of Babel conveys: if I cannot easily grasp what you say, and vice versa, what will I do? Will I hold on to my own language, my own culture, will I build a wall to defend myself against the other threatening my sense of identity, or will I become curious as to the possibilities of getting to know, or even understand, the other? Can I accept the plurality of tongues as cultural enrichment, or do I undertake every possible effort to establish monolingualism, the rule of only one language or a dominant way of living?

These guiding questions might help to define the overarching aim of the book and to situate the various contributions within its overall scope. At first sight, the multiplicity of topics seems confusing. They include (among others): diversity in psychoanalytical theory; linguistic issues such as the benefits of bilinguality in psychotherapy or the limitations of translation; concepts of identity in general or specific identity problems, for example, for women, migrants, or for adolescents exploring cyberspace; cultural differences and how to deal with them; the use of supervision to enhance understanding and to allow emotional speech in psychotherapy. In the process of reading through the book, you might feel as if you are guided through the suburbs of Babel itself. All the different pathways are fascinating and allow new insights. At the same time, the perspectives tend to change rapidly, too rapidly sometimes, and readers might feel lost. But, time and again, they will forget about the other contributions and let themselves become acquainted with the current author's peculiar 'tongue'. And, by and by, they will gladly realize that the diversity of perspectives and arguments slowly builds up patterns that allow orientation while resisting quick and easy answers. Thus, the reader slowly feels at home in this Babylonian book, and begins to realize that maybe he or she might be invited to feel at home in Babel as well.

The book addresses the topic of sameness and otherness that is most important for psychoanalysis. In general and on principle, psychoanalysis favours difference and otherness. It values the omissions, the slips, the infralinguistic subtext of an encounter and talk, and other manifestations of the unconscious as enrichments to self-awareness and understanding. Dealing with unconscious levels of thoughts, representations, and perceptions, psychoanalysis is, on principle, concerned with a confusion of tongues, either intrapsychically or interpersonally, or, rather, with a multiplicity of perspectives.

Intrapsychically, the self is an other, as Arthur Rimbaud put it: "Moi, c'est un autre", and never merely the same. Not only psychoanalysis, but also many scholars of philosophy, such as Paul Ricoeur, Jacques Derrida and Hellmuth Plessner, have stated that it is not possible to understand oneself completely, to get hold of the origin one has evolved from, etc. The notion of the unconscious entails that the conscious mind is not able to totally govern one's thoughts, inclinations, actions, and emotions. Therefore, identity in psychoanalytical terms cannot be regarded as sameness and a trait over time; it always includes the otherness or the 'othering'.

As to *interpersonal relationships*, the psychoanalytic cure allows analysands to become aware of their object images which they have built up throughout their early years and which they tend to project on the persons they are actually in contact with. Eventually, the otherness of the other will be realized more readily and may be accepted as well. But, again, this self-reflective state can be reached only momentarily, only for a while; it will not be durable. The other will again become the object of one's desire or fear and will be identified with one's object representations.

Sameness and otherness are intimately linked to each other, both in intrapsychic and interpersonal terms: the sameness of the self is not complete and, thus, never complete and available. The otherness of the other will again and again be reduced to the needs and wishes of the self. Yet, identity is, nevertheless, a target in our personality development that we cannot dismiss, the acknowledgement of the other is an ethical demand for interpersonal relationships. Obviously, dialectical thinking is necessary. However, it is difficult to conceive of sameness and otherness as poles that cannot be isolated from each other and cannot be reached individually.

Returning to the Babel metaphor, in the end, we all live at the threshold of Babel: always going outside, trying to leave the confusion of tongues, and going back again to experience the multitude and the richness of voices that tend to be mute outside. We commute between places inside and beyond Babel. The book at hand is an important vehicle to enable this dialectical movement.

PART I
Translating, understanding and language confusion

1
INSIDE BABEL[1]

Anna Ursula Dreher

Babylonian language confusion?

In our analytic context, often characterised as 'Babylonian', there are definitely many problems, but there are also potentials worth realising before looking for solutions '*beyond* Babel'. The title "Inside Babel" should elucidate which pole of the field of tension between 'Inside and beyond Babel' this chapter is located on. The Bible story of the Tower of Babel, with the consequence of language confusion among human beings, is understood, in religious interpretation, as a punishment of God for human presumptuousness. The plan, to rise up to God physically, to enter heavenly spheres through the high tower, alludes to an old motive – the aspiration to be God-like – which we find again in manifold ways in the sciences today. However, scientists are, above all, seeking insight and knowledge, that is, to decode God's creation plan of the world through science. Some physicists want to have already discovered 'God particles' and some neuroscientists claim to be able to watch the psyche working by using a scanner. Others are looking for universal natural laws, which can give a causal explanation of all our behaviour and actions. As we know, the God of the Old Testament was 'not amused' by the Tower of Babel and, as a consequence of his punitive action, the negative impact of the difficulty in communicating ensued: chaos, violence, flight and dispersal all over the world – phenomena that are ubiquitous still today.

In psychoanalysis, we are currently living in and with this language diversity, thus we are living 'Inside Babel' in times long after the tower was built. This language diversity does not result only from the many languages that are due to the worldwide distribution of psychoanalysis, but also to the many analytic 'dialects', which are in the background of this chapter. This diversity is, of course, not due to God's punishment, but to the scientific, historic and socio-cultural developments inside and outside psychoanalysis. And it was not our aspiration to rise up to God; our aspiration was and is much smaller, yet not immodest: we want to understand how the human psyche functions, why it is disturbed and how it can be healed. The *language diversity* in psychoanalysis is experienced by many as *language confusion* because one can easily lose the overview. However, one has to distinguish: confusion can, of course, arise when matters become too complex, too contradictory and too unwieldy, but also when there is unwillingness to tolerate, acknowledge and cope with the diversity of other language games. Which aspect is working in the individual case is sometimes difficult to say.

In the Bible story, it is said that there were many conflicts in the time after the tower was wrecked because of the disturbance to communication. But they certainly do not have to be as extreme as those narrated in some Hebrew variants of the Babel mythology, where workers on the tower speaking with other tongues were slain because they no longer understood work orders (Ranke-Graves et al., 1963). The use of language is by far not always as harmless as it might appear. "Flags are optical keywords. National anthems are musical keywords. But the deadly weapon of man is language", Arthur Koestler wrote (Koestler, 1975: 98, translated for this edition). Only think of the sad notoriety that the German word 'Untermensch' has gained; or of the usage of language as a weapon in the yellow press; or only of the highly sensitive nature of an aspect in the enduring argument between the Western world and Russia as to whether the taking of the Crimea may be called 'annexation' or not. The list of the usages of language as a weapon could be arbitrarily continued. Koestler writes further: "Each language acts as a connecting force within the group, and as a repelling force between different groups" (p. 104, translated for this edition) and he sums up pessimistically that, in the course of the history of our species, aggressive, disintegrating forces have always triumphed over those that seek to connect us (p. 104). Regrettably, this is the case. And it is indeed difficult to be optimistic in a world in which the destructive forces are as dominant and ubiquitous as we are currently experiencing. Nevertheless, at least in psychoanalysis, I would want to give the forces of connection a chance and, through that, to the possibility of understanding on the basis of the positive potentials of diversity, not least because we have a common ground worldwide: studying the 'human psyche' through our specific access to psychic phenomena – above all but not only – in the analytic situation.

The special relevance of language is deduced from the well-known fact that we use language in manifold ways: we speak with and about our patients, we discuss our clinical cases, we write our papers, we formulate and modify our ideas, models, theories and *Weltbilder* (worldview). Thus, we communicate with the most different addressees: with ourselves, our patients, our colleagues, the insurance companies, the worldwide associations of analysts, the scientific communities of our competing human sciences, and, not least, with a broad public interested in psychoanalysis. That there can be various barriers to communication is obvious and simple solutions are certainly not in sight. Therefore, I shall attempt to make only a snapshot here, a kind of inventory of some aspects of our psychoanalytic discourse in Babylonian times. In this, I see our analytic Babel as an analogy to the mythological site Babel, within the walls of which a lot of things can happen, constructive as well as destructive. I would like to stroll a bit through this, our town, walk through old and new neighbourhoods and across the squares, and collect impressions, and simply look at what interesting, pleasant, but also unpleasant things one can encounter there.

Reasons for the many voices in psychoanalysis

Psychoanalysis, empirically, conceptually and theoretically, is working with one of the most difficult research subjects in existence: the human psyche. Difficult for many reasons: not least because, in the end, we have only our own psychic apparatus to know how the psyche works. Up to this day, there is no consensual definition of what precisely the human psyche is at all or how it is constructed and how it functions. In the sciences, there is not even consensus about its existence at all, despite it being the name giver of psychoanalysis, as well of psychology, psychosomatics or psychiatry. Even though the whole world often and readily speaks of 'psychic', many people obviously find it difficult to acknowledge an entity, 'psyche', as a scientific subject. 'Mind' has it much easier and even the good old 'soul' is having a comeback. In psychoanalysis, there is certainly a number of schools and traditions of thought, which, based on their specific models and ideas of the psyche, have developed their own dialects. By 'analytic dialects', I mean those tradition-specific language games which are, historically, one of the most relevant sources of our Babylonian diversity and which are apparent mainly, but not only, in the diversity of concept meanings. These dialects distinguish themselves from one another by having developed a number of their own specific concepts and by having given school-specific meaning variants to classic concepts. I think, for example, of the Kleinian concept of 'projective identification' which meanwhile has found recognition in various schools of analytic thought. Or of the 'transference as total situation', an understanding of transference which has remained regional up to now. Most of us, reading or hearing for the first time a text from a different school than our own, will have experienced great surprise upon encountering a concept hitherto unfamiliar to us. For instance, I was flabbergasted when I once heard in a lecture of the 'thinking breast' (Bion).

Behind the many voices in Babel is not only the multitude of specific analytic ideas or models of the psyche; this well-known source of language diversity refers mainly to our internal clinical and theoretical discourses. But, along with these inner analytic discourses, it increasingly also refers to the interdisciplinary discourses, definitely and especially then, when – in the canon of these sciences – psychoanalysis wants to be taken seriously, recognised and, above all, wants to be heard. The broad field of psychic disturbances, as this domain is called in both ICD and DSM, is being differently researched and worked with therapeutically. In addition, we are called more and more to present scientific evidence of the efficacy of our clinical interventions. Whether everyone likes it or not, psychoanalysis actually cannot afford *not* to participate in the field of scientific discourse. However, the different scientific worldviews are evident in this terrain, and they are a further source of diversity, but mainly just another source of confusion. In the same way, how psychoanalysis is scientifically positioned, whether it is a science at all, is seen differently. And even if it is supposed to be a science, there is dissent: what kind of science it is, natural science or human science, cultural or social science, or even a species of its own. And from this stem the controversies about which research methods and aims are the right ones, and which data are relevant at all. This becomes especially obvious with the understanding of what 'clinical research' is, which, since the beginning, has been one of our most important research disciplines. The bow ranges from the traditional understanding of the Freudian 'conjunction research' – the analyst is also the researcher and his research takes place mainly in the analytic situation using analytic methods – to diverse research understandings orientated towards other scientific worldviews, coming from empiricism through hermeneutics up to the neurosciences, which research with scanners, no longer from behind the couch.

Diversity of theories and world views, which is evident in the diversity of discourses as well as in the spoken dialects, is actually quite normal in living sciences and there is no reason why this should be different in psychoanalysis. Different scientific socialisations, different clinical experiences, different reception of analytic and scientific trends, new ideas and findings influence our dialects, which are, moreover, interwoven with the societies and cultures in which they are spoken. And by society, I am not only referring to the regular geopolitical units, but above all to our diverse regional analytic associations. Historically, psychoanalysis was and still is under pressure to continually calibrate and adjust its ideas about the psyche, as well as the ideas about how psychoanalysis can help people. Also, our understanding of the development, diagnostics and therapy of psychic illness was always in competition with, initially, that of medicine, and today also of genetics, of behavioural science and the neurosciences. This has always been the case and will always be that way, certainly for as long as we want to participate in interdisciplinary discourses and keep striving for better solutions – not least of all in the interest of our patients and clients (Dreher, 2014a). We do not treat our patients analytically because we are analysts, but we are analysts because we are convinced that psychoanalysis can help the patients, and that it is definitely not worse than other procedures.

Constructive and destructive aspects in analytic Babel

If you like, you can refer to this ordinary run of things in psychoanalysis, as in all other sciences as 'Babel' – 'Babel' understood in the sense of a never-ending competing *multi-voicedness*; there will never be an 'end of history' in this respect. Competition, however, can have many faces: from bitter rivalry, even hostility, to the constructive search for communication and greatest possible agreement. Babel can be both a fighting arena for dominance and a place for fertile controversy.

If one is optimistic, one can experience the diversity of voices as a resource and the attraction of difference as enrichment. As is familiar to us from the regulation mechanisms of closeness and distance, being constantly confronted with the voices of others not only shapes one's own position with a strengthened identity, but also bestows an increasing readiness to open oneself up to a critical and stimulating dialogue. If one is pessimistic, one can regard the diversity as a barrier at which often unfair battles are fought, which also can often end in emotional injuries due to the devaluations and insults that are exchanged. In this field of tension between sameness and otherness, we encounter different kinds of danger: the impasse of anxiety, defence and exclusion; the danger of fusion and, thus, loss of identity. This dialectic between constructive and destructive moments in all scientific discourses, as well as in our analytic Babel, does not surprise us. At any rate, many of us have been living in this town long enough and want to continue to stay there. It would not be bad if we all got along well, with all our various forms of thought and life, our various beliefs and mentalities. In the German-speaking area alone, all members of so many analytic societies, who have gone through various scientific and analytic socialisations and are working within countless institutions and many fields of practice, belong to the 'psychoanalysts in Babel'. This complexity would increase considerably if we were to take the worldwide distribution of psychoanalysis into account, too. No one has an overview of the *entire* analytic Babel as a whole – we all have limited perspectives on it, as well as, by the way, on our subject, the psyche, even though there are, from time to time, those that act as if they knew 'everything'.

What unites us analysts – apart from our historic descent from Freud's psychoanalysis, never mind how straight or winding these genealogical lines may have been – is that we are all workers on and with the psyche. What can divide us are differences in theory and practice, in mentality and culture, in world views and language games. Most of us speak that analytic dialect in which they were analytically socialised or in which they now feel at home by belief. As tends to be the way with dialects, they signal where you are from and offer a sense of home, a social and emotional 'Heimat'. In the development of our dialects a complicated genealogical tree presents itself. At its branches, one often finds important analysts with their ideas. I cannot trace this branching historically, but can only consider a few aspects of the 'here and now'. The dialects that have had the most powerful effects historically derive from our authorities of the founder generations. Therefore, we find in Babel the old Freudian centre of town, surrounded by a number of old-town quarters where Jungians, Adlerians, Kleinians, Lacanians, Bionians, Winnicottians, etc., live. Next to some of these old centres there are new neighbourhoods, where a 'post-' sign is over the entrance: for example, post-Kleinians. The prefixes 'post' or 'contemporary' signal that things continue slightly differently than has been historically passed on, but without a radical break from the original theories. The old city of Babel is mostly occupied by the diverse '-ians'. Around this old centre of Babel there are areas that are not named by persons any more, but after the dominant perspective on the psyche, whether their inhabitants be object relations or drive theorists, self- or ego psychologists, attachment theorists or intersubjectivists. And there are, of course, not only these relatively homogeneous quarters, there are innumerable single detached houses where pluralists, eclectics, or solitaires live. In the past decades, in the suburbs of Babel, new construction sites can be found; mainly researchers have moved in there, who are dealing with psychoanalytic subjects (e.g., baby watchers, attachment theoreticians, psychotherapy researchers, trauma and brain researchers). Do they still belong to 'our' Babel at all? Are they analysts? Some long-time residents say no, others see them as enrichment. Up to now, they may have a limited influence on the *clinical* discourses in psychoanalysis with their ideas and results; however, they dominate the *scientific* discourses, because their understanding of science and research, of theory and the empirical is closer to the scientific mainstream than the classic psychoanalytic research understanding. Altogether, our Babel is a rather colourful city; its map reminds one more of the organic growth of Rome than of Manhattan's grid designed on the drawing board.

These labels, the analytic quarters in Babel, help us to structure and organise our analytic world. We all know that when we speak with colleagues hitherto unfamiliar to us, the use of some concepts has the function of passwords. Keywords often allow us to open a drawer and this can immediately signal familial closeness or, conversely, even an almost unsurmountable distance. If a speaker talks about "Alpha, beta or omega function", the Bion drawer opens at once. That this can happen even in the case of plain mishearing, a Freudian slip possibly, happened to me recently. When I told a colleague I was working on a paper for a conference titled 'Beyond Babel?', he sceptically asked: "So, are you a Bionian now, too?" He misunderstood 'beyond' as Bion. Anyway, I was able to calm him down: I do *not* live in one of the currently hippest quarters. If one has different beliefs, it is understood that one has to talk and argue with one another. In the field of science there exists, for this purpose, the traditional institution of 'scientific discourse': a rational and fair competition of arguments with the aim that the most well-founded position may succeed. This ideal is advocated again and again, but the lived reality is often so far away from that that we would talk about a disorder if such large discrepancies between ideal and reality showed up in one of our patients. For, mostly, it is not about the best solutions, but about something different: about power, money and dominance; many want to rule over their own little garden patch, and this little garden is supposed to become as big as possible and, above all, no competitor should be in it. The lived practice of scientific discourse, as well as that of analytic discourse, could actually be a subject for analytic social psychology; we find there the whole arsenal of the usual suspects, the well-known narcissistic gratifications such as money, positions, titles as well as the less pleasant motives such as envy, jealousy, or rivalry. It is useful to quote Freud from time to time, for he, of course, has also pointed out this 'dark side' of ours:

> One has… to reckon with the fact that there are present in all men destructive, and therefore anti-social and anti-cultural, trends and that in a great number of people these are strong enough to determine their behaviour in human society.
>
> *(Freud, 1927: 7)*

Let us simply concede that we all have destructive tendencies, which can be observed quite well in our analytic Babel. The aim of communication, or even only an approach to it, is sometimes, unfortunately, not on the agenda – discourses derail much too often. "Bloody duels", André Green calls them in the basic debate with Robert Wallerstein about the common ground in psychoanalysis (Green, 2005; Wallerstein, 2005a,b). In this argument, Wallerstein considers the language barriers in general between Anglo-Saxon and French authors as an important impediment to communication – but can they alone explain the sharpness of the dispute? Green does not think so and sees behind this – and I think rightly so – basic ideological prejudices. "French authors", he says, are "considered as smooth talkers of no interest" (Green, 2005, p. 631). A remark by Otto Kernberg gives us a hint regarding the structure of these prejudices: "cultural dispositions toward empirical research… dominate in the Northern Hemisphere, particularly the Anglo-Saxon and Nordic countries, in contrast to an openness to a more philosophically inspired, subjectivistically focused attitude in Latin countries" (Kernberg, 2006: 921). Then, this is not only about psychoanalysis, but also about different scientific worldviews: Anglo-Saxons are said to be disposed toward empirical research, obviously connected with the claim to generate objective knowledge. The Latins, in turn, are said to possess only subjectivistically focused attitudes. The first do science, the others are good for the arts section. The subtle implication that only one of them could actually be a 'real' scientist while the others are not is a similarly devaluating argument, like the statement that can sometimes be heard in our internal analytic debates, that someone has no 'analytic identity' – this is also a killer argument *par excellence*, because then one does not have to discuss anything further.

How much influence scientific worldviews can have on our analytic language becomes evident in the *Standard Edition*. For Freud's original concepts, as Georges-Arthur Goldschmidt was able to show, the following applied: "in German, the psychoanalytic terminology hardly deviates from general language usage" (Goldschmidt, 2008: 44, translated for this edition). Ricardo Steiner (1994) examined the correspondence between Ernest Jones and Freud's translators, the Stracheys, and has shown very clearly how much Jones wished for the translations of Freudian concepts to be rendered in the professional medical languages of the time, Greek and Latin. This is why, even now, we speak of 'Ego' and not of 'I', why we speak of 'cathexis' and 'anaclitic'. For it was important to Jones that psychoanalysis should present itself as a 'science' in the Anglo-Saxon sense, as a *hard* natural science. It should not belong to the *soft* 'humanities' or 'arts'. He has, by the way, in his letters always capitalised the word 'Science', a spelling only customary in English for words such as 'Lord' or 'King' … or 'Queen'.

Another scientific utopia has left its traces in our language games. Similar to the great world religions, there are also strong monotheistic tendencies in the sciences in the form of the unity-of-science movement: one kind of explanation is sought for all empirical sciences, law-like, causal explanations. In order to achieve this, only a few methods are permitted: systematic observation and experiment. And, of course, research should be quantitative and the theories should be formulated in a language orientated at logic and mathematics. The hope that leaving behind all communication problems by choosing the clarity of a formal language is, in fact then, like waiting for the Pentecostal miracle of understanding. As we know, Bion, too, found the idea of a formal language for psychoanalysis attractive; he explicitly formulated many of his concepts in line with these maxims.

Arguments about the 'right' scientific worldview are restricting, just as are many resources inner-analytically, as the controversies around the analytic common ground or around the 'one right way' of psychoanalysis show. It is too bad how much "anger and bitterness" – so says Green – is produced by this at a time when it would be so much more important to sharpen the profile of psychoanalysis to the outside world, towards other competing sciences and the interested public. And this would really be worth it. For, if one considers the other, the constructive aspect of the diversity of voices, it becomes clear how lively, interesting, and inspiring it can be in our Babel – and that there everyone could learn a lot, inside and outside of psychoanalysis.

Where exactly do the potentials of Babel lie?

In order to illustrate the potentials in Babel, I would like to apply to our analytic dialects a thought of Goldschmidt's, which he had developed for languages in general. Goldschmidt discusses – against the background of the difficulty of translating Freud texts into French – some fundamental problems concerning the interrelationship of language, culture, and world. He writes:

> The myth of Babel is the myth of the 'unity' of the human language: you would never know what a language is missing, what it turns away from, what it refuses to say, what is gradually lost, if there were not the others who spoke about it.
>
> *(Goldschmidt, 2008: 25, translated for this edition)*

In no single language can 'everything' be said about the world, each language has its omissions and empty spaces, its areas of clear sight, but also its blind spots. Each language adapts to just the culture in which it is spoken and lived, and, in its turn, shapes that culture. Each language has – if you look at it pragmatically – its strengths and weaknesses. What one language cannot grasp, another is well able to formulate, and what is lacking in one language, so Goldschmidt says, only becomes visible through the mirroring by another language.

I recognise a similar pattern in our analytic dialects, which centre around *our* subject, the psyche. Two questions can hardly be answered universally: in which language can one best speak *about* psychic phenomena; and, even more basically, in which language does the psyche *itself* actually speak? Henri Bergson tells us about the limited possibilities of the psyche to express in language what is happening *within* it.

Inner experience will not find a precisely fitting language anywhere. It will inevitably return to the concept, by adding, at the most, an image to it. But then the language has to widen the concept, make it pliant and suggest – through the dissipating boundary with which the language surrounds it – that the concept does not contain the complete experience (Bergson, 1948: 61, translated for this edition). There is no 'language of the psyche', not even the *lingua universalis* postulated by Leibniz or the 'language of thought' postulated by computer linguists – as is known, both are conceived as formal languages. What exists and what we are well familiar with through the work with our patients is the often arduous, tentative, fragile and almost always inadequate attempts to first make tediously conscious and then grasp 'in words' what is happening intra- and interpsychically at the moment. Goldschmidt adds, referring to the first question, the possibilities of a best language game *about* the psyche, "All languages are equidistant from that which is meant, just in different ways" (2008: 56, translated for this edition).

Each of our dialects, each of our attempts to grasp the psychic phenomena in language, leaves gaps – one could say Goldschmidtian gaps – because no dialect can grasp everything and say everything about the psyche. Those Babel neighbourhoods mentioned earlier, which do not derive from historic authorities, but from views into the psyche, make this so particularly obvious. Their names already show us what is, respectively, in focus of their view of the psyche: drive, object relation, ego, attachment, or intersubjectivity. But, indirectly, this reveals clearly just what is *not* in focus; thus, which are areas of unclear sight. However, also with the others, the -ians, we tend to know fairly well which areas of clinical phenomena and experience they grasp with great sharpness and with high clarity – and what they see less clearly than others. Each of us is at home in his or her dialect. But when we describe a clinical case where our, up to now, acquired conceptual repertoire reaches its limitations, then we like to fall back on concepts from other dialects, depending on the peculiarities of this case – that is to say, we definitely use the potential of Babel in order to fill Goldschmidt gaps. With narcissistically needy patients, for instance, Kohut's work on idealising transference comes to mind; with patients with oedipal intensity, drive-theoretical concepts come forcefully to the forefront; in heated affects in which yet other patients entangle us, we will surely think of the Kleinian concept of projective identification, etc. Such pragmatic handling of the diversity of our dialects, experiencing them as enrichment, as an asset, presupposes, however, some effort: one must first of all be curious about other beliefs. One must listen, read, and discuss. One must be able to acknowledge what others are saying, and one must be willing to assimilate ideas different from one's own belief system; allow a mixing of one's own dialect with new ideas and concepts. Incidentally, some Bible translations of Babel do speak about a 'mixing' of languages, while the Luther translation, very well known to us, uses the negatively connoted 'confusion' of languages.

Stefano Bolognini describes quite well in an interview which consequence this constructive handling of diversity has on the attitude of an analyst:

> My idea is, that first, at the beginning of the analytic training, there is a split in every analyst between the conscious and official theoretical position and the real internal composition of his or her theory; and secondly there is

an important factor which in reality gives or doesn't give relevance to the success of an analytic identity – this is the harmony of the composition. ... A contemporary analyst can be an analyst listening to many voices, but finally composing a personal way of feeling, thinking, and working – more or less harmoniously. And to evolve this is the personal puzzle and continuous task for each analyst.

(Bolognini, in Dreher, 2014b: 217, translated for this edition)

I consider the – as Bolognini calls it – 'natural pluralism' to be a fitting characteristic, but the transitions from pluralism to eclecticism are in a flow. Because finally there can be as many personal, certainly harmonious, but also idiosyncratic analysis mixtures as there are analysts. A justifiable question is, then: what is the overlap, what remains as common ground? From a pragmatic point of view, I acknowledge that, for clinicians, the diversity on offer of ideas and concepts is really good; they have a choice. And a case-dependent pluralism is by all means adequate, given the current state of our knowledge. However, neither pluralism nor eclecticism is a good resting place and the last word on the subject. From a theoretical point of view, I acknowledge that there is a danger of too great a diversity, and a science, on the level of theory and worldviews, can and must work consequently and systematically towards convergences, mixtures, and synergies. In the long run, an 'anything goes' attitude would not be a good solution, for there would be, in the end, the danger of a sprawling arbitrariness.

The existence, as well as the usage, of all these potentials is made possible through the vagueness and complexity of the psyche. From a clinical and scientific viewpoint, the psyche is an equally fascinating and unruly thing – it successfully resists all simplistic access. It was Freud who opened the door for us to the hidden chambers. But that should not disturb us, because basic concepts of the humanities, such as freedom, life, consciousness, or love, are also not simple to access or have *exact* definitions, and they are still worked with – for they are indispensable for the reflection of the *conditio humana*. I come from psychology, where research has been done for 100 years on intelligence and personality, and since that time a number of theories have competed with each other; each has its strengths and weaknesses, what one cannot do, another perhaps can do. Thus, no one in that field would have the idea not to continue to scientifically research intelligence or personality.

Road signs and stumbling blocks

So, let us stay with the psyche and stay 'inside our Babel'. Regarding the diversity of voices, we are always dealing with *translation*, the manifold facets of which I cannot fathom here. Indeed, various translation efforts are necessary. In the clinical situation, we analysts have always been – in maieutic function – translation assistants of the unconscious into the domain of the conscious and of language, and this normally takes place in the field of ordinary language. In the dialogue among colleagues or in papers, we transport our clinical experiences into our professional language, mostly in that dialect which we individually prefer. Also, between the dialects there is often further need for translation, this time in the inner-analytic dialogue. If we then look to our neighbouring cities, to 'outside Babel', where other sciences are also exploring the psychic disturbances and phenomena, and speak about it in their professional language, we are met with new tasks: when we want to examine if what others have researched is relevant for us, or when we want to make clear to the others what we mean – then, there is a need for translation in the interdisciplinary dialogue. Many tasks are necessary. The chance that a Babel-fish[2] comes swimming by, delivering a perfect simultaneous translation, probably remains science fiction. Except for Babelfish, translation is very hard work, which on top of that is even poorly paid. Translators are – as Camus is alleged to have said – "audacious fighters who attack the tower of Babel relentlessly", and who often perform a Sisyphean task. Luckily, as in any other town, we also have all kinds of regulating services offering orientation, for instance, our textbooks and dictionaries, and last but not least our various professional associations and, of course, individual well-known authors seeking to integrate various dialects. In the 1970s, authors such as Kernberg set up road signs, linking ego psychology with object relations theories, and currently we have authors such as Ferro reading Klein, Bion, and field theory together, just to name two examples out of many others.

One of the typical textbooks of the 1970s was *The Patient and the Analyst* by Sandler, Holder and Dare (1973); both it and the second edition, on which I collaborated in the 1990s, are now not so relevant. But, even textbooks – road signs – are not free of Babylonian communication barriers, of stumbling blocks: at the time, at the publisher's request, our synopsis mainly considered English-speaking authors. From a Babylonian perspective, I regret this limitation, today, for in French, Italian, Spanish and German there were substantial innovations. The strong dominance of the contemporary Freudian perspective, which was due to the socialisation of us editors, I would also judge critically today. While looking through the literature for the updated edition, I also often noticed which tactical and strategic considerations were obvious in quoting. True, I had learned from C. S. Peirce (1931) that authority and prominence were certainly no guarantee for quality, but then had to recognise that, in reality, there are a lot of "citation cartels", as Green ironically describes them (Green, 2005: 629), in which authors from one quarter mutually celebrate each other and simply ignore the rest of the world, let alone consider critical arguments. At the time, we, too, were unfortunately not totally free from these temptations; sometimes one has to struggle quite a bit with oneself in Babel…

Printed textbooks become outdated faster and faster, but the diversity remains – actually, it even increases. The IPA, for quite a while, has been starting initiatives in order to do better justice to communication in Babel. Let me briefly mention two of the more recent projects. A project of the IPA's clinical research committee wanted to work out the essentials of a good clinical research paper all across the three IPA regions, North America, Latin America, and Europe. At a congress panel, therefore, three papers, one from each continent, respectively, were discussed from the vantage point of another continent. A text by the North American analyst Thomas Ogden, for instance, was presented and discussed from a European viewpoint. His version of W. Bion's theory of thought, the depth and subtlety of Ogden's clinical work, and his theoretical reflections impressed us in the committee (Ogden, 2010; Dreher, 2015). On the panel, we were able to show why Ogden's text was, for us, an example of a good clinical research paper. Useful elements for communication purposes are: explication of hypotheses and of the specific theoretical frame of reference, explicit integration of one's own view into the context of analytic theory development, consistent clinical argumentation, supportive illustration of the ideas by suitable case vignettes, as well as a discussion and reflection on the subject of tension between theory and clinical practice. The resonance was very positive. At the very end, however, one of those annoying Babel stumbling blocks appeared: a prominent Kleinian wanted Ogden's original work, as well as our panel contribution, to be very critically evaluated, because Ogden and we, too, failed to mention that he took major ideas from Melanie Klein. She may be right. Ogden refers only to Bion and Winnicott in that paper …. Actually, our research focus got lost as a result of that narrow commenting. Because, on the panel, we were not focusing on what the 'elders' had once said, we were explicitly focusing on how, today, one could develop a pattern for good clinical papers over three continents. Unfortunately, they still exist, these old roadblocks, and we will still have to reckon with them in Babel.

Nevertheless, our project was successful, and there are further ones, which make one optimistic. The IPA is called upon as an institution to offer orientation in this jungle of diversity. No individual analyst, clinicians in private practice far less so than researchers in institutions, has enough resources to maintain the worldwide overview. Recently an Encyclopaedic Dictionary Project has been launched, in cooperation with working groups all over the world, with the aim to put together a dictionary of currently important analytic concepts, which is then generally accessible via the internet. This project is a work in progress, of course, but already a number of Babel-related problems are becoming evident. Initially, there was no consensus about what it means to write in plain and simple language. At first, the target group was also not clear: are we only writing for we analysts or also for other scientists and for interested lay persons, too. There were first text drafts that obviously were drawn up only for readers from one's own quarter – without very good prior knowledge of Bion's, Klein's, or Lacan's theories they were difficult to understand. As was to be expected, for the meaning of some concepts the understanding initially diverged in major ways. For instance, with the concept 'countertransference' a huge range was noticeable: some regarded countertransference as an overarching term for the whole psychic participation of the analyst and, thus, central for the analytic process.

Others only saw individual aspects of this participation, for example, as a response to the patient's transference. Yet others actually considered countertransference marginal – it was only about the patient, and for this purpose the concept of transference was completely sufficient. How does one deal with such differences in writing this dictionary? For this purpose, a set of rules is being developed, the implementation of which, however, presupposes, that one talks to each other and acknowledges the convictions that are other than one's own. Furthermore, what can be done if a working group cannot agree on a homogeneous understanding? Diplomats tend to say in such a case "we agree that we disagree". At the beginning of the project, the Babel mode was applied; different versions continue side by side. I would regard such a case as an indication of a Goldschmidt gap: each version sees something different sharply. This does impede communication at first, but could be turned into a strength because together we would possibly see more than one alone could – but that would mean intensifying our substantial clinical–theoretical dialogues. Of course, such discussions go down to the 'nitty-gritty', to our implicit pre-assumptions, our 'hidden assumptions' of our own analytic worldview. And that quickly leads to discussions about what we want to consider 'innate' in the psyche and what is acquired, when, and in which way. Or about what the relationship is between Freud's 'evenly suspended attention' and Bion's 'reverie', or about what the 'observed infant' could have to do with the clinically 'reconstructed infant', etc.

The psyche between 'inside' and 'beyond Babel'

Some would like to just leave the stress behind and wish they were in a quieter place. It is too confusing for them in the streets and the squares 'inside Babel', perhaps simply too demanding. Those more tranquil places are the 'gated communities' where people live who want, above all, to go back to the roots; "Back to Freud", "Back to Klein", "Back to Lacan", you may read over their entrance doors. The residents are convinced that there are authorities in our analytic history who have already said everything important; research or other input from the outside is actually no longer needed today. Such nostalgic regressions do not really fit into a science where theories and concepts are constantly changing. Motivation for such change has always come from within psychoanalysis itself, and with increasing relevance from the outside, from those sciences also investigating the psyche with a different focus, different methods, aims and concepts. Psychoanalysis has no monopoly on the investigation of psychic phenomena – only our specific access and our 'deep psychological' models of the psyche with special attention to unconscious processes are unique. Access to, and results of, the behaviour-centred, gene-, or brain-centred approaches differ widely from our psyche-centred approach and are, therefore, naturally competing with us, both scientifically, and also in the funding within the health system. No one in psychoanalysis will deny that the psyche needs a brain (and a body, by the way, too) that is structured according to genetic plans, which underlie evolution. And that what is happening in the psyche can also show itself in behaviour and language (and in the body, too). The main work of the psyche, however, happens in secret and is, even for the owner of the psyche, only accessible to a limited extent. The classic unique feature of psychoanalysis, the unconscious, has always pointed to this fact. This non-observability evidently serves an evolutionary purpose, for otherwise nature would have equipped us with sign systems indicating to everyone, and also to us, what is happening *within* us. Reading log-files, as one does with computers, luckily does not work in our case. Also scans of the brain *only* show brain activities, and research is just on the verge of deciphering how these are connected to psychic activities. In any case, the psyche is more than a mere epiphenomenon of brain activities about which one would no longer have to speak separately once one only knew everything about the functioning of the brain. Nevertheless, we must constantly examine whether the findings of the behavioural and neurosciences are relevant for us.

Our current most interesting interface *is* with the neurosciences. The title of an event on the occasion of the presentation of the Kandel Prize in Frankfurt (Eric Kandel Young Neuroscientists Prize) in 2015 can illustrate this trend as well as its dangers: "The brain on the couch. Psychoanalysis on the way into neuroscience". The first sentence, of course, is due to marketing, there are still human beings lying on the couch, and not brains. I would have formulated the second sentence differently: "Psychoanalysis and neuroscience on their way towards a mutual approach". Why should psychoanalysis transform itself into a neuroscience and subordinate its knowledge to the knowledge of the neurosciences? After all, *both* could learn from *each other*. I definitely consider the self-surrender of psychoanalysis just as harmful as the self-overestimation I encountered recently at a conference: psychoanalysis would be the master science, the mother of all sciences, a speaker claimed – such arrogance will certainly not bring us sympathy, or any recognition, let alone friends, for it devalues all others. But the hidden anxieties behind both defence mechanisms – here self-devaluation and there self-aggrandisement – we should attend to assiduously. *The strength of neuroscience* is the investigation of the brain, and neuroscience generates fascinating findings with high relevance for medicine and basic research. The hype of imaging procedures – I also like seeing coloured pictures of the brain – is certainly due to the *Zeitgeist*. As trendy and modern as the neuro-approach is, it is, however, based on a materialistic reductionism that actually does not fit at all for psychoanalysis. *Our strength* is the investigation of the psyche; for that purpose we make a number of substantial assumptions. We assume, for instance, that the psyche mediates between nature and culture, allows us as individuals to survive between our biological physicality and the demands of the society and culture in which we live. A sheer reductionism to hardware does not work for us, because the consideration of both domains is indispensable for our work. Thus, we are dealing – beyond facts and causalities – with meaning and values, with the significance, for instance, of the influence of socialisation and historical conditions.

Human beings are not only generating and processing information, they generate and process meanings, too.

Next, of course, there is our *central* assumption of unconscious structures and processes. 'Unrepressed unconscious' is being studied by many memory researchers, 'repressed unconscious', our dynamic unconscious, still only by us. This dynamic unconscious we see in the context of psychic reality, of instincts and their vicissitudes, of unconscious conflicts, inner object-relationships, defence mechanisms, ontogenetic points of change, etc. The psyche is that agency that, for us and others, constitutes our subjectivity and our inner world, our biographically grown personality through socialisation, our identity. Thus, the psyche is unique for every human being. At first sight, the same seems to be true for the psyche as that which applies to snowflakes: examined in high resolution, none looks exactly like the other, because each individual snowflake shows the history of its origin and development. But there is one important difference. Snowflakes are not culture-dependent products. They have a natural, universal pattern, a hexagon. Whether the psyche, in contrast, is the same in all cultures and functions in the same way is at least an open question. It was Freud who characterised the methodologically most difficult feature of the psyche "Every science is based on observations and experiences arrived at through the medium of our psychical apparatus. But since our science has as its subject that apparatus itself, the analogy ends here" (Freud, 1940, p. 159). The limits of human self-awareness – whether and how the psyche can recognise itself and its functioning completely at all – are an ongoing, so far unsolved philosophical theme. Beyond that, psychoanalysis does not consider the psyche a monad; its full functionality only shows itself interpsychically in exchange with others, usually with the reference persons who are the significant others. Presumably, the psyche differentiated itself evolutionarily only because we human beings as a species are social beings. We make use of this interpsychic moment in the classic variant of analytic treatment: the psyche of the patient and that of the analyst constitute a dyad, a bipolar field, characterised by the interweaving of transference and countertransference, by the interplay of the patient's free association and the analyst's evenly suspended attention. It is only in this field that the unique experiential sphere unfolds which is constitutive for our work. In a special sense, we ourselves, with our psyche, function as diagnostic and therapeutic agents. We analysts not only give a treatment, in the way a doctor gives a tablet or performs surgery, we are an inseparable part of the treatment.

Critics either do not agree with these assumptions or they criticise the lack of scientific grounding of our ideas. And here, suddenly, we are with the scientific worldviews again. For, the relevance of the statement that the phenomena we investigate would be hardly observable objectively, difficult to measure and quantify, is definitely grounded in a specific view of science: the view of modern natural sciences, which have proved themselves to be very successful in their domains. Should we, however, because of this critique, simply give up our assumptions? Or, shouldn't we in turn criticise the improper transferring of this worldview to the domain of the psyche? If we would *only* rely on so-called objective methods in our search for the unconscious, we would not find it at all. And we might experience the same as a drunk man who lost his key and is seeking it under a lamppost. When asked by a pedestrian whether he had lost his key there, the drunk answers: "No, but here I can see something".

Conclusion

My sceptical optimism, that it may be possible to promote the project of psychoanalysis is mainly based on considerations about our traditional subject and name-giver 'psyche'. It is actually not only inspiring and interesting 'inside Babel', there is also a very practical reason to stay here. It is often claimed that the real context of justification of all analytic ideas would be the clinical situation. New ideas and concepts are always tested by us on-site, having regard to both practicability and utility in the analytic work. That this actually constantly happens is illustrated by "natural pluralism" and eclecticism. The German soccer coach Adi Preißler is supposed to have said once about the relationship of theory and practice: "All theory is grey – what matters, is on the field"). We could say: "What matters, is on the couch", even if not all of our patients are on the couch any longer. Our clinical practice remains decisive.

Our models of the psyche are unique and, I think, the best elaborated ones. We have a historically grown treasure of theoretical ideas and reflections *and* of clinical evidence supporting our assumptions about the psyche in essential parts. The complexity of the psyche is probably the essential reason why there is no 'theory of everything', no analytic theory, that embraces everything. Physics, too, is still seeking its theory of everything. Our respective dialects, however, very discriminately grasp partial views of this holistically functioning psyche, and it would be useful to continue working on the constructive mixing of our dialects. And yet, it is not the variety of the dialects that is the problem, for each new dialect possibly adds to the overall picture, the problem is the often observable group-dynamic delineation of the dialect speakers, for whom the distinction is more important than the connective aspects and who would rather remain among themselves.

Living 'inside Babel' is not always easy. But, I think, in all our manifold discourses, one can again and again wring the pleasant from the unpleasant. There are many, perhaps too many, areas of tension: not only inside ourselves, but also within and between dialects, between worldviews, between clinicians and researchers, between psychoanalysis and its neighbouring sciences. It is definitely important to see these areas of tension, and to see them not only as barriers, but as impulses, as an inspiration, and to balance them again and again. Making oneself aware of one's own 'anti-social and anti-cultural motives' alone and keeping them in awareness demands quite some effort. It may be difficult to seek discourse in Babel, but there is only one thing that would cause more difficulties in the long run: that is, not to seek discourse at all.

Notes

1 This is the English translation of the German version, first published in: *Forum der Psychoanalyse* 3(2016). Translation by Eva Ristl.
2 The Babel fish is a literary fiction from the book *The Hitchhiker's Guide to the Galaxy* (Adams, 1979). The Babel fish can simultaneously translate every language in the universe into any other language.

References

Adams, D. (1979) *The Hitchhiker's Guide to the Galaxy*. London: Pan.
Bergson, H. (1948) *Denken und schöpferisches Werden*. Meisenheim am Glan: Westkulturverlag.
Dreher, A. U. (2014a) Wie heilig sind uns psychoanalytische Konzepte? *Forum Psychoanalyse* 30: 11–26.
Dreher, A. U. (2014b) Psychoanalyse international – oder die Kunst, unterschiedliche Welten auszubalancieren. Interview mit Stefano Bolognini, *Forum Psychoanalyse* 30: 213–239.
Dreher, A. U. (2015) Psychoanalytic research with or without the psyche? Some remarks on the intricacies of clinical research, in: S. Boag, L. Brakel & V. Talvitie (eds.), *Philosophy, Science, and Psychoanalysis*. London: Karnac, 219–246.
Freud, S. (1927) *The Future of an Illusion. SE* 21. London: Hogarth.
Freud, S. (1940) *An Outline of Psychoanalysis. SE* 23. London: Hogarth.
Goldschmidt, G.-A. (2008) *Freud wartet auf das Wort*. Frankfurt: Fischer.
Graves, R. & Patai, R. (1963) *Hebrew Myths: The Book of Genesis*. New York: Doubleday.
Green, A. (2005) The illusion of *common ground* and mythical pluralism, *International Journal of Psychoanalysis* 86: 627–632.
Kernberg, O. F. (2006) The pressing need to increase research in and on psychoanalysis, *International Journal of Psychoanalysis* 87: 919–926.
Koestler, A. (1975) *Die Herren Call-Girls. Ein satirischer Roman*. Munich: Droemer/Knaur.
Ogden, T. H. (2010) On three forms of thinking: magical thinking, dream thinking, and transformative thinking, *Psychoanalytic Quarterly* 79: 317–347.
Peirce, C. S. (1931) *The Collected Papers Vol. I: Principles of Philosophy. § 7 The Method of Authority*. Cambridge, MA: Harvard University Press.
Sandler, J., Dare, C. & Holder, A. (1973) *The Patient and the Analyst: The Basis of the Psychoanalytic Process* (2nd edn, 1992, revised and expanded by J. Sandler & A. U. Dreher). London: Karnac.
Steiner, R. (1994) The Tower of Bable or After Babel in contemporary psychoanalysis? Some historical and theoretical notes on the linguistic and cultural strategies implied by the foundation of the International Journal of Psychoanalysis, and on its relevance today, *International Journal of Psychoanalysis* 75: 883–901.
Wallerstein, R. (2005a) Will psychoanalytic pluralism be an enduring state of our discipline? *International Journal of Psychoanalysis* 86: 623–626.
Wallerstein, R. (2005b) Dialogue or illusion? How do we go from here? Response to André Green, *International Journal of Psychoanalysis* 86: 633–638.

2

THE GIFT OF BABEL

Understanding – interpreting – comprehension

Jan Philipp Reemtsma

In his 'trilogy' *The Hitchhiker's Guide to the Galaxy*, Douglas Adams introduces readers to the Babel fish. This small, fishlike creature lives on brainwave energy, absorbing mental frequencies to then excrete a telepathic matrix into the mind. When a Babel fish is placed in someone's ear, then any foreign language heard by the carrier will be decoded into the language they are familiar with. The evolution of the Babel fish is such a "bizarrely improbable coincidence" that some think its mere existence is proof of the existence of God. In any event, the novel tells us, the discovery of the Babel fish and its universal use has led to universal understanding among the populations of all planets – and has thus "caused more and bloodier wars than anything else in the history of creation" (Adams, 1986: 42).

Understanding one another is generally considered to be a good thing, but then one should be wary of simplistic ways of thinking. That is why I began this chapter with the invention described in the *Hitchhiker's Guide*. But before I address the question of what we actually mean by 'understanding', I would like to refer to the original text, the *Urtext*:

> Now the whole world had one language and a common speech. As people moved eastward, they found a plain in Shinar and settled there. They said to each other, "(...) Come, let us build ourselves a city, with a tower that reaches to the heavens, so that we may make a name for ourselves; otherwise we will be scattered over the face of the whole earth." But the Lord came down to see the city and the tower the people were building. The Lord said, "If as one people speaking the same language they have begun to do this, then nothing they plan to do will be impossible for them. Come, let us go down and confuse their language so they will not understand each other." So the Lord scattered them from there over all the earth, and they

stopped building the city. That is why it was called Babel – because there the Lord confused the language of the whole world. From there the Lord scattered them over the face of the whole earth.

(Genesis 11: 1–9)

No matter how one chooses to comment on and interpret this story, it says one thing very unequivocally: Not being able to understand each other (right away) is a curse, and if someone had that capacity (to understand others right away), then there is nothing in the world that could withstand that person, not even a god. So the story is (to my mind) as much indicative of delusions of grandeur as the enterprise of building the Tower of Babel itself. In essence, this is a rather classic neurotic narrative in the guise of a therapeutic reconstruction: That I am unable to live up to my own expectations is because I was thoroughly damaged by someone powerful long ago.

But let us set these thoughts aside. In what Christians refer to as the New Testament there is a counter-narrative called the miracle of Pentecost, which goes like this (in the following, 'they' refers to the disciples of Jesus, the apostles):

When the day of Pentecost came, they were all together in one place. Suddenly a sound like the blowing of a violent wind came from heaven and filled the whole house where they were sitting. They saw what seemed to be tongues of fire that separated and came to rest on each of them. All of them were filled with the Holy Spirit and began to speak in other tongues as the Spirit enabled them. Now there were staying in Jerusalem God-fearing Jews from every nation under heaven. When they heard this sound, a crowd came together in bewilderment, because each one heard their own language being spoken. Utterly amazed, they asked: "Aren't all these who are speaking Galileans? Then how is it that each of us hears them in our native language? Parthians, Medes and Elamites; residents of Mesopotamia, Judea and Cappadocia, Pontus and Asia, Phrygia and Pamphylia, Egypt and the parts of Libya near Cyrene; visitors from Rome (both Jews and converts to Judaism); Cretans and Arabs – we hear them declaring the wonders of God in our own tongues!" Amazed and perplexed, they asked one another, "What does this mean?"

(Acts 2: 1–12)

So you see where the idea of the Babel fish came from.

You have also, no doubt, heard of the evangelical movement called Pentecostalism. Pentecostals believe that they can be empowered to 'speak in tongues', referred to as the gift of 'glossolalia'. The phenomenon in question is a kind of ecstatic frenzy that occurs during religious practices, in which the worshiper suddenly begins to make incomprehensible utterances. Did something similar happen with the apostles? The section of the Acts of the Apostles I just quoted ends like this: "Some, however, made fun of them and said, 'They have had too much wine'" (Acts 2: 13). This is exceedingly peculiar: Doing away with the multitude of languages that is passed on to us because of God's intervention in Babel leads to completely meaningless utterances, which each person can interpret to mean whatever comes into her or his head. The lesson to be learned would be: Understanding without recognizing the principle of separateness is, in effect, pure projection, with some nonsense mixed in for good measure.

I would like to take these stories seriously and retell them by considering three spheres of reflection. I will address (1) understanding, (2) interpreting, and (3) *Verständnis*, the German term meaning a sympathetic form of understanding.

What exactly is 'understanding'? As you know, this discussion has accompanied philosophy more or less since it has existed – why interfere in these debates again now? Because I think that, as far as I can tell, an unproductive mistake is always made in this context to the effect that understanding – I'm referring to understanding language, not to what philosophy calls 'understanding the world' or what is called 'understanding as opposed to explaining' in the theory and philosophy of science, in other words, only what happens when our communication with language (well, all right, as it is accompanied by gestures and shaped by other acoustic elements) simply takes place without any "What is that supposed to mean?" or so much as a "Huh?" – once again, that there is an unproductive mistake, which conceptualizes this type of understanding as something like an activity. In other words, it is conceptualized as something that – even if it just happens and people do not offer explanations for what goes on – can be meaningfully described as a kind of activity. And that 'what happens' can be readily understood, if I describe it in this manner, as an activity. But what activity would it then be? Some people attempt to describe it with words like 'to grasp or determine that' (*erfassen, daß* ...; i.e., that someone speaks at all, what they are speaking about, that the speaker is in this or that state, that what is said is relevant for this or that, and so on). But what does it mean to say someone grasps something, if not exactly the same thing as 'to understand'? In effect, it amounts to the same explanation as Molière's quip about opium, which puts people to sleep thanks to its *vis dormitiva*.[1] Donald Davidson (1973: 313) summarizes things rather drily like this: "Kurt utters the words 'Es regnet' and under the right conditions we know that he has said that it is raining".[2]

Let us pursue the question further along the lines of Wittgenstein's terminology: is understanding a language game? Here is a quotation from the *Philosophical Investigations* (1953: 11–12):

> Here the term "language-game" is meant to bring into prominence the fact that the speaking of language is part of an activity, or of a form of life.
> Review the multiplicity of language-game in the following examples, and in others:
> Giving orders, and obeying them—
> Describing the appearance of an object, or giving its measurements—
> Constructing an object from a description (a drawing)—

Reporting an event—
Speculating about an event—
Forming and testing a hypothesis—
Presenting the results of an experiment in tables and diagrams—
Making up a story; and reading it—
Play-acting—
Singing catches—
Guessing riddles—
Making a joke; telling it—
Solving a problem in practical arithmetic—
Translating from one language into another—
Asking, thanking, cursing, greeting, praying.

'Understanding' does not belong in this list, but, without 'understanding', we are unable to understand what it is about these language games that makes each a language game. 'Understanding', thus, means 'grasping' what game is being played and, as a result, which move is the next possible one. But 'grasping' is, in this context (see above) merely a synonym for 'understanding'. And this 'grasping' is also *not something that I can reconstruct as an activity*. I do not do anything 'in order to grasp something'. I simply learned this language game and now I am capable of playing – or not. Even learning cannot be meaningfully described as an activity. One grows into it. We know that children do not understand irony until they have reached a certain age. And we know that, before that age, all explanations that are supposed to guide them to an understanding are futile. At some point, they understand irony. They are born into a culture with the language game called 'an ironic remark'. But what does it mean to understand an ironic remark? To be able to react to it adequately. There is no other possibility to determine whether someone has understood something. *To understand is when nothing happens*, when no interruption in communication occurs due to enquiries to clarify what is said or objections due to misunderstandings or a lack of understanding – without interpreting what has been said – without the feeling of comprehension. To understand means being able to continue uneventfully on both sides.

To understand is not a language game, nor is it a move in this language game. We call it 'to have understood' when the game is continued. To understand is what one does not notice and what cannot be reconstructed. What one notices, what is conspicuous, is misunderstood. But what does it mean to misunderstand or to not understand?

Many things, no doubt; this and that. But it always means that, all at once, things cannot go on. Those who are talking to each other must consult with each other. A misunderstanding or lack of understanding is a discontinuance of communication, which is called a misunderstanding to distinguish it from a dissent. A dissent has nothing to do with not understanding or misunderstanding – it can only be called that in some cases. "No, no, you just misunderstood me!

We don't disagree at all". Not understanding or misunderstanding is also not recursive, in the sense that something that one previously determined was disrupted is now (tentatively) undisrupted and, presented, as it were, in a completely reconditioned state. You just continue and what can happen next differs considerably: request that a word be repeated more loudly; consult a dictionary; ask for a translation; ask to have the same thing repeated in different words; ask "bear left after the train station or take a hard left?"; allow oneself to be lectured about what it means "to apply for a visa" – the list does not differ much from the one quoted above from Wittgenstein's *Philosophical Investigations*. These are all 'language games' but they differ from one another, and the fact that they all – under certain circumstances – can be categorized as 'rectifying a misunderstanding' does not mean they represent a common type of language game. Here we have the famous 'family resemblances': "… I am saying that these phenomena have no one thing in common which makes us use the same word for all, – but that they are *related* to one another in many different ways" (Wittgenstein, 1953: 31).

This family of rectifying non-understanding or misunderstanding – or perhaps we should refer to recreating understanding – has many different members but, as with understanding, communication always goes on. You don't just do the same thing again until you understand each other; rather, you do something different than you anticipated – but then, when did you really anticipate how things would continue in communicating? Perhaps the way things will continue is that the meaning of a word will be clarified ("What do you mean by …?"), and that, too, can happen in very different ways. You can open a dictionary together or one of the people who is talking can say something like "Well, when I say x, then I always think of …".

The range of possibilities runs from a simple "Huh?" (to which the other replies, "What do you mean by Huh?" or "Why Huh?"); to a "Repeat that please!" (perhaps adding, "I haven't been hearing too well lately"); to asking about a word ("What does 'marginal' mean?" or, in a different mode, "What do you mean by 'marginal'?" or, yet again different, "What do you mean *this time* by 'marginal'?" – *con variazione*); to questions about what the other person is referring to, what they have in mind, ascertaining whether one has seriously and precisely understood what was said in such and such a way; then an offer to say it in a different way ("you probably mean …"), to phrases like "you won't understand until I tell you …", perhaps followed by the story of someone's life.[3]

Everything we can think of in this respect continues communication, rather than repeating it. All of this presupposes understanding or, rather, more precisely, is accompanied by understanding, or, even more precisely, *is* understanding. Understanding is, once more, not an activity; it is not even an activity that can be reconstructed in any way. Understanding happens, understanding is what happens when nothing else happens, when communication does not become redirected into operations that rectify misunderstandings or non-understanding; and such operations as well occur under the premise that understanding is taking place.

Understanding is not 'interpreting'. Interpreting is an activity that interrupts understanding intentionally and with brute force. Of course, interpretation must also be understood; understanding also takes place in this context, but interpreting is, none the less, a declaration of no confidence, and, indeed, a one-sided one at that. Permit me to recount a droll anecdote from Bertrand Russell's autobiography. In the early 1920s, Russell took a trip to China and one of the things he writes about is the following:

> One hot day two fat middle-aged business men invited me to motor into the country to see a very famous half-ruined pagoda. When we reached it, I climbed the spiral staircase, expecting them to follow, but on arriving at the top I saw them still on the ground. I asked why they had not come up, and with portentous gravity they replied: "We thought of coming up, and debated whether we should do so. Many weighty arguments were advanced on both sides, but at last there was one which decided us. The pagoda might crumble at any moment, and we felt that, if it did, it would be well there should be those who could bear witness as to how the philosopher died." What they meant was that it was hot and that they were fat.
> (Russell, 1969: 129–130)

This is, of course, a joke, and Russell tells the story as an example of how similar Chinese and British humor are. Be that as it may, this little anecdote highlights what 'interpreting' is about: the claim is made that what has been said is not what was meant; rather, something else was meant, and the other person involved in communication is able and entitled to introduce this other meaning into the communicative game. This kind of 'interpreting' follows the differentiation that Freud introduced for the interpretation of dreams, as the distinction between manifest and latent content.

But what is at issue here is not the interpretation of dreams but, rather, the interpretative reference to a previous act of communication – and that is something characterized by brute force in the sense that *the person doing the interpreting conveys the message, by interpreting, that the interlocutor does not understand his or her own self at all or that their understanding is, at best, inadequate.* When interpreting is taking place, the interpreter imposes upon the person who is being interpreted a change in the direction of communication.

When someone says, "It's warm here" and someone else answers, "Oh no, it's no more than eighteen degrees", then the subject of communication is the temperature in the room. If the answer is "Should I open the window?", then you might say that this reaction understood the sentence "It's warm here" to be a request to reduce the temperature. The response to "It's warm here" might also have been "Would you like to take off your coat?", which might be interpreted as an erotic offer. Or the answer could be: "Yes, as a sociologist, I know that I am expressing a commitment to the lower classes". ("*Ja, als Soziologe weiß ich, daß ich damit ein Bekenntnis zur Unterschicht ablege*".) No matter how it continues, as long as communication does continue, we call this understanding. If it doesn't, we refer to a misunderstanding. And a misunderstanding will be rectified, one way or the other. If a misunderstanding is to be made explicit through communication, then a communicative act becomes the subject of communication. In other words, communication goes on; it changes through this act, but it does not, in principle, change its character. The situation is different for interpreting – fundamentally different.

We want to distinguish interpretation from the usual kind of interpretative reference that allows communication to continue by one means or another by saying the following: interpreting makes a previous communicative act the subject of communication, of the kind that any object from outside the realm of communication can be its subject. In this way, the communicative act that has been chosen for interpretation is itself no longer capable of easily being continued. Thus, in the case of the exchange discussed above, that is, "It's warm here"; "Should I open the window?", no interpretation has occurred. But in this case, it has: "It's warm here"; "What are you trying to divert my attention from?" None of the possible offers to continue is taken up; the interpreter, who in this case reflects on the preceding communication and points to a perceived problem, does not continue but instead does something else and – this is the important point – forces the person being interpreted to respond to this change in the form of communication, even if he or she has no desire to do so. "I'm not diverting your attention from anything. It's just very warm in here. Take a look at the thermometer!" In order to reject the act of interpretation, the person being interpreted must emphasize the mistakenness of the interpretation – or end communication. *Tertium non datur*, and that is what bestows upon the individual who interrupts communication with an interpretation, at least for the moment, a special position of power within that communication.

Through the act of interpretation, the interpreter gains power over the person who is being interpreted, and this occurs solely by virtue of the act itself. This power is not necessarily long-lasting; the interpreter can soon become the loser, but that does not change the fundamental fact. The act of interpretation is precarious in terms of communication, because what is normally experienced as a situation devoid of power relations (at least, let us assume so in this context) is transformed into a power struggle. One could derive from this the *maxim of a moral code of communication*: interpretations should only occur when the partners in communication have either agreed that interpretations are to have their place in their conversation or that they can be allowed to the extent that an interpretation can only be given if the person being interpreted gives her or his consent to change over to this new communicative status. "It's warm here". "What are you trying to divert my attention from?" "Take a look at the thermometer!" "Excuse me, should I open the window?"

If interpretation is to succeed, in the sense that communication is not interrupted by the act of interpreting but instead continues and does so thanks to the act of interpreting itself, then *the relationship between the interpreter and the person being interpreted must be asymmetrical*. Moreover, where interpreting is allowed and, indeed, called for, no communicative act is excluded from interpretation, whether it is expressed in words or actions. I am referring here, as you can imagine, to a *therapeutic* situation. It is an essential part of therapeutic situations that communicative acts on the part of the person who, potentially, is to be subjected to interpretation, cannot be withheld. None the less, not every offer of communication will be interpreted; a selection will be made on the basis of certain criteria, some specific to the respective personality, and with the goal of familiarizing the person being interpreted with something she or he has as a capacity for but (as yet) has no command of. The asymmetric nature of the communicative relationship is indispensable if this is to occur. If the asymmetry is set aside, communication is blocked. The blockage, in turn, can only be dissolved by an interpretation, by a reflexive reference to the blockage as a communicative act. The therapeutic situation is, thus, not only a situation in which interpretation can and should take place; it must be interpreted – at times – and if the necessary interpretation does not take place, communication is blocked.

This asymmetry – an asymmetry that has been agreed to – is manifested in the fact that an interruption or end of communication can – or even must – also be interpreted. Part of the agreement between therapist and client is the understanding that the client can end therapy, if he or she wants to – otherwise, it would be a kind of confinement – but part of the agreement is also the therapist's right to interpret the client's wish to end the process. Ultimately, it is up to a client to engage with the interpretation of this wish or not. But, at first, an interpretation of the desire to end the therapy means what an interpretation always means: you mean something other than what you are saying; the latent content of your statement is something other than your actual manifest words.

I would like to quote from David Mann's book *Psychotherapy, an Erotic Relationship*.

> This chapter will propose that transgression is integral to curiosity and questioning in creative development. By transgression, I mean the necessary act of going somewhere that previously seemed off limits. Transgression, in the way I use it here, means to denote a pushing beyond the accepted norms, a stepping outside the expected—going past known boundaries. In the therapeutic context, I will suggest that the therapist and analysand need to find themselves in a different place. From this I will suggest that psychotherapy should be considered a mutually transforming process (…) the erotic, by its very nature, will produce the greatest possibilities for transgression.
>
> *(Mann, 1997: 179)*

I would dispute that interpreting is a transgression, a boundary violation (*Grenzverletzung*). Interpreting, like sexuality, is a boundary crossing (*Grenzüberschreitung*). To interpret is to go beyond the boundaries of what has implicitly been agreed to in normal communication that occurs on an equal footing. *Where nothing has been agreed upon is where interpretation* – as in sexuality without consent – becomes a violation of boundaries. To call interpretation a transgression of boundaries in situations in which it is only a crossing of boundaries under consensus conditions can tempt us to overlook where interpretation is a transgression, despite its occurrence in a therapeutic setting. Such seemingly radical pronouncements frequently lead to a process of desensitizing. When violations occur in the psychoanalytical setting, it is not interpretation that is responsible but, rather, those who interpret, for example, when they lack a sense of timing, blurting out their interpretation prematurely.

Freud writes,

> You must wait for the right moment at which you can communicate your interpretation to the patient with some prospect of success. (...) That is a question of tact, which can become refined with experience. You will be making a bad mistake if, in an effort, perhaps, at shortening the analysis, you throw your interpretations at the patient's head as soon as you have found them.
>
> *(1926: 219)*

This is a transgression within a setting, in which, however, there is agreement in principle that interpretation can take place.

But if no agreement has been reached, interpretation is often even more than a mere boundary violation. This is the case at times in politics. Whenever I no longer engage in debate, when I refer to the arguments of my political opponent as communicative acts, rather than confirming them, criticizing them, or refuting them, I have disengaged with him or her as an interlocutor. My interlocutor is now the mass of listeners; I must now get across to them what my rival is *really* interested in. My opponent has now acquired the role of someone who pursues certain interests (which I will expose); a demagogue whose agenda is something different than what is being talked about, or someone who is not quite sound of mind, who doesn't know what they're talking about. In the political sphere, this amounts to a declaration that someone is either unworthy or an enemy.

I'd like to suggest that we reflect on whether the model of appearance and essence that is frequently drawn on to frame the communicative act of interpretation is, in fact, derived especially from the political hermeneutics of suspicion and the desire to 'expose': to unmask someone and reveal their true face. Wherever the desire to expose occurs, we can assume that the underlying motivation is aggressive. Moreover, the aggressive, power-seeking potential of the communicative act of interpretation is revealed, a potential that can be found wherever it has not been contained, that is, where it is permitted as a boundary-crossing act.

Those who interpret the communicative acts of an opponent in the political arena are simulating a political position of power that they do not yet have. If those who are in power are doing the interpreting, then they threaten, by doing so, to use their power. When interpretation takes place in politics, it does not constitute a struggle for power; rather, it makes a distinction between legitimate and illegitimate claims to power. The interpretation aims to offer proof of the illegitimacy of power.[4] The relative share of interpretative communicative acts in political rhetoric is presumably an interesting indicator of the totalitarian tendencies of a political party or movement. (Caveat! As an argument in political debate, this, too, is an interpretation.)

To what extent are interpretations 'right' or 'true'? Students of literary studies, if they have developed a certain degree of sensitivity, experience a crisis that has to do with the question of whether one can distinguish between true and false interpretations. The only answer one can give them is that, of course, one can make a distinction between interpretations that make sense and those that do not (according to criteria but not an entire catalogue of criteria) but that no interpretation will end the potential sequence of new interpretations or variations of earlier ones. Therapies, in contrast, must be finite. One might tentatively say this: they can be completed when the desire for an end does not provoke any further interpretations. And while therapy is still going on? When is an interpretation 'right'? It is right when the process continues, despite the – brutal, boundary-crossing – intervention in communication, the turn that leads to the unexpected and forces one to confront the interpretation of communication. When it continues *differently*, but continues. Perhaps it will at first go on in a mode of refusing to agree to the interpretation, perhaps with agreement (from a "Hm, maybe" to what might be an emphatic "Yes, that's true!").

The response 'true', by the way, puts an end to the classic question of 'interpretation or projection', for if both participants say 'true!', then the projection, which always plays a role (and which then is called 'countertransference') is of no consequence. If the signal 'true' isn't given, then the continuation of communication will have to reveal what has occurred. In a therapeutic situation, a patient's conceivable objection that an interpretation is only a projection on the part of the analyst is, in the first instance, an object for interpretation. The issue of 'projection or interpretation' has a variety of possible practical meanings but is, I would suspect, of no theoretical significance. What determines its significance is the way in which communication is continued or stopped – the therapeutic practice.

During analysis, interpretations are communicative acts. Agreement about whether they are true or not is demonstrated by the way in which one agrees to continue. "That's true" signals the willingness to use an interpretation's communicative input. In the political arena, in contrast, interpretations depend to a significant extent on the fact that the person being interpreted – if he or she is a political opponent and political opponents are the preferred objects of political interpretation – *does not agree* that they are true. The opponent is to be 'exposed', and those who are the target of exposure generally insist that they don't wear masks. (This leads to an interesting twist: one can – assuming one has the capacity to do so – undermine interpretations in the political sphere by agreeing with them and saying "So what?" If the interpretation 'doesn't matter', the interpreter doesn't stand to gain anything by it.) People who interpret in the political arena don't want to hear "That's true!" They aim to exacerbate the antagonisms. They seek a *clash*.

In the therapeutic situation, those who respond with by saying "It's true", in one way or the other, are indicating that they feel they have been understood. This is not in the sense of the mere continuation of communication discussed earlier, but, rather, in the sense that they accept the turn that communication takes with this interpretation – and also accept the distinction between manifest and latent meaning in their statements. Moreover, they do something with far-reaching implications: they accept that the therapist *assigns them a place in the world*, a place that the clients did not previously realize that they occupied. These clients accept that the therapist's understanding of their situation in life is (at least slightly) superior to their own self-understanding.

Now, having discussed 'understanding', 'rectifying non-understanding or misunderstandings' and 'interpreting', finally, the *concept of Verständnis*, the German term that signals understanding accompanied by sympathy. *Verständnis*, thus, denotes sympathy for a situation in life, a place in the world. More precisely, for the life situation, the place in the world of the other, one's counterpart.

Verständnis calls to mind a kind of closeness. Someone has sharpened their senses and now knows (a bit) about who I am (and, in a moment, a little more than I know myself). This creates a *feeling of closeness*. I won't deny that this feeling exists, but it is only half the truth – and not the interesting half of the truth, either. "Yes", the father says to the whining child, "I understand you. You'd like to have some ice cream. But please understand me, too. I have to watch out that you don't eat too many sweet things". In this case, understanding – I know where your standpoint is, now recognize mine – marks a boundary and the demand that that boundary be accepted.

I don't know if any of you are familiar with the film *If…*, which was released in 1968. It won a Golden Palm at Cannes and gained notoriety, among other things, for a wild sex scene on the floor of a seedy café, which supposedly was not acted out. The film is set in a British boarding school and ends in a kind of military training exercise. The protagonists – a few pupils from the school and a woman who works at the café – discover a cache of weapons. They use them to open fire from the school's roof on the parents and teachers who have come together for a celebration and religious service on the school's Founders' Day, before the parents and teachers also distribute firearms and fire back. The headmaster attempts to intervene with the words, "Boys, I understand you!" and is then shot in the forehead with a revolver. Understanding as an unseemly form of rapprochement? Or as a means of assigning people their place, by feigning closeness: you there, me here?

Recognizing someone's place in the world – well, that means suggesting what that person's place might be. If the answer to such a suggestion, as part of an interpretation, seems to be acceptance or, at least, the willingness to imagine oneself in that place, then perhaps it is accompanied by a feeling of closeness. But there is also, at the same time, a *feeling of distance*. One person's place is not the place of another – neither are those places interchangeable. One can see the other person's place in the world, but what is revealed is, above all, this: their place is not my place. Wherever this is not made perfectly clear, an inadmissible form of community building occurs – inadmissible at least in the relationship between therapist and client.

But the same holds true for politics. Political community building is always in danger of leading to totalitarianism. In his memoir *Defying Hitler* (2002), Sebastian Haffner reports on a *Referendarlager*, a summer camp that trainee lawyers were forced to attend, where they were to be indoctrinated in Nazi legal ideology. Many enjoyed the experience of community there, the sense of 'comradeship'. They had been, Haffner asserts, simply too weak for bourgeoisie life (pp. 285–292). Solidarity and comradeship, the glorification and idealization of community, Hannah Arendt writes, are often the virtues touted by threatened communities. But, she notes, they rarely survive the end of the threat – most fortunately (Arendt, 1970: 69).

Experiencing understanding too intensely as closeness and a sense of community (*Gemeinschaftlichkeit*) makes the therapeutic situation a *folie à deux*. Therapeutic communication – which may be accompanied by a strong feeling of closeness and expression of the sentiment "That's true" in response to what is perceived as a fitting interpretation – must, none the less, clarify the separation of therapist and client. This pertains not only to the asymmetry that is the prerequisite for interpretation but also to the need for *accepting separateness* as the necessary precondition for adult life. Aside from symbiotic situations in early life, we all live in "mental solitary confinement", to quote Arno Schmidt (1994), and we communicate, if I may colour in this image a bit more, by using knocking codes and secret messages. Or, to quote Richard Rorty (1991: 204), who expressed the thought a bit less bleakly, we are all monads, but we are "well-windowed monads".

We can, indeed, communicate and understand and rectify misunderstandings; we can even interpret, and, in therapeutic situations, interpretation is even what is called for (then we'll see what happens next), but all of this occurs under the conditions that reign after the Tower of Babel has collapsed – not in the nightmarish setting of glossolalia. That a god has destroyed the tower and scattered us over the earth forces us to recognize the other as separate from us and to recognize every notion of identification as regression to a pre-Babel condition. And it forces us to erect a symbol representing this megalomaniac idea, a condition (an imagined one) of complete symbiosis. This symbol reaches the stars: the formation of the cardinal virtue of coexistence, the *capacity to acknowledge*.

Goethe (and he was not the only one) spoke contemptuously – and quite rightly – about the idea of tolerance: tolerance, he noted, was condescension. Rather than being tolerant, one should acknowledge. In Hegel's opinion, acknowledgement is the perception of another person as free, and the opportunity to be of use to him or her, through my own freedom. *The ability to acknowledge the other in separateness and freedom is the gift of Babel.*

Notes

1 The line is from Molière, *The Imaginary Invalid*, Act Three: "… Opium facit dormire. A quoi respondeo, Quia est in eo Vertus Dormitiva …".
2 In the German translation, published in 1986, the name Kurt has been changed to Geoffrey.
3 Somewhere in this sphere, speaking about "understanding" as it is discussed here intersects with what is addressed in the *Historisches Wörterbuch der Philosophie* in a text written by Hans Apel under the heading *Verstehen* (*Historische Wörterbuch der Philosophie* [2007], edited by Joachim Ritter, Karlfried Gründer, Gottfried Gabriel. Basel: Schwabe Verlag).
4 This raises the issue of how we can differentiate between interpretations in politics and the interpretation of political occurrences in journalism, political science, etc. I consider this to be possible but by no means easy.

References

Adams, D. (1986) *The Hitchhiker's Guide to the Galaxy*, in: *The More Than Complete Hitchhiker's Guide*. Stamford, CT: Longmeadow Press.
Arendt, H. (1970) *On Violence*. New York: Harcourt, Brace & World.
Davidson, D. (1973) Radical interpretation, *Dialectica*, 27: 3–4, 313–328.
Freud, S. (1926) *The Question of Lay Analysis*. SE, XX. London: Hogarth Press.
Haffner, S. (2002) *Defying Hitler: A Memoir*. New York: Farrar, Straus & Giroux.
Mann, D. (1997) *Psychotherapy, an Erotic Relationship: Transference and Countertransference Passions*. London: Routledge.
Rorty, R. (1991) On ethnocentrism: A reply to Clifford Geertz, in: *Objectivity, Relativism, and Truth*. Cambridge: Cambridge University Press.
Russell, B. (1969) *The Autobiography of Bertrand Russell. Vol. II*. London: George Allen and Unwin.
Schmidt, A. (1994) *The Displaced*, in: *Collected Novellas*. Normal, IL: Dalkey Archive Press.
Wittgenstein, L. (1953) *Philosophical Investigations*. Oxford: Basil Blackwell.

3
LONGING FOR CONNECTION

Antje von Boetticher

Introduction

The so-called 'new media' imply enormous changes. Everyday life can no longer be imagined without mobile phones and the internet. In appointments, private and professional meetings and communication, at school and university, today the internet plays an important role. If I want to know something I will "google" it. I send a text message to make an appointment or a rendezvous with somebody. I don´t have to depend on being at home to get a call. And, my message will reach my friend while she or he is on the road. Information, messages, letters, appointments are just a mouse-click away. Nowadays, we often hear the claim that the world is at your fingertips: one click and you have access to the whole world. The generation growing up with 'new media' is called 'generation Y', 'digital natives' or 'generation connected', the era of new media 'digital age' or 'Liquid Age'. A liquid age of a connected generation of digital natives …

Philipp Riederle (born in 1994), one of these natives, denotes the smartphone as today's most important intellectual weapon and says about his generation: "We can tell about us. And this means sharing. And this means: to be a part of this world and find our place. That is what we want" (Riederle, 2013, p. 54, translated for this edition).

Different sources have given rise to unease that is faced by many older people (so called 'digital immigrants'). The alien and unfamiliar surely play as important a role as the alarming results of studies showing that the permanent use of smartphones leads to reduced capacity to learn and concentrate (e.g., Spitzer, 2014), and to the fear of contracting a disorder through seemingly bodiless communication. Seeking for the authentic when all of life is taking place in virtual spaces, many people admit that they don´t know their way around any longer. Do we lose substantial knowledge when information is quickly and easily available?

Is everything becoming superficial and lacking in substance; can we still have deep experiences? Does the World Wide Web offer space for enormous megalomania and oceanic or godlike feelings? Can we see and understand everything, any time?

Freud wrote, in *Civilization and Its Discontents*:

> Future ages will produce further great advances in this realm of culture, probably inconceivable now and will increase man's likeness to a god still more. But with the aim of our study in mind, we will not forget, all the same, that the human being of today is not happy with all his likeness to a god.
>
> *(Freud, 1962: 39)*

Being like god? Understanding everything: beyond Babel

Thus, is the phantasy of the divine or godlikeness at stake? Another presumptuous and blasphemous spatiotemporal delimitation? Where does the virtual quest for recognition lead?

The story of the Tower of Babel marks the end of a series of narratives of transgressions, in which mankind didn't follow the law of god and was therefore punished by language confusion and geographic diaspora. Does the constant availability of the internet, the "digital permanence" (Ball, 2014) cause phantasies of omnipresent power which is able to give solace by being permanently connected? Maybe we can better understand the fascination of the internet medium by noting the apparent overcoming of space and time. But: is it real? Or is it an illusion, a deceit, a simulation of reality, which is not connective but leaves us alone?

Virtual versus real?

The term 'virtuality' creates a problem of definition. Is it an oxymoron? Do reality and virtuality exclude each other or is the issue accepting the digital net as an "expansion of the real world instead of an alternative to it" (Lemma, 2015: 394)? There is no absolute answer to the question if reality and virtuality exclude each other. This has to be examined carefully for each individual case, as so often happens in psychoanalytic thinking. Also whether or in which sense the so-called social networks are really 'social' is a complicated and multi-layered issue.

Löchel (2002) points out the origin of the term 'virtuality' and explains the different ways of using it: (1) the physical optic differentiates real from virtual pictures, (2) referring to the three-dimensional computer simulation, 'virtual reality' is a collective term for all methods and techniques which are necessary to put a person in a computer-generated artificial three-dimensional environment and enable him to interact with the artificial environment (Löchel, 2002: 64, translated for this edition) and (3) the meaning of the word in terms of interactivity, which results from hypertext structure. Löchel is reminding us of using the term in a specific, precise way: "The 'virtual' world of a trainee pilot learning in a three-dimensional flight-simulator surely is quite different from a 'virtual' relationship of a user in a chat room. Both are psychologically significant" (Löchel, 2002: 64, translated for this edition).

Questions of godlikeness, the real and the simulated, and also the opportunities available on the internet will be demonstrated in the case vignette below, too. Between the generations there have always been misunderstandings, otherness, insinuations and lack of understanding – and often it was possible to create something new by demarcation and overcoming the rejection. In my opinion, we have to be very careful not to be sceptical too hastily about the enormous changes caused by the technological development during the past twenty years. Digital interconnection and computerization is a fact of today's life and affects and changes our psychoanalytic treatments – we cannot deny this any more. Instead of obtaining a "dystopic perspective" (Lemma, 2015: 393) we could try to approach this issue from the perspective of both curiosity and the libido, as the 83-year-old French philosopher Michel Serres does in his *Declaration of Love to the Connected Generation* (Serres, 2013).

The mobile phone as a transitional object and the internet as a potential space?

Smartphones are highly attractive. People hold and carry them carefully, they look at them in a loving way and put them in nice covers. Obviously, they are erotically charged. These little tools, fitting perfectly in their owners' hands, appear reassuring to many people. And they give access to the World Wide Web and establish a connection. I am wondering if there is an association between the highly erotic charge of mobile phones and the fascination of the internet and transitional phenomena. Maybe we can better understand the impact of technological changes with the help of Winnicott's concepts.

Transitional objects and spaces – Winnicott

The object relation theorist Winnicott describes transitional objects as a self-chosen object of a young child (between 4 and 12 months), which facilitates the temporary separation from the mother. Usually it is a soft, inanimate thing, such as a doll or a teddy bear, but it may also be another object. This object represents the reassuring closeness of the mother and, at the same time, it symbolizes what transcends the mother's realm. This enables self-calming when the mother is absent. And it soothes the child's separation anxiety and gradually helps him to separate himself from the mother. Yet, it is all about something more essential: the experience that the mother is not part of the child, but a separate being existing outside and independent of him. This experience is bearable by means of a transition, an interspace. The child creatively connects the inside and the outside: "The transitional object is not yet recognized as belonging to the outer reality. Rather it is an interspace of experience between subjectivity and objectivity, between illusion and reality, between the personality and the world" (Kolbenstvedt-Michel & Eggers, 1992: 215, translated for this edition). Therefore, it is not a surrogate or denial of the absent mother, but a symbol preceding or initializing a maturing process. In other words, the transitional object has "a catalyst effect (...) during the period of separation and individuation" (Schlösser, 1990: 6, translated for this edition). That means that the child is in a transitional state with respect to the object's perception and recognition, which involves and requires a subject–object division. For this to be a success, the child needs a 'good enough mother' meaning a 'good enough environment' (e.g., Winnicott, 1969).

Without having experienced a good enough holding environment, the child will develop a "false self" (Winnicott, 1969). The development of object representation is the precondition for turning towards the outside and the creation of a third, or intermediate, space where inside and outside, phantasy and reality are not yet clearly separated. The experience of real separations and calming and soothing by the transitional object promotes and supports the differentiation. The child learns to separate herself from her mother and recognizes the mother as a being existing independently. Thus, the distinction between me and not-me comes in.

Today, the role of the father and the triad from the beginning is much discussed and, in my opinion, very important. I won't go into detail on this issue, but wanted just to mention it.

Case vignette

I'd like to tell you about a patient named Nina, a very young nurse. She came to therapy because of feelings of sadness, alienation from herself and others, the impression of being like a machine without emotions. "I am not really here, everything appears unreal, I'm not in contact with myself and other people", she says.

In her biography we find an extremely clinging mother with a tendency to addiction. The father had several love affairs, and he never really took his place in the family. During the whole childhood and youth of the patient it was not certain whether the parents would stay together. When the was 15, the parents got divorced. The father married again, the mother did not. She never imagined finding a new partner. The relationship between mother and Nina got even closer.

The patient left home at the age of 18. The mobile phone functions as a reassuring connection in their relationship: mother and daughter had installed an 'app', which enabled the mother to always "see" or localize (via GPS) where Nina was (a kind of electronic monitoring, a technique developed for criminals). If Nina slept in and was going to work later, the mother got nervous and worried and called her to ask if everything was okay. Generally, they spoke on the phone several times a day. In the first months of the therapy, the mother called each time after a session, concerned about the well-being of her daughter.

Approximately from the 30th session, narratives about an intensive triangular relationship dominate. The patient spoke much about Tom, her boyfriend, whom she had met via the internet. There is a mutual friend, Mary. Tom and the patient chat regularly and often. Nina 'met' Tom through an internet portal when she was 12. Since then he has been part of her life. Once they met in person when she was 13 and this was the only time that she had seen him 'in reality'. Mary was with them, as she was Tom's best friend. During her apprenticeship, far from home, she ended her relationship with Tom and fell into a crisis. She began to pull men, going to bed with them and then dismissing them. After the break with Tom she needed this 'confirmation' of being attractive and seductive. It felt good for a short time, but soon afterwards she felt shabby, but couldn't stop doing it. Eventually, after a chat session, Tom and she became close again and became virtually engaged. They dream of a future together, chat about interesting topics, mostly about 'detached philosophical views' and moral questions. The time of her one-night-stands was harshly condemned. An ideal of a pure love was built. He was the man of her life, he was so great, the one and only. Mary always knew everything that went on between them, she had an eye on them both.

The couple's relationship is conducted entirely via chat contact – written messages only. They don't call each other, they don't skype and don't write hand-written letters. That they don't meet in person will be explained by a duplicitous deception, which would make meeting too dangerous.

On the other hand, there were real encounters with Mary. They got into intimate contact. After a bottle of wine, they went to bed together. They both told everything to Tom. He was enthusiastic about it and had nothing against it. He was a free thinker and he would accept it if it was good for them both.

The discrepancy between Tom's harsh judgement of the earlier one-night-stands of the patient and the openness regarding the cheating with Mary was not accessible to Nina at first. Following my expressed irritation, Nina began to explain how Mary embodies her consciousness. In a review, she called it an 'externalised consciousness'. It became clearer how harshly Mary and Tom condemned everything regarding the patient's real life and how little freedom she granted herself.

Parenthesis

The social psychologist Döring (2000) says that it is possible to have love relationships exclusively via computer communication. In my opinion, Döring ignores the important differences between an encounter of two people and a bodiless relationship when she says that passion can be created through the shared excitement of formulating sexual fantasies, intimacy through support with personal problems and liability through regular contact (Döring, 2000).

What does it mean for our case vignette? The patient undergoes passion and excitement, intimacy and liability, but she isn't able to connect all this to embodied sensory experiences.

From the point of view of psychoanalysis, there is a tension between the "pleasure principle" and the "reality principle". According to this, the virtual is to the real as the copy is to the original: a reproduction making it possible for what one wishes for to take over reality. This definition of the virtual is usually opposed to the definition of the 'real'. As with omnipotent phantasies, the 'real' loses its physical reality through the 'Virtual' (Lemma, 2015).

Back to the case vignette

After a long latent crisis between the patient and Tom, they ended the relationship. Shortly after that, Nina began a sexual relationship with Mary. First, this relationship seemed playful and good for her until, quite soon, the old patterns of judgement, submission and frequent arguing came up again. Now Tom was the third in the background. The patient was tortured by that. She felt her desire for a real relationship and her own limits at the same time. She lacked the courage to leave the familiar triangle, although it became clearer how this constellation was restricting her.

After a painful period, Nina admitted to herself and to me that she had never met Tom personally. The alleged meeting had never taken place. Any contact has been exclusively via the internet. In the following months, more and more inconsistencies turned up with regard to Tom – or, rather, the patient didn't turn a blind eye to these any more. One day Nina noticed that Mary was writing using Tom's Facebook account. She spoke to Mary about this issue and got the answer: "You don't trust me, you are a bad person. Never ask again!" Shortly after that, Nina got messages about an alleged car crash. Tom was badly hurt. The photos used to document and 'prove' that the accident was real showed different cars. Everything seemed to be dubious and, above all, 'not real'. Nina leaves Mary, too.

Nina got to know that another friend experienced something frighteningly similar with Tom and Mary. This friend was living in shared accommodation with Mary – while being Tom's virtual girlfriend. One day she found a list of several identities and email addresses. She discovered that the photos of Tom actually were photos of another man who was active on Facebook. There was growing evidence that there is no 'real' Tom but a second 'virtual' identity of Mary. Nina was very agitated. On the one hand, she was relieved because her feelings of fake were correct – on the other hand, the whole story was very scary and deeply disconcerting. Numerous questions remain open. Step by step we could better understand why the patient didn't question all the inconsistencies. Nina began to confront herself with her longing for closeness and holding, which was mostly defended before. It became clearer that the virtually encountered grandiosity ('the one and only', the sophisticated detached philosophical discourse) was defending her from real encounters and conflicts. She paid a high price for being caught up in social isolation and a kind of sadomasochistic relationship. After this painful period she said, "Slowly I am arriving in the real world".

Final note

In a way, the patient lost herself in the internet. It took time to clarify how strongly Nina's life was influenced by reading and writing messages via a computer or smartphone. She did her work conscientiously, but without inner involvement. She was socially withdrawn. From this point of view, the technical possibilities allowed the avoidance of 'real' contact. Yet, I think, there is also another view, not opposite but additional: Nina was very disappointed with her first love. The separation process from her mother was quite complicated. She threw herself into sexual contacts in a self- (and other) damaging way. In my opinion, her explanation that she needed such 'confirmation' through feeling attractive and alluring hides her deep longing for contact and connection. The shock in the face of her aggression within the one-night stands and the loneliness without any 'real' contact were difficult to bear. Obviously, a transition was needed.

Did Nina find a transition online? The specific of a transitional object is not the object itself but the way it is used (Schlösser, 1990). I think the patient has used the virtual love as a transitional experience in a transitional space. Her smartphone was an object that was always with her, in her pocket, carefully held in her hand, immediately prior to the session switched off and immediately after the session switched on again. When the patient says proudly: "Today I left my mobile phone at home!" it sounds like a child saying: "Today I left my teddy bear at home" – thereby implying that this is very courageous and exciting. I am a big girl! I am able to leave home, but I will be happy to return my mum and my teddy.

If the mobile phone is understood as a transitional object and the virtual love relationship as a transitional experience, we can suppose that the changes initiated by the confusing technological developments imply promoting both avoidance and good development (cf. Lemma, 2015).

The young patient was in a specific situation of detachment. After moving out of home and leaving the clinging mother, the first love ended in frustrating way.

Subsequently, the patient felt identified with her father's aggressive behaviour, which caused fear. Her relationship experiences were characterised by restrictive closeness on the one hand and, on the other hand, non-binding connections. The ambivalence between her desire for both symbiotic relationship and separation and autonomy, as well as the fear of being alone and separated, have been more bearable with the digital or 'virtual' kind of relationship in the chat room. This seemed to be a transitional space that must not be called into question. The patient experienced something between reality and illusion, you could almost say, reality and illusion at the same time. She felt the illusion of being unseparated and the continuous connection she longed for – without having to come close in a bodily sense, and the illusion that she is able to induce and initiate the activities in the chat room. This may be something like a memory of an early phantasy of omnipotence, which is essential for bearing emotions of reality, dependency and helplessness, as Winnicott has taught us. The reality, on the other hand, is given by the 'hardware': she experienced intense relationships, but at least she spent her time with technical instruments.

According to Winnicott, an intermediate or transitional space is characterized by an interspace between the inner and the outer, the experience between subjectivity and objectivity, illusion and reality, personality and world (Kolbenstvedt-Michel & Eggers, 1992). It is not possible to find definite assignments. Detachment from dyadic closeness and individuation can be prepared in this potential space.

> The Internet as a transitional space can be experienced as an intermediate zone between the self and others, feeling emotions of being held and not abandoned. Herein triangulation cannot succeed, because an object in the virtual world is primarily something to click on: there is only apparent connection because of the principle disconnectedness of the objects in cyberspace.
>
> *(Braun, 2007, p. 11, translated for this edition)*

My patient couldn't maintain the illusion of the perfect, ideal and godlike boyfriend and the power to lead him to live a 'real', 'physical' life with her. Digital communication cannot replace analogue communication: this reality came closer. The illusion or phantasy of omnipotence evoked by the continuous availability of cyberspace was given up. The assumed triangle turned out to be a dyad. With this insight, the patient could detach. The recognition of the border to the 'me–not-me' (Winnicott) enables further individuation. The patient's insight in having externalized her conscience also could have become accessible by experiences within a 'real' relationship. Additionally, this case is characterized by the realization of the 'not-him'.

It would be superficial to simply attribute to smartphones the basic meaning of transitional objects, as well as to say 'the internet' was a potential space.

Through this generalization and widening, the explanatory power is getting lost. Elfriede Löchel pointed out the difference between 'virtuality' and 'reality': "the intermediary space is a subjective space, a potential space related to lively, in person bounded subjects and their psychosexuality and finiteness. Whereas the virtual space first of all is depending on a technical infrastructure" (Löchel, 2002: 65, translated for this edition).

To me, it seems to be essential to consider that transitional objects are not only found but created – in a certain psychological situation.

Alessandra Lemma says:

> today's world is imbued with the use of technical media, and this use defines the world which is no longer virtual or real but characterized by a diversity of combinations within networks. To really face the present at the theoretical and therapeutic level we have to go further than thinking in a binary logic – in order to understand the world today.
>
> *(Lemma, 2015: 395, translated for this edition)*

Psychoanalytic thinking is complicated and mainly stems from a different time. Sometimes it seems to be awkward to apply it to modern questions. In the light of the rapid technological developments, with all their implications, it seems neither useful nor possible to use 'virtuality' and 'reality' as strictly dichotomous concepts. With the concept of transition, integration and differentiation could work simultaneously. As psychoanalysts, we are "familiar with the virtual nature of the real which is filtered by a world of object relations" as Lemma (2015) has beautifully phrased it.

Technological progress is not to be stopped. The stories of our patients are replete with it. New metaphors are created, a new language, which seems to us Babylonically confused and incomprehensible. It will be worth the effort to want to understand the unknown.

References

Ball, R. (2014) *Die pausenlose Gesellschaft. Fluch und Segen der digitalen Permanenz*. Stuttgart: Schattauer.

Braun, C. (2007) Das virtuelle Selbst und virtuelle Andere – was finden wir im Cyberspace? Psychotherapie-relevante Dimensionen der Kommunikation im Internet. Lecture presented to the Institute: C. G.Jung-Institut (19.10.2007).

Döring, N. (2000) Romantische Beziehungen im Netz, in: C. Thimm (Ed.), *Soziales Netz. Sprache, Beziehungen und Kommunikationskulturen im Netz*. Opladen: Westdeutscher Verlag, pp. 39–70.

Freud S. (1962) *Civilization and Its Discontents*. New York: Norton.

Kolbenstvedt-Michel, G. & Eggers, C. (1992) Die Bedeutung des Übergangsobjektes für die psychische Entwicklung des Kindes, *Praxis der Kinderpsychologie und Kinderpsychiatrie* 41(6): 215–219.

Lemma, A. (2015) Psychoanalyse in Zeiten der technologischen Kultur. Überlegungen zum Schicksal des Körpers im virtuellen Raum, *Zeitschrift Psyche* 69(5): 391–412.

Löchel, E. (2002) 'Es könnte etwas dabei herauskommen' – Psychologische Aspekte textbasierter 'virtueller' Realität und Beziehungsmuster jugendlicher Chatter, *Psychosozial* 25(89): 89, 61–72.

Riederle, J. (2013) *Was wir sind und was wir wollen. Ein Digital Native erklärt seine Generation.* Munich: Droemer Knaur.

Schlösser, A.-M. (1990) Übergangsobjekt und Objektbeziehung, *Zeitschrift Praxis der Kinderpsychologie und Kinderpsychiatrie* 39: 6–11.

Serres, M. (2013) *Erfindet euch neu! Eine Liebeserklärung an die vernetzte Generation.* Berlin: Edition Suhrkamp.

Spitzer, M. (2014) Smartphones. Zu Risiken und Nebenwirkungen für Bildung, Sozialverhalten und Gesundheit, *Nervenheilkunde* 33: 9–15.

Winnicott, D. W. (1969) The use of an object, *International Journal of Psychoanalysis*, 50: 11–16.

PART II
Cultural identity and accepting otherness

4

WHAT ARAB AND JEWISH SCHOOL COUNSELLORS REMEMBER FROM WITHIN-GROUP DIVERSITY IN ACADEMIA AND HOW IT AFFECTS THEIR WORK

Lori Greenberger and Ariela Bairey Ben Ishay

Introduction

While Israel's population contains multiple identities, all face complexity in their relations stemming from difference due to religion, culture, social status, and national affiliation, as well as minority–majority relations (Bairey Ben Ishay & Gigi, 2017; Masalha, 2004). The ongoing national conflict permeates all spheres of life, and despite the fact that Jews and Arabs live alongside each other as citizens and meet in commerce, work, and academia, a sense of the foreignness and tension remains (Maoz, 2011). Often the first 'equal' encounters between these two populations take place in academia. Alongside career advancement, the role of academia is to educate toward pluralism and to create an environment that is accepting and nurturing of the various ethnic groups therein (Banks & McGee-Banks, 2010). Unlike in many locales in the world, the practical aspect of the cross-cultural encounter of counsellors in training in academia has not, heretofore, garnered much attention in Israel (Kroyer-Roth, 2010).

The present research was carried out in the context of professional training in educational counselling, at a Masters' program in a leading education college in central Israel. Educational counselling is a humanitarian profession designed to promote advocacy and social justice (Bemak & Chung, 2011; D'Andrea, 2011), and, as agents of socialization, counsellors are expected to improve interpersonal relations between all members of the school's community belonging to differing cultures (Dietz et al., 2017), yet their professional training in Israel is not geared specifically towards this goal (Erhard, 2014). The present study draws from the job definition of educational counsellors in a multicultural environment (Celinska & Swazo, 2016), theories of cultural competence (Lindsey, Robins, & Terrell, 2009; Sue & Sue, 2015), and contact theory concerning encounters of groups in conflict (Allport, 1954, Chapter 16; Maoz, 2011).

Educational counsellor training in a multi-ethnic society

International professional literature directs much attention to multiculturalism and consequent educational counsellor training toward the competence or awareness necessary to effectively deal with it (Harris, 2013; Nassar-McMillan et al., 2009). In the US, it is agreed that cultural sensitivity must constitute an integral part of training for educational counselling and trainees are required to take courses in multiculturalism (Celinska & Swazo, 2016). In Israel, there is no official policy about it (Schwartz, 2008). Educational counsellors must ensure that the school acts with parity toward all its pupils without discrimination or preference. To that end, training programmes offer three components: knowledge, awareness, and practical expertise through which students gain competency via experience and group-as-a whole process (Osbourne et al., 2003). The ethnic and cultural mix of the group and the interactive encounter between students from various cultures is considered to contribute to developing cultural sensitivity and competence (Galassi & Akos, 2007; Sue & Sue, 2015).

In theory and practice of educators and health professionals, the term 'cultural sensitivity' is often misused interchangeably with 'cultural awareness' and other related expressions. Cultural knowledge relates to cognition of counselees' cultures and power relations, oppression, race, ethnicity, and intercultural counselling (Sue & Sue, 2015), while cultural competence refers to understanding counselees' expectations of other cultures and the use of techniques appropriate to these (Pederson, 1987). Lindsey et al. (2009) detail specific skills and capabilities of the culturally proficient educator that entail ongoing reflective processes on individual, group, and organizational levels that promote the development of consistent language, values, and praxes (Collins & Arthur, 2007). Israeli literature refers primarily to empathy and sensitivity as the skills necessary for working with culturally diverse populations (Dwairy, 1998; Tatar & Horenczyk, 2003).

In addition to cultural competence theories, Allport's Contact Hypothesis addresses the intergroup encounter and conditions under which it is likely to improve relations of groups living in protracted conflict (Lewin, 1989; Sonnenschein, 2008). This social-psychological theory sustains that intergroup encounters can reduce prejudice and stereotypes if the following conditions exist: (1) equal status between the groups; (2) superordinate goals to generate cooperation; (3) intimate, ongoing and non-compelled interpersonal interaction enabling familiarity beyond superficial acquaintanceship; (4) a social climate that supports the intergroup contact; (5) initial openness to intergroup relations.

Research population and methodology

In the two-year Masters programme where the present study was conducted each cohort is composed predominantly of women, approximately 70% Jews and 30% Muslim Arabs. The ages range from 20–55, and the Arabs are usually much younger (20–30) than the Jews (25–50). A total of twenty graduates, equal numbers from each national group, were interviewed.

This research sought to learn from the retrospective accounts given by educational counsellors in their second year after graduating, concerning their experience of co-education in a multicultural group while training to be educational counsellors and what they learned from it. Using qualitative research methodology, semi-structured in-depth interviews were co-conducted (by both researchers, fully recorded and transcribed) and thematic content analysis was applied (Shkedi, 2011). The subjects were asked to share.

Research findings

Previous to the current study, as became clear during the interviews, the issue of the encounter between the two groups and its significance had not garnered the graduates' conscious attention. A central issue that arose was the encounter itself and the choice (or lack thereof) to co-study with students of the 'other' cultural or national group. The second issue of central importance entailed the students' silence concerning difficulties in talking about related conflictual issues in the classroom.

The choice to study together

When asked about the multicultural encounter, all the respondents indicated that it had definitely been significant to them. However, it emerged that having purposefully chosen to study together had a positive contribution to the experience and to their willingness to derive benefit therefrom. Arab students had consciously chosen to enrol in a college with Jews, hoping that the encounter would improve their Hebrew and that studying at a Jewish College would contribute to the quality of their training and their chances of getting a job. One Arab student related to her choice:

> This was a good opportunity to get to know the other [Jews]. It was not the first time I'd meet Jews as students. It's good to be in a group representing various cultures and worldviews; it adds to the experience, especially in the case in educational counselling.

Another Arab student enrolled with the hope of reliving her positive multicultural experience abroad:

> When I lived with my family as refugees in Kuwait, it was a kind of "mini United Nations", people came from around the world, causing me

to be open. Being with people of many cultures was fabulous. I expected the education counselling programme to be the same.

Unlike Arabs who had enrolled deliberately in the program and looked forward to a positive experience with Jews, all the Jewish students had neither intentional awareness of the multicultural mix nor expectations of it:

> I knew it was a good programme, but I didn't know it was so mixed. My mother told me that there are lots of Arabs at this college, but I didn't give it any thought. I just wanted to study education counselling.

From the beginning, the differences were present in the room but were not spoken of. Both Arab and Jewish interviewees described what they saw on the first day of class, relating differences they noticed in the sitting configuration in the room. An Arab student recounts:

> I recall it exactly: the Arab girls sat as a group. All of the Jews on one side, and all of the Arabs on the other, except for me. I took a seat, then some Jews sat beside me, but the other Arabs stayed on "their" side. It bothered me that they sat separately.

This interviewee discerned by means of visual identity, or outward appearance, that her fellow students sat with members of their own group. This student was dressed in Western style, with no head covering. Unlike her fellow Muslim students, her ethnic identity was not visibly discernible. In contrast, a Muslim student dressing traditionally noted:

> When I entered the classroom the first day, my eyes scanned the room and found a few students wearing headscarves. I immediately sat with them. Despite the fact that I knew I'd be studying alongside Jews, I didn't feel comfortable. My Hebrew wasn't good, and I was afraid of not fitting in.

Among the Jewish students, who had not made a deliberate choice to study with Arab students, it was prevalent that those who had been exposed to previous multicultural encounters, either locally or abroad, were more curious about getting to know Arab students. A Jewish student whose family had lived in several countries growing up, stated:

> You can be an educational counsellor your entire life here and not have one conversation – certainly about your profession – with Arabs who are fellow educational counsellors. I really wanted to get to know them. I jumped at every opportunity to join in conversations and do projects in mixed groups.

First impressions remained, unspoken openly in class. Furthermore, Jewish students who lacked previous multicultural experiences, shrank from the encounter:

> I didn't expect it. I wasn't prepared for it. I was in shock. I saw lots of Arabs in our building, and I felt I was in the minority group.

Unspoken tensions

As students interacted and relationships developed, underlying tensions increased but were not expressed verbally. One Jewish graduate recalled angrily:

> We [Jews] would arrive on time, as opposed to their [the Arabs'] tardiness and their constant absences. It really bothered me. They were always late, and they always had excuses for not showing up to class.

Concerning the feelings in the room, a Jewish participant said:

> We didn't talk about them. Perhaps out of politeness. You don't want to embarrass anyone. We [Jews] didn't say anything, nor did the instructors. It was irksome.

Furthermore, Jewish participants felt that teachers' expected more of them than of the Arab students:

> I recall the instructors requiring more from us [Jews] to adhere to the schedule and meet deadlines. In grading, also, instructors went easy on them [the Arabs].

Simultaneously, the Arabs had their own frustrations and interpretations of the encounter. One Arab saw her Arab friends struggling in class, which annoyed her:

> Samira [an Arab, fictitious name] volunteered for role play. The Jews laughed and smirked as she stood up, maybe because she doesn't speak Hebrew fluently. As the instructor interviewed her and she shared her feelings, the Jews giggled, but the instructor said nothing. I saw she was hurt. After class, she said that she'd never again speak up in class, that she'd rather stay silent.

This silencing affront, though unspoken, took on both personal and collective significance, affecting the entire joint group. She continues:

> The Arabs learned to stay silent and not to share their experiences, fearing they'd be ridiculed and make fools of themselves. They learned to be quiet, and the Jews learned to keep looking snidely. Such a shame …

The lack of response on the part of the instructors to these underlying feelings and thoughts appeared to have legitimized them. Interviewees spoke of the need for sensitivity and active intervention and modelling on the part of the instructors, especially since Hebrew, the official language of instruction, is not the Arab students' mother tongue:

> I didn't want to show my weakness in Hebrew. One instructor never even got to know what my Hebrew level was, as I didn't say a word the entire year. Though I'm usually an active learner, I needed the teacher to approach me, especially in Hebrew, since it isn't my mother tongue.

Teachers sometimes required students to work together on assignments. A Jewish interviewee remembered:

> There were Arab students who were very bright, although they were quiet and didn't talk much. Doing assignments with them was a real "treat". I worked with nearly all of them, in contrast to other Jewish students. Still, it was obvious that in a sense, we were "piggy-backing them along", particularly surrounding writing papers in Hebrew.

The use of the term 'piggy-backing' refers to group written assignments that Jewish students had to put more work into due to their competence in Hebrew. Despite good intentions, the term 'piggy-backing' testifies to a sense of burden or resentment on the part of the Jewish students for having to work harder than their Arab colleagues in writing the papers, though, paradoxically, Arabs had to work harder to keep up in the Hebrew. The complexity of 'simply' writing a paper together created mixed unspoken feelings and thoughts. An Arab interviewee explains:

> I wanted to do group assignments with Jews but the Jewish girls broke up into groups right away. My friend and I asked two Jewish girls, but they said that they'd rather work together. Perhaps they feared we'd lower their grade, or that we would not do enough work or pull our weight. I don't know.

These interpersonal and intergroup unspoken difficulties of working together represented the tense elephants in the room. The silence was broken when the unavoidable 'season' of national and memorial days commenced.

Silent tensions explode

The unspoken tension between the two groups was referred to by interviewees as the 'ticking bomb' in the room. It peaked during the national and memorial days that are commemorated nationwide, and occur one after the other: Holocaust Day, Memorial Day for Fallen Israeli Soldiers, Israel Independence Day, and the

Nakba Memorial Day (the Palestinian Tragedy), unrecognized officially. These days trigger strong emotions in the Israeli context, and are known to catalyse conflict in Arab–Jewish settings (Arieli, 2015).

An Arab student, attempting to understand the Jewish instructor, was upset as she spoke of an incident in class that occurred on Holocaust Day:

> I remember that after the ceremony, our instructor addressed the entire class, angrily pointing out that some students hadn't stood for the minute of silence during the siren. The Jewish students began whispering. It was really uncomfortable. It looked like the instructor and the class had a problem with it, but didn't want to talk about it.

A week later, Memorial Day for Fallen IDF Soldiers was to be traditionally marked by a loud, two-minute nationally heard siren. A Jewish student related a class incident, a few days before Memorial Day:

> Salua said she wanted to say something that she'd never dared talk about openly with Jews. On Holocaust Day, she said, she identifies with the Jewish people's suffering and stands respectfully with everyone else. Yet, on IDF Memorial Day, it is too difficult for her to leave home. She doesn't want to see Jews, particularly soldiers, who she sees as murderers of her people. Everyone was silent, and the class ended.

Underestimating how difficult it would be for Jewish students to contain her words, she did not expect what ensued. The Jewish student continued:

> Two Jewish students protested that an Arab student "allowed herself" to disrespect the state in class. [They said that] she needs to "understand where she is", in a Jewish State and a Jewish College, and should be grateful that a 'Jewish' college allows her to enrol in their programme. Israel should strip them of their Israeli citizenship, she said. I was shocked!

Another Jewish student described the mounting argument:

> A heated debate began, the two Jewish students stood up to leave the room, but the instructor insisted they all remain in the room and talk about what bothered them. Tension rose, and the argument became heated between the Arabs and Jews, and among the Jews themselves.

Some of the Jewish students defended the Arabs' right to freedom of expression, to study at the predominantly Jewish college, and attacked their fellow Jews for their behaviour towards their Arab classmates. Others were shocked that their dear ones, sons and husbands, were seen as murderers by the Arabs, who remained silent.

The interviewees referred to the incident as the 'explosion' of the 'ticking bomb' in the room, as one nervously explained:

> Prior to lobbing a ticking bomb into a classroom, you have to know how to detonate it before it explodes. If you don't know how to handle them, it's better not to use explosives at all.

For some, the fact of studying together in the same classroom was the 'ticking bomb':

> Learning education counselling would be best done in a homogenous enrolment. Their schools are utterly different than ours. We don't work in their schools, and vice versa. So, what's the point of co-education?

For others, the 'ticking bomb' was not knowing the meaning and relevance of a mixed classroom:

> The instructors should have addressed it from the first day, they should have said something about the significance of Arabs and Jews studying together, the philosophy and its importance, and [should have] used the daily encounter in order to model its benefit.

Furthermore, the 'ticking bomb' was placing students in a conflictual mixed classroom without teaching them skills to cope with its complexities:

> … especially concerning Jews and Arabs, since every year there's a war and many terror attacks. When our teachers do not talk about it in any of the courses, they are making a statement! Regardless of our own political opinions, we must be prepared to hear divergent voices in the room.

Especially experiencing that Arabs and Jews in one classroom are, paradoxically, simultaneously both potential friends and potential foes:

> … there are two nations here, between whom is a bloody conflict, and it won't simply end over time. I realized the conflict goes much deeper, and that interpersonal friendship isn't enough to solve it.

The overwhelming majority of interviewees saw the importance of learning to speak openly as a skill necessary for educational counsellors:

> It's incumbent upon the educational counsellor to be able to talk about conflictual issues. This is a skill that educational counsellors must develop. I learned that you don't just walk out of a discussion; you must stay and cope, even if it's hard.

With the following metaphor, one of the interviewees summarizes:

> It's important to talk. Because if we don't, it [the conflict] will simply continue. It's like a gash that you must disinfect with alcohol: it stings, but you've got to do it so that the wound will heal. It's painful, but painful things have to be talked about.

According to the testimonies, identifying the 'ticking bomb', learning to cope with it and being able to discuss its tensions were clearly essential skills that must be learned in a mixed setting, especially when in training as educational counsellors.

Discussion, conclusions and recommendations

The Jewish–Arab encounter was the most significant for all of the interviewees, yet it was also the least spoken about throughout their training. How can this disparity be explained and what can be learned from this dissonant finding? One possible hypothesis rests on Allport's conclusion that "contact is not enough" for forging meaningful relations, when conflicting groups encounter each other (Allport, 1954). Only three of Allport's five conditions existed during the educational counselling training programme. Indeed, all were citizens of Israel holding the common goal of becoming successful professionals. Second, the college supported bi-national encounters in the classroom. Third, the students interacted interpersonally, though the research noted difficulties and unspoken tensions when required to write papers together, and the relationships were characterized by correctness and politeness. Two essential conditions were not in place: an *a priori* openness to the encounter and symmetry between the groups. Whereas the Arab students, who chose to study with Jews and commenced their studies with willingness and openness to the encounter, the Jewish students had not made that choice and were taken by surprise by it. Although the profession advocates social justice, activism and equal rights (American School Counselor Association, 2012; Dashevsky, 2009) the findings show that the training itself made no connection between these values and using the opportunity of Arabs and Jews in the same classroom to reduce stereotypes and learn professional skills to cope with the conflict. If the encounter is to be of mutual benefit, students should know about it in advance and understand its professional significance as they consciously make the choice to enrol in the mixed programme.

Finally, in terms of Allport's condition that there be equal status or symmetry on other existing aspects between both groups, the study points to a multitude of challenges for which no easy solutions can be found. The Arab–Jewish encounter in the programme is asymmetric on various levels: numbers, age, life experience, socio-economic background, civic status, and, most notably, language asymmetry (lower proficiency of Arab students in Hebrew, and no proficiency of Jews in Arabic). Despite the fact that full symmetry may not be feasible, we recommend creating a classroom wherein more symmetry is created between Arabs and Jews studying together, beginning by recruiting equal numbers. Furthermore, since the faculty presently comprises solely Jewish members, we recommend building a balanced team that ethnically reflects the student populace, thereby providing role models for both national groups. If these basic issues are not properly addressed, one may wonder if anything is gained at all when Arabs and Jews study together in training.

Based on our findings, we recommend preferring students, both Arab and Jewish, who have some multicultural past experience and who, in full awareness, choose to study in a mixed setting. Past research supports the claim that previous experience with multiculturalism indeed tends to create a predisposition to view these encounters as opportunities (Aga Mohd Jaladin, 2013). Despite the fact that literature shows that students who have high scholastic ability tend to decode cultural meanings with greater ease even without instructors' mediation (Hladik, 2016), it appears necessary to provide all students with more specific skills in order to derive professional capacities from the multicultural encounter. In order that the tensions can be addressed proactively, tools must be provided to cope with difference and conflict, including the learning of a professionally relevant language.

It is essential to remember, especially in the case of students lacking this experience, that additional guidance will be required for them in noting differences and making these available for enquiry. In any case, it is necessary to go beyond empathy, being 'considerate', 'patient' and 'respectful' and acting from a desire to 'keep the peace', in the spirit of 'cultural sensitivity' (Dwairy, 1998; Tatar & Horenczyk, 2003). Dealing with difference must go beyond 'cultural blindness', that is, seeing cultural differences yet not addressing them, pretending they are not there (Lindsey et al., 2009). We strongly recommend that faculty and administrators are properly trained to engage cultural differences in the room and versed in teaching students how to transform it into resources for the group. Thus, they can serve as role models and inspire their future pupils accordingly.

Most importantly, a coherent philosophy of learning objectives must be developed by the Ministry of Education and specifically by every educational counselling programme. Given that the profession espouses a worldview of social justice, advocacy, activism, and humanism (Bemak & Chung, 2011; Gonzalez et al., 2018), each programme must decide how the training process and curriculum are to address these issues and what pedagogy is to be practised to provide consistency and coherence to what is gained by the multicultural encounter.

Until the necessary conditions detailed above are achieved, and given that most educational counsellors will work in their respective communities in any case, it is not clear that studying together, Arabs and Jews in the same classroom, is of much benefit. More comprehensive research is necessary to gain a deeper understanding of the skills and knowledge that educational counselling faculty and students must develop to cope effectively with the encounter, both personally and as educators. From this research, it is apparent that the potential of the bi-national encounter has, heretofore, only begun to be utilized.

References

Aga Mohd Jaladin, R. (2013) Barriers and challenges in the practice of multicultural counseling in Malaysia: A qualitative interview study, *Counseling Psychology Quarterly* 26(2): 174–189.

Allport, G. W. (1954) *The Nature of Prejudice*. Boston, MA: Addison Wesley.

American School Counselor Association (2012) *ASCA National Model: A Framework for School Counseling Programs* (3rd edn) Alexandria, VA: American School Counselor Association.

Arieli, D. & Friedman, V. (2015) Between conflict and dialogue: On intervention processes in the encounter between Arabs and Jews in Academia, *Social Issues in Israel* 19: 9–36. [Hebrew]

Bairey Ben Ishay, A. & Gigi, M. (2017) From personal awareness to social consciousness and action: Changing consciousness among students after participation in an academic course, in: D. Golan, Y. Rosenfeld & T. Or (Eds.), *Bridges of Knowledge: Academic–community Cooperation in Israel*. Tel Aviv: Offset Tal, of the MOFET Institute. [Hebrew]

Banks, J. & McGee-Banks, C. (2010) *Multicultural Education: Issues and Perspectives* (7th edn). Hoboken, NJ: Wiley.

Bemak, F. & Chung, R. (2011) Applications in social justice counselor training: Classroom without walls, *Journal of Humanistic Counseling, Education, and Development* 50(2): 204–219.

Celinska, D. & Swazo, R. (2016) Multicultural curriculum designs in counselor education programs: Enhancing counselors'-in-training openness to diversity, *Journal of Counselor Preparation and Supervision* 8(3): 288–310.

Collins, S. & Arthur, N. (2007) A framework for enhancing multicultural counseling competence, *Canadian Journal of Counseling* 41(1): 31–49.

D'Andrea, M. (2011) Expanding the understanding of the complementary nature of humanistic principles and social justice practices in counseling and education, *Journal of Humanistic Counseling* 50: 133–135.

Dashevsky, E. (2009) Standards for professional praxis in education counseling, Education Ministry Education Counseling Division, Psychotherapy Department. Accessed December 10, 2017. [Hebrew]

Dietz, S. S., Dotson-Blake, K. P. Enselman, D., Jones, L., Sexton, J., Edward, H., Waller, M. S. & Richardson, M. (2017) An international learning experience: Looking at multicultural competence development through the lens of relational–cultural theory, *Journal of Counselor Practice* 8(1): 22–44.

Dwairey, M. (1998) *Cross-cultural Counseling: The Arab–Palestinian Case*. New York: Howorth.

Erhard, R. (2014). *School Counselling - A Profession in Search of identity*. Israel: Mofet Institute.

Galassi, J. P. & Akos, P. (2007) *Strengths-based School Counseling: Promoting Student Development and Achievement*. Mahwah, NJ: Lawrence Erlbaum.

Gonzalez, L. M., Fickling, M. J., Ong, I., Gray, C. & Waalkes, P. L. (2018) Learning to advocate: Evaluating a new course, *Journal of Counselor Leadership and Advocacy* 5(1): 13–26.

Harris, H. L. (2013) National survey of school counsellors' perceptions of multicultural students, *Professional School Counselling Journal* 17(1): 1–19.

Hladik, J. (2016) Assessing multicultural competence of helping-profession students, *Multicultural Perspectives* 18(1): 42–47.

Kasan, L. & Kormer-Nevo, M. (Eds.) (2010) *Data Analysis in the Qualitative Study*. Beer Sheva, Israel: Ben-Gurion University Press. [Hebrew]

Kroyer-Roth, M. (2010) Willingness for social relations between Jewish and Arab college students as per a distancing–closeness scale. Final paper toward degree, Jezreel Valley College, Israel. [Hebrew]

Lewin, K. (1989) *Resolving Social Conflicts: Selected Papers on Group Dynamics*. G. W. Lewin (Ed.). New York: Harper and Row.

Lindsey, R., Robins, K. N. & Terrell, R. D. (2009) *Cultural Proficiency: A Manual for School Leaders* (3rd edn). Corwin: Sage.

Maoz, I. (2011) Does contact work in protracted asymmetrical conflict? Appraising 20 years of reconciliation-aimed encounters between Israeli-Jews and Palestinians, *Journal of Peace Research* 48(1): 115–125.

Masalha, S. (2004) Individual counseling in a multicultural society, in: R. Erhard and A. Klingman (Eds.), *School Educational Counseling in a Changing Society*. Tel Aviv: Ramot, pp. 229–245. [Hebrew]

Nassar-McMillan, S. C., Karvonen, M., Perez, T. R. & Abrams, L. P. (2009) Identity development and school climate: The role of the school counselor, *Journal of Humanistic Counseling, Education, and Development* 48(2): 195–214.

Osborne, J., Daninhirsh, C. & Page, B. (2003) Experiential training in group counseling: Humanistic processes in practice, *Journal of Humanistic Counseling Education, and Development* 42(1): 14–28.

Pedersen, P. B. (1987) Ten frequent assumptions of cultural bias in counselling, *Journal of Multicultural Counselling and Development* 15: 16–24.

Schwartz, A. (2008) Training educational counselors in Israel: A peek behind the scenes. Masters' Thesis, Tel Aviv University, Israel. [Hebrew]

Shkedy, A. (2011) *The Meaning Behind the Words: Methodology in Qualitative Research – Implementation*. Tel Aviv: Ramot. [Hebrew]

Sonnenschein, N. (2008) *The Identity-challenging Encounter*. Tel Aviv: HaKibbutzha Meuchád. [Hebrew]

Sue, D. W. & Sue, D. (2015) *Counseling the Culturally Diverse: Theory and Practice* (7th edn). New York: Wiley.

Tatar, M. & Horenczyk, G. (2003) Dilemmas and strategies in the counseling of Jewish and Palestinian Arab children in Israeli schools, *British Journal of Education and Counselling* 31(4): 375–391.

5
WOMEN TODAY
When equality turns into a trap

Daniela Lucarelli and Gabriela Tavazza

Introduction

Social and cultural changes

Many things have changed and are changing in the organization of society and in culture and are affecting the transformation of family structures. We feel it is important for our work as analysts to try to understand better the effects of these changes on the psychic functioning of individuals and on intersubjective links such as those found in families and couples. Starting from a comprehensive view of the effects of social and cultural factors on psychic functioning and on the forms of intra- and interpersonal suffering, in this chapter we would like to dwell in particular on the difficulties women encounter in their family relations and at work, despite the great transformations of their role and position in society, in couples and in families.

We think it is useful to start with mentioning that Freud stressed, in some of his works, that he had tried to establish a tighter link between social psychology and individual psychology (Freud, 1925). From the earliest times he had reflected on the connections between psychic disorders and civilization (1908) and introduced the idea that psychic suffering is not only psychogenetic but has a social origin, in civilization, and derives from the mutual relations between men (1908). It cannot, therefore, be dissociated from civilization.

In his so-called anthropological essays (*Totem and Taboo* (1912–1913), *Group Psychology and the Analysis of the Ego* (1921), *The Future of an Illusion* (1927), *Civilization and its Discontents* (1929) one of the recurring themes is that psychic reality rests on intersubjective and social links and finds a sublimating outcome in the objects and terms of culture (Kaës, 2012). *Civilization and its Discontents* is the work that best shows Freud's sensitivity to the social, cultural and political milieu where the psyche is organized and structured.

In this essay, we can see how Freud, in addition to his well known way of thinking about individuals and conceiving the unconscious according to the internal functioning of the individual psychic apparatus, was able also to identify what connects individuals to social functioning and to the needs of society.

A century later, taking for granted the connections between psyche, culture and society, Kaës presents a very valuable approach to this issue, suggesting that civilization and the unconscious are in a relation of mutual transformation (Kaës, 2012). We think it is extremely interesting that he states that the process of civilization is not carried out only by single individuals, but is a collective work that mobilizes specific psychic processes and formations different from those of the individual psychic apparatus. This work is conveyed through transformations from one generation to the next. In particular, a confrontation with non-elaborated collective traumas and losses allows us to see the importance of extra-subjective symbolizing functions.

Starting from these considerations, we must assume that the concept of endogenous determinism of the psyche explains only imperfectly the cultural and intersubjective conditions of psychic life.

It is, therefore, important to try to understand how the organization of civilization is currently contributing to the emergence of new psychic configurations, such as narcissism or identity problems or to the prevalence of certain defences, such as splitting, denial, ambiguity, idealization, omnipotence, or to the more and more frequent emergence of phenomena such as the failure of the preconscious, a widespread lack of affectivity, difficulty in keeping in contact with one's own and the other's psychic reality, and a widespread tendency to get rid of psychic life. We could ask, with Kristeva (1993), "is the psychic space, this darkroom of our identity where the evil of life, the joy and freedom of Western men are reflected at the same time, going to vanish?"

So, if on the one hand, it seems that we are seeing new psychic organizations and new forms of subjectivity that are probably also determined by the functioning of our civilization, on the other we have to face new complex civilization processes that affect the human condition and shape the forms of psychic pain.

The great social changes under way in our times seem to have infected the functioning of the shared unconscious and the mythopoeic function that generates and structures families. So, at times, we see a dearth of myths or the creation of defensive myths with rigid forms that protect us from the intersubjective invasion of destructive and rupturing elements that are, however, not sufficient to build sense. The rules of behaviour thus imposed do not correspond to a possible psychic work.

The ensuing psychic distress is caused by the confusion of myth and reality, when myth prevails on reality, instead of accepting its metamorphosis. Instead of providing structure and feeding thinking, it risks becoming sterilizing, omnipotent, and sclerotizing.

The role of families, whatever their structure, is to make it possible to treat psychic reality and, in particular, the constant crisis caused by the comparison between individual desires and the needs imposed by the group. This work of adaptation, regulation, and transformation can be done only as long as the continuity of links is guaranteed (Granjon, 2001).

Is there parity between men and women today?

The general considerations we presented above should help us to frame more precisely the question we intend to discuss: that is, the changes and difficulties concerning women, in particular, from the point of view of both intra- and interpsychic functioning and of their social reality.

Many situations show that women today experience specific and particular difficulties in trying to reconcile their professional lives with their family and personal needs.

For a long time, women's goal has been to reach parity with men in work. They started from a very unbalanced situation where it was difficult to access qualified professional jobs, which were mainly occupied by men. The importance of work does not reside only in economic factors, but also in the wider meaning and value attributed to it. To reach economic autonomy, avoid social isolation, and receive psychological support from colleagues, these factors turn work into a resource, a tool for security and a source of social identity.

This goal seems to have been reached, as there are women in all professions and roles with skills and competence equal to those of men. But we still see much dissatisfaction and distress, so that we think it is important to try to understand what this means.

We are aware that our effort at understanding forces us to face the great diversity of contexts in the different countries of the West. We see great disparities in terms of social organization, family structures, female and male roles, and also ideas and representations of this issue. But despite this diversity, we think that there are some major themes, some recurring aspects that are present with lower or higher intensity in many contexts.

It seems that, even where the aim of professional accomplishment has been reached, the problem is on what conditions and if it can be experienced without conflict with the investment in family life.

With regard to workplaces, it is well known that there is no longer attention paid to the reproductive function of women, but, rather, that this function is seen as a threat to the continuity of work, with the attendant costs for companies.

We read news reports that suggest that the models of success imposed on social life, in this case concerning work, tend to intrude heavily on private life, in particular of women. Those very women who, in the past century, fought to obtain equal rights in society and at work.

We will present a few examples from different countries and cultures that seem to show situations with various contact points and highlight a problem that seems to be present in most developed countries to varying degrees.

Recently, we read in the news that some high-tech companies in Silicon Valley (USA) are providing free cryogenic conservation of oocytes to their female employees wishing to defer pregnancies to a later age, since many of them were already having recourse to this service at very high cost. Japan does not lag behind: a shocking survey of the ministry of health showed that 30% of women in their thirties have not had sexual relations and do not plan to have children in order not to endanger their careers or lose their jobs.

There is a very obvious difficulty for women in reconciling work and private life. The very fact of being a female of reproductive age can lead to exclusion from a possible career, just as the ability to respond to a baby's needs is subject to the rhythms of her mother's work. The bias imposed to women by work is such that, in Japan, a movement emerged based on a new word, 'Matahara', made by joining two English words: maternity and harassment, that describes one of the main forms of abuse – along with sexual and power abuse – of Japanese female workers. They, in fact, risk being fired at the time of pregnancy or, more and more often, they suffer miscarriages caused by psychological and physical pressures. So they end up having to choose between a job and a family.

(In the six years of life of the Matahara Net, the number of women reporting harassment from their employers increased.)

In other cultural contexts things can go differently. It is not always possible to find forms of support and association to defend oneself and rebel against the lack of recognition of women's rights and needs in the workplace.

It seems that, despite efforts at making one's voice heard, the kind of demands coming from society and from the workplace in particular have started to create defensive drifts in the way women think of themselves, up to the point where giving up maternity or sexuality is felt as a choice to be proud of, since it allows them to attain professional success. For about ten years, all over the world, groups have been developing that call themselves 'No kids'. In Italy, for example, a 'Childfree' group emerged under the slogan "We do not want any children".

The choice of not having children seems to emerge from the difficulties posed by reality to the reconciliation of work and childbearing that determines what we could call, with Amati Sas (1992), a "defensive ambiguity" that produces an acquiescence to the demands of the social cultural milieu that are perceived as unavoidable. The concept of ambiguity refers to an "ambiguous core" (Bleger, 1972), a residue of "primary undifferentiation" that remains in mature personalities. This core must be projected and deposited in external "repositories" through a symbiotic link. This forced unconscious dependence on the external context provides subjective feelings of safety and belonging.

The violence coming from society causes subjective adaptation phenomena that provide obviousness and familiarity to any context and give rise to a "defence through ambiguity" that leads to an "adaptation to anything". In the state of ambiguity, there is an alteration of the capacity for critical thinking and of alarm mechanisms, so that the subjects tend to be easily penetrated and manipulated.

Participating in a 'No kids' movement might also favour the rationalization of suffering due to not having become a parent. It seems that some participants have acknowledged that their choice was also determined by a feeling of inadequacy deriving from an idealized model of maternity.

If maternity is experienced as an obstacle to one's life, this should be attributed also to the fact that the social organization does not support working mothers. Or, in a still rather widespread, if changing condition, to the fact that paternity is still often expressed at a narcissistic level or as a confirmation of one's identity, rather than as assuming responsibility for child care. All this makes it hard for mothers to put together different dimensions and needs: "It seems that we lost the connection that should unite generatively being a mother and being a woman" (Saraceno, 2017: 43, translated for this edition).

In couple relations, the problems experienced by women are reflected in the difficulty in assuming their role and in the subdivision/differentiation of parenting functions. It seems that once they lost the role they had in past decades, women struggle to form a different identity and risk giving up meaningful aspects of their realization connected, in this case, mainly to maternity, pressed both by the hurdles created by external reality and by the fear that leaving room for these aspects can threaten the professional role that they acquired with great effort.

On the other hand, the parenting function seems to be seen in a more and more idealized way and there is still an idea that maternity can be lived to the full only if protected from other interests, wishes, and activities. This corresponds to the ideal of a totally dedicated mother that is hard to escape, even for those women who fought so hard for the right to have a family and a job. Women seem to find it hard to share their management of children and of the house with their partner because they fear losing the centrality of the traditional female role that implied a sense of obligation, against which they rebelled, but which also provided the gratification of being the only experts. Let us remember that women were called "the queens of the house".

Let us now see some clinical examples.

Chiara and Paolo

They met at a demonstration when they were students: she was a lively and talkative girl, he was a quiet and composed man. After a short while, they moved in together.

When they came for consultation, their little child, Sofia, was still small and they had been apart for three months.

She seems to be the one requesting help. Paolo, on the contrary, from the very first meeting, says that he does not think psychotherapy can help their coupledom: "If I need to let off steam, I go and have tea with a male friend", but he accepts participating since Chiara attributes so much importance to it: "It's our last resort, we must try it", she will say more than once during psychotherapy.

There follow some excerpts from a therapy that lasted for three years.

The choice to live together after a short period was made mostly by Chiara, with great resolve. Paolo's doubts about this "big step" were seen as a lack of commitment. "He did not love me enough!" The day they entered their flat for the first time, she cried all the time, seized by strong anxiety, afraid of having made a rash choice. In lieu of the initial resolve, there emerged a fear that she could not explain. Paolo's doubts, however, vanished as she took responsibility for their home. Her choice of painting it herself marked her sense of belonging.

At the time, Paolo was a maths teacher in high school. Chiara was on the dole. This disparity in the production of income had serious implications for the couple, especially for Chiara. She felt her joblessness was devaluing her. She had been a brilliant student and gained her degree with the highest marks. She recalls that she spent months writing and sending application letters and meeting prospective employers that ended almost inevitably in the employer seeing that she was a very good candidate, but too qualified for the position they offered.

Often her frustration caused great unease in her relationship to Paolo. Comments from her relatives or friends such as: "You are lucky to have so much time for you", "There's no hurry for a job, you are young, enjoy your freedom" caused deep conflicts that put a strain on their relationship. Paolo found it hard to accept her emotions oscillating from anger to sadness. The lack of professional recognition made her feel her image, identity and deep self were in peril. Chiara's parents were both in academia and also her grandparents had been well known public figures. The myth of autonomy, independence, hard work and dedication to it had accompanied her growth.

Finally, one day she finds a job that requires very long hours and great flexibility. She is offered a one-year contract, renewable, and a very high salary.

She plunges into work with a total commitment in terms of time. Her job fills her days completely and she demands recognition for her new role from Paolo, from her parents and her friends.

During therapy, she will say: "I was drunk on work, I couldn't see anything else". This infatuation lasts for a year and gives place to a painful disappointment due to the loss of the previous idealization.

In this context, Paolo decides to ask for shorter hours at school. They could afford it without giving up their lifestyle since Chiara earned really well. Although he enjoys teaching he would like to have more time to dedicate to his voluntary work in environmental causes aimed at sensitizing public opinion. For Paolo, work is functional to pursuing his interests and ideals. He does not seem to idealize anything, while he offers a pragmatic interpretation of his professional activity.

For Chiara, however, it is difficult to reconcile her investment in work and in the family. First of all, she needed to secure her professional persona.

Only after achieving this could she dedicate herself to caring for her daughter and to couple life, as if these were pleasures she could not afford otherwise. Paolo's willingness to look after the baby and the home, since he had more free time, on the one hand was welcome, but, on the other, made her feel jealous and excluded from her daughter.

Paolo's wish for shorter hours was supported by Chiara, who felt that this would lead to parity between them, since, at the beginning of their shared life, he had been the only breadwinner. The fact of being economically stronger now allowed her to satisfy her competitive need that protected her from a feared dependence. But if Paolo seems to have chosen taking his own needs into account, we could ask if Chiara has truly evaluated the implications for her of his part-time work. Will her stronger position in the couple allow her to acknowledge and express the various aspects of herself and her needs? Or could it turn into a trap?

Caterina

Caterina is 45 and came to analysis through her son's therapist. This therapist had referred both parents, but the father was never available so she came alone. At the beginning, she did not have a clear motive for starting psychotherapy but, rather, she complied with the request. She is, in fact, a gentle person who follows the advice given to her. This aspect might seem in contrast with the determination she showed, for example, in attending university and getting a law degree and gaining a position in the judiciary at the early age of 24, rating first in her group of peers. She is still a judge, and works with great passion. She also has three children aged between six and 12 years. She seems to be better at work than at home as a mother and wife, although she loves her children dearly. She cannot admit that looking after their needs all the time is too absorbing and frustrating for her. In fact, from the birth of her first son onwards, she is the parent who looks after the children, the home and all the issues that emerge there, leaving her husband free to pursue his career as a lawyer that takes up all his time. Her husband did not have, in his family culture, the concept that a father could take care of his children. For his family of origin, roles were set and immovable: father works and mother looks after the children.

Caterina found it hard to do everything alone, but never thought of asking her husband for greater participation or sharing of chores. Only after the beginning of analysis can she manage to ask something of him. At first, he tried to avoid responding, but as time progressed, does try to listen, at least in part.

It seems that Caterina, despite having reached autonomy at work, cannot acknowledge it and feels it is in conflict with her role of mother.

To be a mother and, at the same time, a professional is extremely hard to reconcile and she feels guilty for not having enough time for her children. Although she is quite resourceful and knows how to take care of others, she has a very idealized view of motherly functions and built a link with her husband that is reinforcing her guilt because she is investing in work.

She says she is lucky in having a job that gives her a lot of freedom and that she can perform in part at home (writing her judgments) and she tends to devalue a role and function that are, in fact, quite difficult. Her husband, on the contrary, always stresses the importance of his work and the many engagements that do not leave him time for anything else.

Families are a historical–social construction, so they are varied and their forms and the rules that define them change in space and time. We could say that too rigid and univocal family models that do not leave room for alternative forms can reduce the capacity to create a family. They can prevent the establishment of supportive, affective and mutual relations in contexts where, although these models are felt as too restrictive and inadequate, they still remain reference points because the symbolical tools that make it acceptable and legitimate to elaborate new modes of links and roles seem unavailable (Saraceno, 2017). It seems that it is difficult to adjust the mythical heritage of families to the evolution of its reality and of society. Their mythopoeic and structuring function is no longer guaranteed, and this blocks the circulation of fantasies, the individual psychic elaboration, thus disproving the subjects' identity references.

A top professional couple: work as alienation of oneself

Tina and Stefano have been married for 11 years. They met through work in Russia (she is Russian, he is Italian). From the beginning, their relationship has been characterized by the wish "to conquer the world" and initially by his promise: "I will give you all you want". In their life together everything took place very fast: the move to Italy (because of his job), the birth of their first child and of a second one after a year, a change of company (a better one) for her, everything has been determined by the requirements of their work. Their own and their children's needs (a third child was born after three years) have always been submitted to the requirements of their respective careers. This is why they have lived long periods apart: he was in Russia and she was in Italy. He was in southern Italy and she was in Rome until the present arrangement: she is getting ready to move to the US, where he will join her but it is not clear when because he needs to find a proper job there. Their union is based on the need to form a perfect family that neither has had (her father, manager of a coal mine in Siberia, was an alcoholic, while her mother was a sanitary inspector at the mine, while he was the son of "perfect" parents that never saw him). In fact, they both picked a partner who does not see them and have tried to compensate for the "non perfect" couple they built with a perfect career. Their relationship is characterized by a very competitive aspect where, at the beginning, he was better at work, but later she became the one set on a stellar track and still ascending. This push forward led her also to have an affair with a colleague that made him feel dejected. This is why the couple is coming to therapy.

Somatizations are a hallmark of the family: she has a migraine about 20 days in a month, he has become diabetic and stammers slightly, cannot sleep and has panic attacks, in addition to suddenly gaining and losing weight. The first son has type 1 diabetes and is insulin dependent. These mostly psychosomatic symptoms have the function of repositories also for the children.

The break he suffered in his career prospects is compensated by a massive investment in his body, which he strives to improve mostly by swimming every day. Actually, this daily activity prevents the family from finding some time to share. She comes back home at seven in the evening when he goes to the pool with the children. When they are all back there is time only for a quick dinner and they all go to sleep, because the next day starts very early, at 5.00 a.m. We are reminded of Kristeva's words (1998: 26): "In this everyday life we don't have the space and time required to grow a soul" (translated for this edition).

They cannot be together but they cannot separate: the fantasies of closeness and separation are counteracted by the chances offered in professional life: "Come to the US with me and we'll be united as in the past", she says, "but in the meantime I go and I don't know if you will follow me".

In this couple's situation we notice in particular the importance of a career and of success in our society and the acceleration of time induced by the effort of reaching these goals.

It seems that, for them, the use of these myths was aimed at the need to deny individual and couple areas that are deficient but also unthinkable.

We could say, with Erlich (2005), that the inevitable tension between everyday experiences of society and the omnipotent fantasies of love and happiness, beauty and wisdom, peace and a life free from suffering contribute largely to the feelings of disappointment, dissatisfaction and betrayal.

Conclusions

Starting from the big changes that have occurred to the role and function of women in the past decades, which certainly changed the conditions of equality between men and women in many countries, we tried to identify some critical areas.

- If, on the one hand, it appears that women can now express themselves and be successful at work, there is still a difficulty in reconciling work and maternity because the latter is seen as an obstacle and a pregnant woman's professional prospects are jeopardized by the interruption of work continuity and/or career. On the other hand, there is a risk that women do not contest this hostility and adjust to the demands for uninterrupted efficiency of the companies they work for, giving up maternity, as they can no longer be in contact with their wish for/choice of maternity.
- With regard to the possibility of being a mother, we see that today an idealized image of mothers prevails that captures women's imagination.
- When they try to reconcile maternity and their career, they often feel inadequate in both areas, but mainly in the family. It is as if, when they cannot dedicate themselves totally to either role, they feel inadequate as mothers and wives, as if they could not get away from that idealized image.
- Men, in turn, after having seen their old image disrupted, have tried to change: the most recent generations are certainly changing their models. There remains, however, a certain resistance in men to taking care of their children and their homes, as if they lacked internal reference models, or as if it was difficult to find a new role that is not just a "copy" of a mother's role.
- In the situations where the social and work environment and the partner's availability favour maternity, allowing women to accommodate work as well as family, women can find it difficult to leave their central role at home to their partners.
- There are also difficulties in metabolizing the changes that have already occurred and are still occurring in society due to their swiftness, so that we could ask if the individual's internal organization and relations have had enough time to change while still retaining continuity.
- In a time of great changes like ours, the mythopoeic needs might tend to increase in order to integrate these changes. But it seems that today it is more difficult to create myths. Often, they are not produced by the family but are taken from society, as substitutive myths that have lost their peculiarities.
- Some families are unable to adapt their mythical heritage to the evolution of their reality and of society. So the container function of myths is disproved and the transformation of family thinking, starting from experiences and emotions, defaults and leaves some aspects of reality still raw.

References

Amati Sas, S. (1992) Ambiguity as the route to shame, *International Journal of Psychoanalysis* 73: 329–334.

Bleger, J. (1972) *Simbiosi e ambiguità*. [Reprinted 1994, Loreto: Edizione Lauretana].

Erlich, S. (2005) L'insoddisfazione del soggetto e il benessere della civiltà, in: *Psiche, Rivista di cultura psicoanalitica, Volume 2*. Milan: Il Saggiatore.

Freud, S. (1908) *La morale sessuale "civile" e il nervosismo moderno. OSF* 5. Turin: Boringhieri.

Freud, S. (1912–1913) *Totem e tabù. OSF* 7. Turin: Boringhieri.

Freud, S. (1921) *Psicologia delle masse e analisi dell'io. OSF* 8. Turin: Boringhieri.

Freud, S. (1925) La negazione. *OSF* 10. Turin: Boringhieri.

Freud, S. (1927) *L'avvenire di un'illusione. OSF* 10. Turin: Boringhieri.

Freud, S. (1929) *Il disagio della civiltà. OSF* 10. Turin: Boringhieri.

Granjon, E. (2001) Mitopoiesi e sofferenza familiare, *Rivista Interazioni* 1: 15.

Kaes, R. (2012) *Il malessere*. Rome: Borla, 2013.

Kristeva, J. (1993) *Les nouvelles maladies de l'âme*. Paris: Fayard. Italian translation, *Le nuove malattie dell'anima*. Rome: Borla, 1998.

Saraceno, C. (2017) *L'equivoco della famiglia*. Bari: Laterza.

PART III
Families and children at risk

6
PSYCHODYNAMIC FAMILY THERAPY OF ANOREXIA NERVOSA

Günter Reich, Antje von Boetticher, and Manfred Cierpka+

Current developments in family therapy of anorexia nervosa

There is a long tradition in connecting anorexia nervosa to family interactions and family issues, especially problems of separation–individuation in adolescence.

Each relevant style of family therapy – be it psychodynamic, structural or systemic – in some way has its origin in the struggle to overcome this chronic and, in many cases, deadly illness and in understanding its mechanisms (Cierpka & Reich, 2010).

Contemporary family therapy methods prefer to focus on the consequences of anorexia nervosa to the parents and siblings and try to coach mainly the parents to deal with the eating behavior and related issues with the patient. They avoid examining the possible contributions of family relationships to the origin and maintenance of the illness, among other reasons in order not to accuse the parents of being the cause of the illness and make them feel guilty (Lock et al., 2013; Reich, 2015).

This approach is in contrast not only with a psychodynamic one, which postulates that childhood and adolescent experiences in close relationships have a strong impact on the psychic development of individuals, but also with a series of empirical findings which show an indisputable influence of family factors on the development of eating disorders, such as a strong relationship between disturbed parental attitudes towards eating, a preoccupation with dieting and slimness and the corresponding behaviour and eating disorders of the children, as well as a negative body image, especially in girls (e.g., Cierpka & Reich, 2010; Field et al., 2008; Kluck, 2010; Quiles Marcos et al., 2012; Neumark-Sztainer et al., 2010; Reich, 2015).

Indeed, an accusing or judging attitude against parents of disturbed children and adolescents is, in most cases, not helpful in building a therapeutic alliance and keeping the parents in a therapeutic process, be it an individual or a family approach. Our multigenerational view of family processes, which includes at least a look at three generations as relevant for the development and maintenance of severe psychic disorders, may enable us to see parents' developmental issues and needs and their historical and social circumstances and, thus, keep us from judging instead of exploring.

The question of specificity

The discussion about family dynamics and family therapy for specific illnesses also touches on the question of specificity vs. non-specificity. Indeed, no specific family pattern of relationships or interaction has a particular impact on the development of an illness and neither does it function as a direct cause of certain symptoms.

The biological, individual, family and social levels of psychosomatic illnesses such as anorexia each function according to their own genuine mechanisms. They influence each other, but follow their specific regularities. So, every level of the system, respectively, each system involved in the anorexic process, must be investigated in its own right. For example, media and peer group influences, which contribute to body dissatisfaction, are only partially, if ever, under the control of the family or the individual. On the neurobiological level, anorexia is characterized by a series of structural and functional differences compared to healthy controls, some of which persist after weight restoration, for example, the reduction in the grey matter, as compared with the volume of white matter. Deficits in the volume of grey matter are reported for areas heavily involved in the regulation of emotions. Deficits in dopamine (important for eating behaviours, motivation, reinforcing behaviour and reward) and serotonin (important, e.g., for the regulation of obsessional behaviours, anxiety, and impulse control) are reported, too. The decreased level of leptin may be responsible for compulsive hyperactivity (Phillipou et al., 2014; van Elburg & Treasure, 2013). These results of starvation and cachexia reduce the potential effects of psychotherapeutic interventions and can only partially and very indirectly be influenced by changes in family interaction. Psychodynamic psychotherapists may tend to underestimate the consequences of neurobiological dynamics.

The psychosomatic family model

The most influential family model for anorexia is the psychosomatic family model created by Minuchin and his co-workers (1978). Against rumours postulating the contrary, the group never saw such family factors as conflict avoidance, enmeshment, overprotection and rigidity as the 'cause' of anorexia, but both the anorexia and the family interaction characteristics as a co-evolving process, which needed to be interrupted by family therapy interventions. The model inspired many empirical studies in family interaction, at least parts of it being validated for subgroups of eating disorder patients and their families (e.g., Kog and Vandereycken, 1989). Although not being applicable as a whole for families of anorexics, the characteristics described can, at least partly, often be found in clinical work. They are, therefore, still worthwhile subjects for clinical observation. In their further elaboration of the Minuchin model, Beatrice Wood and co-workers (Wood et al., 2000) described feedback mechanisms between dysfunctional family interaction and the vulnerable child suffering from asthma, colitis ulcerosa or Crohn's disease formulating 'biobehavioural reactivity' as a link between psychological and biological processes in a biobehavioural family model (Wood et al., 2008).

Family relations and the 'inner family'

Psychoanalytic object-relations theory offers a suitable concept for understanding the interactive development processes between the individual and the family. "Identification processes with the psychosocial formulation of compromise in the family determines what the individual internalizes as the 'inner family'" (Cierpka et al., 1998: 321).

> The child may be born into a family, but she or he assimilates the concept of the family in general and the specific family of his origin gradually over time. During their entire development, children contribute to the evolution of the family system by imposing change upon their parents, who must adjust to new development tasks and accept appropriate roles.
> *(Cierpka et al., 1998: 321–322)*

This active relationship-inducing role of the child

> means for the family that the child does not simply identify with the functions and processes of the family – he or she contributes to the development of these functions. Interaction patterns, as family representatives, are identified with and internalized, which the child himself has helped to create.
> *(Cierpka et al., 1998: 322)*

In the following, the identification processes and the co-evolution of individual, familial and social factors is shown for the etiopathogenesis of eating disorders. We emphasize a longitudinal view of the development of eating disorders. In the continuum of causal factors, the family may play a very important role, but not the only one. Besides hereditary factors, such as temperament and affectivity (Strober, 1991; van Elberg & Treasure, 2013), social factors, such as the slimness ideal and sex-role issues of women (who are overwhelmingly more at risk), developmental factors, especially the transitions of adolescence and early adulthood, and the self-reinforcing dysfunctional eating behaviour itself, with its neurobiological implications, also play an important role (Cierpka et al., 1998).

Adolescent development

Adolescent developmental tasks require reorganization in the individuals, not only the adolescent her- or himself, but also the siblings and parents, and in the family system as a whole. For the individual adolescence is a crucial phase for self-development, gender and sex-role identity, and for the integration of familial and cultural role expectations.

> The body and the outer appearance changes, often dramatically, girls having a high increase of fat cells. Body esteem seems to decrease or to fluctuate considerably. Comparison with social standards, either imagined or real, represented by media and peers, intensifies. The cultural thinness schema, linking slimness to attractiveness, social and professional success, and thus to self-esteem becomes very important. The risk for eating disorders increases the more self-esteem is connected with the thinness schema... the more the sense of achievement is felt to be threatened and the more their self-definition emphazises "success in multiple roles in order to secure an identity through external approval".
>
> *(Smolak & Levine, 1994: 51)*

> Family interaction preforms the way the slimness schema is adopted and internalized and the way conflicts of self-esteem are experienced and handled.
>
> *(Cierpka et al., 1998: 322)*

Family influences on the development of eating disorders

Eating disorders are often interwoven with dysfunctional family processes (Cierpka & Reich, 2010; Holton–Viesel & Allan, 2015; Reich, 2003a,b, 2015; Tetley et al., 2014).

There are several pathways of influence:

1. We have already pointed out the relationship between disturbed parental attitudes towards eating, a preoccupation with dieting and slimness, and the attitudes towards eating, dieting and slimness ('appearance focused families') and the corresponding behaviour and eating disorders. So the family has a very direct impact on pathological eating attitudes and behaviours.
2. There is empirical evidence for linking individuation–separation difficulties and eating disorders (Cella et al., 2014; Cierpka & Reich, 2010; Friedlander & Siegel, 1990; Reich, 2015; Kog & Vandereycken, 1989; Vandereycken et al., 1989). Anorexics especially seem to have tight bonds to their family of origin.

> In families with permeable interpersonal and intergenerational boundaries and a high degree of interpersonal control both factors do also manifest themselves in eating behaviors and rituals. Often the

boundaries between these families and the outside-world are closed. These family systems do not give enough room and encouragement for the adolescent striving for autonomy, eating becoming the secret or open battlefield.

(Cierpka et al., 1998, p. 323)

3. In family systems, where basic needs for affective responsiveness, consolation, recognition and emotional support are not met, these needs are warded off. They tend to manifest themselves in more global dysphoric affect states, which the subject has difficulty in differentiating and handles in subtly diversified ways. The intake or the refusal of food can become the main method for the regulation of affects. In families of 'classic anorexics' the expression of affection is often combined with attempts at control and negation of their separate needs.
4. Systems with permeable intrafamilial and closed family environment boundaries and high interpersonal control are likely to promote individual tendencies of high harm avoidance, low input seeking and high reward dependence, as Strober (1991) describes for anorexic individuals. The protection and control of the self–other boundary and of self-esteem is then likely to be displaced to the intake of food and thinness, both visible inside and outside the family, and to lead to anorexia nervosa (Cierpka et al. 1998; Reich 2003b).

Besides self-reinforcing interactional vicious circles, anorexia also leads to physiological vicious circles, which again reinforce maladaptive intrapsychic and interactional patterns. Starvation leads to disturbances in hormonal balance and a drop in serotonin, which increases the likelihood of depressive mood states.

Our family therapy approach

In our family therapy approach the treatment of anorexia nervosa follows three steps or stages:

1. Stabilisation of weight and the intake of food, including the prescription of steps for weight gain and, according to that, the decision about the continuation of outpatient treatment or the necessity of inpatient treatment.
2. Working on the relational issues of the family, dealing with family conflicts mostly about separation–individuation, and their possible resolution. In this phase also, multigenerational issues and the individual development of the parents in their families, as well as a couple, are often explored, with efforts to induce changes in rigid beliefs, phantasies, feelings and interaction patterns.
3. A phase in which problems of individual and peer development, for example, issues of sexual feelings, body image and relationships, become the focus of individual therapy sessions for the diagnosed patients and possibly couple sessions for working on conflicts between the parents.

The case of Julia: a multigenerational family therapy

A case example may illustrate this.

> Thirteen-year-old Julia was referred to us by her individual therapist, where she was treated with cognitive behavioural psychotherapy because of compulsive rituals and anxieties and where she developed anorexia with a body mass index below 14 (1.66 m; 37 kilos).
>
> For the first two sessions she came with her mother, a nurse in her mid-thirties. The parents divorced about a year before, although they had separated when Julia was about seven years old.
>
> During the first sessions we learned that Julia and her mother had moved into a separate apartment in the house of Julia's grandparents, that the grandfather had died about a year before, that the anorexia developed then, and that the grandmother spent much time with Julia, transporting her to school, friends, private lessons, and preparing a great part of the meals for all three.
>
> We arranged separate individual sessions for Julia, focusing on her body image, eating behaviour and peer development. We also invited the grandmother to join the family sessions, which was gratefully accepted by her as a chance to inform us about her point of view in respect of the development not only of Julia, but also of Julia's mother, with which the grandmother was absolutely dissatisfied.
>
> During the first sessions with the grandmother, we observed loud disputes between her and Julia, whereas the mother kept calm, answering only direct questions and contributing verbally very little to the understanding of the dynamic, mostly downplaying possible conflictual themes. We saw Julia as a possible delegate of her mother in her unresolved conflict with the grandmother about her own individuation and position in the family, acting this out on a non-verbal level.
>
> When we saw mother and grandmother for two separate sessions, the grandmother reproached Julia's mother for her refusal to achieve in school, receiving a qualification of only minor value in the eyes of her mother, not making an academic career but being a nurse, and marrying a good-for-nothing, who turned out to be a heavy drinker, suffering from many anxieties and phobias and having problems with controlling aggressive impulses. The escalation of conflict between Julia's mother and her former husband, watched by Julia, led finally to a retreat into her parents' home. Julias mother still maintained contact with her ex-husband, helping him out with money, sometimes shopping for him, even for liquor, much to the disapproval of the grandmother. She remained in a co-dependency relationship with him, defending this against the pressure of her mother, Julia's grandmother.

The grandmother was an architect and worked for a big building contractor in a leading position, supervising huge building projects until she retired. After her retirement, she helped her husband in his own smaller building firm, which was taken over partly by one of her sons (Julia's uncle, brother of her mother) about five years ago, and fully after the death of the grandfather. The other son (Julia's mother's second brother) was a successful lawyer in a larger German city.

The grandmother seemed to be very capable of imposing her will on others, in the building firm, where she was called 'the Iron Helen', as well as in respect to her husband and sons. The only persons she did not succeed well with this were Julia's mother, with her passive resistance, and Julia, with her more active resistance.

We also suggested seeing Julia's father for a session, in order to become more acquainted with his role in the family interaction and his attitude towards Julia's difficulties, a suggestion which was strongly opposed by Julia's mother, who expected only more trouble from this, and which was strongly supported by the grandmother, who expected "more clarity in the matters", which, as we supposed, meant more division between Julia's father and Julia, her mother and the grandmother.

As we did not want to side with the grandmother against Julia's mother in this central issue, we left the decision to Julia's mother.

Exploring the triad of Julia–mother–father in the following session, we found Julia in a strongly parental role in respect of her father, who phoned her and her mother at least once a day, telling both of them about his problems and anxieties. Julia was very concerned about her mother, too.

At this point, the therapy came to an impasse, not so much with respect to Julia's progress in eating, gaining weight, and improving her relationships with peers, but with respect to work on the family conflicts. Julia's mother reacted very evasively, downplaying and reluctant. In this transference–countertransference process, we seemed to take more and more the role of the grandmother, pointing to the difficulties, flaws, incompetence and mistakes of the mother in fulfilling her role towards Julia. We fell into the roles of family judges, who should determine who was right and who was wrong, and of better parents for Julia.

In this phase, we decided to involve Julia's uncle, her mother's brother, who lived nearby, in a therapy session. He had a good relationship with Julia's mother and, therefore, might be a support for her and eventually bring new perspectives into the family dynamics.

In a joint session with him, Julia's mother, the grandmother and Julia, we learned about the mediating role of the grandfather for the whole family, especially between Julia's mother and the grandmother and his caring role for Julia. Julia's anorexic symptoms evolved soon after his sudden death, also her anxiety about suffocating, since he died by suffocation after suffering from chronic obstructive pulmonary disease. Obviously, Julia was strongly identified with him.

The session also shed a new light on the grandmother's course of life. Coming from a big farm, which was run by her father's family for generations, she was allowed to get a higher education and to study, while her younger sister had to marry a farmer and take over the farm. For her school education, the grandmother was given to a teacher in the nearby city, with whom she lived and by whom she was raised and educated from twelve years onwards, and where she visited the high school before she left for the university in another town, where she met the man who would become her husband. When she became a mother herself, she did not want to interrupt her work and took her former foster mother and educator into her family as a governess for her children, especially for Julia's mother, who suffered from the rigour and the punishments, also sometimes the abuse, doled out by that lady, and who rebelled against this with disobedience and rejection of schoolwork.

The younger sister of the grandmother, who took over the family farm, had a very unhappy marriage with a violent drunkard, from whom she finally divorced with the support of the grandmother. Soon after the divorce she died of cancer, with extreme suffering.

The grandmother feared a repetition of her sister's fate in her daughter, which came partly true, and in Julia, whom she feared to be too weak and too impressionable, and would fail in school, as Julia's mother did, and through this would become too dependent on a man.

This session was an important turning point in the whole therapy. The revelations of this session brought relief to Julia and her mother, the mother from now on more clearly contradicting the grandmother in some central aspects of their living together in the grandmother's house and the intergenerational enmeshment.

As Julia's mother became less avoidant of conflict during the following session, some points at issue could be spoken about more clearly between them and without Julia being in the role of an intermediary between her mother and grandmother, gaining more room for her own development. She overcame her anorectic symptoms and her anankastic rituals and also some of her anxieties.

The multigenerational approach

As in many families with severe psychic symptoms, we also see here an intergenerational 'repetition compulsion', a tendency to repeat problematic, conflictual relationships over several generations and a strong defence against their surfacing and being settled.

We also can see that conflicts with separation–individuation and loyalty often develop in the course of not only two, but three or more generations, and that problems in the generation of the children, our diagnosed patients, can be more effectively resolved by also working on the conflicts between the parents' generation and that of the grandparents.

References

Cella, S., Iannccone, M. & Corufo, P. (2014) How perceived parental bonding affects self-concept and drive for thinness: A community based study, *Eating Behaviors* 15: 110–115.
Cierpka, M. & Reich, G. (2010) Familien- und paartherapeutische Behandlung von Anorexie und Bulimie, in: G. Reich & M. Cierpka (Eds.), *Psychotherapie der Essstörungen* (2nd revised edn). Stuttgart: Thieme, pp. 164–198.
Cierpka, M., Reich, G. & Kraul, A. (1998) Psychosomatic Illness and the family, in: L. L'Abate (Ed.), *Handbook of Family Psychopathology*. New York: Guilford Press, pp. 311–332.
Field, A. E., Javaras, K. M. & Laird, N. M. (2008) Family, peer and media predictors of becoming eating disordered, *Archives of Pediatrics and Adolescent Medicine* 162: 574–579.
Friedlander, M. L., Siegel, S. M. (1990) Separation-individuation difficulties and cognitive-behavioral indicators of eating disorders among college women. *Journal of Counselling Psychology* 37: 74–78.
Gale, C. J., Cluett, E. R. & Laver-Bradbury, C. (2013) A review of father–child relationship in the development and maintenance of adolescent anorexia and bulimia nervosa, *Issues in Comprehensive Pediatric Nursing* 136: 48–69.
Holton-Viesel, A. & Allan, S. (2015) A systematic review of literature on family functioning across eating disorder diagnoses in comparison to control families, *Clinical Psychology Review* 34: 29–43.
Kluck, A. S. (2010) Family influence on disordered eating: The role of body image dissatisfaction, *Body Image* 7: 8–14.
Kog, E. & Vandereycken, W. (1989) Family interaction in eating disorder patients and normal controls, *International Journal of Eating Disorders* 8: 11–23.
Lock, J., LeGrange, D., Agras, W. S. & Dare, C. (2013) *Treatment Manual for Anorexia Nervosa: A Family-based Approach*. New York: Guilford Press.
Minuchin, S., Rosman, B. & Baker, L. (1978) *Psychosomatic Families. Anorexia in Context*. Cambridge, MA: Harvard University Press.
Neumark-Sztainer, D., Bauer, K. W. & Berge, J. M. (2010) Family weight talk and dieting: How much do they matter for body dissatisfaction and disordered eating behaviors in adolescent girls? *Journal of Adolescent Health* 47: 270–276.
Phillipou, A., Rossel, S. L. & Castle, D. J. (2014) The neurobiology of anorexia nervosa: A systematic review, *Australian and New Zealand Journal of Psychiatry* 48: 128–152.
Quiles Marcos, Y., Sebastián, M. J., Aubalat, L. P., Ausina, J. B. & Treasure, J. (2013) Peer and family influence in eating disorders: A meta-analysis, *European Psychiatry* 28: 199–206.
Reich, G. (2003a) *Familientherapie der Essstörungen*. Göttingen: Hogrefe.
Reich, G. (2003b) *Familienbeziehungen bulimischer Patientinnen. Eine Vergleichs-Studie zu Patientinnen mit Anorexia nervosa und einer nicht-essgestörten Kontrollgruppe*. Heidelberg: Asanger.
Reich, G. (2015) Familientherapie, in: S. Herpertz, M. de Zwaan & S. Zipfel (Eds.), *Handbuch der Essstörungen und Adipositas*. Heidelberg: Springer, pp. 255–262.

Strober, M. (1991) Disorders of the self in anorexia nervosa: An organismic-developmental paradigm, in: C. L. Johnson (Ed.), *Psychodynamic Treatment of Anorexia Nervosa and Bulimia*. New York: Guilford Press, pp. 354–373.

Tetley, A., Moghaddam, N. G., Dawson, D. L. & Rennoldson, M. (2014) Parental bonding and eating disorders: A systematic review, *Eating Behaviors* 215: 249–259.

Vandereycken, W., Kog, E. & Vanderlinden, E. (1989) *The Family Approach to Eating Disorders*. New York: PMA.

Van Elburg, A. & Teasure, J. (2013) Advances in the neurobiology of eating disorders, *Current Opinion in Psychiatry* 26: 556–561.

Wood, B. L., Jungha, L., Miller, B. D., Chea, P., Zwetsch, T., Ramesh, S. & Simmens, S. (2008) Testing the biobehaviorial family model in pediatric asthma: Pathways of effect, *Family Process* 47: 21–40.

Wood, B. L., Klebba, K. B. & Miller, B. D. (2000). Evolving the biobehavioral family model: The fit of attachment, *Family Process* 39: 319–344.

7

HELLO/GOODBYE NEW FAMILIES! GROUPWORK WITH LOOKED AFTER SIBLINGS

Heather Lee-Messner and Elizabeth Stevenson

Introduction

We are going to discuss our experiences of working with a sibling group of five children over a period of one and a half years fortnightly for a total of 32 group sessions. The children in the sibling group are all from the same family and ranged in age from three to nine years; they were all in foster care together awaiting separate adoptions. There were also two children in the family who had been adopted before the oldest of the five children in our group was born.

Our focus is to look at the themes of sameness and difference, omnipotent functioning and the confusion involved for the children in moving from their family of origin to foster carers and, ultimately, to a new family. An earlier version of this chapter was presented as a paper to a conference focusing on Freud's 'Mourning and melancholia' (1917) and that version was published in the *Journal of Child Psychotherapy*, December 2014. 'Mourning and melancholia' and sameness and otherness have some overlap in that to truly mourn, one must have achieved enough separateness or a sense of otherness to bear the pain of the loss, whereas Freud's melancholic remains attached to the lost object. Boston and Szur (1983) described characteristic patterns in looked after children's personalities, which include an omnipotent denial of helplessness and loss, confusion about intimacy, generational confusion, uneven development and a marked distrust of parental figures. Hindle and Shulman (2008: 17) wrote, "For these children, their experiences may be so fragmented and disorganised that it is difficult for them to gather a sufficient sense of who or what has been lost even to grieve".

In the group, we hoped to create a thinking space to contain the experience of being in transition and to enable mourning alongside emotional development. Susan Reid (1999: 251) wrote,

> Seeing the siblings together can facilitate the exploration of the ways in which they see one another, their parent or parents, and the ways in which

one may be a carrier for particular feelings or experiences for the others. It can be particularly helpful when one child has been 'scapegoated', enabling the exploration of projective mechanisms and allowing a healthier redistribution of feelings and even cognitive capacities.

Along similar lines, Canham and Emanuel (2000: 284) described the usefulness of groups allowing,

> the trajectory of a projection to be followed and explored and also enables the recipient of the projection to examine his/her vulnerability to being used by other people in this way. The group as a whole can also examine why they allowed this exchange to take place.

Referral

The children were referred to a small multidisciplinary team funded by local social care to address the mental health needs of looked after children. The referral held little information about the children in the early years, but we were aware that drugs and alcohol featured prominently and the children were often left with other adults while drugs were being procured from abroad. The children were found living in squalor and were noted to have been subjected to years of neglect and emotional abuse. Their foster carers had been involved throughout unsuccessful attempts to work with the children's mother and grandmother. Our team was asked to assess the children with recommendations for placements following care proceedings. The results from those assessments showed no significant cognitive impairments or any psychiatric disorders, although all of the children were several years behind their peers academically. Assessment findings are shown below.

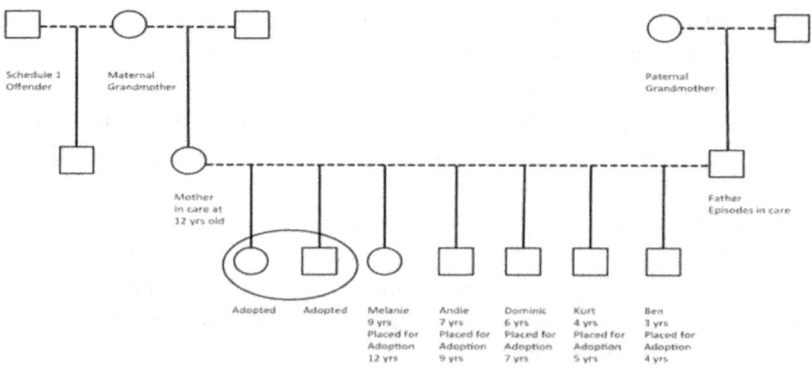

FIGURE 7.1 Genogram: the Green family

After Assessment

Melanie	Andy	Dominic	Kurt	Ben
Bland	Acting out	Little sense of identity	Avoidant	Afraid
Denial	Adults are useless	Didn't express emotion	Underlying despair	Traumatised
Wish to control feelings & others	Children find own solutions	Chaotic story stems	Reckless	Over familiar
Adults not helpful	Grown ups don't notice or care	Lost	Strong personality	Object seeking
Trick others	Distress not noticed		Attention his way or not at all	

FIGURE 7.2 After assessment

The network

The children's removal, followed by the intervention and confusion of the many professionals involved, the court processes, the people making decisions about the children's care could all be seen as a confusion of tongues, leaving the children with fears of what would happen to them now. When we met the children after the assessment, we thought about the children's sense of loss, which appeared to have more to do with the question Rustin (2006: 125) posed: 'Where do I belong?' How could these children allow themselves to know about losses and do the work of mourning without knowing who would be looking after them in the long term? The adults around the children, their carers and the professionals, had to face and metabolise the losses for them first. Networks surrounding children in care are notoriously complex (as many have described: Britton (1981), Reder et al., (1993), Sprince (2000), Lanyado (2008) and Rustin (2006)) as the adults and professionals reenact conscious and unconscious communications relating to the plight of the children and how this affects them.

Following assessment, our team recommended that, as the individual children's needs were so great, it would not be in their interests to be parented together as a sibling group. We pointed to the high risk of placement breakdown in a situation of one family attempting to manage the needs of these five children. We raised concerns about the unhealthy ways they relied on each other to meet their emotional and physical needs, often excluding adults as inconsequential. The social workers and foster carers initially argued against our recommendation and became distressed and angry with us as they found it unbearable to think about the children losing each other.

The Family Finders helped the social workers and foster carers to manage their grief by talking to them about how relieved they were not to have to find a family who could take and manage all five children. Having come to terms with the need for the children to be placed separately for adoption, the adults could approach the children with this decision.

The network took up our offer of a psychotherapy group alongside regular meetings for the foster carers, which we hoped would prove to be a transitional containing space. As the children departed, we were aware that each set of adoptive parents would meet the siblings who hadn't yet been placed, giving them a real and personal experience of them and of their child being part of a family of children. This would enable them more readily to relate to the sense of loss and deprivation the child they adopted would inevitably feel about their siblings over their lifetimes. It might also support their willingness to continue meeting for sibling contact.

The children

At the time the group started, the children had settled well in their foster family, who solidly provided the essential maternal and paternal functions they had missed out on in their early lives. This allowed us to help the children work towards separation and to engage in the work of mourning. They needed to develop as individuals in order to mourn that which they had not had in their early lives and the loss of each other in order to be available to make a relationship with a new family. The process of individuation proceeded alongside the mourning process, rather than sequentially. This was a dynamic process where each child moved between times where s/he was more integrated and separate in the working through of feelings and times where there was a return to reliance on the others for the management of unbearable feelings of grief, rage and sadness.

'Hello/goodbye/new families', the title of our chapter, is taken from the words written on the whiteboard in the group room at the start of every group meeting. The children added to it to announce important events such as holiday breaks, the introduction of the new adoptive families and the goodbyes to the specific children as they left to join their new families.

In the early group sessions, we found ourselves talking to each other when we were often ignored and treated as irrelevant. This was a clear communication to us about the children's experience and lack of expectations of parental figures. The sibling group often took over all parental functions omnipotently, excluding us as they remained in denial of the need for the adults in their lives. Canham (2002) described 'ganging up' in groupwork as being a way of avoiding the pain of dependency and ambivalent feelings in mourning. In the first three groups, the children all joined together to mock us and gathered together making silly noises, saying loud nonsense words and giggling at us.

Figure 7.3 shows our understanding of some of the aspects each of the children held for others. In the early groups, it was hard to keep the children individually in mind apart from the oldest, being the only girl, and the youngest, who was very clearly the smallest and still more like a toddler.

Summary of Differentiation/roles After Three Group Meetings

Melanie	Andy	Dominic	Kurt	Ben
8 years	7 years	6 years	4 years	3 years
Carer	Angry	unnoticed	Ideas	Undeveloped
Parental authority	Scape-goated	peacemaker	Grievance Determined	Fearful Left out
Controlling /bossy	Out of control	Disappear Fits in	Loud Susceptible	Babied Lost
Bully/bullied	Provokes 'Bad one'	Lacks independent Play	Clear	In the way
Harsh Super ego	Punished		Independent	Traumatised Anxiety 'Poor one'

FIGURE 7.3 Summary of differentiation/roles after three group meetings

As the only girl, Melanie was often called Mummy, while Andy and Kurt appeared to alternate taking on the paternal function for the group. We saw this occurring regularly. The following is an example:

> Andy got angry and shouted, "Look at this mess!", as he glowered at them all. Melanie then became a bossy teacher/parent who shouted and threatened, "If you don't clear that up you'll get a point taken off!" Kurt joined Melanie at the whiteboard where they proceeded to work out a system to earn points for being tidy. The others started to clear up to earn their points with Andy drawing their attention to himself calling, "Look what I've done". The others followed suit. (6th session).

Melanie, Andy and/or Kurt joined up as a parental couple at times to agree a way forward for the others, encouraging them to behave or else threatening punishments. Jennifer Silverstone (2006) described how siblings in families where mothers have been unable to offer containment attempt to take on an inappropriate parenting role, placing pressure both on themselves and the other siblings.

Melanie could become bossy, controlling and, at times, cruel towards her siblings. For example, in session 5:

> Melanie started furiously to move the furniture around the room, interfering with the ball game and all the activities the others were doing. They all complained but didn't stay with their protest. She arranged the furniture into beds, determinedly putting baby dolls roughly to sleep in each bed.

It was clear, in her use of the dolls representing the boys, that they were being punished and sent to bed as Melanie became the dissatisfied, cruel teacher/mother. At other times she could be solicitous, caring and generous, helping her brothers as they frequently turned to her for assistance and offered comfort to those who needed it. Her important and varied functions on behalf of her siblings were present in the group sessions from early on and the burden of this on her was substantial. This was an area of important work with Melanie in the group that slowly began to change over time, to the point where she encouraged the boys to ask us for help rather than always providing it for them. She became more in touch with her upset feelings that triggered her controlling behaviours towards them.

Andy was the scapegoated child at home and in the group; he appeared to hold the anger for most of the children. He spent a lot of time attempting to provoke others or interrupt their games, as in the third group:

> Andy smiled nastily while he loudly taunted the others. He spent most of the meeting looking for someone to wind up, first Kurt, who this time managed to resist, and then Dominic, from whom he took the ball. He kicked it repeatedly so that it wiped off the children's names, surrounded by their friends' names, that Dominic had spent a long time writing on the board.

Andy began to move towards an understanding of how the others used his volatility for their own purposes when, in the fifth group, Andy heard Liz and Heather talk about how he seemed to get angry for everyone even when he was not angry. Melanie then got angry and we talked about how she was now angry and Andy had immediately calmed down. This proved to be a turning point for him, as he became more thoughtful and less angry. Andy continued to be better able to resist the bossy, controlling demands on him made by his sister and resisted her attempts to wind him up. This development for him was evident by the time we prepared to say goodbye to the first child going to their new home.

> Andy sat with Heather, who said to him that he was sad today and couldn't play. He stared at the board (which had the usual 'Hello/Goodbye/New Families' with the addition of 'Goodbye to Kurt' and 'Hello to Kurt's family') and nodded. Heather said it was hard to know what to do today or what to say. He looked through his folder, found the paper rings, and Kurt came over to help him with them (session 12).

The paper rings had been understood in the previous meeting to be addressing the children's concern about how they would remain linked together, played out by using our help to make rings for everyone, linking the two ends of paper together. All of us had to have our own rings and wear them displayed on our fingers.

In the group, Dominic was hard to reach; he seemed more depressed and mainly fitted in with whoever asked him to join them in their activity. He did not initiate his own activities and neither did he say no to the others' demands. It wasn't until the ninth session, when we all knew Kurt was leaving shortly, that

> we could finally get a sense of what Dominic was feeling, as he let us know that he was sad because he knew Kurt's new adoptive father was a

footballer. He indeed looked crestfallen. Dominic later stood up to Melanie trying to boss him around with play in the dolls house and eventually told her he wouldn't play any more and went off to find his own activity.

In the same group, he became angry for the first time with Kurt, who made him an aeroplane as asked, but it didn't fly as well as the one he had made for himself. He was beginning to emerge as an individual presence within his sibling group and could better communicate his different feelings to his siblings and us. In group number seven, he said there were, "No new families for me and Andy". The implication we felt was that we had not sorted it out as we should, revisiting a regular theme; we spoke to him about feeling let down and fed up. It is important to note that this was, indeed, the first time he had expressed anything directly for himself in the group.

Kurt was the first child to move to an adoptive family, so we had less time to get to know him. In the second group meeting:

> Kurt drew himself with a new mummy and daddy on the board and said this was what they were here for. He began using the pens to draw a picture and he talked about it being his house on an island in the sea; the colours of the sea were a vivid series of blues and greens, conveying movement. The island appeared to be listing, with the house and island both coloured in carefully and a rocket drawn along the side of the paper. We spoke together about the picture and Kurt listened – pleased at our noticing. We talked about Kurt being clear in his mind that he was to go to a new mummy and daddy in a new house and we wondered about the potentially unsafe island and about what the rocket might mean, is it to take you away from worries about new families, or is to blow up the whole island?

Kurt could communicate his thoughts and feelings, which enabled him to be the clearest in his plans and intentions. We felt he held for the group the sense of agency and desire by being the capable one who could know about what he felt. Despite this, he was also susceptible to being easily wound up by his siblings' states of mind, which completely hijacked whatever he might have been feeling and doing. Over the course of the group, he became better able to withstand the provocations from his siblings.

Ben, the youngest child in the group, was often left out, ignored or babied by his siblings. He was the one who held the fear for all of them, as his traumatised state was evident by his fearfulness of the noises outside the room, his avoidance of police car toys, his clinging to Liz, fears of the crocodile toy and utter dependency on his siblings for help to get his coat or shoes off and on. All of his siblings agreed they never felt afraid. Ben slowly developed a sense of confidence:

> Ben was drawing carefully, connecting the lines of the kidney-shaped figures he often drew. He turned to Liz and said, "I love you". He said,

"We have the same glasses" (8th session). We commented that he wanted parents like us and was thinking about whom he fitted with and what he needed. We contained the ball game a little and Ben suddenly announced, "I'm in charge".

Later on, in a different group, he had overcome his fears about angry feelings:

After the return from the holiday, we were struck by Ben's continuing with his movement towards a sense of agency and possession of his own capacity to organise and demand of others. He was in charge of inviting others in the group into play and Andy allowed this without taking over the ball game as usual. Ben also managed to enjoy playing ball on his own at times in the meeting and stood up to Andy later when he knocked over the castle he had built. Ben made fists and growled at him, impressing us all (session 10).

Goodbyes

The time between each child's departure and the number of group sessions each child attended is shown in Figure 7.4.

In the groups leading up to Kurt's departure, the children were confronted with the reality of their situation and the loss of each other. All of the children had been working on reintegrating the aspects of themselves they had invested in each other, as we have described. They had moved from a state of undifferentiated sameness to a sense of otherness. The imminent loss of Kurt changed the group's functioning from one where we, as the leaders, were at times treated by the children as good and useless and, at other times, we were more consistently functioning as a containing couple who could facilitate a working group. Bion described the 'work group' as a group where there was an understanding

Order of Departure

- Kurt: 8 months in group
  12 sessions
- Dominic: 9 months in group
  16 sessions
- Ben: 13 months in group
  21 sessions
- Andy: 18 months in group
  32 sessions
- Melanie: 18 months group + 6 months fortnightly individual
  32 sessions

FIGURE 7.4 Order of departure

of the need for development as individuals, to co-operate, to face reality and to acknowledge emotional need.

Kurt's sense of purpose and determination meant he could imagine and prepare for belonging to a new family. This was not as pronounced in any of the other children at the time he left. The reality of his departure meant that the remaining children started to struggle in earnest with issues of loss. However, Kurt appeared to be in denial of the impending loss of his siblings until the very last session before he left.

We felt that Kurt's pleasure at being wanted was in danger of tipping into a manic defence, where his being full of good things left little room for thoughts about losses. Instead, we felt his sister held the negative feelings on his behalf, as she fell out with us over not being able to take home a picture she'd made for a friend or being able to give Kurt the soft giraffe toy he'd liked from the first group meeting (12th session). Melanie was able to say no to Kurt about asking her for help, and directed him to ask Heather. Dominic was upset and angry as he struggled with his chatterbox game that didn't work out as well as Kurt's. Andy expressed some of the sadness for the group at this time when he began to wonder about why he always thought he'd be last to leave the carers. Andy attempted to find ways to link himself and his siblings together by returning to the play with the rings, evocative of the connection between them. Ben fell over a lot in the meetings leading up to Kurt's departure. He held for his siblings a sense of how destabilising it felt to face this momentous change for them all. In the last group with Kurt, the children struggled to find 'lost' things from their box, such as the rubbers and scissors, which we felt was a communication about being severed from one another and not being able to rub this knowledge out.

Kurt spoke about being with his new family for the next Christmas and promptly became angry, which we linked with it being an exciting idea but also scary to think about so many things being different for them all by then. The children managed to use us, both in coming near to us in order to ask for help and making sure we would notice their play in the house or football game, for example (session 10). We felt there was now more change and thinking space available with the inevitability of the imminent loss of Kurt moving on to his new family. The constellation of the projective functioning of the sibling group was now more fluid, as the children could individually express their own anger and sadness.

The children all became interested in creating cut-out pictures. These were drawings we were to make for them of trees, flowers, rabbits and other animals, which the children then cut out and glued on to another paper to create different pictures. Where they placed the cut-outs and how they coloured them in became things they at first copied from Melanie and then began individually to organise how they each wanted their own pictures to look. We felt they had found a creative means by which to explore and be in charge of fitting into a new family. They may also have been managing feelings about the loss of Kurt, who had been cut out from the group.

Following a long break due to holidays and a missed group meeting, we heard that Dominic had spent the weekend before the group in his new home. We realised as we started the group that the children would then be saying goodbye to each other in the waiting room after the group. Here is a summary from our notes of that last group meeting with Dominic.

> They raced ahead of us to hide in the room but didn't wait to be found, instead popping up to tell us that Dominic was going. Dominic looked different; his hair was longer and not gelled as it usually was, he looked bigger, his face was red and his clothing stood out as being different from the others. Andy told him he should get his hair cut but Melanie said maybe he liked it longer. Melanie wanted 'Bye bye Dominic' added to the board. Melanie organised Liz, Heather and herself to have telephones together and we talked about wanting to stay in touch, be reachable and to know we were thinking about them. Melanie could turn to us in the face of the loss of Dominic and express her need to seek continuity. The group was dominated by a loud football game played by Andy and Dominic which took over and made it impossible to think or concentrate'.

Dominic and Andy took flight from the painful reality of the loss of each other, making it impossible for the others to process their feelings about losing Dominic. We felt the ball represented the unbearable feelings that no one wanted as they shouted angrily at each other and threw it back at their siblings (session 16).

Melanie hid her head, needing us to notice and ask after her. She hid behind a chair and eventually responded to Heather trying to reach her by phone. She told us she dropped Kurt (referring to the giraffe toy he liked from the first group meeting); "Is the giraffe Kurt?" Heather asked Melanie; she told us that the giraffe toy wasn't named Kurt, he *was* Kurt as she cuddled him close. We spoke about sadness and not being able to care for him any more while feeling angry about having to say goodbye, angry at the ball game and with Dominic, who was so busy today. Melanie turned to drawing flowers with the cut-outs again, something she knew how to do and could control. Ben announced he was king of the castle and didn't mind his brothers ignoring him. We felt he avoided becoming involved in any feelings to do with the loss of his brother, as those would dent his newly found sense of power.

There was mayhem in the waiting room with the children saying goodbye to each other, the foster carers wanting to tell us they will miss another group and the new adoptive parents looking our way. With hindsight, more meetings with the network to prepare for and plan Dominic's departure might have been useful.

There were only three group meetings between Dominic leaving and Ben going to his new family. The group meetings up until Ben's last one were uncharacteristically cooperative, with all three children joining together to play a variety of games. Ben continued to develop his capacity to assert his thoughts and wishes within the group and Melanie and Andy responded to his initiatives. Ben spoke proudly about his new family and they all thought about meeting them. Session 21, Ben's last group with his siblings:

> Ben asserted his right to choose strawberry cake for his goodbye party, not chocolate as Andy had wanted, and said no to playing Bingo. Melanie and Andy were full of angry feelings that played out between them in their teacher game, where Melanie made unending demands that could never be satisfied by Andy. We spoke about Ben saying goodbye, which Melanie responded to by becoming increasingly bossy and overexcited. She started to dance madly around the room, upturning chairs, shouting, then drawing with black pen over her hands and fingernails. We spoke together about it as a difficult meeting, sad big goodbyes and how it wasn't possible for anyone to be in charge or keep things in control. It hurt too much to think. Andy couldn't sort out the paper or anything else. He did manage to break free of Melanie to try to help clear up the room. Andy put some of his own pictures into Ben's folder and spoke about the next group doing more sorting out of his folder after the summer holiday. He helped Ben put on his shoes and carried his coat for him. Melanie left after reminding us that they would be away for three weeks.

There were nearly four months before Andy left the group. Melanie and Andy began to work out what they called a 'map' together on the whiteboard of their family (session 22).

Figure 7.5 is a photograph of the family map drawn on the whiteboard (hence the handwritten heading). The names and initials of the children, including the two children of the family who were adopted before we met these children, have been changed, while the numbers refer to the ages the children thought everyone was.

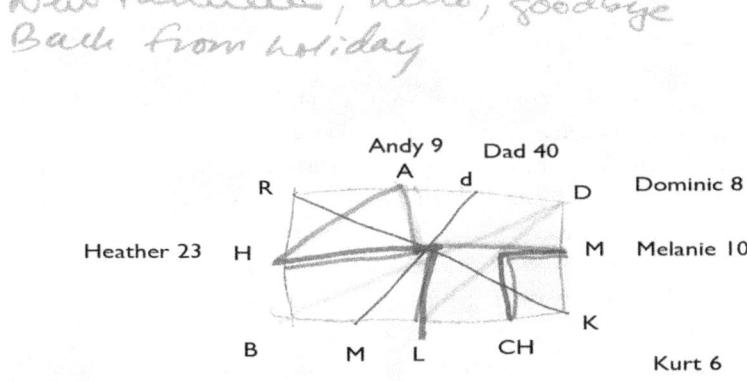

FIGURE 7.5 New families, hello, goodbye. Back from holiday

The family map consists of a series of lines interconnecting and identifying different family members and ourselves. This was created painstakingly by both children and redrawn over several group meetings. They concentrated on this activity to the exclusion of all others until they were satisfied with it. We felt the joint effort to create the family map represented their acknowledgement of their shared history, to be kept alive in each child's mind.

The other important activity they developed together was a series of lessons on fractions that had to be figured out and reworked over and over by us.

> A deal was struck between Melanie and Heather that Heather would do the fractions and then Melanie would talk with Heather. She came near but still could not make eye contact. Heather said it was too difficult to talk about the fractions. She looked at Heather and said she was ready. Melanie said, "What will I do when Andy goes and I'm the only one left?" looking at Heather, tearing up. Heather said it was a big and difficult upset and very hard to be alone with. It was so hard to be the oldest, seeing each one go, even if they were happy. Heather said she knew Melanie would really miss Andy and couldn't keep in mind hope that a family or mother would be found for her. We spoke about how she needed to be able to talk to us and to her carers about her feelings (session 26).

Melanie was in touch with the awful reality of being the last out of the five to go to a new family. We were surprised and touched by her capacity to communicate her distress and fears, also by her ability to turn to adults for help, so different from the bossy girl we first encountered.

Both Andy and Melanie could talk to us about their concerns about fitting into a new family and what would happen if it didn't work out. Andy thought about what the reality would be like when he thought of living with his new family. There was a lot of talk about cats and dogs, which we spoke about as learning to live together, like living with different people in their new families and getting on with each other in our group (session 28). Andy wondered about how to manage that his new family are Arsenal fans when he is a Manchester United supporter. We spoke in the group about how he could still be different and fit in. Andy was grappling with divided loyalties between his link to his siblings and his need to make new allegiances. He told us a long narrative about the plans for him, the goodbye to his school, his holiday coming up. We spoke about his now having a story he could tell about his new family (session 31).

In the last group meeting, our 32nd session, Andy had met his new family and was full of information about them. He looked forward to meeting the family animals, which he hadn't met yet. 'Goodbye Andy, Goodbye Heather and Group/Hello meetings with Liz' was written on the board (this referred to our agreement that Melanie would continue to have fortnightly individual sessions with Liz once Andy left). Both children hugged Heather as if it were all really about her leaving, not the more difficult Andy going. Melanie started the family map while Andy kicked the ball around and talked about his new parents. The family map was very painful to do and we felt the fullness of Melanie's pain at the losses. The last thing done was Melanie making another Christmas card which Andy had liked so much and had asked her to make one for him. She wrote, 'Goodbye, lots of love Melanie', managing to stay with the excruciating feeling of sadness. She remained patient with him while he became giggly and started being disruptive, taking pens off her. She told him calmly to stop and managed to finish giving him her card. The feelings of pain over the losses of each other had grown as they became more integrated; "to have a memory you have to have separated sufficiently to bear the pain of absence" (Case, 2008: 131).

Conclusion

The literature about looked after children acknowledges the complexity of the development of the children's internal landscapes, given their early deprivation, neglect and abuse. The emotional development of the five individual children and their growing capacity to differentiate from their siblings enabled them to recognise their losses and to begin to mourn. The group could be seen to stand at the border between mourning and melancholia, or between sameness and otherness. From the ruins of the chaos of their difficult start in life, the children began to develop as individuals and find new ways to relate to others.

We considered the importance for the children of the adults around them helping to contain and metabolise the losses they faced before they could individually experience mourning. The children were able to turn to the adults in their lives for this support once they had relieved their siblings of providing the essential parental functions for them. These children, with help from the network and the group, were able to look forward to, and prepare for, their new families. They experienced delight when they knew a family had been found for them and could imagine belonging. They had not hardened up in denial of their dependency needs, and neither had they turned inwards towards a lost object, away from life and new relationships.

References

Boston, M. & Szur, R. (Eds.) (1983) *Psychotherapy with Severely Deprived Children*. London: Routledge and Kegan Paul.

Britton, R. (1981) Re-enactment as an unwitting professional response to family dynamics, in: S. Box, B. Copley, J. Magagana & E. Moustaki (Eds.), *Psychotherapy with Families: An Analytic Approach*. London: Routledge and Kegan Paul.

Canham, H. (2002) Group and gang states of mind, *Journal of Child Psychotherapy* 28(2): 113–127.

Canham, H. & Emanuel, L. (2000) Tied together feelings. Group psychotherapy with latency children: the process of forming a cohesive group, *Journal of Child Psychotherapy* 26(2): 281–302.

Case, C. (2008) Moving towards reality after trauma, in: D. Hindle & G. Shulman (Eds.), *The Emotional Experience of Adoption: A Psychoanalytic Perspective*. Abingdon, UK: Routledge.

Freud, S. (1917) Mourning and melancholia'. *SE* 14: 243–258. London: Hogarth.
Hindle, D. & Schulman, G. (2008) *The Emotional Experience of Adoption: A Psychoanalytic Perspective*. Abingdon, UK: Routledge.
Lanyado, M. (2008) Playing out, not acting out. The development of the capacity to play in the therapy of children who are 'in transition' from fostering to adoption, in: D. Hindle & G. Shulman (Eds.), *The Emotional Experience of Adoption: A Psychoanalytic Perspective*. Abingdon, UK: Routledge.
Reder, P., Duncan, S. & Gray, M. (1993) *Beyond Blame: Child Abuse Tragedies Revisited*. London: Routledge.
Reid, S. (1999) The group as a healing whole: group psychotherapy with children and adolescents, in: M. Lanyado & A. Horne (Eds.), *The Handbook of Child Psychotherapy: Psychoanalytic Approaches*. London: Routledge.
Rustin, M. (2006) Where do I belong? Dilemmas for children and adolescents who have been adopted or brought up in long-term foster care, in: J. Kendrick, C. Lindsey & L. Tollemache (Eds.), *Creating New Families: Therapeutic Approaches to Fostering, Adoption and Kinship Care*. London: Karnac.
Silverstone, J. (2006) Siblings, in: P. Coles (Ed.), *Sibling Relationships*. London: Karnac.
Sprince, J. (2000). Towards an integrated network. *Journal of Child Psychotherapy*, 26(3): 413–444.

8

THE CREATION OF IDENTITY

The way to gender distinction and identity in the family

Anne Loncan

Gender distinction appears, is constructed and acquired within the family. Drawing its reference points from the previous generation's inheritance, the couple produces, in turn, its specific psychic life, which becomes a family life by giving birth to children.

First, I would like to define the notion of gender and its current evolution. It is now a concept discussed and called into question in sociological circles, as well as historical and psychoanalytical ones. Several authors would like to give it a prominent connotation, to deny the sexual implications attached to it, or to delineate its limits and go further into the processes used. I examine here how the feminine is transmitted in order to try to understand how gender identity is dependent on societal myths and norms, but, above all, on the family psychic world.

A few definitions

Gender comes from the Latin 'genus', and from the Greek 'γενος'. This origin works equally well in French, in English and in modern Latin-based languages. In Latin, according to the Gaffiot dictionary, genus means, first and foremost: origin, extraction or birth, second, and by extension, 'race, species or type'. We see here that sexual identity is not involved at all.

In modern French, the word 'genre' today contains a variety of meanings. The Larousse dictionary refers the most frequent meaning of the word genre to biology (roughly, a group of species which have some characteristics in common). Masculine and feminine are linked to genre only in grammar, to mark the 'sex' of beings or things.

In English, and according to Webster's dictionary, 'gender' mainly refers to grammar, like genre in French, but the second meaning of gender is 'sex', as in the expression 'the feminine gender'.

So, we can observe the traditional semantic nuances between French and English and understand the changes, which happened in French. In French, little by little, a shift in meaning occurred under the influence of gender studies developed in the USA since the 1960s. It was differentiated, at the same time, from biological determining and from classic psychological and psychoanalytical constructions. Environment and family impact on the gender experience of the subject seemed decisive, particularly in a feminist positioning which denunciated the masculine domination (Butler, 1999).

This introduction explains the use of 'gender identity' instead of 'sexed identity' or 'sexual identity'. According to French professor Colette Chiland (2011), sexed is just on a biological level, sexual is about sexual relations and 'gender' is about any element linked to social roles. I believe that gender identity is wider than sexed or sexual identity, and includes the former, corresponding to a partial overlap. According to the theory of unconscious intersubjective links, I think that external sources, such as social models, habits, ideas and representations, are not enough to explain gender identity merely by assignment. Ideals and identifications and their opposites are constantly working to forge the subjective world, regulating introjection and projection processes. So, I will use the locution 'gender identity' to talk about gender attitudes, mostly socially determined, as well as about the deep feeling of being a male or a female. Wanting to examine mainly the origin of female and feminine identity, I first look at the history of ideas and myths about women through the centuries to estimate the weight of societal assignment in the building of feminine and female identity. Second, I investigate what comes from the unconscious transmission of family essence.

Transmission of feminine and societal myths

I am broaching the transmission of the feminine following the progression of this legacy within the family on the basis of social perdurable myths, then looking for their infiltration in psychoanalytical thought. All these myths contribute to the building of the cultural envelope, which itself contains the psychic family envelope. All of us have inherited them, including beliefs and ideals which have founded our practice of couple and family psychoanalysis. At the heart of the links, which are considered as vehicles, myths are associated to fantasies, dream thoughts and feelings at the same time.

In the light of the links theory, I list the ways which lead to the feminine and female in women, over and beyond the Oedipal triangulation, and include genealogic depth.

In Greek Antiquity, we can see in Plato (*Timaeus*) the myth of women's inferiority and animal nature, which is confirmed by Aristotle: women are 'beings naturally made to be obedient'. They are defined by their lacks, and considered as just physical, good only for procreation. Considered to be without the necessary abilities, they were not given access to knowledge or power, which are essential tools for transmission.

The first Christian thinkers perpetuated similar ideas, but in the 16th century, Luther and the Reformation granted women a relative dignity, recognizing their virtues in the matter of spirituality and education, but only to teach little girls the Gospel. The Reformation left their position within the couple unchanged: "…like a nail stuck in the wall, the woman stays at home […] since she has not the abilities to conduct external and public affairs" (translated for this edition).[1]

During the Enlightenment, glimmers of the beginning of a more egalitarian concept of relationships between genders appear, at least in the narrow circle of philosophers. Among them, Jean-Jacques Rousseau dreams of snatching human beings away from nature and of leading them towards a new freedom by means of the "social contract". Following this thought, he thinks about women's education, but provided that it develops "the female virtue of dependence", and he reasserts male prerogatives: "everywhere she [the woman] asserts her rights, she has an advantage; everywhere she wants to usurp ours, she stays underneath us" (Rousseau, 1762, translated for this edition).

The underlying myths in the ideas mentioned can be regrouped according to the viewpoint of transmission:

- The myth of a strong anchoring of women in nature and of their animal nature leads to them being confined to the tasks of breeding and raising the young.
- The myth of women's inferiority justifies the subordination of women to men. Power and transmission of knowledge are major tools, which have to remain a man's prerogative.
- The myth of the spirituality specific to women gives them the task of transmitting faith and religion.

On the whole, these myths are found right up to modern days, when they suddenly shifted.

The feminine in psychoanalysis

Regarding theories about the feminine in psychoanalysis, up to what extent have these myths survived and infiltrated the psychoanalytical thinking? This question contributes to estimating their ability to orientate psychic life and throw light on the living context of transmission of feminine identity.

Freud and his contemporaries

Freud's work is shot through with references to women, which are organized from a viewpoint influenced by the previously mentioned societal myths. Be they about sexual theories in children, their fantasizing life, their entering into, and disengagement from, the Oedipal position, for Freud, the father remains the main magnet, even if chronologically the mother is the first one. In girls,

Freud thinks that entering the Oedipus complex is dependent on an elaborate construction, which, unlike what happens with boys, requires a change of object. Not only is the father prominent, but also libido "is of male essence". In his own words, his concept of the psychogenesis of the feminine is "unilateral". His emphasis on father and male could be understood as an attempt to restore the father's authority, which he feels is threatened. In line with the most innovative trends of his time, he develops and supports the main themes of Western thinking, as an heir to a tradition, which he fights, justifies and renews all at the same time. Nevertheless, he does not ignore that social factors would inflect psychic development, as we can read in *Zur Einführung des Narzissismus* (Freud, 1914). According to him, an increase of narcissism is parallel to pubertal development in the girl, especially when it coincides with an increase in beauty. This leads to "a state where the woman is self-sufficient, to compensate for society denying her free choice of object".

These last points are tied to the myths of the power of nature and male domination (whose corollary is women's inferiority). Women's inferiority is a notion consistent with the weak Super Ego, which is attributed to them. And we know that this instance, transmitted through generations, controls everyday life.

Among works of contemporaries and followers of Freudian thinking, even female psychoanalysts also refer to the same myths.

As a pupil of Freud, Helene Deutsch continues the master's thinking. A bit condescending with regard to women, she considers women's accomplishment to be in their biological functions ('Psychologie des Weibes in den Funktionen der Fortpflanzung', 1925). She tries to bring out a female specificity just as noble as that of men. She thinks that the quantity of libido is proportional to the volume of genitals, so that women are able to keep, like children, "polymorphous perverse features" (translated for this edition).

For her, female achievement reaches its highest point during pregnancy and delivery, the last being described as a true "masochistic pleasure orgy" (translated for this edition). Sadistic drives are at their peak at the time of the expulsion of the baby and the Ego-Ideal will be embodied in the child. Deutsch, with psychoanalytical tools, succeeds in confirming the traditional Latin saying: "*Tota mulier in utero*".

Post Freudian theories

I can summarize post Freudian theories. Roughly, they state that feminine which preludes the later feminine identity, is built by archaic sexing determined within the dyad of motherchild because the mother's belongs to the world of women: this is the quintessential narcissistic link, orientated by the attraction of sameness. A maternal harmonious mastery actively maintains the investments necessary to the blossoming of the child's primitive omnipotence, in a context of maternal homoerotic seduction.

We have seen that later, the child is classically a place of various identifications in the context of Oedipal development, and these processes start again and carry on during adolescence.

More recently, some theoretical research emphasizes the couple as a focus of maturation, which leads women to fully integrate their gender. Schaeffer (1997), a French psychoanalyst, suggests the significant role of a "pleasure lover" who becomes the decisive agent of women's erotic fulfilment in sexual life. Schaeffer extends, with conviction, Freud's energetic point of view. For her, the quantity and constancy of the surge of libido play a major role. She doesn't disclaim the preliminary processes that, from the very beginning, prepare this "initiating experience", in particular the co-excitement linked to wishing for the mother's attention. The first organizing work of the drive is to seduce, and then contribute to building an "erotic masochism, not perverse, nor acted […], as guardian of sexual pleasure" (translated for this edition), which allows the Ego to let in large quantities of non-linked excitement. This author recalls Freud's words about dependency and underlines the similarity in the situation of women and children with regard to a love object. She considers masochistic pleasure as being a female specificity which would soften the biologic bedrock's hardness, and give the key to the enigma: if man can be the cause of such pleasure, he can access the feminine through identification with women.

I would underline that, according to Schaeffer, women become truly themselves only in couple transmission through relationship with a "pleasure lover" under the aegis of submission. Motherhood, even fantasized, seems to have lost its historical statute.

According to all these studies, men and fathers remain the initiators of couple and family functioning. They mobilize the driving forces which lead women to their female identity.

During the past few years, we have seen that the Oedipal complex keeps the main role, while new theories about the roles of the mother or the couple extend this point of view. These last theories renew ancient arguments, serving as a stepping-stone to reaffirm women's submission, which would characterize their gender.

In the world of Anglo-Saxon psychoanalysis, we must remark on how important and worthy of interest is the work of Juliet Mitchell. This author has highlighted, as early as 1974, in *Psychoanalysis and Feminism*, and later in 1985 (*Feminine Sexuality: Jacques Lacan and the École Freudienne*), the extent to which the unconscious and sexuality Freud was talking about came under psychic construction and not immediate data. Further on, she broaches the role of the siblings in these constructions (2003), notably as she reconsiders and broadens the significance of the Oedipus complex. She then develops the importance of transversal relationships between siblings (whether biological or not), making a link with the vertical axis of filiation, and this on a level which is not exclusively sexual.

In the United States, the works of the philosopher Judith Butler (1999, 2004) fall within the continuity of anthropological studies on gender started in the 1960s. Her point of view is that gender is built in a complex relationship with biological sex, the existence of which she doesn't deny, but she thinks that its definition "needs a framework of intelligibility". As Mitchell before her, she thinks that gender is not a foregone conclusion given by nature. She insists on the social norms, which weigh heavily on the construction of gender, infiltrating the fantasies. According to her, each person has to "negotiate" with these norms to concur with them, reject them or live their ambivalence.

We can see that, depending on the author, the ideas foster differing factors, establishing each person in a gender, whether it corresponds partially or totally to his biological sex.

Contribution of family psychoanalytic theories

The parameters involved in gender access are multiple, either pertaining to family environment (pre-Oedipal, homoerotic or homosexual, Oedipal, amorous, maternal), or to social environment. While classical psychoanalytic works emphasize intrapsychic agencies and processes, as well as object relations, the more recent studies consider mainly environment and contemporaneous factors.

Family psychoanalysis includes them all and leads to a coherent conceptual set about the ways of gender transmission and access. All the processes superimpose and are closely intertwined, thanks to simultaneity or succession of various outlooks, and seem easier to understand if we use the theory of intersubjective unconscious links within the family. Our point of view encompasses a temporality beyond individuals, otherwise transmission effects would remain scattered or condemned to proximity relationships, in particular about genders.

The origin of the concept of link, as we use it, comes from the 1960s–1970s, when Pichon Rivière, an Argentinian psychoanalyst, defined it thus: it includes the relationship of reciprocal objects as well as the psychic representation of their assembly. As early as 1962, Bion mentioned three types of links (hate, love, and knowledge). For him, they are "emotional experiences" lived by *the subject in relation with another*, in an active perspective, the affect being considered as a fact. The link comes under a whole where the elements are interlinked and influence each other in the subject's psyche, and it is in the subject's psychoanalysis that this can be seen.

From the viewpoint of family psychoanalysis, with Alberto Eiguer I consider that the psychic formation, which is the link, includes reciprocity, mutuality and acknowledgement. The intersubjective link works then 'in between', in an unnamed area, sometimes called 'extra-topical' (Kaës, 2005), outside the psyche. Personally, I would like to stress that, if the link develops in intersubjectivity, it resolutely dives into the intrapsychic and unconscious, where it anchors itself. The texture of the link is made of various and variable psychic contents: affects, fantasies, myths, ideals… It is also the seat of various processes, and among these, the unconscious alliance developed by Kaës. Subject to temporality, the link can be modified without disappearing. The vestigial link is then fed into an other's intersubjectivity after a split-up or a death (I developed this theory in 2008); thus, it is accountable for transgenerational identifications.

The unconscious intersubjective links can be of filiation, alliance or fraternal, and are preferentially marked by narcissism or objectality. Combining the links, through pooling and sharing the contents transiting there, ensures transformation and transmission within the family group. In our study, they are, therefore, in the foreground of the construction of gender identity, along a metaphorical line.

To complete my viewpoint, I will also mention the transpsychic register, which enshrines significations waiting to be taken up to the level of the family psychic envelope. This last concept was posited by Anzieu (1991, 1993), as an extension of the *moi-peau* (*The Skin Ego*, Anzieu 1986, tr. Engl 2016) and the individual psychic envelope (1990). Obviously, we should also think in terms of exchanges made between the cultural envelope, the family group and each person's subjectivity.

Whether gender is being refused or rebelled against, its transmission works through family myths, which are strong beliefs constructed and passed on from one generation to the next and which define the family-self, the feeling of belonging to the family, while the societal myths form the background of our cultural envelope. The impact of societal myths on the family, and on each one of us, will depend on the permeability, suppleness and definition of the family envelope. A 'high definition' envelope, where the filters are precisely defined by the family myths and ideals, will better protect the family from societal myths it disagrees with. Conversely, a family envelope badly defined because of failing myths and ideals, or torn by traumatic impacts, will more easily let in societal myths conflicting with the family's psychic organizers.

A synthesis-shaped conclusion

I think that the construction of gender identity remains to be considered according to the drives mobilized in the developing subject, to the identifying processes, the vectors and places of transmission: the links, their apparatus, how they are enshrined in the family and cultural psychic envelopes. Transmission takes place in accordance with two complementary lines: the vertical line, represented by filiation links and links to ancestors, is the main theatre of Oedipal play and constructions of the SuperEgo (among others) in a diachronic mode. At the same time, the horizontal line of sibling links opens also to the world of pairs in a synchronic mode. It prepares the acceptance of the alterity of the other as a subject, contributing to leading towards societal life.

Additionally, it is very important to understand that family or societal contributions concerning gender identity are not passively received, but that the subject metabolizes and transforms them at each new stage of his/her psychic building. The diversity of the means used takes into account the potentially fluid and mobile side of gender identity, but without making it easily unstable.

I should conclude by broadening the theme towards the building of the feeling of identity: gender identity constitutes a decisive part of this.

Note

1 *Commentaire du livre de la Genèse*, in Luther, M. *Œuvres*, Vol. XVII. Geneva: Labor et Fides, 1955–1993.

References

Anzieu, D. (1986) Le moi peau, *Journal de la Psychanalyse de l'Enfant*, 2: 12–24.
Anzieu, D. (1990) *A Skin for Thought*. London: Karnac.
Anzieu D. (1991) La peau psychique, *Gruppo* 7: 137–139.
Anzieu D. (1993) Le moi-peau familial et groupal, *Gruppo* 9: 9–18.
Anzieu, D. (2016) *The Skin Ego*. London, Karnac.
Bion, W. R. (1962) *Learning from Experience*. London: Karnac.
Butler, J. (1999) *Gender Trouble: Feminism and the Subversion of Identity*. New York: Routledge.
Butler, J. (2004) *Undoing Gender*. New York: Routledge.
Chiland, C. (2011) *Changer de sexe: Illusion et réalité*. Paris: Odile Jacob.
Deutsch, H. (1925) Psychologie des Weibes in den Funktionen der Fortpflanzung, *Internationale Zeitschrift für Psychoanalyse* XI, 1.
Freud, S. (1914) Zur Einführung des Narzissismus, *Gesammelte Werke*, X, 138–170, 1946, English translation: *Standard Edition, XIV,* 73–102, On narcissism: An introduction (1957).
Kaës, R. (2005) Pour inscrire la question du lien dans la psychanalyse, *Le Divan familial*, 15: 73–93.
Mitchell, J. (1974) *Psychoanalysis and Feminism*. London: Allen Lane.
Mitchell, J. (1985) *Feminine Sexuality: Jacques Lacan and the École Freudienne*. New York: Norton.
Mitchell, J. (2003) *Siblings*. Cambridge: Polity Press.
Pichon-Rivière, E. (1971) *Teoria del vincula*. French translation: *Théorie du lien suivi de le processus de création*. Toulouse: Erès, 2004.
Rousseau, J.-J. (1762) *Emile, ou de l'éducation*. Paris: Poche, 2009.
Schaeffer, J. (1997) La belle au bois dormant: comment le féminin vient aux filles? In: *Le refus du féminin*. Paris: PUF.

9
MISUNDERSTANDING AND CONFUSION: EDUCATIONAL AND PSYCHOTHERAPEUTIC WORK IN A KINDERGARTEN

An outreach project

Christiane Ludwig-Körner

Children growing up in low socio-economic circumstances are, for several reasons, more prone to misunderstanding and confusion. Often, they attend kindergartens together with children from various cultures who speak different languages, many of whom are unable to speak the local language. Additionally, the children's point of contact throughout the day in these kindergarten groups are the kindergarten teachers, many of whom have their own individual cultural identities and linguistic backgrounds. In the light of these factors, relationships and interactions in this multicultural setting tend to be overly complex and challenging. Furthermore, at home, these children typically experience parents who are not attuned and are not able to meet their needs. There is an added tendency in these families for complex family dynamics to be passed down from generation to generation. Many of the parents or the grandparents have either been refugees, or faced terror, violence and helplessness themselves. The severe mental distress in the parents caused by such traumatic experiences are often passed down to their children. As a consequence, children in need of care that would allow them to develop self-regulation and mentalization are often left with parents who lack those capabilities themselves.

Generally, the kindergartens in low socio-economic areas (in Berlin) are unable to provide sufficient support and adequate care. Neither are they able to even partially compensate for the deficiency present in the familial construct. The result is carers who are overworked and over challenged by their daily tasks. Their time and qualification is mostly inadequate for the complexity that unfolds in their groups and the specific developmental needs of the individual children. High turnover rates in staff, coupled with a lack of budgets for specialized practitioners, further reduce the likelihood of adequate support and care.

After much observation and study, the problems of this early 'Babel' were narrowed down to the following three areas: adult education, early prevention and early intervention. As each of these is in physically different locations, an idea was formed to implement and bring together all three areas directly into the kindergarten setting. The aim would be to provide support to the parent–child relationship in overburdened families. We focused on the most drastic cases, as there was a real risk that some of the members of such families, especially the children, would end up in psychiatric clinics. To this end, we worked with specialized pedagogic–therapeutic support in the kindergarten. By inviting the mothers and fathers to be present together with their children on a daily basis in the kindergarten and be supported by qualified staff in an appropriate and professional manner, we hoped the parents would overcome their resistance to educational help. The hope was that they would adopt, through an exemplary manner, more functional educational behaviours and, thereby, develop a better relationship with their children. In Germany, in contrast to other countries, for example, Scandinavia, the integration of parents into the everyday educational processes in the kindergarten is almost non-existent. Unfortunately, kindergarten care is often still limited exclusively to the 'care' of children and does not support broader educational processes. Additionally, most carers are largely under-qualified and, therefore, unable to support parents psychologically. Since Germany joined the UN Convention on the Rights of the Child in 2009, awareness is growing that all children have the right to equal treatment, yet, in reality, children growing up in poverty and/or whose parents suffer from mental disorders have significantly less chances of healthy development and of becoming educationally successful (Kluge et al., 2015). There is a growing aspiration for an inclusive pedagogy in which all children can grow up together, with specialists knowing that new paths have to be taken. Is it worth looking backwards into the history of psychoanalysis for suggestions on how to deal with the present?

Experiences of a psychoanalytic therapeutic–pedagogical work in kindergartens

In 1950, Anny Katan founded a kindergarten (nursery school) in Cleveland, Ohio, which is now part of the Hanna Perkins Center. Together with Erna (Poppy) Furman, a psychoanalyst trained by Anna Freud in London, and Liz Dauton, she set up the "treatment via the parent" programme in which she worked closely with parents and teachers to impart to them the necessary skills for dealing with children (Furman & Katan, 1969). From these experiences, she further established therapeutic nurseries, such as the Lucy Daniels Center for Early Childhood in Cary, California, the Allen Creek Preschool in Ann Arbor, Michigan, the Harris School in Houston/Galveston, Texas and the Hanna Perkins Center for Child Development (Cleveland Therapeutic Nursery) in Ohio (Ludwig-Körner, 2014). Experience with projects such as The Abecedarian Early Intervention Project, conducted in 1972 by the Frank Porter Graham Child Development Institute in North Carolina, USA – where children from early infancy to the age of three were closely looked after by specialists in a special nursery school (carers' key in infancy: 1:2, just before school entrance 1:5) – illustrate the effectiveness of such intensive care (Campbell & Ramey, 1994). However, as early as in 1941, Augusta Alpert (1941) offered therapeutic groups for nursery children. According to Rosenblitt (2005) different psychoanalytic work can be carried out in a kindergarten setting. For one, a more or less classical variant can be utilized, in which a psychoanalyst carries out therapy with individual children. Alternatively, a combination of individual and group therapeutic activities can be integrated into the educational framework. Currently, Inge Pretorius (Pretorius & Karni-Sharon, 2012) is working as a child psychoanalyst in a kindergarten located in a blighted district in London, where she conducts parental counselling, parent–infant–toddler psychotherapies, individual child psychotherapies and advises the pedagogical team.

Strengthening the parent–child relationship within the kindergarten

Focusing, as just outlined, on the support of the parent–child relations of overburdened families, the main project goals were the fostering of the child's development, as well as strengthening the parent–child relationship and parental skills. The aim of the pilot project was to offer the children opportunities for better development. We hoped that by experiencing a different quality of relationship, the parents themselves might be able to develop an improved relationship with their children. With this in mind, the parents were treated benevolently and received supportive assistance from a qualified counterpart in a warm and accepting manner. By means of individual training and support, we expected their parenting skills to improve in a way that would be more beneficial to their children.

To summarize the intended effects, we might say that the project strove to enhance understanding and minimize confusion in early childhood through direct experience. In the long run, we hope that this work will serve as a model that would combine the three financially separate departments of finance, health, and education. Until now, each public institution worked individually. In this way, the support for overburdened families would be more efficient and effective.

Our project could rightly be called multilateral, as there were a number of heterogeneous participants: the kindergarten and its staff, families, children, our practitioner and students to support the research. The kindergarten in which the project took place is located in Neukölln, a low socio-economic area in Berlin. In the Kiez – the colloquial term for the surrounding quarter in Berlin – where the kindergarten is located, the percentage of temporary residents is 31.9 – more than twice the Berlin average. In addition, another 16.1% of the residents are immigrants from other countries. The kindergarten was located in four separate and very small apartments, albeit in close proximity. Seventy children attended the kindergarten, of which 72% were non-German speakers. With all due respect to the carers, the kindergarten is archetypal for low socio-economic areas in Berlin. Although there are many low-socio-economic areas in the city, the average carer–child ratio in Berlin is 1:6, which is very bad for German relations. These figures fail to take illness, holidays or training of the carers into account. There are far too few well-educated carers in Germany who, especially in view of the stressful work, would rather work in the districts where not so many stressed families live. Therefore, the educators constantly changed so that the children again and again had to experience breaks.

Five families with a total of eleven children participated in the pilot project. Originally, the project had been planned for three families only, but two additional families were strongly recommended by the youth welfare office and the children's psychiatric day hospital. In retrospect, five families were too many. Four families participated voluntarily, while one was forced to participate in order to avoid the removal of the children. All families faced substantial problems and urgently needed support in the parent–child relationship. The living conditions of the families were very rough. Besides being financially very limited, they lived in cramped flats (e.g., six people sharing two and a half rooms).

The parents showed a wide cultural and linguistic variance. All parents were traumatically burdened by at least one of the following: sexual abuse, domestic violence or early loss of a parent. Some of them faced chronic illness or lived in unstable families, some of them had severe difficulties in rejecting their traditional parental behaviour (e.g., hitting their children). They were torn between different cultures and disappointed by reality, regularly exhibiting negative emotions that adversely affected their children. As they had rarely met people who showed empathy and compassion, they hadn't developed the competence to be sensitive toward their children and their needs. One mother, for example, told us that one of the best times for her had been the short time she had spent in a children's home, because she had met people there who for the first time treated her kindly and were empathic.

As expected, all the children had an exceptionally high need for support. At the beginning of the project, nine of the children exhibited insecure attachment styles (one child was born during the project period and another child was also simply too young for an attachment measure). All children exhibited a general lack of development in varying degrees. They had substantial problems in concentration, learning and verbal expression. Some of them showed extreme aggressive behaviour and were considered unsuitable for attending kindergarten. Due to their difficulties, some of the children were unable to participate in the psychological evaluations.

At the beginning of the project, only one child was classified by the 'I-Status', that means that he or she officially needed special integration. The reasons for this low rate were that the carers in low socio-economic areas develop a different benchmark for what is considered 'normal', not to mention the deficit of specially trained carers who should have been working in this kindergarten. The NUBBEK study by Tietze et al. in 2013 shows how children of high-risk families often end up in low-quality kindergartens and, therefore, show an even greater need for specialized care.

In order to accomplish our goal, a qualified colleague was needed, someone who had both therapeutic and educational skills, and was well versed in early preventions and interventions. This pedagogical therapy trained practitioner needed to be able to address the often complicated personality structures of the parents and to enhance their mentalization capacities. Additionally, she was required to support the carers onsite in dealing with the parents.

As all parents showed structural deficits, they needed a counterpart, a kind of 'helping ego', with whom they could identify and learn from by example to identify situations and react as the practitioner did. Instead of acting in a psychotherapeutic setting, the psychotherapist worked in the field, that is, onsite in the kindergarten and in the domestic environment of the families. Going beyond traditional psychotherapy and counselling, she accompanied the parents sometimes to important diagnostic and medical appointments. Notably, she visited the families at home even in critical situations or during illness. Working in the field was more difficult and challenging because the setting and the working alliance were much less structured. Despite this, the unique experience with the families and the accompanying observations provided invaluable insight into the lives of these families.

Each day, the psychotherapist spent a few hours training the parents in an attempt to bolster the parent–child relationship. We proposed forming 'mindful parenting groups' introduced first by Grienenberger in the Center for Reflecting Parenting in Los Angeles (Grienenberger et al., 2005). However, and although the strengths and weaknesses of each parent varied, most parents were disinclined to partake in group activities. What's more, the 'Babel' cultural differences and languages presented added challenges. For these reasons, we decided to do the trainings mostly one-on-one.

For the work with the parents, the psychotherapist used a number of methods. The promotion of mentalization skills was induced through the psychotherapist's empathic understanding. The parents learned to get in touch with their inner mental state and to develop a representation of their own sense of self. They gradually learned to put these into words and to express them to others. Through training, they became more proficient in understanding their own and their children's psychological processes and gained a stronger ability to react more sensitively to their children's needs. If the parent didn't perceive her or his child's signals, the psychotherapist directed their attention to her or him – in a sense of a 'helping ego'. If the child was too young to talk about his or her mental state, the psychotherapist lent her/him her voice and told the parent what the child might feel. The parent was sometimes invited to partake in an imaginative exercise in an attempt to aid them in developing a representation of the child's feeling and experience.

Quite often, the parents had difficulties observing and perceiving their child differentially. Either they were too occupied with their own problems and self-care or they hadn't experienced good enough parenting themselves, so that they never had the opportunity to develop intuitive parenting capacities. Sometimes, the children were functionalized to meet their parents' needs. For example: the parents played functional games with their child with the single objective of training the child's capabilities. In these cases, there was no space or awareness for what the child was currently preoccupied with. With the help of the psychotherapist, the parent observed the child and described her or his perception. The psychotherapist asked questions such as, "What can you see?" "What is your intuition say?" "How do you think your child feels?" and "How could you know, how your child feels?"

A very powerful method utilized was 'Watch wait and wonder' (Cohen et al., 1999). This is an attachment-focused activity between parent and child. In playful interactions, the game starts with the initiative of the child and only then are the parents invited to join in. Watching, waiting and wondering, the parent provides space and time for the child to find his self-determined play. In the project, the parents felt encouraged to create more child-led play in the families' daily lives.

The video work introduced by McDonough (1995) was utilized and showed the parents their own best-practice example of interaction with their child. For this purpose, playing scenes of a parent–child interaction and, if possible, of both parents with the child, were recorded and discussed. Using the principles of STEEP™, (short for 'Steps toward effective and enjoyable parenting', Egeland and Erickson, 2004), self-reflection of parents who didn't have adequate access into their own inner world, and to the inner world of their children, was nurtured by visual feedback, in a sense of 'seeing is believing'. Many parents didn't sit opposite their children while playing together. This complicated the child's language acquisition, as the child was unable to see the parent's mouth, which hindered real dialogue, not to mention, that there wasn't any eye contact or affective tuning. To change this, the psychotherapist introduced the dialogue work. Spontaneous and real-life situations were used to practise joint moments of parent and child face to face. The parent was instructed to wait for and watch the child's reaction in his or her eyes and body language and to react accordingly. By using this form of dialogue regularly herself with the parent or the child, the psychotherapist acted as a model for the parent. And sometimes starting with the basics is necessary. Psycho-education concerning parental practice and behaviour enhanced the parents' capacity to think about their parenting style and develop and test alternatives.

While working with the parents, the psychotherapist faced ongoing complexities. To work effectively for the benefit of the child, it was necessary for her to find a joint focus on the development of the child with everyone who participated in the child's development process –especially the parents – as precisely and as early as possible, that is, at the beginning of the relationship. The immediate application of the training to the family's daily life demanded alternatives to current familial situations. Much effort was needed to make the transfer from trainings in the kindergarten to changes in the home.

A unique challenge in the psychotherapist's work was the cooperation with the carers. In the kindergarten, there was a high turnover rate of the carers already, before we started the project. This required the psychotherapist's integrative action to counteract the resulting turbulence and destabilized group settings. By acting in the carers' home turf, the psychotherapist was confronted early on with expressions of mistrust and scepticism as opposed to reflexion and joint responsibility. Showing acknowledgement for their engagement in the multicultural work and the improvisational abilities of the carers, as well as corrective experiences with each other, gradually enhanced the relationship. It became obvious that a well-planned and proper structure of the day was a basic necessity for the work of the project team. It was equally important, and substantially reduced the stress for the parents and children, to benefit from a proper structure.

In summary, the role of the psychotherapist was to understand and give support to all the various groups. Furthermore, she had to be flexible in her work, alternating between counselling, therapy, pedagogy, psycho-educative and social work.

The results of the pilot phase showed that the project was clearly successful. Depending on the amount of parental cooperation, the tests showed visible improvement in the children's development. When starting the project, we quickly realized that we need to reach many more families than we were able to do with our small pilot programme. Thus, we decided to continue by implementing a student mentoring project.

The mentoring project, 'K-IPU', began with 38 students of psychology from the International Psychoanalytic University, who became mentors for 36 children in the project kindergarten for at least one year. They were supported by seven volunteer supervisors (psychoanalysts) who met them in groups every fortnight and helped the mentors to cope with the sometimes very difficult interactions with children and their families. Finally, the effects of mentoring were investigated by a concomitant research project.

The questions posed were related to the development of the children while having a mentor, to the quality of mentoring, and to the development of the mentoring students themselves. ET-6–6 (Petermann et al., 2006) was successfully used to measure the development of the children in their widespread age from 18 months to six years. There was a direct relationship to the quality of the care on the part of each mentor and the development of their respective mentees/children.

In the specific context of the project, the mentors showed a more altruistic and trustful attitude, as well as having a tendency to avoid conflicts. Their positive strategies, particularly in coping with conflicts, such as social exchange, their openness for new experiences and their own positive relationships to their parents and friends seemed to contribute to a good mentoring base. Qualitative analysis showed that their ability to keep the relationship alive was essential for successful mentoring. Their attitude towards the relationship with the child had been challenged by the ongoing necessity to clarify their roles with the parents, the careworkers and other children. This seemed to be most successful when their own attitude was positive and closeness and distance were well regulated.

The students themselves regarded the mentoring as a very valuable part of their education. The mentoring programme provided them with an opportunity to use and put into practice their theoretical knowledge in developmental psychology, diagnostics and clinical psychology. It also opened up the chance for them to reflect on their own attachment styles and their capacities with regard to relationships. One of the conclusions was that reliability and continuity were significant for the development of a relationship with a child and that long breaks and holidays were a hindrance. This innovative project has only been possible with the help of a team that was fully committed to the project and worked together to overcome numerous obstacles. Finally, the project and its implementation could not have been possible without the generous financial support from the Hamburger Foundation for Science and Culture (Stiftung für Wissenschaft und Kultur) and the foundation Bild hilft.

References

Alpert, A. (1941) Education as therapy, *Psychoanalytic Quarterly* 10: 468–474.
Campbell, F. A. & Ramey, C. T. (1994) Effects of early intervention on intellectual and academic achievement: A follow-up study of children from low-income families, *Child Development* 65(2): 684–698.
Cohen, N. J., Muir, E., Lojkasek, M., Muir, R., Parker, C. J., Barwick, M. & Brown, M. (1999) Watch, wait and wonder: Testing the effectiveness of a new approach to mother–infant psychotherapy, *Infant Mental Health Journal* 20(4): 429–451.
Egeland, D. & Erickson, M. F. (2004) Lessons from STEEP™: Linking theory, research and practice for the well-being of infants and parents, in: A. J. Sameroff, S. C. McDonough & K. K. Rosenblum (Eds.), *Treating Parent–infant Relationships Problems* (pp. 213–242). New York: Guilford Press.
Furman, R. A. & Katan, A. (1969) *The Therapeutic Nursery School*. New York: International Universities Press.
Grienenberger, J., Kelly, K. & Slade, A. (2005) Maternal reflecting functioning, mother–infant affective communication and infant attachment: Exploring the link between mental states and observed caregiving behavior in the intergenerational transmission of attachment, *Attachment and Human Development* 7(3): 299–311.
Kluge, S., Liesner, A. & Weiss, E. (Eds.) (2015) *Inklusion als Ideologie. Jahrbuch für Pädagogik*. Frankfurt: Peter Lang.
Ludwig-Körner, C. (2014) *Frühe Hilfen und Frühförderung*. Stuttgart: Kohlhammer.
McDonough, S. C. (1995) Promoting positive early parent–infant relationships through interaction guidance, *Child and Adolescent Psychiatry Clinics of North America* 4(3): 661–672.
Petermann, F. I. A., Stein, I. A. & Macha, T. (2006) *ET 6–6. Entwicklungstest 6 Monate bis 6 Jahre*. Frankfurt: Pearson.
Pretorius, I. & Karni-Sharon, T. (2012) An audit and evaluation of the Hammersmith & Fulham CAMHS Child Psychotherapy Outreach Service at the Randolph Beresford Early Years Centre, *Infant Observation* 15(2): 65–184.
Rosenblitt, D. L. (2005) Translating child analysis from playroom to the classroom: Opportunities and choices, *Journal of the American Psychoanalytic Association* 53(1): 189–211.
Tietze, W., Becker-Stoll, F., Bensel, J., Eckhardt A. G. & Haug-Schnabel, G. (Eds.) (2013) *Nationale Untersuchung zur Bildung, Betreuung und Erziehung in der frühen Kindheit*. Weimar/Berlin: Verlag Das Netz.

PART IV
Cyber
New forms of communication

10

ZOOM, SKYPE, THE UNCANNY THIRD ONES AND PSYCHOTHERAPY

Irmgard Dettbarn

We experience the uncanny "… when the border between fantasy and reality is blurred…", Freud writes (Freud, 1919: 258). It accompanied my thoughts whenever I have dealt with the topic of the internet or video telephony and psychotherapy in recent years, and that was quite common; for example, when I sit in front of my computer and Skype. I have been using internet telephony for therapy hours for eight years, sometimes four days a week. 'Skypen' has become a term for this technique, which makes it possible to call over a computer network on the basis of the internet protocol (Wikipedia, 18.11.18 enforced, VoiP = voice over internet protocol).

Skype was the first software for visual telephony on the internet. The software has been in use since 2008 and, at the end of 2016, it was used by around 25 million people in Germany. In 2017, the estimated number of registered Skype users worldwide was 1.33 billion. For some years now, the data uncertainty of the software has been pointed out, "because its users not only have to agree that Microsoft uses all transferred data at will, but also that this actually happens and that the company does not reveal what exactly it does with this data" (Beer, 2013; Skype, 2018). Zoom, a newer software, is so far considered secure and does not have these requirements for its users, but demands a minimum user fee in contrast to Skype. However, our daily experience of new scandals tells us that all software is hacked in the long run.

In Germany, the legal situation for the use of internet telephony and telephone since November 2018 is regulated as follows

> …. the principle has been maintained that psychotherapy takes place in direct, personal contact between psychotherapist and patient. Remote treatment can, however, be used as a supplementary measure within the framework of psychotherapy. The prerequisite is that indispensable quality

standards of the psychotherapeutic treatment are adhered to. Before starting treatment, each patient is entitled to have his/her psychological complaints clarified. The professional standard continues to be diagnosis and indication in *direct personal contact*.
(Resolution 33, German Psychotherapists' Day, 17 November 2018)

In a study on teletherapy in 2001, Richards and Goldberg reported that 83% of therapists had used telephone therapy in the preceding two years (quoted in Scharff, 2013: 227). The American Psychoanalytic Association reported in 2011 that, of 859 analysts who answered a questionnaire, 28% used the telephone for psychotherapy and 9% used Skype. "Analysts often report their phone or Skype analyses behind closed doors. They are afraid of criticism from their colleagues, e.g. instead of analyzing separation anxiety with the analyst's dependency wishes collusion to enter" (quoted in Scharff, 2013: 232).

In the book *Psychoanalysis Online* (Scharff, 2013), some trained analysts report on their experiences with phone or Skype analyses in their training. They live in areas which are far away from any psychoanalytical training centre, for example, in the US or Panama. The training analysis takes place generally on the telephone or at the computer with internet telephony and is supplemented by personal sessions in the office of the analyst, for example, every four weeks for two hours with an hour break in between (Scharff, 2013: 211). Another analyst writes about her four-hour telephone analysis, which was interrupted by five one-week stays a year for personal analysis sessions (two hours a day) (Scharff, 2013: 198) In general, everyone confirms that they would have preferred a personal analysis to distance therapy if it had been possible.

After I had the opportunity to live in Asia for three years, and being the first training analyst of the IPA to carry out training analyses with nine candidates, the question occurred to me whether the work could be continued by shuttle analysis with a stay of several weeks at the location twice a year and interim bridging with internet telephony.

In the 1990s, the use of the telephone for analyses was already being discussed in detail in the professional journals. In the meantime, there were further publications on the subject of remote therapies, etc. Personal discussions with colleagues on the subject could not be more contradictory. On the one hand, total rejection, for mostly different reasons; on the other hand, references to the fact that anonymised telephone and video telephony session minutes cannot be distinguished from minutes spent face-to-face sessions from some analysts.

A colleague from Kazakhstan compares personal and internet hours with breast or bottle-feeding a baby. Giving the bottle requires greater effort; the mother needs a lot more preparation, as does the analyst for a Skype session, who has to install the technology, etc. But both hold the baby lovingly in their arms, whether they are breastfeeding or giving the bottle (Kudiyarova, cited in, 2013: 187).

I use video telephony of necessity, but I have mixed feelings towards it. Doubt and fascination seem to go hand in hand, which has led me to think further about my experiences with this new tool. My thoughts revolve around what I have noticed and what has occurred to me when I am sitting (and just after I have been sitting) behind my laptop, talking with the analysands who are thousands of miles away in another part of the world. I am very interested in finding out more about the influence of Skype on my analysands, on me, and on the analytic process itself. The two Skype contacts that I had on the day when I first started writing this text could not have been more different. The technical difficulty with Skype in each case was experienced *sometimes* differently, depending on whether the context was a negative or a positive transference.

Today, I am able to log on to Skype straightaway, without encountering any difficulties, but sometimes it's not like that. For me, in Berlin, the first session is at 7 a.m., but for my analysand the local time is 1 p.m. It is a beautiful sunny spring day in Berlin. 8,000 kilometres away, it is lunchtime, and I have no idea if the analysand is looking out the window at smog, sunshine, or rain. Is it important to know this? Neither of us shares the same space nor the same time zone, and yet we are both in our own individual real time. We are both part of the digital revolution. What does this mean for us, our work, psychoanalysis and psychotherapy?

When I 'boot up' the computer, I am greeted from time to time by messages on the screen from the software companies, telling me that there is an update of this or that program, and asking whether I want to load it now or later. I am faced with making decisions, unprepared, but forced to answer the message with 'yes' or 'no' or 'later'. Today I managed without any difficulties to reach the internet domain immediately.

On the screen, I can see all the names and photos or icons of the people whose addresses are stored in my Skype address book. I can also see who is available on Skype right now and who is not. Although I do not know where my Skype contacts actually are, I am still informed as to whether they are currently available, busy or not online. So, every time I click on Skype, I get to know who is online. However, Skype also offers its subscribers the option of showing an 'offline' message, when in fact they are still online, or they can activate a red icon requesting others not to disturb them. So, my experience of Skype has taught me that the information presented by the displayed icons does not always coincide with the facts. For example, the small green 'cloud' beside my Skype address indicates that I am online, but the analysand's display may tell him something else. So neither the analysand in Asia nor the analyst in Berlin can be sure if either of us is online at the time of our appointment. When the analysand clicks on my Skype address on his computer, it should cause my laptop to ring. But here I am, sitting in front of my laptop, and it fails to ring.

How will the new media affect us and our society, and to what extent can they be put to use in psychoanalysis? In the 1950s, the media theorist McLuhan, author of the famous quote "The medium is the message" (McLuhan, quoted in Grampp, 2011: 175–218) noted the close connection man makes to the tools he has made to enhance his capability and make his life easier. As Carr puts it, "We shape our tools and thereafter our tools shape us" (Carr, 2010: 323). As Kramer puts it,

> Whenever we use a tool to gain greater control over the external world, we change our relationship to this world ... The medium is not simply the message but it really perpetuates the message of the mark of the medium ... as the unconscious is in relation to what is accessible to the consciousness.
> *(Krämer, 1998: 81)*

But Carr warns, "If a carpenter takes a hammer in his hand, he can only do with this hand what the hammer allows him to do [with it]. The hand becomes a device to hammer in and pull out nails" (Carr, 2010: 323). So, if, as analysts, we use technology, does this mean that we will find our analytic sensibility constrained by technology or that we will respond to technology with a creative, flexible adaptation of our technique in sync with the changing society in which we live?

As participants in one of the greatest technological changes that humanity has undergone since the invention of the clock that fragmented our time, the printing of books that expanded our memories, industrial production, mass production and wealth, we can observe how the media revolution that has already begun through radio, telephone, film and television continues into the rapid developments of cyberspace and becomes part of our lives, conscious and unconscious.

So, imagine how it feels to read the Cyberspace Independence Declaration at the World Economic Forum in Davos on 8 February 1996 from the internet pioneer, John Perry Barlow:

> Governments of the industrial world, you tired giants of meat and steel, I come from cyberspace, the new home of the spirit... where we gather, you have no more power. Our world is different. Cyberspace consists of relationships, transactions and thinking itself. Ours is a world that is both everywhere and nowhere, but it is not where bodies live. Our identities have no bodies, so ... we cannot obtain order by physical coercion. There is no matter in cyberspace.
> *(Barlow quoted after Rötzer: 35)*

And this was 1996!

When I contemplate a matter-free world of thinking, I recall Freud's description of "magic and sorcery, the omnipotence of thoughts ... all the factors which turn something frightening into something uncanny" (Freud, 1919: 243). Is that what technology is? The writer Arthur C. Clarke thought so: "Any sufficiently advanced technology is indistinguishable from magic" (Herbold, 2012: 25). Before I continue with the uncanny and magical aspects of the new strange world we occupy, I would like to consider the influence Skype has on the setting and the analytic pair in psychoanalytic practice.

Zoom, Skype, the uncanny and psychotherapy

By eliminating the geographical distances created by locations spaced far apart, Skype removes barriers to analysis for analysands who live in remote areas without access to analytic centres. However, Skype, with "its flickering screen" (Carr, 2011: 18) can be problematic and physically strenuous. At the same time, Skype connects the analytic pair by means of a machine. The vertical relationship (in the traditional setting) between analyst and analysand arises from the fact that the analysand actively seeks, and then makes his way to, the analyst. In turn, the analyst awaits the analysand and provides him with a safe room in which the analysand can enter a psychological space for work. With the advent of technology, this has all changed. Instead, a peer-to-peer communication is created. Both sit in front of the computer, both touching the keys. The similarity in the arrangements is that the analysand calls first. Usually, I switch on my video for the greeting at the beginning of the session, then close it until I put it back for the farewell at the end of the session. There is a difference between so-called analytical internet sessions and therapy sessions. In the latter, the video remains on for the whole session.

Returning to my example, I am in my office waiting at the appointed time for my analysand to call. I wonder why my machine does not ring. However, I know that the icons can sometimes be wrong or misleading. So I call him myself. Behold, the analysand had tried several times to reach me, but, according to his computer, I was not connected to Skype. The machine, a third party that suddenly determines the rules, becomes a part of our work. We are both affected by this, both of us are unprotected from the intrusion as we would be if the analysand who meets us in person has a road accident on his way to the analyst or the analyst's next door neighbour begins to play the piano, or a handyman is drilling in the apartment above the practice. However, these disturbances come from a very understandable reality and we know what is to be done, whereas a malfunction in the computer is something that "very few of us would understand, even if the hidden codes were revealed to us" (Carr, 2011: 20). Unexplained computer malfunctions and broadband interferences that may interrupt and terminate the conversation at any given time, combined with the possibility that the person we are talking to may do so by happening to touch a key on the keyboard, leaves us questioning our reality.

Here I would like to insert a small note from an analysand on the subject of therapy rooms. The patient has moved and has a very long journey to the practice, over two hours. In an emergency situation a telephone session was the only possibility left. Afterwards – again in the protected therapy room – the patient reports: "When I am here, I can try to pack all my thoughts at the end of the session, leave them on the couch in your room and turn off the carousel in my head. When I was at home, that was not possible. Then the thoughts cannot be turned off". The artificial third, the computer, restricts the protection of the room or does not allow it, in this patient's experience.

The video telephony, the third party that not only participates in the internet contact but also determines it, to a degree, is an *inanimate object* that is rapidly spreading itself throughout the world, especially among the younger generations and revolutionizing their way of being. It is becoming an *evocative object*.

> My laptop computer is irreplaceable, and not just for all the usual reasons. It's practically a brain prosthesis. Besides, I love it. I would recognize the feel of its keyboard under my fingers in a darkened room. ... I carried it on my back all over England, Cuba, Canada, and the United States. When I use it in bed, I remember to keep the blankets from covering its vents so it doesn't overheat ... It doesn't just belong to me; I also belong to it. ... It just so happened that I had early romantic experiences with machines, and so computers make me think of love.
>
> *(Newitz, 2007: 88)*

When I read this text I am, of course, reminded of Winnicott's (1971) *transitional object*, and of Habermas's (1999) *personal objects* that accompany us in life. Newitz's descriptions of her relationship to her laptop provide an impressive and vivid example of Habermas' definition of personal objects However, her text also reveals just how the object sets its own conditions; for example, when the author describes protecting it from overheating. Writing before Skype was invented, Habermas (1999) defined these personal objects as follows:

> Personal objects mediate not only between man and nature and between man and culture, but also thirdly, between the individual and his fellow man, especially his significant other(s).
>
> A) Personal objects can remind us of a significant other and therefore the relationship with him or they can even represent him. Personal objects help to symbolically maintain the connection to another or others; they make him present, even when he is no longer there following separation or in situations of separation.
>
> B) Personal objects can also serve as a medium to connect with others by acting as a common object, organizing joint activities or by making communication over long distances possible, i.e. technology such as the telephone and car.
>
> *(Habermas, 1999: 500)*

The device that is programmed to use internet telephony fulfils these personal object functions. In its technical existence, it mediates between man and culture, and when used as a means of communication, it not only links the analyst to the analysand during sessions, but it can symbolically make and potentially maintain the connection eternally, as when a Skype participant looks to see if his analyst is online around the clock. The patient no longer has to go for a walk in the residential area of his therapist out of curiosity or for shopping – now he/she can look at his/her smartphone and ask, may be at midnight, who is my analyst talking to?

I can think of a mobile phone in connection with an anxiety patient. It is so important for her that when she realizes in the subway or on the train that there is no internet connection, she has difficulties not to panic. For her, no internet contact means that if she had a panic attack, she could not call anyone close to her. Has the technical device helped her to be less anxious or has a pseudo-dependency developed which would not exist without the technical facility?

The *personal object* has, as it were, become a living object, having settled somewhere between living and dead matter. Once again, I hear the ring of the magical and uncanny. The uncanny is that which exists between life and death and creates the impression of living. Why do we treat or deal with dead matter as if it were 'alive'? In addition to psychological explanations, perhaps the neurosciences can be materialized, too? According to Mitchell (2009),

> Evolution has imbued our brains with a powerful social instinct … a set of processes for inferring what those around us are thinking and feeling … Recent neuroimaging studies indicate that three highly active brain regions … are specifically dedicated to the task of understanding the goings-on of other people's minds.
> As we've entered the computer age, however, our talent for connecting with other minds has led to an unintended consequence!
> *(Mitchell, 2009, quoted in Carr, 2010: 213)*

Mitchell says: "Chronic overactivity of those brain regions implicated in social thought … can lead us to perceive minds where no minds exist, even in inanimate objects" (Mitchell, 2009, quoted in Carr, 2010: 213).

Inanimate objects may be thought to assume the functions of human abilities. The creepier they seem, the more we project vitality into the inanimate object, and the more perturbing it is to us. Just as the child, with the help of the transitional object, in imagination learns how to bear the absence of its mother, the adult tries to bring the mighty inanimate object to life, and, in doing so, hopes to evade the uncanny, the terrifying absence of life, and the imagined encounter with death.

> In addition, there is mounting evidence that our brain naturally imitates the spirit of those with whom we interact, whether real or imaginary. Such 'neural mirroring or reflections' explain why we so quickly ascribe human characteristics to our computers and computer properties to ourselves.
> *(Carr, 2010: 213)*

"Even as the larger system, into which our minds so readily meld, is lending us its powers, it is also imposing its limitations on us" (Carr, 2011: 19).

Let's return to the Skype session: the computer has given us the power to overcome a seemingly insurmountable distance for a short time but its technical possibilities have limitations, such as presenting false information concerning the presence of the internet user. The computer has created a relationship of equality, as previously described. It has also put us into the realm of disembodiment, which John Perry Barlow celebrated in his Manifesto as a basis for greater, freer communication. Do our voices become disembodied on the computer? Are they ghostly voices? But who still believes in ghosts? Surely we have long since left this notion behind us. Or have we? Perhaps technology throws us back into an encounter with the uncanny "when infantile complexes which have been repressed are once more revived by some impression, or when primitive beliefs which have been surmounted seem once more to be confirmed" (Freud, 1919: 249). As the normally vibrant mark of our presence, does the voice lose its vitality in the absence of the body, or does it lead us into an emotional area between the living and the dead? A witness to history in the making impressively describes his feelings about the disembodied voices of the first talking machines:

> You can't believe it dear friend, what a strange sensation and impression it made on us; hearing a human voice and human speech for the first time ever which did not seem to come from a human mouth at all. We looked at each other in stunned silence, and afterwards we openly admitted that during those first few moments a secret little shiver had run down our spine.
> *(Macho, 2006: 136)*

In 1878, Edison enthused about the voice of a dog which he had recorded:

> One day, a dog came passing by and began barking in the hopper, and… this barking was reproduced in such fantastic quality. We have removed the roll well and now we can let him bark at any time. As far as I'm concerned this dog may die and go to dog-heaven… but we have him – everything that has a voice survives … This dead apparatus presented the dead voice as the overcoming of death.
> *(Edison, 1878, quoted in Macho, 2006: 139)*

"Since time immemorial, human beings have tried to use voices to humanize inanimate matter. Animals, plants, objects, dead people or abstract entities were given a voice, so as to provide them with human characteristics" (Macho, 2006: 139). The lifeless should be brought to life and technical inventions are supposed to refute the statement that all of us are mortal. "… but no human being really grasps it, and our unconscious has as little use now as it ever had for the idea of its own mortality" (Freud, 1919: 242). This is the deadly sinister side of technology, laptops, notebooks or smartphones. Didn't computer freaks from Silicon Valley create a new movement to explore the immortality of the human body, the so-called 'transhumanism'?

Computer technology puts us at the mercy of an apparatus that we do not properly understand: it functions according to its own laws and, therefore, it can be controlled only to a limited extent. When the connection fails in a Skype session, this may be a minor obstacle for some people. However, for others it might mean the reactivation of a trauma, or it might even cause a trauma with associated feelings of powerlessness, helplessness and vulnerability. Both analysand and analyst are equally exposed to this: maybe there is even the risk of a seductive symbiotic 'joining of forces' against the uncanny third. In turn, this can prevent the working through of conflicts within the analytical process. The ensuing potential aggression and fear should not be underestimated. It can be a relief not to be left alone at the mercy of unpredictable technology. In terms of the analysand, this can also mean disillusionment, if he has attributed magical powers to the analyst. On the other hand, this traumatic situation can lend support to mutually complicated and negative feelings being experienced in the transference: if the analyst is experienced as a bad object, malfunctions or disruptions in internet telephony are interpreted as confirmation of the analyst's aggression towards the analysand. For example, in an analytical session, in which technical disturbances occurred frequently, the analysand is claiming: "You did that, you turned off the computer". The projection could hardly be edited. Since the technical problems with Skype cannot really be controlled, the field of magic and the uncanny is activated.

Another small detail in internet telephony, so to speak, is that scenic possibilities are offered by the icons, the symbols in the address list of internet users. Sometimes they are suddenly changed by the participants during the course of the therapeutic work; for example, an empty page appears where the favourite flower was visible before. The empty page announced the willingness to change and, at the same time, the uncertainty about in which direction it should go.

In another Skype session, a patient raised a very touching but also troubling issue. My eyes are closed as I listen to him. I often do this during in-person sessions to tune in to my analytic reverie. I realize that I am deeply moved by what he is telling me. When I open my eyes again and look at the Skype images on the screen, I see that the patient is crying. I do not doubt the sincerity of his or my own emotions for one moment; the closeness and proximity between him and me, which, with the help of technology in a virtual world, happened at this very moment, even though we are far apart. I am not only surprised, but positively impressed by the possibility of this experience of emotional presence in a Skype session.

A few hours later, another connection is established without any initial difficulties, until a text bubble from Skype appears on the screen, announcing that it has found a fault and is trying to reconnect. Even so, the conversation continues. I endeavour to understand what the analysand is saying. But despite all my efforts, I often have to ask him to repeat or explain himself again, because our words are being lost somewhere in cyberspace. I can't quite connect to what he is saying. Both of us are really annoyed. Alternately, we try to call each other again and again. The analysand asks me to stop asking him to repeat himself so often. He suggests that we should try to guess what each other has meant. I understood this as an attempt to install an *illusionary symbiotic* form of communication, rather than submit to the dictates of technology. Needless to say, this particular session took place with a *negative transference* in the background. The problems are piling up: the computer forces us to constantly focus on restoring the connection, and we are both upset at the lack of continuity. Should we stop or just switch to the telephone? But, on this occasion, the phone also fails to work properly. The analysand, who already would have preferred to do anything else other than have a session, is now full of anger. It seems to me that the creepy third has allied itself with her. Neither of us can change the situation. We are both angry, the patient in particular, as the hour draws to a close: "That's unfair", she says. I waited during the time when she tried to call me. I also think it's unfair: technology is just unfair. It seems to me like a double negative transference with a real background. As the word 'unfair' proves, I also succumb to the temptation to humanise technology.

When I found the term "machine-loathing" (Ellrich, cited in Ziemann, 2011: 116) in literature, I could only confirm that someone had found the right name for my current feeling.

With regard to the voice, silence is also an aspect of speaking. In the last session described, the troubled or malfunctioning technology made it impossible for any "sense-perceptible silence" to occur (Gehring, 2006: 91). In any case, internet telephony makes it difficult for any 'silent understanding' to take place. If neither the analyst nor the analysand is speaking, we cannot tell whether the silence is due to a technical problem or if it is an active silence on the part of one of us. This can result in an unwanted 'forced-to-speak' situation for both parties. A poor internet connection can create distortions of the voice so that it repeats like an echo. 'Echo', who needs to speak, but can no longer say anything other than repeat the words of others (Gehring, 2006: 106). Her voice cannot communicate any sense. It can neither really 'live' nor 'die'. Internet telephony guides us back into the uncanny space between life and death.

The next day, I have another Skype session, also of poor technical quality. So we change to the phone without difficulty. During this session there is a *positive transference* mood and any technical problems with Skype are irrelevant. Although the patient finds the change of media somewhat distracting, he is so intent on his thoughts and feelings that not even this change seems to cause any kind of disruption.

Geoffrey Anderson reports from his training phone analysis that he had the impression that projections, transmissions, were particularly easy to develop. He describes how the analyst's real image was lost from memory on the phone and how images of his mother, wife and other important carers were pushed into his memory. He saw this experience as a special advantage of remote treatment, as projections were subject to few restrictions by reality (Anderson, in Scharff: 213). This could also be understood to mean the opposite.

What role does the room or space play? Gumbrecht addresses this as follows:

> [This is] the most difficult existential consequence of the electronic age...
> eliminating the spatial dimensions at various levels of our experience, our

behavior ... Thereby, we encounter a fascinating paradox: With the help of electronics, globalization has, on an unimaginable scale, expanded and strengthened our control over the space on earth and at the same time, it has almost completely excluded this space from our existence.

(Gumbrecht, 2010: 42)

With the elimination of space and distance comes dislocation. According to Attali (1992) the highly mobile residents of the global village seem to live like nomads equipped with communication devices that he refers to as *nomadic objects*. Is Internet telephony a nomadic object? Are analysis and analysts also nomadic objects? On the one hand, anonymity on a large scale, on the other hand 'eternal life', because an internet address could not be deleted at first. The EU's basic data protection regulation has been in force since 2018. Article 17 gives data subjects the 'right to be forgotten', the right to delete their own data. Attali again:

> "To use these devices, they only need to be connected to global electronic information and trading networks, the oases of the new nomads... It does not matter where you come from; a number or name is enough to identify the nomads of the Millennium". ... Like the objects of pagan antiquity, the nomadic object of the future will be an *inanimate object*, however, they will embody the life, spirit and values of those who develop and use them. Basically, they are branches of our senses and our bodily functions. For example, computers supplement the human brain.
>
> (Attali, 1992: 26, 107)

Now I would like to go back to the beginning of this text: the first internet telephony software. It was supposed to be called Skyper, but had to drop its 'r', so that it could enter the stage of the World Wide Web. We can use Skype to overcome distances and hold real-time conversations with the intense quality of analytical sessions. Then again, a disrupted internet connection can remind us of Echo's punishment: that she is forced to speak the words of others again and again, however senseless this may be, her never-ending repeating voice preventing her from taking or giving any comfort or relief from silence.

Just as an echo must repeat itself and cannot be silent, the punishment's distinguishing feature is its immortality: it never ends. Using this metaphor, it seems internet telephony is becoming a punishing superego. In any case, a man-made machine superego cannot be merciful to the human ego. Do we submit because "the digital revolution is irreversible and because we can no more hold back the impact of technology than we can dismiss the sun or the sky?" (Schirrmacher, quoted in Carr, 2010: 1, translated for this edition). Talking metaphorically of sky reminds me of another metaphor – the cloud, a name for repositories of data that are stored in geographically remote data centres that can be accessed via the internet. Again, to the technology neophyte, it sounds uncanny.

Before communication satellites appeared on the scene, stars, angels, spirits and the gods were to be found in the clouds. In *Clouds*, a comedy by Aristophanes (423 BC), a middle-aged Athenian tells Socrates that he wants to know the truth of the divine and communicate with the deities in the clouds. In the post-modern Western world, we are caught between the clouds of Aristophanes and the clouds of the computer world. Although they are separated by more than 2,000 years, they still have one thing in common. They are there where "it often seems to be uncanny, when the line between fantasy and reality is blurred, when something real steps out in front of us, which we hitherto had considered fantastic" (Freud, 1919: 244).

Internet telefony takes us into the man-made digital world that is based on the number line between 0 and 1, is programmed to decide automatically between right and wrong. In contrast, psychoanalysis addresses ambivalence and the constant inner conflict between right and wrong. The computer can only function when the user makes a clear decision: Yes or No. This is in complete contrast to the unconscious, which does not differentiate between contradictions. Yet, a function as binary as internet telephony is asked to support the complexity of psychoanalytic process.

Unlike analysis, Skype guarantees a special identity for eternity. A Skype address is unique and never deleted. Even though there can be anonymity on a large scale, there is also eternal life. Does this give us some narcissistic gratification? Or does its virtual reality abandon us to a new kind of solitude? We can be reached at all times and everywhere, but we are not actually together, physically present in the same room.

We have lost not only the 'r' in Skyper but also the bodily presence of analyst and analysand. This negative can also be a positive in some cases in that it can eliminate the threat of physical aggression or potential sexual attacks. "When two bodies come close to each other geographically, this reinforces the sexual (or aggressive) attraction, and simultaneously the visual perception of the overall shape of the other person begins to blur.... Close spatial proximity implies emotional closeness" (Habermas, 1999: 64, translated for this edition). The gain of reduced threat is countered by the loss of closeness. In analysis by internet telephony, is it "a dangerous illusion, if in a 'broad present' (now), we are robbed of our physical presence?" (Gumbrecht, 2010: 130, translated for this edition). The emotional closeness that promotes the analytical process remains limited to the closeness that the therapist's hearing and verbally expressed understanding can develop. The voice becomes an analytical space, a container in the analytical process, guaranteeing the liveliness of the therapeutic dialogue. A colleague wonders whether not every therapeutic space, be it the therapist's treatment room, the computer screen or the telephone receiver, is an *artificial space*, detached from everyday life (Scharff, 2013: 12). It seems that there is danger and opportunity whether the body is present or not. Extreme acts of physical violence, including sexual abuse and murder, are not a literal possibility as they are in traditional in-person analysis. Internet telephony provides a particularly safe setting that may eliminate the stimulus for passionate declaration, or it may facilitate its expression because there is no possibility of actual violence.

Although we do not share a common physical space, now we can always be reached. Does this spare us the *pain of separation*? Gumbrecht suggests that "we have replaced the pain of loneliness caused by physical absence with the *permanent semi-loneliness* of unlimited availability" (2010: 130, translated for this edition, my italics). Does this affect the *process of mourning*?

Technology, as a tool, reduces the workload and increases possibilities: it leads to experiences and facilitates processes that, without devices, would be not simply weakened but would not exist at all. On the downside, the goal of media technology seems to be global reach rather than improved performance (Krämer, 1998). So much interaction across distance in real time is now possible, but what if, sitting at our computers and speaking to each other on Skype, "everything merges into one another, *everything is fusion*" (Gumbrecht, 2010: 130, translated for this edition, my italics)? How do we differentiate and adapt the technology to our use without fooling ourselves?

Is that enough for good *containment*? Can the real absence in crises lead to dangerous states of despair of the patients? Does this limit the possibility of necessary regression? We are in a new world: "World production is the productive sense of media technology" (Krämer, 1998: 85, translated for this edition). Can and do we want to use this newly created world for psychotherapy, or do we want to use it as an uncanny third, threatening and at the same time dangerously illusory, when we are deprived of our physical presence, in a "broad present" in which much is possible at the same time, but "everything merges into one another, everything is fusion" (Gumbrecht, 2010) sitting at the computer and talking to each other via video telephony?

"When we begin to live with objects that question the boundaries between the naturally and artificially created, between the human and all others, we have to tell ourselves new stories", Turkle suggests (2007, p. 326). Will we invent new stories and will they be useful for our therapeutic work on the "border between fantasy and reality" (Freud, 1919)?

References

Aristophanes (423 BC) *Clouds*. http://records.viu.ca/~johnstoi/aristophanes/clouds.htm 250

Attali, J. (1992) *Millenium*. Düsseldorf: Econ.

Barlow, J. P. (1996) Cyperspace Independence Declaration. http://www.eff.org/~barlow

Beer, K. (2013) Vorsicht beim Skypen – Microsoft liest mit, in: *Heise online*. Verlag Heinz Heise.

Carr, N. (2010) *The Shallows – What the Internet Is Doing to Our Brains*. New York: W. W. Norton.

Carr, N. (2011) Wie das Internet unser denken verändert, *Du* – April:14–21.

Freud, S. (1919) The 'uncanny', *Standard Edition*, 17 pp. 217–256. London: Hogarth.

Gehring, P. (2006) Die Wiederholungs-Stimme. Über die Strafe der Echo [The repeating voice. On the punishment of Echo], in: D. Kolesch, & S. Krämer (Eds.), *Stimme*. Frankfurt: Suhrkamp.

Grampp, S. (2011) *Marshall McLuhan*. Konstanz: UVK Verlagsgesellschaft.

Gumbrecht, H. (2010) *Unsere breite Gegenwart* [Our broad presence]. Berlin: Suhrkamp.

Habermas, T. (1999) *Geliebte Objekte* [Loved objects]. Frankfurt: Suhrkamp.

Herbold, A. (2012) Bezaubernde Siri (Enchanting Siri), in: *Der Tagesspiegel* 18.1.2012. Berlin.

Krämer, S. (1998) Das Medium als Spur und als Apparat [The media as trace and apparatus], in: *Medien Computer Realität* [Media, computer, reality]. Frankfurt: Suhrkamp.

Macho, T. (2006) Stimmen ohne Körper. Anmerkungen zur Technikgeschichte der Stimme [Voices without body. Comments to the technical history of voice], in: D. Kolesch, & S. Krämer (Eds.), *Stimme*. Frankfurt: Suhrkamp.

Newitz, A. (2007) My laptop, in: S. Turkle (Ed.), *Evocative Objects*. Cambridge, MA: MIT Press, pp. 88–91.

Scharff, J. S. (2013) *Psychoanalysis Online*. London: Karnac.

Schirrmacher, F. (2010) Preface, in: Carr, N. *Wer bin ich, wenn ich online bin ... und was macht mein Gehirn solange? Wie das Internet unser Denken verändert* [German edition of *The Shallows*]. Munich: Blessing.

Skype – https://de.wikipedia.org/w/index.php?title=Skype&oldid=97893968. Accessed on 18 November 2018.

Turkle, S. (2007) *Evocative Objects*. Cambridge, MA: MIT Press.

Winnicott, D. W. (1971) *Playing and Reality*. London: Tavistock.

Ziemann, A. (2011) *Medienkultur und Gesellschaftsstruktur* [Media culture and the structure of society]. Wiesbaden: Springer.

11
LIKE OR DISLIKE

Questions and challenges in the consulting room of a 'society 2.0'[1]

Angelo Bonaminio, Domenico Scaringi, and Giusy Daniela Spagna

Introduction

The digital era has brought about many changes in the way we live, some of which have probably not been completely understood yet. It may be that, for the first time, the younger generations are more expert than those that have preceded them. The metaphor of digital natives consigns adults to the position of 'immigrants' in a foreign land (the digital world), and produces a real confusion of tongues. This rift between the generations may result in different outcomes: on the one hand, it may generate a fearful reaction which stigmatises certain increasingly pervasive phenomena, on the other, one may observe a complete denial of this generational gap, tending to support the illusion of being able to nullify any differences.

According to communications scholar Marshall McLuhan (1964), the medium is the message, in the sense that the medium transforms the message and is able to produce psychological changes in the individual using it. However, the exact social and psychological ramifications of the digital era, to the extent that we are now talking about Society 2.0, is still an open question. One thing is certain: we are at a point of no return. Reflection on these themes is a highly complex matter and the arguments put forward in the debate usually take the form of value judgements, which are fundamentally dichotomous. What is certain is that cyberspace plunges the user into a paradoxical experience of connection and disconnection in relation to the self and the other, leading to either creative or defensive outcomes, according to the way it is used (Kieffer, 2011).

This matter is still an open question in the psychoanalytic field, even if, generally, the prevailing tendency seems to be to mainly consider the defensive and potentially psychopathological dimension of the new technologies (Griffiths, 2012). Nevertheless, many recent authors have been opposing this tendency, highlighting a transitional aspect of these devices and clearly proposing optimism (Tisseron, 2004, 2012; Tisseron et al., 2006; Virole, 2012). However, in general, attitudes fluctuate widely between curiosity and suspicion.

Changes in society, changes in the psyche

At the moment, psychoanalysts are thinking about how certain changes in society can lead to more profound changes in the individual's intrapsychic and relational organisation. On the basis of Touraine's considerations (1997), Kaës (2005, 2009) highlights the deep crisis in traditional social aspects such as roles, hierarchy and the institution of the family, which are seen as the effective guarantors of the functioning of society; any fracturing or restructuring of these aspects would significantly alter the 'guarantors' of psychic functioning (the so-called meta-psychic guarantors); that is to say, they would modify the formation of the fundamental interdictions and intersubjective contracts upon which a subject's psyche is based and structured.

Moreover, our present-day culture seems to be bringing to light new forms of psychopathology which can be understood if we allow for models of psychic functioning which see the mind as exposed to further types of conflict beyond the intrapsychic one (Kaës, 2005, 2009). Furthermore, changes in society in the direction of enhancing individualistic and hedonistic aspects, place human beings in the contradictory position of needing to re-establish a dimension of broader social relations; cyberspace and virtual reality may represent a surrogate solution to this quest, especially in younger age groups (Akhtar, 2011).

Virtual communities, however, radically differ from traditional communities in the patriarchal mould; instead, they display the functioning typical of brotherhoods (Forest, 2009), in which anti-authoritarianism is one of the predominant features: these communities branch out horizontally and consist of individuals who are all on an equal footing. Identity is amorphous and reaching out to an external third party is considered problematic, if not superfluous. Such communities base themselves on controlling the relationship rather than on moral imperatives (Forest, 2009). This form of regulation works by blocking or allowing communication, as in the case of 'banning', which is the only type of sanction or normative feature used by these communities.

The unrestricted circulation of messages seems to offer an antidote to the anxiety of solitude and being disconnected: something similar to the reassuring word pronounced to a child in the dark, enabling a sense of contact through proof of the existence of the other, regardless of the content of the message. It would, however, be ingenuous to neglect the other side of the coin: besides the potential risks inherent in the use of the new technologies, these also offer new kinds of opportunity to young people (Tisseron, 2004), facilitating subjectification.

Some considerations on cyberspace in adolescence

One of the salient aspects of this phenomenon, among the many characterising the use of cyberspace in adolescence, is the question of identity formation. Trying out different identities and seeing how other people relate to them in the virtual world allows young people to become more aware of certain less explored aspects of self. Nevertheless, in the digital world, identity is more subject to being influenced by the actions and reactions of others, with the paradoxical consequence of a diminished capacity to define one's own social identity.

Another issue raised by the relationship between cyberspace and adolescents is that of drives. In puberty, the sensorial and perceptive dimensions are brought to centre stage once more through specific, new inputs defined by Gutton and Bouchet (2004b) as the archaic genital. Thus, the adolescent might be trying to control and articulate the increased sensitivity to sensory perceptions through the use of technological means (Bonaminio, 2014). In effect, the adolescent is attempting, through mastery of the various perceptive and sensorial stimuli associated with new technology, to dominate the excitement originating in his or her own body. The adolescent who immerses his/her self in cyberspace is not seeking to be absorbed by a plethora of stimuli, but is, rather, seeking proof of being able to remain firmly in control of them at all times.

Third, the early adolescent, lacking the processes of symbolisation, representation and sublimation, can see the use of cyberspace as the first opportunity for psychic representation (Botella & Botella, 2001) of those aspects of the adolescent's psychic and corporeal functioning which he/she experiences with amazement and surprise, or anxiety and preoccupation (Bonaminio, 2014). These non-represented elements are not only linked to a body overwhelmed by sensations, emotions and drives, but also to the void associated to the absence of the object, resulting from the process of separation–individuation at this stage (Blos, 1962), which is potentially traumatic because of the impulses of disinvestment and detachment. None the less, as Monniello (2014) effectively points out, the protraction of excessive reliance on both the sensorial and the perceptual processes may delay and even paralyse the psychic processes of representation of genitality. However, the close support of a psychoanalyst, providing the adolescent with an intersubjective dimension based on a commonly held sensoriality, may gradually stimulate the activity of personal fantasising, initially perceived in the other and later internalised.

Cyberspace in the adolescent patient setting

Based on the above, it can be postulated that it is precisely through immersion in the visual and sound effects of digital devices that the early adolescent, within a therapeutic setting, may be able to discover both sensorial traces belonging to the experience with the primary objects and indications of new objects which are beginning to emerge, as well as the various aspects and states of the self in flux.

In particular, the visual images appearing on the screen with which the adolescent can interact, and which, for this reason, can become found–created images, enable representation and, therefore, a kind of containment which can be shared with the therapist and which can stimulate the psychic work of symbolisation.

The use of digital devices in the analytic setting, can, therefore, acquire meaning, and promote insight and elaboration by fostering the processes of subjectification (Cahn, 1998, 2009), through listening, sharing and the interpretative function of the therapist. However, the therapist will have to face "working in situations of limited differentiation from the primary object, and of psychic functioning dominated by the sensorial and the perceptive in which conflict is, however, barely tolerable by reason of a lack of stable investment in self" (Monniello, 2014, translated for this edition).

Of course, an analytic encounter is therapeutic when it allows for an exchange between the therapist and the patient resulting in dialogue, and in the patient's finding room for reflection on self. However, in those cases where there is evident difficulty in using verbal language as the means of narrating oneself, then it is possible to use, during the session, a technological medium in which the patient is emotionally invested and which may, therefore, represent parts of the patient's self.

In fact, adolescence in itself implies dynamics of peripheralisation and externalisation of the psychic life, which, through the use of the external reality of cyberspace in the session, contribute to the creation of an extended psychic space (Jeammet, 1992). It is precisely through sharing the experience of new technologies with the therapist in the therapeutic space that transitions come about between internal and external, between body and mind, between past, present and future, and that processes of integration and subjectification can be activated.

Clinical vignettes

For the purpose of aiding reflection on what has been said so far, there will now follow some extracts from clinical material in which the patient brought a technological device to the session. The diverse situations will be commented on in order to illustrate different ways of conceiving this material in therapy.

> ### Marco
>
> Twelve-year-old Marco was referred for therapy because of learning difficulties and a tendency to isolate himself. He moves slowly around the room during the consultation, looking all around; he briefly stops at the toy box and lightly fingers some of the ones on top. He then directs his attention to the white sheets of paper lying on the desk and, with a pencil, begins to sketch a figure that never takes shape. He drops into the armchair, almost collapsing, and whispers, "Everything seems empty".

Like or dislike: questions and challenges 131

The therapist comments that he is trying to find his own way to express himself, but perhaps he is no longer used to playing with toys, or drawing and talking is difficult.

For a moment his expression comes to life and he comments, "That's exactly it… I'm bored", For a while he remains in a state of hesitation, of expectation. Then he takes his Nintendo DS out of his pocket and begins to play a Pokemon video game commenting that he no longer collects the cards although his mother continues to buy them for him, as though he were still a little boy. However, he still likes to play the Pokemon video games.

Marco describes to the therapist what he's doing and the characters that appear on the screen; then he becomes progressively absorbed in this activity, becoming silent and concentrated, while the therapist stays next to him in a discreet and attentive way.

The therapist formulates the hypothesis that, by using the video game during the session, Marco is adopting a defensive mechanism, not only because he has difficulty in regulating the proximity–distance in the relationship, but also, because of a tendency to fill up the emptiness he feels with familiar and habitual sensations, movements and images. The lack of meaning and representation that the boy perceives, together with his disorientation in the here and now, are characteristic of the developmental passage of puberty, when physical and psychic alterations begin to be vaguely and disturbingly experienced. Reference is being made to the unsettling dynamic state of the pre-pubertal boy effectively described by Sapio (2008) as the no longer and not yet: no longer totally dependent on the primary objects and not yet sufficiently autonomous, no longer completely identified with them and not yet separated, no longer a child and not yet an adolescent. In a defensive mode of functioning, the tendency is to avoid the pain of separation and the absence of the object, which compromises the adolescent's ability to symbolise and introject.

It is interesting to consider that, during the session, Marco re-emerges from his state of total absorption and tells the therapist, unexpectedly and spontaneously, that some of the Pokemon evolve, growing in size and strength, while others remain the same and show no sign of change.

Tuning into the theme of the evolution–non-evolution of the Pokemon, the therapist attempts to enlarge on Marco's comment by hinting at the desire for, and fear of, growing up, and the urge for change and the security of staying the same.

Marco, getting excited, asks, "Do you like video games? Do you have any? Do you play with them? Well, not now because you're grown up but at my age? I think you did, maybe you played with Games Cube or the first DS".

In this way Marco is prompting the therapist to re-encounter his own puberty, his own adolescence, in order to find genuine acceptance and reflection in him. In this way they begin to discuss the evolution over time of video games and the successive modifications in the Nintendo console. In their shared experience they begin to explore the themes of sameness and otherness, union and separation, identity and change. These themes will, in the course of the therapy, enable the creation of further narratives of experience capable of promoting the articulation of self and of the relationship; this will allow Marco to realise the absence of the object, open up to the experience of mourning and, as a result, to the possibility of symbolising.

Franco

Franco is 17 and was referred to the therapist because of attention deficit and difficulties in relating to his peers; most of the time when he is studying, whether at school or at home, Franco is totally absorbed in his daydreams to such an extent that he has been named 'the dreaming poet'. Endowed with a special talent for music, he can play a number of instruments proficiently and gives live performances with his band as well as performing on social networks. He maintains several active profiles (Facebook, Instagram) and a channel on YouTube where he publishes his videos, but he seems obsessed by the number of views, likes, dislikes and comments he gets from his followers. The therapist reflects on how what may seem to Franco to be a need in fact comes at a high price, as it involves a disquieting kind of reciprocity: being in control at the cost of being controlled.

During the first session, the young man identifies the start of his difficulties with the onset of puberty at age 13, when he changed schools from one based on few rules and creativity to another characterised by a more 'classical' approach to education: Franco feels inadequately prepared to respond to the demands made on him in the new environment, which he perceives as urgent and pressing. Alongside this, he begins to manifest excessive anxiety about his physical appearance, accompanied by persecutory experiences: he is afraid of being photographed and filmed by his companions in embarrassing situations and also that his physical defects are being 'fixed' on video and in photos which are then posted on Facebook or YouTube. Franco's anxieties seem to be preventing him from establishing meaningful relationships with his peers in which he can feel welcomed and accepted. Franco also spends many hours checking out the Facebook pages and YouTube channels of his friends in order to reassure himself that they do not contain any images of him. The therapist thinks that Franco's use of social networks implies a narcissistic fragility, which puts him at risk of distancing reality. Continuity and omnipresence are characteristics of cyberspace which can contribute to the fetishist use of social media, feeding into fantasies of the continuity of the object and omnipotent control of it; it is important to note that, in the most extreme cases, this determines a lack of engagement with external reality and hyper-investment in the fetish that substitutes for it.

Despite the feelings of disquiet that Franco's remarks produce in the therapist, it appears that the young man is immediately posing a forceful question: will the therapeutic space be able to accommodate the more embarrassing aspects linked to the sexual body he experiences as monstrous, as well as the more infantile, grandiose or idealised aspects? The therapist, at this early stage of the treatment, by means of a mirroring functioning, aims to promote investment in, and recognition of, the self, even as a body.

Daniele

Daniele is a 16-year-old with serious difficulties in socialisation and performance related anxiety. The boy immerses himself in daydreams to an extent which risks distracting him from the present moment and from reality. He is obsessed by the idea of wanting to remain connected to infancy and tends to discredit those in his age group, cynically describing any really adolescent aspect and using such contemptuous terms as "corruption" and "depravity" to refer to the experiences of other boys he knows. He often indulges in grandiose fantasies about himself and his future. In the course of the therapeutic process, during a session in his second year of therapy (three sessions a week), Daniele gets out his smartphone and surfs the internet for an app which will allow him to simulate the working of an old video game device that he used to use as a child. He then tries to install one of his favourite video games from that time, in which it was possible to make fantastic creatures fight, controlling their every move at will. As Tisseron (2004) points out, the use of social networks and video games enables someone to escape temporarily from an unbearable situation. Daniele's fantasies seem to be an attempt to evade an anxiety, which he is, at the time, unable to symbolise. Out of the blue, Daniele affirms that certain childhood experiences are extremely important and can impress themselves on a child's mind, for instance, promoting creativity. Immediately afterwards, he goes on to describe a version of the game slightly different to the one he is looking for, which, in Japan, supposedly caused serious harm since the background music was capable of making children psychically unstable to such a point that they committed suicide. Having found the video game he was looking for, Daniele begins playing without involving the therapist and progressively isolating himself. The therapist is, at that point, in contact with feelings of solitude, anger and impotence. Once he finishes the game, Daniele again starts to talk to the therapist as though nothing had happened. A short time later he has an outburst of rage when he realises that he has failed to save the game. After this, and still during the session, he begins to use an app on his smartphone which enables him to transform everything the camera focuses on into a drawing. This time, however, he does involve the therapist in his activity by asking him if there is a problem with remaining attached to his childish self. At that point, the therapist, who, up until then, had allowed Daniele to play by remaining in silent expectation, can reconstruct for the boy the mental functioning that was at play in the session: his withdrawing from the relationship, regressing to an infantile functioning full of omnipotent fantasies (manipulating the characters whose destiny he controls), to then revert to feelings of impotence and extreme frustration when his state of withdrawal makes him unable to manage reality (forgetting to save the game). This profound frustration induces him to re-immerse himself in fantasies of omnipotent control by his action of digitalising reality through the app on his smartphone. Daniele's acting-in will enable him, through the therapist's verbalisation, to render thinkable modes of primitive functioning that would otherwise not be easily accessible to the boy.

Marina

A 14-year-old girl, Marina presents clear signs of social inhibition underpinned by a deep core of depression. Marina's 'entrance' into adolescence proves to be particularly arduous: her unelaborated mourning for the death of her father, when she was five, and her identification with her depressed mother, are hindering the investment and integration of her sexual body, recognition of her own desire and that of the other, as well as the processes of subjectification. Marina appears to be stuck on the 'edge' of adolescence.

The progressive 'silent' investment that is created in the relationship over the course of the first year of twice weekly therapeutic sessions provokes the first movements inside a psychic dynamic which is 'frozen'.

In an extended transfer, Marina begins to show interest in Paolo, a classmate, who, however, treats her as an inferior, with indifference and disdain.

At this stage, a number of questions confront the therapist: does Marina find in Paolo a specular attitude to her own attitude with regard to the opposite sex? Has she 'chosen' a boy who corresponds to her strong unconscious feelings of guilt at detaching her psychic investment from her 'dead father' and her 'depressed mother'? Does the reintroduction and re-creation of feelings of depression in the context of the therapeutic setting serve defensively to 'cool down' the climate of lively emotion which is beginning to be felt in the consulting room?

A significant turning point along the therapeutic route is reached when the internet makes its appearance in Marina's life and is introduced into the analytic setting, a kind of found–created space, a medium which helps to create a transitional area (between the inner and outer worlds and also between self and the therapist). The girl begins to log on to and use a social network called 'Ask.fm', one of whose functions allows you to contact other users anonymously or not. In fact, its forum and chat rooms allow you to interact differently from in reality by admitting anonymity and allowing you the possibility of withdrawing at any time you please. This need not be read simply and solely as an inability to form a relationship in a normal way, but also as an attempt to establish contact with the Other at one's own pace.

The internet, and social networks in particular, may not only provide a way of distancing oneself from certain affects, fantasies and preoccupations, but also a means of gradually confronting these in a reassuring way by apparently allowing a greater possibility of controlling them. In certain cases, for example, encounters on the internet constitute a kind of complex learning process which allows the adolescent to gain progressive familiarity with the stages of the most feared and desired encounter, the romantic one.

To return to Marina, her use of 'Ask.fm' seems to provide her with a 'malleable medium', both concrete and virtual at the same time, as it allows her to contact Paolo maintaining her anonymity and temporarily removing the presence of a body which is experienced as inadequate and sometimes repugnant, and to control the motions of closeness and detachment and, thus, permit the emergence of feelings, emotions and thoughts from behind the excitement of a protective screen.

In this new and special place, it is possible to carry out research, discovery and exploration of the self and the other, and also of the relationship between self and the other. On and through the internet, the relationship between Marina and Paolo begins to acquire interest, pleasure and intimacy. This is the stage at which the interpretative activity of the therapist intervenes respectfully 'within the transference' and not by means of 'transference interpretation'. A second decisive moment is reached when Marina spontaneously decided to reveal her identity to Paolo, an identity which has come to life and assumed shape precisely through this specific experience, and which has been felt, reflected on and integrated within the therapeutic space. This revelation also assumes the form of 'self-revelation'. Marina's initial feeling of incredulity at Paolo's positive reaction seems to be a manifestation of the discovery of being a source and object of desire for the other, and also the discovery of an incipient integration of the psyche and the body, a body 'taking shape'.

In the consulting room, as in Marina's inner world, a new stage has been reached, in which the Oedipal dynamic and all its associated emotions can be played out.

Conclusions

To summarise, among those working with adolescents, it is a common experience that looking at photos or videos together does not, in itself, bring about therapeutic change. The therapist has to try to show interest and curiosity, but also gradually to bring what happens in session to the level of narrative and meaning. Nevertheless, in certain circumstances, he/she should not avoid getting involved in the use of technological devices, given that the adolescent might not be able to reveal parts of self in any other way. On the other hand, it is important, as therapists, to pay attention to the various aspects that such use implies in order to promote development and not collude with defensive or pathogenic actions.

It is particularly important, for the evolution of the therapeutic experience, that the therapist treating adolescents should assume the emotional and mental disposition highlighted by Novelletto (2009) – which allows him/her to detect, accept and interpret primitive functioning as an internal process, without focusing on the infantile dimension, but, rather, following the thread of the adolescent's present development, that is to say, pubertal transformation and sustaining him/her in carrying it through.

What is required is to recognise a positive and creative use of new technologies while, at the same time, acknowledging their potentially psychopathological aspects. In order to achieve this, the therapist must succeed in constantly maintaining that 'sufficiently good' distance which enables him/her, on the one hand, to avoid excessive identification with the adolescent, and, on the other, not to fall into the trap of the "professional hypocrisy" Ferenczi (1932) talks about, which, in this precise case, could be a false interest in video games or social networks and which the adolescent would detect immediately.

The difficulty in approaching the issue regarding new technologies and their potential repercussions in the clinical and therapeutic field is attributable to two interwoven factors. The first of these can be traced to an epistemological attitude that tends to relegate to the background, if not altogether repudiate, external reality and its objects. To paraphrase Tisseron (1998), most clinicians manifest a striking resistance to pursue Freud's interest in everyday objects, and so, with the sole exception of those artistic works that are commonly considered 'noble', 'plebeian' objects are snubbed.

The second factor, which concerns more generally the attitude of society and the adult world, is on a far deeper, unconscious level. Despite their widespread use, in reality, the new technologies remain outside of, and unknown by, the adult world except with regard to their most superficial aspects and functions. On the contrary, they typify the adolescent's world, reflecting, in many respects, its functioning. The adult's ambivalence in the face of these devices reflects fear of novelty, and of the unknown, which adolescence inevitably brings with it.

Given these premises, it is up to the psychoanalysis of adolescence to provide the most significant contribution in this matter, to provide, that is to say, the new maps required by psychoanalysis in order to be able to find its course in these psychic and social territories that are still unexplored and in continuous transformation.

Note

1 This paper received the award Best Paper Presented by a Trainee at the conference Beyond Babel? On Sameness and Otherness, 26–28 June 2015, Berlin, Germany. The conference was organised by the EFPP in cooperation with DGPT, DPG, DPV, DGAP, DGIP, VAKJP, D3G, BvPPF.

References

Akhtar, M. C. (2011) Cyberplay: The pros and cons of a "macrosphere", in: S. Akhtar (Ed.), *The Electrified Mind* (pp. 63–72). Plymouth, UK: Jason Aronson.
Blos, P. (1962) *On Adolescence: A Psychoanalytic Interpretation*. London: Free Press.
Bonaminio, A. (2014) Attraverso lo schermo e quel che l'adolescente vi trovò, *AeP Adolescenza e Psicoanalisi*, IX(1): 101–122.
Botella, C. & Botella, S. (2001) *La figurabilité psychique*. Paris: Delachaux et Niestlé.
Cahn, R. (1998) *L'adolescent dans la psychanalyse. L'aventure de la subjectivation*. Paris: Presses Universitaires de France.
Cahn, R. (2009) Una vita di lavoro con gli adolescenti, *Quaderni del Centro Milanese di Psicoanalisi Cesare Musatti*, N 12.
Ferenczi, S. (1932) La confusione delle lingue tra adulti e bambini, in: *Fondamenti di psicoanalisi, vol. III, Ulteriori contributi*. Rimini: Guaraldi Editore 1974.
Forest, F. (2009) La communauté des frères branches, *Adolescence* 27: 667–677.
Griffiths, M. D. (2012) La dépendance aux jeux vidéo sur internet: une revue systématique des recherches empiriques disponibles dans la literature, *Adolescence*, 1–79.
Gutton, P. & Bouchet, S. (2004b) L'archaïque genital, in: *La naissance pubertaire* (1–10). Paris: Dunod.
Jeammet, P. (1992) *Psicopatologia dell'adolescenza*. Rome: Borla.
Kaës, R. (2005) Il disagio del mondo moderno e la sofferenza del nostro tempo, *Psiche* 2: 57–65.
Kaës, R. (2009) *Les alliances inconscientes*. Paris: Dunod.
Kieffer, C. C. (2011) Cyberspace, transitional space, and adolescent development, in: S. Akhtar (Ed.), *The Electrified Mind* (pp. 43–62). Plymouth, UK: Jason Aronson.
McLuhan, M. (1964) *Understanding Media: The Extensions of Man*. New York: McGraw-Hill.
Monniello, G. (2014) Un giorno questa adolescenza ti sarà utile, in: G. Montinari (Ed.), *Adolescenza e psicanalisi oggi nel pensiero italiano* (pp. 47–59). Milan: Franco Angeli.
Novelletto, A. (2009) *L'adolescente: Una prospettiva psicoanalitica*. Rome: Astrolabio.
Sapio, M. (2008) Tra il non più e il non ancora: l'enigmatica articolazione tra latenza e adolescenza, *Richard e Piggle* 16: 5–21.
Tisseron, S. (1998) De l'inconscient aux objets, *Les Cahiers de médiologie* 6: 231–243.
Tisseron, S. (2004) Le virtuel à l'adolescence, ses mythologies, ses fantasmes et ses usages, *Adolescence* 47: 9–32.
Tisseron, S. (2012) Clinique du virtuel: rêvasser, rêver ou imaginer, *Adolescence* 79: 145–157.
Tisseron, S., Missonnier, S. & Stora, M. (2006) *L'enfant au risque du virtuel*. Paris: Dunod.
Touraine, A. (1997) *Critica della modernità*. Milan: Il Saggiatore EST.
Virole, B. (2012) Exil, combat et mascarade, *Adolescence* 79: 101–106.

PART V
Babel in psychotherapy

12

IS THERE SUCH A THING AS 'PSYCHOANALYTIC IDENTITY'?

Towards a theory of indivualised interaction in our sessions

Michael B. Buchholz

Introduction

What I would like to say here is structured into two sections. In the first section I flash back to some historical moments during which the concept of identity appears. In this context, I support the thesis that this concept is burdened with attempts at coping with historical traumata; however, in a way which cannot be deciphered by the concept itself. Rather, the concept of identity is a symptomatic consequence of grave historical crises of violence. The concept hides the possibilities of historical remembrance.

In a second section, I transfer these considerations to psychoanalytical practice. The thesis of this second section is that good psychoanalytical practice means being capable of handling fundamental human paradoxes unfolding through the transference. For this, we do not need the concept of identity. Furthermore, our profession has the task not only of 'maintaining' but of contributing to the further development of our discipline; for this, the concept of identity is rather an obstacle because it aims at maintaining always the same.

Section I: The historical burden of the concept of identity

Let me start with a nice little story.[1] At the beginning of the 19th century, in 1807, Jean Paul wrote a novel with the bold title *Flegeljahre* (The Awkward Age). It tells about two authors working on a novel of exactly that title. The author watches his invented characters while writing his novel. It is full of flirtation and bright humour. And to this there fits a funny story from real life.

Two university students from Halle wanted to steal the idea of the 'double novel'. They were Karl August Varnhagen and Wilhelm Neumann. Both roam through the salons, chatting and charming, and one year after the battle of Jena and Auerstädt, that is in 1807, in Berlin they have made quite some progress with their project of a double novel, one of them writing a chapter which the other one has to continue, and then it is the first one's turn again. They have finished ten short chapters when they start a walk to see Friedrich de la Motte-Fouqué in his Nennhausen Castle in the Havel country (about this Nennhausen Castle, by the way, a poem will be written at a later time, about a certain Mr Ribbeck and his pears). Fouqué was an author who loved romanticising soldierly life; Arno Schmidt dedicated a biography to him.

Fouqué now becomes interesting for Varnhagen and Neumann because he has a salon hosted by his wife, who is not really happy with her marriage. Anyway, the two wanderers are welcomed quite heartily. They read from their book project and Fouqué is enthusiastic; also, the headmaster of the local grammar school, Bernardi, is present, and, thus, the two visitors agree to extend the project to four authors. A first part is actually published in 1808. Of course, there are many allusions, among others to Goethe's *Wilhelm Meister*, with a personal appearance of Wilhelm Meister in the four authors' novel, as if this literary character was able to move from one book to the other. Literature becomes real life, real life is literature. Goethe appears, although code-named. Jean Paul, the inventor of self-writing, several authors' novels, is mentioned by his full name, and now in this novel it happens that he no longer understands all the confusing events and strange connections between the various levels of reality, and, overwhelmed by heaps of piled metaphors and other excursions, he completely loses himself. A complete loss of identity!

Thus, this is a case of psycho-pathological emergency. A serious identity crisis. Desperately somebody is trying to find himself, but how and where? In the novel, the ambiguous question is: Where, after all, could he have *misplaced* himself? At which place, in which publishing house? This is the playful way in which these authors formulate their story. Jean Paul makes clear that our expression 'looking for identity' – taken so much more seriously – is just a metaphor. Only – a metaphor for what? In any case, this holds: if one has lost something, one must look for it.

Here the search for identity which plagues us every day is taken *literally* and is dealt with literarily, not therapeutically: he writes an arrest warrant; as a detective he is in pursuit of himself. Being a detective, he must arrest himself if he finds out his own whereabouts. Now, one does not only get an idea that there might be a connection to the detective stories on television, but one also knows what is meant by a paranoid–schizoid position. If one senses being followed, there must be someone following, and even this is oneself.

Some analysts (Carveth, 1984; Spence, 1993), as well as one literary scholar (Thomé, 1998), will show us later that Sherlock Holmes is a literary guiding character, representing Freud, who observes the way in which Dora handles her handbag as precisely as Dr Watson tells us what his friend does. Both Freud and Holmes, as Spence believes, have a very similar way of observing in common. However, there are also differences. Freud, the detective, in *The Interpretation of Dreams* (Freud, 1900) does not only communicate the insight of the symbolism, shift and mechanism of dreamwork but he *investigates himself*. The initial dream of the psychoanalytical interpretation of dreams, the dream about Irma's injection, is, as we know (Bonomi, 2013), an act of self-justification not only because he was involved in an amateurish surgical mistake made by his friend, Wilhelm Fliess, but also because of Freud's knowledge of female genital mutilation as a widely discussed and applied therapeutic treatment in Vienna. Freud analyses this dream not only through the double epistemological function of subject and object, but also by the double juridical function of prosecutor and defendant. This results in strange loops and paradoxes. In the first one of his *Lectures* (1916/17) he tells his audience to give up on their previous academic preparations; in *The Interpretation of Dreams*, he asks the reader to make his, Freud's, interests his own, and one asks oneself (Buchholz, 2006) how, after all, any reader could be made interpret his *own* dreams? Who, as in Zweig's *Chess Story*, plays chess against himself must get lost among the paradoxes of self-reference.

Owing to the insolubility of such involvements and the strange loops, Ernst Cassirer (1927) made the statement that the Western religions were only about the redemption *of* the I, whereas the Eastern religions are about being redeemed *from* the I. As we now see, there are also other ways out of such involvements: a literary–humorous one, as in Jean Paul, and a theoretically demanding one, as in Freud. In Freud, the solution is the observation and working out of suppression – this is the conceptual sword that makes the Gorgon of self-reference weak. Freud is not awestruck by Medusa, but makes use of the reflection in the mirror. Through the concept of suppression, the epistemic order of one thing recognising and one thing being recognised is re-established.

I insert this remark on paradoxes here because, in the second section, I would like to come back to it in more detail. For now, I shall briefly give some more historical, astonishing parallels between Jean Paul's time and the founding history of psychoanalysis. We can say even more about this time of doubled and lost fictitious identities. There already existed a Wednesday Society, with E. T. A Hoffmann and his brothers from the literary group known as Serapion participating. The discussions there, and also the consumption of tobacco, are said to have been as extensive as later in the Viennese Wednesday Society founded by Sigmund Freud in 1902. And also, taking us right to the heart of our topic, the concept of the *original self* was invented by a man we can hardly imagine as being connected to it: Turnvater Jahn wanted to find German equivalents for "un-German" terms, such as replacing the word 'original' (Germ.) by the German term 'Ur-Selbst' (original self). The term 'Selbst' (self) did not refer to anything psychological but served to distinguish from an enemy.

Applied to German-ness, now the process was psychologised and existentialised. German-ness was imagined as an inner and, at the same time, collective essence, found only in the Germans and connecting them across the borders of the various small German states. In 1916, in the midst of the First World War, Floerke published a book on this, *Deutsches Wesen* [German Essence], in praise of this feature (Floerke, 1916). In 1937, a certain Detlef Holz published a book *Deutsche Menschen* [German Humans], an epistolary novel whose motto is shown on its cover: 'On Honour without Glory, on Greatness without Splendour, on

Dignity without Payment'. Such sentences form a contradiction to the praise of everything German; Detlef Holz was the alias of Walter Benjamin, who this way hoped to smuggle the book from Switzerland to Germany, avoiding censorship, because it presented a panorama of the bourgeois world and civil virtues between 1783 and 1883 which radically contradicted the Nationalsozialismus [National Socialism] (NS) terror. The identity formula of 'German humans' already served as a camouflage for Benjamin (Klapdor, 2007).

When returning to the pathos of essence, we note: if it was the inner essence, why then was educational work necessary? Why these efforts to make reference to it? Why was it possible to tell people that they should say 'Ur-Selbst' instead of using the term 'original'? After all, their essence would have been sufficient to make them use the correct German word. Of course, soon one took notice of this contradiction. It is an experience from the period after the wars of liberation against Napoleon's foreign rule.

Still Freud (1919), at the Budapest Congress of 1918, formulated the object of the cure by saying "the patient is supposed to be educated not towards becoming similar to us but towards liberating and completing his own self" (GW XII, p. 190, translated for this edition). The word 'educate', however, does not really fit with 'liberating' and also not with one's 'own self'. This paradox has not yet been resolved.

Well, it does not really come as a surprise when William James (p. 330) formulated in 1890 that this was, as he put it, 'the most puzzling puzzle with which psychology has to deal'. How right he was becomes obvious if one looks at the list of publications on the self and on identity. In the almost 30 years between 1950 and 1979, only 7,759 dissertation theses were written on this topic; between 1990 and 2006 it was already 20,190. On the topic of identity, the figures are: 571 works between 1950 and 1979, 3,802 works between 1990 and 2006. During half of the respective span of time, the number of works tripled (Owens, 2006). And we may refer to yet another study, by Moser, presenting biographical interviews (Moser, 2000), who was able to investigate 3,899 metaphorical ways of speaking about the self among university students. Are there any reasons for this boom in studying the concept?

On the history of the concept of identity

The philosopher Hans Blumenberg, in his book *Life-Time and World-Time* (Blumenberg, 1986), observes how somebody remembering the First World War states that one had to live as if "nothing could be taken for granted anymore, and that who has lost that what has been taken for granted is condemned to improvising his life". This experience can easily be generalised; the loss of what has been taken for granted is our experience of modernisation in essence. Blumenberg formulates: "Only the surprise given the fact that things have changed indicates what it used to be like, without the latter having been 'stated'" (1986, p. 23). As long as we are living in a world we take for granted, we do not 'state' it, but it is our 'lifeworld'; only if we are thrown out of it do we look back and 'state' what this world used to be like. Man before the catastrophe of the second Thirty Years War on German soil was different from man after that. At the end of his heart-rending interview, a survivor of Auschwitz has a message for the interviewer:

> At Auschwitz, as well as at other extermination camps, the illusions of the Western civilisation were shattered. Everything which up to then had looked human, noble and just disappeared into an abyss of nothingness. Auschwitz represents the breakthrough of that which must not be. It was the place where mankind did not make sense any longer.
> (Quoted in Poppe, 2014, p. 32)[2]

Some date the beginning of this catastrophic loss of humanity to an earlier date. In his novel *Middlesex* (Eugenides, 2003), which deals with the human body being influenced and shaped by medicine, among other factors, Eugenides formulates, in an almost melancholic manner:

> Historical fact: in 1913 humans stop being humans. That was the year when Henry Ford had his cars being made on rollers and the workers had to adjust to the speed of the conveyor belt … But in 1922 it was still something new to be a machine.
> (Eugenides, 2003, p. 139)

This way, the chronological limits of the space of experience can be marked, when the concept of identity as a "collective identity" experiences a "haunting boom", as historian Lutz Niethammer (2000) has it. Identity is a subtle synonym for 'affiliation'. At that time one starts identifying oneself as belonging to nations, races or religions, while, at the same time, identifying outward affiliation as the realisation of some inner core. In the already mentioned book *Deutsches Wesen* (Floerke, 1916) the concept of collective identity appears as a concept of delimitation. Still on the pre-war markets in Galicia, from the Russian villages as far as to Pomerania or the regions around Berlin, Prague or Brünn, the cattle traders had spoken at least five languages, if only imperfectly, to be able to do their business. One knew where one belonged, but one did not need any 'identity' to define one's 'social place' (Bernfeld, 1929).

It was a colourful jumble of social categories of affiliation, as it is once again the case in the present time, and from Wolfgang Herrndorf's novel, *Tschick* (p. 98), I quote a passage which shows how two bright 14-year-olds playfully handle social categories, not identities (Herrndorf, 2012).

Two boys at the age of 14, one of them the Russian who is new in the class, discuss Tschick's identity:

> "Now, what are you then, after all? A Russian? Or a Walachian or what?"
> "A German. I've got a passport".

"But it's where you're coming from".

"From Rostov. That is Russia. But the family is from everywhere. Volga-Germans. Ethnic Germans. And Banate Swabians, Walachians, Jewish Gypsies –"

"What?"

"What what?"

"Jewish Gypsies?"

"Yeah, man. And Swabians and Walachians –"

"No way".

"What do you mean, no way?"

"*Jewish Gypsies*. You're talking shit. You're talking shit all the time".

"Not at all".

"Jewish Gypsies, that's like English Frenchmen! They don't exist".

"Of course there are no English Frenchmen", Tschick said. "But there are Jewish Frenchmen. And there are also Jewish Gypsies".

"Gypsy Jews".

"Exactly. And they're wearing these things on their heads and travel around Russia and sell carpets. You know them, with these things on their heads. Kippe. Kippe on their heads".

"Kippe your arse. I don't believe a word".

"Don't you know that film with George Aznavour??"

Now Tschick wanted to really give me proof.

"A film is a film", I brushed him off. "In real life you can only be either Jewish or Gypsy".

"But Gypsy is not religion, man. Jewish is religion. Gypsy is somebody who has no place to live".

"As a matter of fact, those having no place to live are toe-rags".

"A rag is a carpet", Tschick said.

As we see, here social categories are intelligently ironised and, at the same time, the processes of the description of affiliation are made transparent. This had a very serious historical background. The historian Leonhart (2014) writes:

> On Crete and in Macedonia there were Muslims speaking only Greek. On the other hand, many Anatolian Christians spoke only Turkish. In some Northern Greek regions, farmers had been forced to convert to Islam, but still they celebrated Christian holidays, and in Thessaloniki there were the Dönme, a sect of Islamic converts practicing Jewish rites.
>
> (Leonhart, 2014: 18186ff.)

When, in the years preceding the First World War, such a jumble was called "chaos" and nationally minded circles, by inventing collective identities which almost always were connected to languages, started to establish orders which previously had not existed, a powerful potential for violence was unleashed.

The idea of making such orders *reality* cost the lives of many humans. There is no need to describe the earlier situation as an idyll, and one should not forget about the Tsarist pogroms. Of course, it had been unwise for Jews to appear in the street at Easter or on Christmas Day. But, on the whole, one had somehow found ways to get along with each other. But then suddenly it counted if one was Jewish or German, a Christian or a Muslim, a Ukrainian, German, Galician or wherever else one had come from. A tool for establishing such orders, 'ethnic engineering', had become a means of resettlement recognised by international law through the Treaty of Lausanne, and, by referring to it, there started the murderous actions between Greece and Turkey, linguistically belittled as an 'exchange of populations' with the goal of creating 'ethnically homogeneous' states. Two and a half million Greeks were expatriated from Turkey, 400,000 Turks from Northern Greece, which was practically depopulated. In the name of 'identity' multi-ethnic regions were homogenised. Still, today, the dead have no names, no memorial. In 1950, as another historian (Ferguson, 2006) summarised it, nothing was left of an originally multi-ethnic East Europe except a disturbed nostalgia (Schwartz, 2013).

My thesis drawn from the historical experiences is that the concept of identity is burdened with historical traumata of violence. Still, Jean Paul wanted to play with it literarily; he loses himself, literally loses his identity in 1807, that is, one year after the battle of Jena and Auerstädt in 1806, just at the time of the Napoleonic conquests from which the contemporary population suffered so much. Turnvater Jahn reacts to the victorious expulsion of Napoleon from the German lands in 1812–1813 and, by way of identity concepts, establishes national German gymnastics. William James reacts to the extreme experience of violence during the American Civil War, in the course of which his brother Henry was seriously injured. There were purges carried out according to identity, meaning that the First World War went on until 1925, rather than ending in 1918, which is a Western–European perspective that ignores what happened in the East. The boom in publications after the Second World War demonstrates the same connection. Identity becomes a topic if it experiences a crisis, such as after historical violence and defeat. But the concept as such does not open up this connection but hides it. It feigns an order that never was. And its restoration has then the potential to unleash new violence.

Following Niethammer (2000), we may distinguish at least three ways of applying the concept of identity:

(a) In the *political* context as an argument for social homogenisation – then some speak of religious, racial or national identity, thus trying to naturalise affiliation. This makes people easily move towards right-wing populist discourses.
(b) Identity serves for the construction of *cultural* difference – then collective identity, such as in Maurice Halbwachs, refers to a feeling coming from the encounter with other ethnic groups, thus emphasising the continuity of one's own group. Today, we would speak of the experience of being alien.

(c) A third way of applying the concept of identity uses it as a tool for the criticism of mass civilisation, thus making the fear of the dissolution of one's own civilisation a topic of discussion, by at least maintaining one's own identity as a *cosmic* universality. This latter way of applying the concept does still today easily connect to some esoteric meanings.

Thus, we understand why Freud avoided the concept of identity ever more carefully.

Psychological transfer

The origin of the concept of identity from the policy of the collective, from violently organising homogenisation, from the defence of cultural difference and the criticism of civilisation, has become obvious by its transfer to *psychological* applications. It is certainly no coincidence that Erikson's book *Childhood and Society* was published in 1950, marking the beginning of the new, now *psychological*, boom of the concept of identity. This is the time when emigré social scientists, such as Solomon Ash or Kurt Lewin in social psychology, start their studies on the way in which social influences may distort correct individual perceptions and attitudes in a group-conforming way – all were driven by the question of how the catastrophe had become possible. From this, there developed films such as *Let's Spoil the Party*, by Roman Polanski. In 1957, this director hired hooligans to storm a party, and he filmed what happened, the event taking such a violent direction that the authorities of the film academy where he was studying at that time gave him a warning. We know how much he was traumatised by experiences he had, as a child and young man whose mother was murdered at Auschwitz (Mahler-Bungers, 2010; Stroczan & Bayer, 2004). The same topic is dealt with not only by the film but also scientifically: for example, the famous Milgram Experiment or the Stanford prison study by Philipp Zimbardo, whose results haunt the researcher still today, because, in retrospect, he must consider himself a 'mad scientist' (Zimbardo, 2007). It was Zimbardo's then girlfriend who informed him that something was going terribly wrong between those persons in the study who were acting the prison guards and those acting the prisoners – in recent times we saw the images from Abu Ghraib or Guantanamo in our daily newspapers.[3] The experiences of the Zimbardo experiment have also been made into a film, titled *Das Experiment* [The Experiment] with Moritz Bleibtreu.

Identity in psychoanalysis?

Thus, are we supposed, above all, to use such a concept as a description of what makes the psychoanalytical practice? Do we not run the risk of just closing off from the outside without defining our practice in detail on the inside? I would like to pursue these questions and to make some appropriate suggestions.

The psychoanalytical use of the concept of identity is first of all based on logic which stubbornly, but boringly, states that A=A. This is the premise of identity, which we will not deal with here. We will not make much progress by referring to the premise that A=A.

However, above all, one must ask why a concept aiming at continuity and equality at all times is claimed to be coping with gigantic transformation crises of both the social and the individual kind? The question alone makes us assume that the concept of identity is burdened with something that cannot really be understood this way. Thus, for his description of his theory of seven stages, from basic trust to generativity, Erikson had to introduce a number of additional terms, such as 'I-identity', and must again delimit them from psychosocial identity, whereas at the same time he is trying to grasp the transformations of the individual's life.

Seiffge-Krenke (2014) starts her essay 'Identität im Wandel' [Changing identity] by quoting a definition which Erikson used for identity: "Identity, that is the interface of that which an individual wants to be and what the environment allows him/her to be" (Erikson, 1970, quoted in Seiffge-Kenke, 2014, translated for this edition). Now, I wonder, would the message of the sentence change if identity was replaced by 'compromise', for that is exactly what is described: a compromise between that which an individual wants to be and that which he/she is allowed to be. To describe such a psychologically important circumstance, the concept of compromise would be sufficient. Here, identity rather obscures it. This is of significance for psychoanalysis because Freud did not understand 'compromise' at all in the sense of rational negotiating. Neurotic symptoms, as his first formula on their development states, are, like mistakes, 'compromises' between struggling psychological forces – could it thus be that the concept of 'identity' is actually a neurotic symptom? To make myself quite clear: nobody is supposed to be deprived of his/her identity; it is not about those conceptual tools provided or, indeed, taken away by such a term. The term 'identity' is not more enlightening than the term 'compromise', but instead is more opaque.

One remark may be added here. When psychoanalysts try to define their profession with the help of the concept of identity, at once the violent potential of such a concept becomes obvious, as those whose behaviour can be rejected or even defamed as being 'non-psychoanalytical' may be excluded (see Blass 2010). A topical definition of this behaviour, however, is hardly possible. Let me consider two examples:

a) Is it really a fact that the representatives of depth-psychological schools work more, or more clearly, 'anti-regressively' on the 'current conflict'? Can "psychodynamic" therapy be excluded because they do not work psychoanalytically? Who can define with worldwide acceptance what "psychoanalytic" is?
b) There are not only voices expressing doubt that regression can be controlled to such a degree, there is also empirical research making clear that these differences, which are believed to be 'true', are not at all succinct. At least the study featured in *Forty-two Lives in Treatment* (Wallerstein, 1986) has shown

that with both methods, depth psychology and psychoanalysis, supportive measures or change through realisation exist to the same degree. This was a serious blow to the international psychoanalytical community, and later research has changed only little. One must conclude: Identity definitions are not suitable for defining differences, but they have the violent potential to undermine group affiliations.

It is remarkable that, in a new essay by Andreas Herrmann (2014), we read that Freud had connected psychoanalytical identity to a 'group identity', that is, a kind of affiliation that we would describe as loyalty pressure. Then, non-conformity can always be understood as dilution, or it may even be defamed as being 'wrong', that is 'non-psychoanalytical', but not as a source of inspiration and innovation. Thinking in terms of loyalty results in preserving–narrowing ties to tradition and origin (on whose couch one has been lying). Then it is less competence or skill what defines psychoanalysis, but a kind of "belonging" that can be taken away any time. This threat inhibits every new thought. New thought can be defamed as "non-Freudian" from what follows that theoretical or practical innovation always runs the risk of being excluded as non-conformity, as long as we think in terms of loyalty. Herrmann writes that this narrow understanding of psychoanalytical identity is somewhat paradoxical; I add, psychoanalysis lacks rules for the changing of rules, concepts for the changing of once defined conceptual dispositions. From such calamities there result paradoxes, logical levels are confused, which, as is my thesis, even affects psychoanalytical practice. The concept of one identity hides these paradoxes far too much. What a computer scientist who deals prudently with our questions (Hendriks-Jansen, 1996) has expressed with the formula 'Catching ourselves in the act' seems apposite. This means that for our situational activity, as well as for interactive emergence, we may create sense, producing better understanding of the small and fabulous solutions for paradoxes, achieved because, so to speak, the situation itself offers them. We would lose them, had we an omniscient theory. That is why Merton Gills once said that who wants to *apply* a theory, must have his/her Third Ear blocked by earwax.

As far as we describe our situational activity, as well as the interactive emergence of good solutions, the process evolves, and human thought is provided with new thinking. A patient, however, does not *experience* identity, but the creative development of new, helpful aspects of self-perception. Then he/she will not be 'educated' towards his/her own self, but experience and recognise him/herself through that which has previously been alien. If this process of recognising the other and alien is able to continue, at its end there will be the insight that self-preservation and preservation of the world do not contradict each other, that the other is not object but subject: self-preservation and preservation of the world require the same effort. Here, I will not further discuss Erikson or other topics explored under the keyword of 'identity', but, rather, I shall turn to the question of which experiences of the psychoanalytical practice could be usefully described while giving up on the concept of identity. It is about unsolved paradoxes.

Interestingly, when it comes to coping with paradoxes, there is never only one solution but many. This might make why we have a pluralism of therapeutic offers plausible. However, to which problems are these theories meant to provide solutions? Which are the paradoxes that seem to be solvable in so many ways? These are the questions that allow us to trace the paradoxes with which we are confronted every day.

I summarise this section by saying that, by and large, equating identity and affiliation indicates that this concept is a contingency formula for the purpose of increasing the cohesive power of the members of the group of psychoanalysts. But identity formulas have no operative value. Speaking of identity serves the purpose of maintaining an association, as David Tuckett wrote years ago (Tuckett, 1993). We may gain operative power, however, only if we turn towards the paradoxes of psychoanalytical practice and towards the questions of how they could be coped with.

Second part: paradoxes of psychoanalytical practice

Now I shall proceed by picking out some of these paradoxes which I believe to be significant here – without any claim to completeness.

First paradox – sovereignty as recognition of dependence

The first paradox is that of the *expert's sovereignty*. Therapists are experts as a result of a long period of training; however, at the same time they must also have had the important experience of being badly clueless, of having to give up illusions after their training. Each new case ensures that we have this experience. In the context of his famous package deal formulation, Freud (1927) writes not only about "healing and researching" but about that no treatment is possible "without learning something new" (p. 294). Thus – no earwax in our Third Ear! The new is due to the individual's uniqueness, which we may not consider a 'case of …' because that means the uniqueness is missed. The individual patient needs to be provided with a chance *against* common theory, because otherwise we would never learn anything new. At the same time, however, we are seen as experts on such 'cases', addressed not about the individual but the typical. Those vocational–political seductions trying to tell us that we have to conceptualise 'interventions' into 'disorders' ignore the other, the individualising side, without which professional practice would not be capable of doing what it does. Here, the paradox results from the fact that therapists must cope with a double dependence. How? By way of conversation. By not suffering from such dependence but by *recognising* it we will gain sovereignty. Here, there are some remarks on the concept of sovereignty.

We are psychoanalysts, not because we own a certificate, but through our attitude towards our patients, and only if they make it possible and allow us to be psychoanalysts; only if they allow us to analyse them can we be analysts.

Sovereignty, which I explicitly differentiate from autonomy, develops from *recognising* this dependence. Sovereignty is an emotional *position*, knowing that it must constantly put itself up for negotiation if it wants to survive. It defines self-preservation not as *cogito*, but as maintaining insecurity (Brothers, 2008). Thus, it cannot do without communication, while knowing at the same time that it is incommunicado (Winnicott, 1974). It is *alone* in the presence of the other and only in this way capable of stimulating the therapeutic conversation. At the same time, it is deeply connected (to the other), and only if this is so will it find the right words. Whereas an analyst looks at himself to find answers to the unspoken questions of his/her patient, inevitably what he/she does is introspection, and, as far as he/she does so, he/she leaves the field of interaction – while still exploiting it as a hidden asset. Connectedness reaches as far as psychic dimensions, which are difficult to introduce into language and speaking. It is, so to speak, a self going far beyond individual limitedness, it is a "dyadic state of consciousness" (Tronick, 2007), while being on its own at the same time. Even through analytical conversation the human basic paradox, as Camus had it, if "solitaire" or "solidaire" is to gain the upper hand, is decided. Sovereignty must be *communicated* as the recognition of dependence – an identity concept would interfere precisely with this essential demand. We are a different person with and for each individual patient. For me, it has become deeply satisfying to speak in a different rhythm, with different resonances, in a different tone to each individual patient, different from hour to hour.

Second paradox – coenaesthesia

Here, is the second paradox: that of *communication which cannot really start* because any pre-understanding is lacking. We know that everything a patient tells us has a highly unique meaning about which we would have to reach an understanding beforehand, but this could only happen by way of communication which will never catch up with itself. Some (Ferro, 2004) give an elegant description of psychotherapy, using melancholic metaphors, saying that therapists prepare highly individual dishes for their clients – there, individualisation is clearly recognised as a necessity. But how, after all, is a chef to know what a guest likes? How could we know something about the other that could safely be distinguished from our own projections? Daniel Stern (2004) explains this as follows: let us imagine (p. 174) that two young people who hard know each other are having their first date, going out for dinner. It is winter, and on their way to the restaurant they pass a skating rink. They decide to get skates and have a try on the ice. Unsteadily they are standing on the ice and moving cautiously; she almost falls to the ground, he reaches her in time and supports her in a helpful way. When he raises his arms because he is almost falling to the ground, she reaches out her hand at the correct height, so that he can grasp it and avoid falling. They laugh, they have fun – and they get to know a lot about each other without speaking about it. The crucial thing is that intuitively they know what the other needs just at that 'present moment', and this becomes an extremely important, enriching experience: "They have vicariously been inside the other's body and mind, through a series of shared feeling voyages" (Stern, 2004, p. 174).

Being vicariously 'inside the other' – is that observation? Is it reality or a metaphor? The fact that this question cannot be answered in the context of our discursive thinking creates the paradox. The other need not 'express what he/she means', he/she need not 'symbolise', need not discursively 'represent' his/her experience – no, it is about shared knowledge coming from the "shared feeling voyage". The paradox creates dyadic, not identitary, but *participatory* knowledge.

When now the young couple arrives at the restaurant, they are already looking back at such a "shared feeling voyage", and what they say then will be spoken against this background, will be evaluated by the question of whether it moves this experience forward or if it blocks it. Speaking becomes a continuation of physically 'moving along'. Their bodily choreography is, so to speak, transferred into language choreography; linguistic kinetics – Sebastian Leikert (2011) spoke of coenaesthetic semantics – saying that they are based on physical kinetics. The body, as Christian Morgenstern said as early as 1927, translates the soul into the visible.

Such picturesque experiences address something. One can imagine it. One is sitting in a railway compartment and knows; intuitively; that the person just entering is 'excited' or even 'dangerous'. One is sitting in a still empty lecture hall. By and by the people are arriving. Even without turning around one has a comparatively good idea of how they are distributed among the room – and one can even check this out. Somebody is standing in the queue behind oneself, and one knows that he/she would need more distance, which one then tries to provide. Lovers are lying in bed, they twist their limbs, and even if one of them feels comfortable, nevertheless he/she 'knows' that the way in which their knees bump into each other or their arms intertwine may be inconvenient or even painful for the other. There is, to use an older expression, a *coenaesthetic shared feeling*. One knows something about the other, even if it has never been said.

What I try to say is that the paradox of a communication which will never catch up with its own beginnings or, at best, for a 'present moment', is constitutive for therapeutic practice. This paradox cannot be taught, it can only be discovered. The difference between knowledge that can be taught and the fact that experience cannot be taught has effect here as something unidentical. That is why all of us *perform* our practice in quite different ways, even if we use the same expression and *call* it 'psychoanalytical'.

Third paradox – the name of the transference: used relationship

The third paradox, *that of information and performance*, follows easily. In the course of therapeutic communication our clients provide us with a lot of information, and in the course of training we are told to act as collectors of information. For some, the medical file is what the botanizing drum is for the biologist. However, what a client *makes* of his/her therapist is often more important than the problem of presentation. What counts is not only information, but performance; our sensibility to the fact that, during conversation, there is some kind of performance (Buchholz, 2002; Danckwardt, 2013), some kind of stage presentation of hardly remembered dramas which, in the form of staging or re-enactment, has been much developed in recent years. It is painful, but we had to learn that our *throwing light on the situation* is not really helpful. If – to give a simple example – a young man relives an authoritarian father–son conflict with his therapist, should the latter simply tell him that he is mistaken? Rightly so, the young man would answer that he knows himself that the therapist is not his father and that he doesn't like being taught lessons of this kind – and this father–son conflict would be continued throughout its discursive clarification. No, it indeed distinguishes psychoanalytical therapists that, in such a situation, they learn how to handle the paradox in a different way: that they are father and *not* father at the same time. Basically, it is this that therapists are constantly communicating: "No, you can't do that with me"; "Yes, you may make that out of me". There are many nice little examples of the skilfull analytical handling of this paradox. If, in the course of our training, we are told to accept the transference, at the same time we must learn how *not* to accept it. Transference is our name for a complex paradox of intimised, individualised interaction. Our debates on the concepts of transference provide us with a variety of solutions. But solutions for what? For the transference being a '*used* relationship' in the double sense: it is second hand *and* it is urgently needed.

Fourth paradox – individualised, intimised interaction

Inevitably, there occurs another paradox, that of *personal encounter within an impersonal, formal space*. Right from the beginning, the whole treatment is permeated by this; every client wants to know what kind of person his/her therapist is, beyond the limits of the professional – but beware if the therapist gives in to such curiosity! Clients want to be treated professionally, they want to learn about method and technique, in order to take them with them. If everything were just method and technique, the extra something would be lacking. According to my experience, younger therapists have too much of a tendency to overemphasise either the personal *or* the technical aspect; more experienced therapists know that moments of personal encounter should, rather, be embedded in periods of productive work. Over the years, psychoanalysts have emphasised neutrality, rather existentially orientated schools have emphasised personal encounter, others have emphasised 'technique'. Today, we see the dilemma of how to formulate the unity of these differences, and we are not always successful, but we know how to better handle the paradox. Usually, we find a solution for the paradox when discovering the playful dimension of therapeutic communication.

Too much personal contact at the beginning of a therapeutic encounter might mobilise too much shame, too little prevents the therapy from really starting. We see that it is not about identity but about the *individuality* of the therapeutic dyad, with a high degree of *intimacy* and the skilful *handling of interactive density* (Buchholz, 1999).

Fifth paradox – the therapist is still a patient

Here now, the next paradox comes into force. It is about *the therapist always being a patient to a certain degree*: the therapist will only survive if, at the same time, he/she is always also a patient, if he/she finds something about him/herself which is close to what the patient is speaking about, something he/she understands and knows, yet whose different nature he/she can nevertheless accept. Only by 'loving' the other will he/she become neutral. In my opinion, this is due to the fact that a mother already knows what it was like to be a baby; but the baby does not know what it is like being a mother. This asymmetry creates many dangers, for, of course, it provides the therapist with the grandiose opportunity to project whatever he/she likes on to the patient, in the belief that he/she must have experienced all this. But, like mother–baby interaction, this will do no harm if the resulting wrong perceptions can be promptly and sensitively 'fixed'. At least, the micro-analytical studies of therapeutic processes show us clearly how things are mended while basically the perception missing in the other looks inevitable. Why is that so? Because the perception of the other always includes an attribution of meaning. Only if the actions of children and patients are attributed intentionality and meaning is the expectation confirmed that what others do is intentional. Expecting purpose and meaning as essential regulations constitutes the humane, as such (Levinson, 2006), but always it may go off the tracks.

Sixth paradox – the reality of illusion and the illusion of reality

Meaning and the attribution of meaning indicate a specific dimension of therapeutic communication: it happens within a space of the creation of illusion, which, at the same time, is experienced as being very much real. This *paradox of the reality of illusion* is indispensable. A patient who could not believe that the therapist addresses him (or her) personally would never benefit from the therapy. Emotions of affection and dislike of the therapist are experienced as being very much real. In this context, neutrality (Pizer, 1998) might be defined as the therapist's communicative responsibility for maintaining the illusion in the sense of a potential space (Odgen, 2004) – for the purpose of further negotiations. Always, everything must be *possible* without ever being realised. Analysts support that this was what Robert Musil had in mind when connecting the "sense of possibility" to the "sense of reality". Only the illusion of constantly having somebody else by their side helps some heavily disturbed people with becoming real. Spatial metaphors of an 'inner world' confronting an 'outer world' are our standard solutions for this paradox, and we should consider whether we should go on thinking in such metaphors or if we should get completely rid of them – one may indeed 'have' thoughts, but in which sense are they supposed to be 'inside'? Speaking of one's own thoughts and emotions in contrast to those one has taken up or which have been forced upon oneself provides a helpful difference; it reveals power relations which remain invisible by means of spatial metaphors.

However, it is only the safety of the therapeutic relationship which keeps everything *possible* without the need of being realised which enables patients to break out and start towards that degree of freedom that can be achieved by therapy; only under such conditions may patients protest against mistakes by their therapists and increasingly dare to criticise him/her. If finally they have achieved this, they will notice that they do not need him/her any longer – and (under otherwise happy circumstances) they may be deeply thankful to him/her.

Other paradoxes

I have sketched some paradoxes which we know how to handle more or less skilfully during the process of establishing with a patient that communicative system we then call 'psychotherapy'. Other paradoxes, such as the "art of being natural", as described by Heimann (1978) or the paradox of therapeutic authority, which both leads and follows, could be easily described. Under these paradoxes happening in our consulting rooms we might also file those coming from overall societal development. On our way towards being professionalised as a result of the Psychotherapists Act of 1999, social scientists believe that we are, at the same time, hit by de-professionalisation thrusts for which we hardly develop any discursive sensitivity (Thom & Ochs, 2013). If a once emancipatory ideal such as self-fulfilment has become a normative division line, separating the healthy from the ill, if self-perfection becomes the new psychotherapy-supported guiding word for that which, in the past, was called pressure to perform, if a therapy culture (Flick, 2013) has resulted in the universal spread of psychotherapeutic discourses, and if talk show hosts have become the most qualified masters of the once emancipatory lifting of taboos, then, paradoxically, one must definitely ask if, taking everything together, psychoanalysis is becoming a victim of its own success?

What are the conclusions?

If we stay with the internal paradoxes, with those we encounter in our consulting rooms, then we will see that each skilfully[4] handled paradox, so to speak, catapults us to a higher level of functioning. We make experiences and inevitably process them by thinking. And if we do not make them, still we must start thinking – or the system will collapse. Then therapy will just be flat conversation, a chat over a cup of tea, or faked concern. We afford psychic sovereignty in order not to drown in the confusion of the communicative jungle.

The therapeutic relationship within the potential space is constantly threatened by two dangers: by order and by disorder. In my opinion, identity is a concept that takes the side of a violently created order too much. Individualised and intimised interaction is the counterpart. Not to get lost in its disorder is an art in the context of which finding safety on 'Identity Island' would be the same as running away. If there is something like a paradox, if still we cannot see it, we must imagine it. And it will only come into being by thinking. Once discovered, it can only be lived and reflected within living. If we are not broken by the paradoxes, we will inevitably develop therapeutic resilience, we will, to state another paradox, increase our hardiness and sensitivity at the same time. We move into a new paradox, formulate new metaphors for a solution, but in the end we will not escape ourselves. Then we will be given back to ourselves.

Notes

1 Many more historical details on this are found, for example, in Bruyn (2010).
2 Poppe (2014).
3 Only a few days after I had given the lecture that is the basis of this chapter, the press published similar images from German homes for refugees.
4 "Being capable of" – with my professional theory (Buchholz, 1999) – this makes the crucial difference between profession and scientific 'knowing'.

References

Bernfeld, S. (1929) Der soziale Ort und seine Bedeutung für Neurose, Verwahrlosung und Pädagogik (Neuauflage 1974), in: L. v. Werder & R. Wolff (Eds.), *Antiautoritäre Erziehung und Psychoanalyse Bd. 2*. Frankfurt: Ullstein.
Blumenberg, H. (1986) *Lebenszeit und Weltzeit*. Frankfurt: Suhrkamp.
Bonomi, C. (2013) Withstanding trauma: The significance of Emma Eckstein's circumcision to Freud's Irma dream, *Psychoanalytic Quarterly* 82(3): 689–740.
Bruyn, G. de (2010) *Die Zeit der schweren Not. Schicksale aus dem Kulturleben Berlins 1807–1815*. Frankfurt: S. Fischer.
Buchholz, M. B. (1999) *Psychotherapie als Profession*. Giessen: Psychosozial-Verlag.
Carveth, D. L. (1984) The analyst's metaphors. A deconstructionist perspective, *Psychoanalysis and Contemporary Thought* 7: 491–560. [Reprinted in German (1993) in: M. B. Buchholz (Ed.), *Metaphernanalyse, Vandenhoeck und Ruprecht*.]
Cassirer, E. (1927) *Individuum und Kosmos*. Darmstadt: Wiss.Buchgesell. (Unveränd. Nachdruck 1977).
Danckwardt, J. F. (2013) Performance. Zur Begriffsentwicklung, Konzeptgeschichte und zum Erklärungs- und Gebrauchswert in der Psychoanalyse, *Jahrbuch der Psychoanalyse* 66: 147–170.
Erikson, E. H. (1970) *Jugend und Krise*. Stuttgart: Klett.
Eugenides, J. (2003) *Middlesex*. Reinbek: Rowohlt.
Ferguson, N. (2006) *Krieg der Welt. Was ging schief im 20. Jahrhundert?* Berlin: Propyläen.
Ferro, A. (2004) Interpretation: Signals from the analytic field and emotional transformations, *International Forum of Psychoanalysis* 13(1–2): 31–38. https://doi.org/10.1080/08037060410026490
Flick, S. (2013) Paradoxien der Psychotherapie. Psychoterapeut_innen und die Kultur des Therapeutischen. *Zeitschrift für das Unbewusste in Organisation und Kultur*, 16(3+4), 111–128.
Floerke, H. (1916) *Deutsches Wesen im Spiegel der Zeiten*. Berlin: Otto Reichl Verlag.
Freud, S. (1900) *Die Traumdeutung. G.W., 2–33*. Frankfurt: S. Fischer.
Freud, S. (1916) *Vorlesungen zur Einführung in die Psychoanalyse. G.W., 11*. Frankfurt: S. Fischer.
Freud, S. (1919) Wege der psychoanalytischen Therapie. *G.W., 12*: 181–194. Frankfurt: S. Fischer.

Freud, S. (1927) *Nachwort zur Frage der Laienanalyse*. G.W., 14: 287–296. Frankfurt: S. Fischer.
Heimann, P. (1978) Über die Notwendigkeit für den Analytiker mit seinen Patienten natürlich zu sein, in: S. Drews, R. Klüwer & u. a. (Eds.), *Provokation und Toleranz. FS f. A. Mitscherlich zum 70. Geburtstag*. Frankfurt: Suhrkamp.
Hendriks-Jansen, H. (1996) *Catching Ourselves in the Act: Situated Activity, Interactive Emergence, Evolution, and Human Thought. Complex Adaptive Systems*. Cambridge, MA: MIT Press.
Herrmann, A. P. (2014) Warum es so schwierig ist, in psychoanalytischen Institut(io)nen gedeihlich zusammenarbeiten, *Psyche – Z Psychoanal* 68(2): 97–121.
Herrndorf, W. (2012) *Tschick: Roman* (1. Aufl). *Rororo: Vol. 25635*. Reinbek bei Hamburg: Rowohlt Taschenbuch Verlag.
James, W. (1890) *The Principles of Psychology*. New York: Dover.
Klapdor, H. (Ed.). (2007) *Ich bin ein unheilbarer Europäer. Briefe aus dem Exil*. Berlin: Aufbau-Verlag.
Leikert, S. (2011) Kinästhetische Semantik. Der Wahrnehmungsakt und die ihm korrespondierende Form der psychischen Organisation, *Psyche – Z Psychoanal* 65: 409–438.
Leonhardt, J. (2014) *Die Büchse der Pandora. Geschichte des Ersten Weltkriegs*. Munich: C. H. Beck.
Levinson, S. C. & Enfield, N. J. (Eds.) (2006) *Roots of Human Sociality. Culture, Cognition and Interaction*. Oxford, UK: Berg.
Mahler-Bungers, A. (2010) Film-Revue: Tanz der Vampire von Roman Polanski (1967), *Psyche – Z Psychoanal* 64: 359–367.
Moser, K. (2000) *Metaphern des Selbst. Wie Sprache, Umwelt und Selbstkognition zusammenhängen*. Lengerich: Pabst.
Musil, R. & Frisé, A. (1987)[1978] *Der Mann ohne Eigenschaften: Roman* (Neu durchgesehene und verb. Ausg). Reinbek bei Hamburg: Rowohlt.
Niethammer, L. (2000) *Kollektive Identität. Heimliche Quellen einer unheimlichen Konjunktur*. Reinbek: Rowohlt.
Owens, T. J. (2006) Self and identity, in: J. D. DeLamater (Ed.), *Handbook of Social Psychology* (pp. 205–233). New York: Springer.
Paul, J. (1975) *Siebenkäs. Flegeljahre (I); Werke in 12 Bänden*, hg. von Norbert Miller, Band 3. *Reihe Hanser: Vol. 200*. Munich: Hanser.
Pizer, S. A. (1998) *Building Bridges: The Negotiation of Paradox in Psychoanalysis*. Hillsdale, NJ: Analytic Press.
Poppe, C. (2014) Doing testimony: Recipient Design in Zeitzeugeninterviews (Bachelor Arbeit). International Psychoanalytic University, Berlin.
Schwartz, M. (2013) Imperiale Verflechtung und ethnische 'Säuberung'. Zur Transformation der osteuropäischen Vielvölkerreiche durch ethnonathionalistische Gewaltpolitik im Ersten Weltkrieg, in: P. Hoeres, A. Owzar & C. Schöer (Eds.), *Herrschaftsverlust und Machtverfall* (pp. 271–292). Munich: De Gruyter Oldenbourg.
Seiffge-Krenke, I. (2014) Identität im Wandel und therapeutische Herausforderungen, *Forum der Psychoanalyse* 30(1): 85–108.
Spence, D. P. (1993) Die Sherlock-Holmes-Tradition: die narrative Metapher, in: M. B. Buchholz (Ed.), *Metaphernanalyse*. Göttingen: Vandenhoeck & Ruprecht.
Stern, D. N. (2004) *The Present Moment in Psychotherapy and Everyday Life*. New York: W. W. Norton.
Stroczan, K. & Bayer, L. (2004) Es gibt keine Eltern. Vom Drama zur Tragödie in Polanskis Filmen, *Psyche – Z Psychoanal* 58: 1182–1196.

Thom, J. & Ochs, M. (2013) Der Typus des postmodernen Professionellen – ein Porträt Psychologischer Psychotherapeuten, *Psychotherapeutenjournal*, 4: 382–390.

Thomé, H. (1998) Freud als Erzähler; Zu literarischen Elementen im 'Bruchstück einer Hysterie-Analyse', in: L. Danneberg & J. Niederhauser (Eds.), *Die Darstellungsformen der Wissenschaften im Kontrast: Aspekte der Methodik, Theorie und Empirie* (pp. 471–493). Tübingen: Mohr.

Tronick, E. Z. (2007) *The Neurobehavioral and Social-Emotional Development of Infants and Children.* New York: W. W. Norton.

Tuckett, D. (1993) Some thoughts on the presentation and discussion of the clinical material of psychoanalysis, *International Journal of Psychoanalysis* 74: 1175–1189.

Wallerstein, R. S. (1986) *Forty-Two Lives in Treatment. A Study of Psychoanalysis and Psychotherapy.* New York: Guilford Press.

Winnicott, D. W. (Ed.). (1974) *Reifungsprozesse und fördernde Umwelt.* Munich: Psychosozial Verlag.

Zimbardo, P. G. (2007) *The Lucifer Effect: Understanding how Good People Turn Evil.* New York: Random House.

Zweig, S. (Ed.). (2013) *dtv: 2688 : Bibliothek der Erstausgaben. Schachnovelle (Nachdruck der Original-Ausgabe, Buenos Aires 1942)* (Orig.-Ausg). Munich: Dt. Taschenbuch-Verlag.

13

IS PSYCHOANALYSIS IN A STATE OF 'BABYLONIAN CONFUSION'?

Heinrich Deserno

Introduction

The overall subject 'Beyond Babel' is used to organise some considerations of the present situation of psychoanalysis and its future, restricted to a special topic: the tension between psychoanalysis as a psychotherapeutic profession (organised in several national, European, and international associations), and psychoanalysis as a part of different academic faculties (in departments of psychology, medicine, and social sciences, etc.). I have run through psychoanalytic training according to the standards of the International Psychoanalytic Association (IPA) and have worked for more than forty years in scientific institutions, for most of this time in the Sigmund-Freud-Institute (SFI), Frankfurt M, finally as professor of clinical psychology and psychotherapy of the International Psychoanalytic University (IPU) Berlin since 2009.

T. Fydrich, professor of clinical psychology and behavioural psychotherapy, delivered one of the welcome addresses when the IPU was opened in 2009; he commented: "It is just the way it is: psychoanalysis is not psychology, it is just a theory among many others". Seen as one of the many theoretical languages in psychology, medicine, social sciences, and others, highlights the actual restrictions of psychoanalysis, and, at the same time, its progressive project as a transdisciplinary science.

The multilingual quality of contemporary psychoanalytic theory is in the centre of the following consideration. In the plurality of voices the author point to the tension between psychoanalysis as a psychotherapeutic profession and as part of academic faculties. Reading Amati Mehler et al's. (1993) monograph, *The Babel of the Unconscious* (1990, 1993), we find important contributions, which compare psychoanalysis as practised in mother tongue *and* in foreign languages. Amati Mehler is quoted because her contribution is not plural but it subsumes the myth of Babel under Margaret Mahler's theory of symbiosis and separation in respect of individuation (Amati-Mehler et al., 1993: 14–18, translated for this edition):

> Like the major myths of Oedipus and of the Lost Paradise, the myth of Babel is two-sided. On the 'progressive' side, the myth postulates an impossibility – in our case it means the exclusion of universal communication. On the 'regressive' side, it reconstructs in the imagination an ideal state which once existed but is actually lost – an original kind of interpretation follows: mythical unity which gives rise to the narcissistic claim of total communication. Each of these myths actually affirms the need for exile and separation resp. castration as a sine qua non condition for future knowledge [...] Babel represents the moment when detachment from what is similar to us takes place. It thus corresponds to that crucial core for individual development in which – starting from the original fusional situation – separation, individuation and differentiation are experienced at a mental level.

The Babylonian tower is a metaphor of 'vertical' logic

Amati Mehler's interpretation is a stereotypical one which means that you may apply it to whatever you want. Methods of application such as this one follow what can be called the logic of subsumption. It is, nevertheless, important because of the 'vertical' logic it applies by referring to the vertical axis of regression ('down') and progression ('top'). This is just what happens in the myth of Babel. Amati Mehler's use of Mahler's formulations corresponds with the vertical logic. But is that all we have to think about, while reasoning beyond Babel? History teaches us, that mankind is always struggling to overcome vertical versus hierarchical organisations in favour of more freedom, which can be lived in horizontal ways of communication.

A Babylonian 'confusion of tongues' is never restricted to language as such, but it comprehends language in a metaphorical way, too. The vertical perspective implies a split between the regressive tendency of preverbal (figurative) thinking and the progressive move toward verbal (conceptual) thinking. Besides this, an interesting example of conceptual research would be a systematic account of vertical and horizontal orientation in different psychoanalytic schools and their theories. Gödde and Buchholz (2011) describe the favoured vertical perspective of the unconscious and added the horizontal perspective to it.

The most prominent theoretical schools of psychoanalysis, such as drive and ego psychology, object relations theory, and self psychology, were carefully evaluated (see Mertens, 2010; Pine, 1990, 1998). The prominent vertical logic is decreasing in this line, but the Kleinian–Bionian or contemporary Klein approach, which becomes increasingly important in Germany, too, followed by Lacanian thinking, adhere to the vertical logic. Yet, the definition of a particular school that follows the theories of a leading name is, in itself, an instance of vertical logic. Why speak of Kleinian–Bionian or Lacanian psychoanalysis? There seems to be a parallel between orthodoxy and pluralism, as Cooper (2008) alludes to in the title of his paper: 'American psychoanalysis today: A plurality of orthodoxies'.

There are also contradictions caused by the previously mentioned subsumption logic. Kleinians, for instance, speak continuously of symbolic equation in psychic states, which are not symbolic but desymbolised. Of course, we know what they want to say, but the illogical name of the concept persists in the same way that the problems with projective identification still exist. Apparently, the character of thinking a Kleinian thought seems to be more important than the empirical and logical convergence of the facts that are addressed by the concepts. This is reminiscent of Freud's tendency to identify the 100% (female and male) psychoanalyst by shibboleths (marks of identification); for example, by her or his adherence to the concepts of the Oedipus complex, drive theory, the unconscious, and transference. A question of authority has become a vertical logic of theory, which is, at least, a question of control. This does not fit with the need to have interdisciplinary dialogues to maintain the state of being a transdisciplinary science, and it does not fit with the two different sides of psychoanalysis in Brumlik's (2006) view, being, on the one hand, a new kind of anthropological philosophy, and, on the other hand, a science which is in need of being validated and falsified.

The next steps go back to the myth and the history of Babel and then forward to its significance as a metaphor for the actual situation of psychoanalysis, especially its contemporary plurality or pluralism. According to the first, we have to consider two aspects: (1) the metaphor of the destruction of a tower, which probably can be situated historically about 1700 BC, and (2) the so-called Babylonian exile or captivity, that is, the forced detention of Jews in Babel after the conquest of the kingdom of Judah in 598–586 BC.

After the fall of mankind, with the loss of Paradise (*Sündenfall*) and the deluge, or universal flood (*Sintflut*), the tower of Babel and its destruction is a similar mythical narrative of pre-scientific age, mixed up with historical and religious motives. In fact, towers like the one of Babel served for orientation, observation, and, of course, for demonstrating power. There follows the original narrative in Moses XI 1:

> And the whole earth was of one language and of one speech. / And it came to pass, as they journeyed from the East, that they found a plain in the land of Shinar; and they dwelt there. / And they said to one another, Go to, let us make bricks, and burn them thoroughly. And they had brick for stone, and slime they had for mortar. / And they said, Go to, let us build us a city and a tower, whose top may reach unto heaven; and let us make us a name. / And the Lord came down to see the city and the tower, which the children of men builded. / And the Lord said, Behold the people is one,

and they have all one language; and this they began to do: and now nothing will be restrained from them, which they have imagined to do. / Go to, let us go down, and there confound their language, that they may not understand one another's speech. / So the Lord scattered them abroad from thence upon the face of all the earth: and they left off to build the city. / Therefore is the name of it called Babel.

Historians assume that the word 'Babel' derives from the Akkadian *bāb-ilim*, which means gate or door of divinity; there does not seem to be evidence of thinking of 'Babel' coming from the Hebrew word *balal*, which means to 'baffle' (i.e., to confuse). More important is that we know two different narratives. In the first one, God causes directly a confused communication among the workers, followed by serious and deadly accidents so that the tower could not be finished. In the second, God caused thunderstorms leading to the destruction of the partly built tower, with the same consequence: that the workers took flight, lost social cohesion, and ended in mental confusion. As survivors they had to learn a new language far away.

In *Folk-Lore in the Old Testament,* James Frazer (1923) described 'widespread' narratives with similar elements, in which God retaliates against mankind. He tells us a more elaborate version in the Jewish lore, in which pregnant women do not stop making bricks during delivery, and workers who argued up in the air on the tower lost their balance and crashed down. At the end of the story, we learn that anyone who passes the destroyed tower will forget everything he knows (see Frazer, 1923; Bamm, 1955). African folk-lore reports of piled up trees which collapse and kill men who climbed up. The Mexican pyramid of Cholulo ended at the height of 60 metres when God chastised the workers with lightning and thunder.

The element of confusion led to discussions about a language 'primara' or unitary. Was it Hebrew? Dutch? Turkish? The question here seems to be: can the confusion of tongues be connected with the previously mentioned logic of 'top down and bottom up' in both former and contemporary psychoanalytic thinking? Looking back, we see since the 1970s and 1980s (1) a decline of orthodox ego-psychology, and (2) the creation of a variety of different psychoanalytic 'schools' or 'models of the mind', and, in detail, different branches of object relational theories and self psychology; contemporary Kleinians and Lacanians; relationalists, interpersonalists, intersubjectivsts (for details, see Mertens, 2010–2012).

Can this development be interpreted as a 'confusion of theoretical languages'? To give a well founded answer, it could be necessary to study systematically how the differences are expressed, for example, in the malicious attacks by Jacques Lacan against protagonists of object relation theory such as Michael Balint and Donald Winnicott, combined with the programme 'back to Freud', which is reading and re-reading Freud. Reading Freud is, of course, an intellectual adventure through the knowledge of the 19th century, but reading and re-reading

Freud should not be exclusive reading. The admirable translator of Freud's work into Hebrew, Eran Rolnick, noted recently (2015: 531) that we do not need to like Freud or to understand him, "because reading Freud is in the same sense worthwhile as a pianist's exercising scales" (translated for this edition). This points to theoretical exercises in respect of 'exercitia'. Rolnick's device, that we need not like Freud or understand him while reading his oeuvre causes irritation, especially if we are convinced that transference and countertransference happens while reading and thinking, too.

When, for example, I became acquainted with some impressive readers of Bion (and of Lacan, too) for the first time, it influenced his further reading negatively; he felt as if someone or something superior was talking 'down to him', as if in a religious congregation. Why? Latent 'vertical' logic manifests itself when one side insists that they have 'superior' arguments to others and that the reader is a pupil who is in need of reading just these works to become a correct or proper analyst.

A book that calms negative arousals like those described above is *On the Shoulders of Giants* by Robert K. Merton (1965). The basis of his arguments is an aphorism, attributed to Isaac Newton: "If I have seen farther [than others], it is by standing on the shoulders of giants".

Merton's main topic is an ironical critique of 'serendipity' (in German: *Gelehrsamkeit*) and the satisfaction gained through serendipity. Of course, each generation leans or relies on predecessors. But the main topic of Merton's work is to criticise the vertical logic: history does not evolve in a linear way but in diversions, digression, or zig-zag patterns. So, the subject matter of historiography is not history, but lots of stories, which cannot be subsumed as one single and eternal story.

As we know, towers reaching to heaven are fascinating: we feel big being on top of them, and small looking up at them; in their presence we may feel and think 'vertically', becoming a part of timeless truths, participating in an epiphany. Or, to put it more simply, we may become like children, thinking and feeling in a magical mode. Of course, Freud himself has become a symbolic figure, and his greatness is impressive. Significant elements of his theory are apparently vertical: the developmental line of drives, the ups and downs of consciousness and unconscious, the term 'depth psychology' itself, vertical directions between progression and regression, or between superego and id. These are represented as psychic reality in vertical logic. To be sure, it is seductive to believe in this logic. Is reading and re-reading Freud satisfying the wish to believe and to repeat that we believe?

Concerning 'confusions of tongues', the late Sandor Ferenczi comes to mind, already, in 1933, describing the dangerous aspects of vertically organised relations in his paper 'The confusion of tongues between adults and children: The language of tenderness and of passion'. In abusive relations in childhood and in psychotherapeutic practice, he found effects of dominating or indoctrinating vertical logic.

Exile experiences and fantasies

The Jewish exile ended in 538 BC, when the Persian conqueror of Babylonia, Cyrus, permitted the Jews to return to Palestine. The exiled upper 10,000 had a good living for about 50 years in Babel. They participated in richness and highly developed sciences and earned a good living. But they were excluded from religious ceremonies. We are told (Bamm, 1955; Brumlik, 2009), that the Jews were sitting "at the waters of Babylon" and weeping while the processions to the wonderfully decorated "Ishtar-door" took place. Having been released, they proclaimed their belief in the *one* and *invisible god*. As Brumlik (2009) points out, this is where the real history of Jewishness begins.

Contemporary psychoanalysis includes a history of exile, too. Without the political and professional support of psychoanalysts who survived the Holocaust, psychoanalysis in Germany (and Europe) would not been as well established as it is. But those who escaped were not always welcomed in their exile. They had, as the sad example of Otto Fenichel shows, to work until they were exhausted. Others, such as Erik Homburger Erikson participated politically in the decision to rebuild Germany and to 're-educate' the people. My generation is more or less consciously identified with analysts like Erikson, Balint, and others, but this is not the whole story. A very important consequence of the political situation after the Second World War is that this generation had to rebuild psychoanalysis and felt obliged to 'save' it. Besides this transgenerational order (German: *Auftrag*), psychoanalysis has been undoubtedly the best for the medical, social and psychological institutions, with their history of being contaminated by ideology and the cruelty of Nazi fascism.

Today, we can experience conflictual tensions in psychoanalysis ourselves, being (1) professional psychoanalysts and (2) representing psychoanalysis in psychology, medicine or other disciplines. From its beginning, psychoanalysis has claimed to be a scientific theory and a psychotherapeutic profession at the same time. Will there be more young psychological and psychoanalytic academics in future? Can psychoanalytic training become a part of university departments? These and more questions are actual and urgent.

Does there exist, in psychoanalysis and in psychoanalysts, a latent exile fantasy, which is, in a reminiscent – melancholic or nostalgic – way, negatively influencing our efforts to transform psychoanalysis so that it has a good and successful future? Is this supposed latent exile fantasy expressed in the pessimistic belief of not being accepted, not recognised, not understood? Remember Freud's dictum, psychoanalysis has mortified mankind by its discovery of unconscious psychic reality, and remember his quotation at the beginning of his *Interpretation of Dreams*, that he will stir up the underworld if it is not possible to change the superiors. Are these continually (German: *gebetsmühlenhaft*) quoted sentences part of a latent exile fantasy? Beyond all references to Freud and to Babel, it seems necessary to say that the majority of psychoanalysts nowadays are living in social systems that do not persecute them. We can earn our living through very comfortable contracts with the insurance companies. Psychoanalytic associations are spread all over the world. The question is: does the exile fantasy defend the conflict within professional psychoanalysis, which provides the education of the next generations of psychoanalysts on the one hand, and, on the other, psychoanalysis as a discipline which is in need of scientifically trained successors?

Convergence of empirical studies and 'horizontal' logic

New empirical studies in developmental psychology by psychoanalysts following Winnicott, Bowlby, Stern, Fonagy, Target and others have brought a 'horizontal' logic into consideration. They point to the interplay of a "competent baby" (Dornes, 1992) and his mother in a relation of "joint attention" (Tomasello, 1999). They reconstruct the way from interactive regulation of affects to their modulation by representations (inner interactions) and symbolic modes. This knowledge is transforming psychoanalytic theories, practice, and education.

Nowadays, psychoanalysts like to speak of 'clinical' psychoanalysis. My generation had learned to be sensitive to a social process of 'medicalisation'. This generation had pulled out their white overalls in psychiatric and psychosomatic institutions. The expression 'clinical' is preferred by Anglo-American members, especially of the Klein–Bion school. Their main concepts, such as the 'autistic–contiguous', 'paranoid–schizoid' and 'depressive' positions sound very clinical, but in a disturbing way: they claim that even the very small child starts life as a person with a severe personality disorder, almost psychotic, and we wonder how this child will acquire normal functioning later on. Moreover, scientists outside of psychoanalysis cannot deal with these concepts. What is their function? What is their attraction? Is it possible to prove them? Is it possible to transform the concepts into operational elements and in naturalistic research designs (see Schöpf, 2014, Chapter 8)?

The answer will be surprising, and the question is rhetorical: the desired research has already been done! The starting point was 1985, when Stern's book, *The Interpersonal World of the Infant: A View from Psychoanalysis and Development*, was published and followed by a flood of studies on attachment, self-development, affect regulation, mentalisation, and so on. In the eyes of some analysts, such as André Green, this flood of research seems to be a contemporary deluge (*Sintflut*), a movement destroying psychoanalysis, as his plea against baby observation shows (Green, 2000). This movement has been compiled, evaluated, and discussed by the tireless Dornes (1992, 1997, 2000, 2006, 2012). These studies deal with the same period of human development that Klein and Bion described, and which is addressed by Lacan in his concept of the "mirror state" and the establishment of "*l'imaginaire*". Mirroring, in mentalisation, is completely different from Lacan's mirroring. The result of Fonagy and Target's (2003) studies is: there is no Kleinian baby, although there are analysts and patients who imagine babies in their adult patients the way Melanie Klein started to conceptualise them.

My own explorations (Desorno, 2006) in the field of symbolisation, mentalisation, and representation showed that before mentalisation came up, symbolising was mainly thought of as a means *to master the absence of a significant object*. The couch situation simulates the absence of a present important object, the analyst. But the concept of mentalising activity added to the former view the helpful condition of a present and empathising object. A contemporary conceptualisation of psychotherapy should integrate both views, in psychoanalysis, too.

Epilogue

Tomasello (1999) does not address the Kleinian 'baby' and the Lacanian *infans*. We do not any longer think that babies are 'autistic', 'symbiotic' or 'psychotic'. Instead, they are psychologically "competent" (Dornes, 1992). Before speaking in words, they use affective expressions to interact and communicate. They 'emphasise', and they draw conclusions. Tomasello describes the development of cultural thinking with his studies comparing human babies and the babies of anthropoid apes. Cultural thinking develops in repeated "situations of joint attention" between two agents, who communicate to attune to each other, and to relate to something of the world around. Only human beings develop externalised memory, and they do it by communicating. The difference between human beings and apes is a kind of communication that enables an intersubjective concentration and its intergenerational transmission. On a horizontal level, one takes over the perceptual perspective of the other, which leads to a social perspective, by which both direct their attention to an indicated object. They gain shared knowledge about the object they observe and identify interdependently.

Mentalisation theory adds to this more cognitive view the exchange and shared experience of affects: in a horizontal communication, a mutual negotiation of sense and meaning is going on and on, between a baby, a toddler and the adult carer. Our new knowledge of joint attention and mirroring of affects has fundamental therapeutic consequences.

Buchholz (2008: 563) tells us that we have to use metaphors as long as we talk about mind or psyche. In psychotherapy, we cannot function without metaphors, and an alternative to metaphor is not the term 'concept', but 'alternative' metaphors. Here, Buchholz refers to Gregory Bateson, who defined metaphor as an "organizing glue in the world of the mind which processes the body" (Buchholz, 2008: 563).

The preverbal, sensorimotor, affective coordinations and the pictorial or presentative symbols may be our shared 'proto'-language (*Ursprache*), which was unknown and articulated in religious and mythical beliefs in pre-scientific times and was searched for in the 19th century without success. Instead of treating Freud's, Klein's or Bion's oeuvre as holy texts through repeated reading, we may see them as down-to-earth pre-languages (*ur*, "primary") of psychoanalysis, stimulating a lot of new ideas, studies, etc., as happens today. Psychoanalysis will have a good future, if we are able to recognise the creative power of confusions and, to repeat, give up our latent exile fantasy and move to 'integrative' pluralism (Kendler, 2005). 'Integrative' was the intention of Miller, Duncan and Hubble (1997) to look out for a common language in psychotherapy.

In his book, *Nach Babel. Aspekte der Sprache und des Übersetzens* [After Babel. Aspects of language and translation], Steiner (1975, 1992) stated that translating is part of any communicating activity, in sending and receiving any form of

> meaning [...]. Understanding means to decipher [to encode]. Hearing meaning is translating. In consequence, the decisive structural and practical means of translating are part of any act of speaking and writing and of any pictorial encoding. Translation from one language into another one is nothing more than applying a configuration, a model, which [also] determines human speaking in a single language.
>
> *(Steiner, summarised and translated for this edition)*

At least Steiner presents an argument for differentiating between mythological and evolutionary perspectives. There is no mythology, he summarises, which does not describe the shattering of an original language into fragments, cacophony, and isolation as a catastrophic punishment by God on mankind for rebellion and vanity or hubris. At first sight, a universal language seems to have material, economic and social benefits, but on looking at this again we learn, following Steiner, that it is the constructive power of language which enables us to build concepts or ideas of the world and to survive. This power of language, and, we may add at this point, its symbolic and metaphoric capacities, enables us to say 'no' to reality and to construct fictions of what we dream of and wish for and expect, making our consciousness naïve and trustful in this constructed world. In short: the wasteful plurality of languages is essential and indispensable for the psychic life of man.

Steiner advocates this perspective, for less dogmatic and vertical organised thinking (Cooper, 2008) in favour of horizontal and heuristic argumentation, especially in the most sensible and responsible activity in psychoanalysis, in education and training, and, therefore, a combination of training and research from the beginning of training and in cooperation with the departments of psychology, medicine, social sciences and others would be helpful to reduce the conflictual tension between profession and disciplines.

References

Amati Mehler, J., Argentieri, S. & Canestri, J. (1990) The Babel of the unconscious, *International Journal of Psychoanalysis* 71: 569–583.

Amati Mehler, J., Argentieri, S. & Canestri, J. (Eds.) (1993) *Das Babel des Unbewussten. Muttersprache und Fremdsprachen in der Psychoanalyse.* Gießen: Psychosozial-Verlag.

Bamm, P. (1955) *Frühe Stätten der Christenheit.* Stuttgart: Kösel.

Brumlik, M. (2006) *Freud. Der Denker des 20. Jahrhunderts.* Weinheim: Beltz.

Brumlik, M. (2009) *Kurze Geschichte Judentum.* Berlin: Jacoby & Stuart.

Buchholz, M. B. (2008) Worte hören, Bilder sehen – seelische Bewegung und ihre Metaphern, *Psyche – Zeitschrift für Psychoanalyse*, 62: 552–580.
Cooper, A. (2008) American psychoanalysis today: A plurality of orthodoxies, *Journal of the American Psychoanalytic Association*, 36: 235–253.
Deserno, H. (2006) Die gegenwärtige Bedeutung von Symbotheorien in der psychoanalytischen Theorie und Praxis, in: H. Böker (Ed.), *Psychoanalyse und Psychiatrie* (pp. 345–357). Heidelberg: Springer.
Dornes, M. (1992) *Der kompetente Säugling*. Frankfurt: S. Fischer.
Dornes, M. (1997) *Die frühe Kindheit*. Frankfurt: S. Fischer.
Dornes, M. (2000) *Die emotionale Welt des Kindes*. Frankfurt: S. Fischer.
Dornes, M. (2006) *Die Seele des Kindes*. Frankfurt: S. Fischer.
Dornes, M. (2012) *Die Modernisierung der Seele*. Frankfurt: S. Fischer.
Ferenczi, S. (1933) The confusion of tongues between adults and children: The language of tenderness and of passion, *International Journal of Psychoanalysis* 30 (1949): 225–230.
Fonagy, P. & Target, M. (2003). *Psychoanalytic Theories. Perspectives from Developmental Theories*. London: Whurr.
Frazer, J. (1923) *Folk-Lore in the Old Testament*. New York: Tudor.
Freud, S. (1900) *The Interpretation of Dreams*. Standard Edition, 2–3. London: Hogarth.
Gödde, G. & Buchholz, M. B. (2011) Das *Unbewusste*. Giessen: Psychosozial Verlag.
Green, A. (2000) Science und science-fiction in der Säuglingsforschung, *Zeitschrift für psychoanalyrische Theorie und Praxis* 15: 438–466.
Mertens, W. (2010–2012). *Psychoanalytische Schulen im Gespräch*. Bd. 1: *Strukturtheorie, Ichpsychologie und moderne Konflikttheorie*; Bd. 2: *Selbstpsychologie, Post-Selbstpsychologie, relationale und intersubjektive Kritik*; Bd. 3: *Psychoanalytische Bindungstheorie und moderne Kleinkindforschung*. Bern: Huber.
Merton, R. K. (1965) *Auf den Schultern von Riesen*. Frankfurt: Suhrkamp, 1983.
Miller, S. D., Duncan, B. L. & Hubble, M. A. (1997) *Jenseits von Babel. Wege zu einer gemeinsamen Sprache in der Psychotherapie* [Beyond Babel: Paths to a common language in psychotherapy]. Stuttgart: Klett-Cotta, 2000.
Pine, F. (1990) *Drive, Ego, Object, and Self*. New York: Basic Books.
Pine, F. (1998) *Diversity and Direction in Psychoanalytic Technique*. New Haven, CT: Yale University Press.
Rolnick, E. J. (2015) Vor Babel. Freud lesen, *Psyche – Zeitschrift für Psychoanalyse* 69: 551–569.
Schöpf, A. (2014) *Philosophische Grundlagen der Psychoanalyse. Eine wissenschaftshistorische und wissenschaftstheoretische Analyse*. Stuttgart: Kohlhammer.
Steiner, G. (1975, 1995) *Nach Babel. Aspekte der Sprache und des Übersetzens* [After Babel. Aspects of language and translation]. Frankfurt: Suhrkamp, 2014.
Stern, D. (1985) *The Interpersonal World of the Infant*. London: Karnac, 2014.
Tomasello, M. (1999) *Die kulturelle Entwicklung des menschlichen Denkens. Zur Evolution der Kognition*. Frankfurt: Suhrkamp, 2006.

14

LINGUISTIC CONFUSION IN THE PSYCHOANALYTIC PROCESS

About understanding and communication

Annemarie Laimböck

Let us imagine the psychoanalytic work as the building, or, better, remodelling, of a tower with analyst and patient. The tower would symbolize the patient's personality, which is a sediment or fortified structure from the interactive psychodynamic events of childhood. The aim of the analysis would be a new, different and enriched history and personality of the patient, which would integrate the formerly unconscious and supressed aspects. The analysis aims to repair the cracks and gaps in this structure, which were caused by earlier unsolvable conflicts, empathy gaps and adversities.

Like the work at a construction site where all the workers and their activities are organized and connected to each other, the psychoanalytic procedure is interactive. The hard structure of the personality is retrospectively structured in an interactive process that resembles the original one from childhood. We return, so to speak, to the developmental phase of the patient's personality. As in a type of 'living history', old experiences are reanimated, but in the knowledge of its restaging or new edition under present conditions. The, by now, unconscious childhood scenario is fitted into modern conditions, the adult personality and the present phase of the psychoanalytic treatment, so that the old structure is not recognizable at first glance. The present scene does contain the earlier events, but the scenic function of the ego integrates the new with the old, or re-forms the new, so that it harmonizes with the old. Therefore, in spite of the ubiquitous phenomenon of transference, the actual scenes don't seem fundamentally crazy; they do make sense. Without the scenic abilities of the ego, our communication would be a total disaster. The construction of the tower, as in the history of the tower of Babel, would be a dismal failure every time.

This poses the question of how you can recognize, in the psychoanalytic scene, the hidden and, therefore, not directly observable old stories in the patient's unconscious motives, wishes and fears.

So, how do we make use of the scene?

From what has been said, it becomes obvious that we analysts, by approaching the hidden, subjective relationship experiences of our patients, turn to the psychoanalytic scene. The word 'scene' describes the many-sided motivational interactions between several people and can be signified by a title such as 'The drama of Oedipus' or by the description of the back and forth of the interacting people. The actual psychoanalytic scene, I call it the meta scene, is all encompassing. There is no communication, verbal or non-verbal, that is independent from the scene. Everything is a contribution to the dramatic development of the scene between analyst and patient. According to Watzlawick and colleagues, it would be impossible, however hard one might try, to not communicate (★Watzlawick et al., 1969: 51). When you transfer this to the scene, it is impossible not to make information a part of the scene. It is also impossible to give just information. Here, you can use the process of building a tower to illustrate the specifics of a psychoanalytic scene. The meaning of the workers' labour in the construction scene is derived from the goal to build a tower according to the rules of an objective building technique. In an analysis, on the other hand, the general and objective aim to treat a patient takes a back seat, and the relationship of the participants moves into the foreground. The actions of the players derive their significance from the dynamic of the relationship and not from objective clinical theories or a diagnosis. This also differentiates a psychoanalytic treatment from a medical one. It is not the treatment according to scientific insights, as occurs in a doctor's surgery, but the understanding of the analyst–patient relationship within the actual scene.

I would like to illustrate this special perspective by describing an initial consultation.

On the phone is a woman who speaks in a suffering tone. She says that she has problems and that her physician referred her to me. There is something in her way of talking which keeps me from enquiring further about her problems, as I usually do. My ignorance about her problems leads to an unusual beginning. In the waiting room, I meet a suffering, but controlled woman of about 50, with an expression of reproach. I see that her leg is bandaged and that she probably walks with a limp. I can see right away that, for this patient, the three flights of stairs to my office are a chore. There is an elevator, but it only works with a special key. Had I known of her difficulties, I would have met her at the elevator and she would have been spared that difficult ascent.

Her reproachful look gives me feelings of guilt but also a certain antipathy towards that woman. My feelings of guilt make me mention my surprise, and I tell her that I would have met her at the elevator if I had known about her difficulty in walking. She contradicts right away, this was not necessary, she gets along fine, and then she takes her cane and drags herself with difficulty but on her own feet into the consultation room and sits down. Now I sit across from her and wonder how I can help a woman who does not need help. She is obviously hurt, but wants to get along by herself.

From a psychoanalytic perspective, one can look upon this scene and its ingredients in a very subjective way.

The evaluation of the entire first consultation indicates that this patient showcases in this scene a central, unconscious Oedipal conflict with her mother. It hurts her above all that she had not been properly cared for by her mother, so that growing up would have been easier. Now she must lean on crutches and make the difficult ascent. Also, the elevator takes on a new meaning, as an opportunity to master the ascent directly and without effort. All you have to do is become the wife of the boss and everything moves along smoothly, as she told me later in that first consultation. But this way, too, was blocked to her, and in a 'sour grapes' reaction, she does not even want to hear about this possibility. The analyst's feelings of guilt mirror those of the mother. Instead of supporting the patient in her sense of being poorly equipped and to help her deal with the fantasized handicap, she recommends the elevator.

In the episode, it is obvious how the external circumstances and the analyst, too, are used to staging the unconscious conflict, without tearing apart or disfiguring the conscious scene of the consultation.

The analyst deciphers the scene by looking upon it as if the patient had created it to illustrate a central problematic situation in a relationship. Everything that becomes visible and audible in this scene derives its meaning from the scene itself. Nothing is beside the point or insignificant.

Cracks and gaps in the scene – non-understanding

In human relationships, and especially in the analytic one, complete harmonic scenes without any gaps and riddles never exist, because of the activity of conscious or unconscious conflicts, ambivalences and fears, in addition to the possible overtaxing of the scenic function of the ego.

In these situations, the actions of a participant in the scene appear unmotivated; there is no sense to them, and they are puzzling. What should I do with a hammer a co-worker throws to me while I am in the process of painting the façade? This is how, in the metaphor of building the tower of Babel, the puzzling scene might look, and the analyst has to make sense of it.

In contrast to everyday human contact, where these gaps or, let us say, areas lacking in sense, are marginalized for the sake of a smooth process, in the psychoanalytic situation they are of high interest, because they indicate the influence of unconscious processes.

The hermeneutic play, the interpretation (Deutung)

The analyst starts her search for a solution at the point when the question arises of why the patient acts in this or that manner, what is he trying to achieve and what does he want. As mentioned earlier, this question, in the framework of the metaphor of the tower, could be this: what is my fellow worker's intent when he throws me the hammer, which has no connection to my present job of painting the façade? The moment this riddle emerges, we begin to play with the materials at our disposal, in order to find a hypothesis, an explanation, an interpretation. If we stay within the framework of the metaphor, it may be that the painter, whom we assume to be the analyst, looks around to find an explanation in this larger context. Perhaps she deduces that the thrower needs to get rid of his hammer in a hurry, but does not really want to throw it away. Therefore, he throws it to the painter in the hope that she would take charge if it, hide it and keep it for him. This could be a motive for the enigmatic action. Another possible creative turn of events would be if, for example, as in a dream, the hammer stood as a symbol for something else, like a momentous piece of news, as in the German figure of speech, 'this is a real hammer'. This would change the entire scene into one where the patient, so to speak, throws a hammer at the head of the analyst by announcing something that is supposed to knock her over. This would strongly point to a motive of aggression.

This possible interpretation illustrates the following short sequence of a psychoanalysis:

> At an analytic session on 9/11/2001, the patient arrives at the usual time, we greet each other, he lies down on the couch, waits a few seconds as usual, and says "Just now, in New York, the World Trade Center has collapsed". "Huh", I experience irritation, Can this be true? What is he talking about now? I wonder. My "huh" and the ensuing pause make the patient add that two aeroplanes had crashed into it. Pause. This news heightens my irritation and adds to my problem as to whether this can be true, and if not, why this pronouncement? What aggressions are driving this man, what unleashed this phantasy in his head, I ask myself, more and more unsure if I was dealing with a phantasy or a reality. After another pause, the patient clears up my uncertainty and enlightens me by relating more details.

From a psychoanalytic point of view and with the scene in mind, it shows how the patient uses the scene in order to inject his subjective intentions. He puts his analyst in a helpless, disorientated state. He throws the hammer to knock her out. Not only does he want to seduce her into interpreting a mega-objective event in analytic terms, but he wants her to be laughed at and to parade her and her analysis in their full ridiculousness. He also causes an exchange of the relationship in the scene, as he evidently perceives it: it is not he who is helpless, disorientated and the object of ridicule, but the analyst, a person, whom, in this phase of the analysis, he perceives or at least fears as someone who exploits her superiority. In this case, he can show his power by having access to information before the rest of the world does.

This example illustrates that the patient's motives in the framework of this scene are of interest, in spite of the fact that these events actually did take place and the causes had nothing to do with the analysis. Also, the assumption that every patient in that situation would have related these events – they were simply too overwhelming to be ignored –does not negate the more subjective point of view, which shows the way that this patient makes use of the circumstances to form his own scene, and how the meta scene lends even such objective events their very own significance.

We can see how the negative experience (★Gadamer, 1960), the non-understanding, sits in the hermeneutic process, which requires the inner freedom of the analyst to 'play' with what she has seen and heard and to put it together in a different and new way. In order to gain material for her creative ideas, she pulls apart what seems to belong together. The conscious scene, the Gestalt,[1] easily falls apart along the gaps of meaning – such as contradictory actions, outstanding and not understandable behaviour, etc. These elements of the fallen apart scene become materials for the hermeneutic action of understanding. The guideline for putting together the materials in the direction of a new Gestalt or scene is its capacity to explain the gaps of meaning. In the new scene, the former riddles should be solved. This process, the distortion and the creating of a Gestalt, a scene, characterizes the process of understanding.

The participation of the analyst in these processes, his fear of no longer being in control of the event, to no longer understanding the patient, is not just a bothersome side effect, but a precondition for the creative interpretation. On the one hand, the agitation pushes the analyst to an interpretation, on the other hand, the riddle, and also the analytic attitude, prevent him from coming to a hasty or bad interpretation. This inner tension between the wish to find a solution and the resistance of the material to clinging together as a harmonic Gestalt is the fertile ground for new and creative thoughts and interpretations. These so-called critical passages (★Laimböck, 2007) within a psychoanalytic process take on an existential attitude because the constructive process can fail. For this creative work of the analyst, the unconscious interplay between analyst and patient is a never-ending resource.

(Different authors from different psychoanalytic schools have dealt with this phenomenon. Examples are ★ M´Uzan (1996) with the "paradox system", ★Ferro (2005) with the co-narrative transformation or the transforming co-narration, ★Bion's (1990) concept of reverie or ★Stern's (2005) so-called now-moments.)

The interpretations deriving from this networked situation have a special evidence for both the analyst and the patient, more than any clinically founded interpretation, because they originate from a real, existing critical situation within the relationship. From the scenic angle of perception, the interpretation is not only information about the recognized, unconscious drama and the patient's role in it, but also another action in the framework of the scene. This scenic point of view, therefore, leads to disillusionment in regard to the knowledge and the neutrality of the analyst. Whatever insight he gains, it is also a part of the unconscious play and, in this respect, an action of yet unknown meaning. Aware of this situation, the analyst does not give up on the idea of drawing the right conclusions about the motives of the patient. He pursues his quest of understanding, fully aware of its relativity and of the dialectic between understanding and acting.

Similarities and differences between psychoanalysis and everyday psychology

Psychoanalytic procedure, as an understanding of the whole scene, puts it in the vicinity of everyday psychology. It appears as a special form of everyday communication and no longer as a derivative of psychoanalytic meta theory.

In everyday scenes, it is assumed that the other participants act in a psychological, motivated fashion. This assumption leads to constant interpretation because the participants in the scene do not directly verbalize their intentions. They have to be deciphered. Freud expanded this everyday formula of understanding, against the scientific thinking of his time, by applying it to symptomatic actions, and so discovered a universe of preconscious and unconscious connections.

Although psychoanalytic understanding of scenes is closely related to the everyday understanding of scenes, there are specific deviations and limits within the psychoanalytic framework:

Analysts are used to not understanding everything immediately, but to postponing understanding. This fact causes additional gaps in making sense, irritation and even fear.

Furthermore, subjectivizing in the psychoanalytic scene is a speciality in contrast to everyday psychology. In this revival and emphasis on former thinking as a child, objective reality plays a small role. Primary process, egocentricity, aggrandizement and self-objects play a leading role here. The early childhood egocentric thinking is revived in psychoanalysis. It is applied methodically and leads to a world of self-centredness and phantasy and not to a world of reality, ruled by the laws of objectivity. By the very distance from reality, this subjective thinking reveals the mostly hidden motives for behaviour and actions that seem irrational on the surface. In addition, creative ideas, which are valuable in eliminating gaps by creative interpretations, are intertwined with the primary process. Loosening up objective logic is a precondition for the development of new connections.

To sum up, the unorthodox aspects in psychoanalytic communication are the delay in understanding, the limitation to subjective explanations and the usage of only material derived from the scene. These deviations from everyday understanding intensify the dynamic, support the actualization of inner conflicts and force their solution into the framework of the actual scene. The methodical limitations, as part of the framework as a third factor, enforce a constant new orientation and prevent a symbiotic agreement and stagnation.

Summary

At the end of this chapter, I return to the metaphor of the Tower of Babel. Analysts don't work beyond Babel, which means outside the scene, and its linguistic confusions. They do not interpret the entangled events from a secure point of view outside the scene with the support of clinical theories. What they do instead is work as part of the scene, in the middle of Babel, and, thus, lose a neutral and secure point of view. With the loss of neutrality and the so-called scientific method, there arises the possibility of influencing the action with an immediate knowledge of experience. The process is one of understanding; the interpretations must prove themselves by means of their plausibility and the dynamic effect in the actual scene. The emotional participation of the analyst creates a tension between the concentration on letting the gaps remain and the inner urge to eliminate them to put an end to the non-understanding. Playing exclusively with material from the scenes in the session, which excludes the systematic application of clinical theories, leads to creative pictures and connections to new scenes, where the gaps are closed. The process of understanding is a continuous pendulum swinging between deconstruction and construction. In addition, the concentration on one participant in the scene, namely, the patient, is considered a psychoanalytic speciality. In the interpretation, the scene appears as if the patient alone had formed the scene in this or that way for subjective reasons. This subjective reasoning leads to more intimate, and even more subjective, deepest domains of his personality, which are far from any objectivity. In retrospect, they can be seen as the former unconscious, repressed relationship experience from early childhood. Theory follows method.

In the end, we have to say that the analyst and the patient begin the construction of their tower somewhere, and, guided by the urge to understand, they end up in unexpected places. Analysis is a continuous construction site, where creative potential erects ever new, unusual buildings and where, again and again existing buildings are torn down or remodelled. Analysis is not a scientifically secure place, but also not one of randomness. The new constructions and remodelled ones proceed within certain limitations. It is not a case of 'everything goes'.

Note

1 About the connetions of psychoanalysis and Gestalt psychology, see Waldvogel (1992) and Laimböck (2007, 2011).

References

Bion, W. R. (1990 [1962]) *Lernen durch Erfahrung*. Frankfurt: Suhrkamp.
Ferro, A. (2005) Einige Überlegungen zur Deutung, *European Psychoanalytical Federation Bulletin* 59: 47–48.
Gadamer, H.-G. (1960) *Wahrheit und Methode. Grundzüge einer philosophischen Hermeneutik*, GW Bd I. Tübingen: Mohr Siebeck.
Laimböck, A. (2007) *Schwierige Passagen. Herausforderungen an die psychoanalytische Methode*. Frankfurt: Brandes & Apsel.
Laimböck, A. (2011) *Das psychoanalytische Erstgespräch. Überarbeitete und ergänzte Neuauflage*. Frankfurt: Brandes & Apsel.
M´Uzan, M. (1996) Zur Formulierung der Deutung, *European Psychoanalytical Federation Bulletin* 47: 51–61.
Stern, D. N. (2005) *Der Gegenwartsmoment. Veränderungsprozesse in Psychoanalyse, Psychotherapie und Alltag*. Frankfurt: Brandes & Apsel.
Waldvogel, B. (1992) *Psychoanalyse und Gestaltpsychologie*. Stuttgart–Bad Canstatt: Frommann-Holzboog.
Watzlawick, P., Beavin, J. H. and Jackson, D. D. (1969) *Menschliche Kommunikation: Formen, Störungen, Paradoxien*. Bern: Hans Huber Verlag.

15

'TO HEAR SIGNIFICANCE IS TO TRANSLATE' (GEORGE STEINER). PSYCHOANALYTIC CONSIDERATIONS ABOUT CAPABILITIES AND LIMITATIONS OF TRANSLATION PROCESSES IN LITERARY AND CLINICAL WORK[1]

Angela Mauss-Hanke

Common grounds

In 1996, for the first time ever, a chess computer succeeded in defeating then-reigning world champion chess player, Gary Kasparov, in the first game of the match. The most crucial feature of the chess computer, named Deep Blue, was the evaluation function it employed to determine and evaluate specific parameters of the game of chess (for example: the importance of a safe king position compared to a space advantage in the centre, etc.). By analysing thousands of master games, Deep Blue was thus able to determine and execute the optimal moves for any given number of situations in a game of chess.

So, would it not be possible to analyse a large number of translations in the same fashion in order to develop a viable speech and translation computer? However speech computers may or may not function, one might assume that when the international internet company Google offers a computer translation programme for fifty languages, it should be capable of producing a more or less viable translation.

By way of testing this idea, I entered that last sentence into Google's translation service, requesting a translation from German to English. The result: 'If Google as a global Internet company a translation computer offering for fifty languages, is surely one of the reasonably produce useful translation'. Then, I entered this result into the same programme, requesting a translation from English to German, and received the following reverse translation: 'Wenn Google ein globales Internet-Unternehmen eine Übersetzung Computer Angebot für fünfzig Sprachen, ist sicherlich einer der vernünftigerweise produzieren nützliche Übersetzung'. The result produced by Google's translation service translated back into English was: 'If Google a global Internet company a translation computer offer for fifty languages, is surely one of the reasonably produce useful translation'. This was in 2015. Now, four years later, Google Translate is able to translate the sentence perfectly well!

The point here is not to take the comparison between computer programmes for chess and computer-generated translation to the extreme, but, rather, to shed light on the fact that language, that the translation of even the simplest words and word sequences, is obviously predicated on much more complex terms than those governing the game of chess, so these processes can still not sufficiently be accounted for and reconstructed by the digital or mechanical means that have since been applied to so many other human activities. Svetlana Geier, a Russian–German translator, described translation as one of those "primal activities" that rank among the "fundamental needs of human existence" (Geier, 2008, p. 125).

> It is perhaps the most human activity of all. Each of us is always in search of the other, always driven to understand it. And it always eludes us. (…) There is probably some longing living within us as humans. Although interpretations of what that is may vary, it seems safe to say that it is a search for identity, for perfection, for wholeness. For the archaic, the original. Because everything in our lives is filled to the brim with compromise. Everything. Our cognizance, everything. Everywhere you look (…) you find something missing. It is never what it actually is, *it is never identical, it is never the original thing.* And just as human life is finite—and there's surely a connection between these two things—*human beings are forever at the mercy of the eternal compromise.* And, of course, that is also the attraction, and precisely what makes translation such an archaically human activity. Because—because, whether we know it or not—we are constantly engaged in the process of translating. (…) And no matter how well we may think we know one another: we are still not the same as any other.
>
> (Geier, 2008: 111)

But it is not only the *wish to understand* the Other in order to bridge the gap between 'Me' and 'You' – there is also the urgent, sometimes violent human *need to be understood*. Without the mother's understanding of the infant's preverbal messages, the infant cannot survive. Without the translator's understanding of the author's verbal message, there is no translation of his original text. And without a basic trust of both, analyst and analysand, that the analyst is doing her best to understand the non-verbal, preverbal and verbal messages of the patient and that, beyond all defences, a wish in the patient exists to grasp what the analyst is trying to get across – our analytic work would remain meaningless.

If we imagine that the original text is something important (to anybody) and that this transcript has become the only existing version of it, I guess we all feel a similar shock, perhaps like when an ancient sculpture is being destroyed, or a species of animals disappears, or when we put ourselves into the position of somebody losing his memories. And, furthermore, we might also see a parallel between this last version of something that originally was much more differentiated and had many aspects that got lost or have been transformed into something bizarre and the material that some of our patients bring to us, that they express in their sessions. Then our task as analysts is – and here is a fundamental difference between translator and analyst – not to add another version of translation, but to '*de-translate*' (Laplanche, 1992) what the patient brings, in order to help him to come as close as possible to something that he can consider as more 'true', less fixated to a defence that may have been felt as life-saving until the present (I leave open here whether you want to conceptualize this as a new construction or finding an inner existing truth, or a mixture of both: in Bion's terms I mean the transformation of beta-emotions and material in alpha-emotions and content).

... Looking back

The earliest known representation of a translator is to be found on an ancient Egyptian relief, where the translator is depicted as a double figure in his role as listener and as speaker. Ever since the introduction of cuneiform script about 5,000 years ago, the translator has assumed the role of reader and writer. As analysts, we have appropriated for our profession this archaic double figure who listens passionately and speaks, and each of us internalizes and puts it into practice in his or her own way.

However (as we all know and have heard several times these days), the historical–mythological point of origin for deliberations on the subject of translation is to be found in the Book of Genesis. The story of the Tower of Babel envisions all human beings in a primal state in which everyone spoke the same language and there was no room for misunderstanding between them, and the Tower of Babel became the material symbol for this state of existence. As the story goes, God saw in this human capacity for mutual understanding such a threat to his inviolable power that he 'came down' and "there confounded their language, that they may not understand one another's speech. So the Lord scattered them abroad from thence upon the face of all the earth and they left off to build the city" (Moses I: 10.11) To this day, the myth has inspired linguists and psychoanalysts to reflect upon the meaning of this primal state that was destroyed by God, to ponder the unconscious dynamics and the psychic state it represented.

We know from baby research that infants actually do imitate[2] all the 'language' they perceive (e.g., auditory and mimetic forms of communication, etc.), and that they possess a reflexive faculty of perception which is soon lost, and which is why we must develop psychic and intellectual capacities for translation in order to develop relationships with one another. So, even at the ontogenetic level, there does indeed seem to be a sort of biologically determined proto-linguistic faculty that, paradoxically, diminishes in the course of the maturation process and must subsequently be painstakingly reconstructed. 'Not here' is the first thought (Bion) – this is the first thought in the mind of every human infant; however, according to Bion's understanding, like every other original thought, this thought stems from the universal potentiality in an already extant treasure chest of thought/s. Is it possible that the myth of the Tower of Babel expresses the roots of our longing to regain access to this proto-linguistic faculty? Does it concern the realization that we will never completely understand ourselves, much less anyone else; is it the awareness of a loneliness, a solitude, an (a)lonesomeness that is fundamentally structural in nature? Or, to put it in Lacanian terms, a recognition of the impossibility of direct communication between the unconscious and the unconscious (Pagel, 55)? The way translator and author Esther Kinsky has expressed it in her wonderful book, <u>Fremdsprechen,</u> is: what "was destroyed with the Tower of Babel was not merely everyday language, not some common language used to identify things, but rather *language about languages*, a common language for articulating creative intent" (Kinsky, 2013: 14; original emphasis, translated for this edition). After Babel, human beings have felt compelled to develop capacities and faculties to overcome the obstacles preventing them from understanding one another. And yet this is also precisely the point at which we begin coming into being as human beings; it is a blessing and a curse, for, as Kinsky elaborates, "the loss of innocence also signalled the loss of stasis" (p. 15).

The Tower of Babel ranks among those myths human beings employ in their attempts to navigate the sense of being thrown into a world of development, differentiation and transformation.

> This confusion of languages is seen as a punitive act – following the expulsion from Paradise and the Flood, it is the third and final universal punishment imposed on the human race, stripping them once and for all of the possibility for any form of unhindered mutual understanding, and it anticipates misunderstanding as a constitutive human experience. This third punishment inflicted on humanity is nothing less than the creation of 'Otherness'.
>
> *(Kinsky, 2013: 15f.)*

It is this often so urgent desire to overcome the otherness of the other, the foreignness of the foreign, to enter the world of the incomprehensible and render it comprehensible that is at the core of what translators, psychoanalysts – and patients! – have in common.

Miss May[3]

I hope that the following vignette sheds a light on two issues: (1) on the limitations of comparing the role of the translator and the role of the analyst; and (2) on the analytic process between de-translation (mostly the role of the analyst) and learning a new language in order to find new translations (mostly, but not only, the role of the patient).

Miss May came to seek psychoanalytic treatment because her isolation, her patent rejection of any sort of emotional overture, had become unbearable for herself. At the age of 29, in the beginning of the analysis with four sessions per week, Miss May was still living with her parents. There were no friends, no visits from relatives; neither she nor her sister (12 years older) or her brother (ten years older) ever had a sexual relationship. Any contact with others was strictly instrumental. The family kept to themelves, living in close quarters – and yet none of them knew anything substantial about the others' personal, emotional lives. After her sister strangled herself, my patient could no longer ignore the tremendous lack of communication and love that characterized her life. But neither did she know how to extricate herself from the transgenerational *terra cremata* that she and her family lived in.

From the beginning, Miss May spoke very little, and when she did, it was in a dismissive, largely indifferent tone that was intent not on addressing me, but on excluding me. There were times I felt robbed of my thinking faculties, as if I were made of air and barely existed. In the transition between this state of mind and the return of my ego-functions, I sensed all the misery and aggressively mute indifference her family was entrenched in over generations, and what it must have unleashed inside her: an eternal back and forth, vacillating between desperate helplessness, irredeemable outrage and resignation. Whenever I tried to interpret this projective identification, whenever I tried to put words to what she sought to tell me with her silence, she agreed with me, but nothing changed. She confirmed, too, my readings of her silence as a withdrawal strategy, fear of intimacy, of shame, of being discovered, etc., then continued to say nothing: nothing occurred to her, or she wasn't thinking anything. After the sessions, something would come to mind, but when she was with me she would lose track of it. 'I don't want to be bothered with myself!'

Nevertheless she was always on time and never missed a session. I always had the feeling that she was watching me closely, registering my reactions, as if she wanted to climb inside me and inspect me from inside without my noticing it. Gradually, I came to understand that the patient's clinging to the fusion with me, while at the same time avoiding contact, did also represent her attempt to provide shelter for what was dead inside her. Through transference, she sought fusion with her elder sister, and, in the process, projected her own 'deadness' as well as the desperate sense of helplessness that welled up to resist this inner process of annihilation. It felt as if I had 'corpselike capacities' and was suspended between life and death. I *had to* listen to her silence in order to 'meet' her and to understand her inner *terra cremata* and existential despair. I had to contain her inanimateness before it could be identified as such and questioned. Gradually, it became apparent that *her silence was a weapon against speaking as a form of communication.* Using language robbed it of its function as a means of power in the sense of refusing to communicate: speaking and being understood is *what the other hopes for:*

182 Angela Mauss-Hanke

PATIENT: My mask is so good, it fools even myself. If I were to let you see inside, you would see just how confused I can be. Like a pile of misery. Well, that's a bit of an exaggeration. It's sort of like this: if you show the other and let them see – who's in charge, who is the winner?
ANALYST: What makes a win?
PATIENT: Simply not answering. Because that means you're stronger and triumphant.

I hope this gives you a first impression of the manifest 'text' within this patient, and why it could not be 'translated', but, rather, why it would have to be 'de-translated'. For a long time I could only do this through 'micro-interventions' (Erika Krejci), that is, through the sort of little interventions that Stefano Bolognini described so beautifully at the International Psychoanalytical Association Congress in Prague, 2013.

Six dimensions of the translation process

Let us now switch into the minds of translators. The empirical material in the content I have situated here in the framework of these six dimensions is derived from a small sample study I conducted in preparation for the lecture that is the basis of this chapter.[4] I interviewed five translators, four of whom are also analysts, and also took into account interviews with, and texts by, other translators who have reflected extensively on their engagement with their work. Against this backdrop, the process of translation can be described as a 'morphological process' (Salber, 1981) involving the following six dimensions (Figure 15.1):

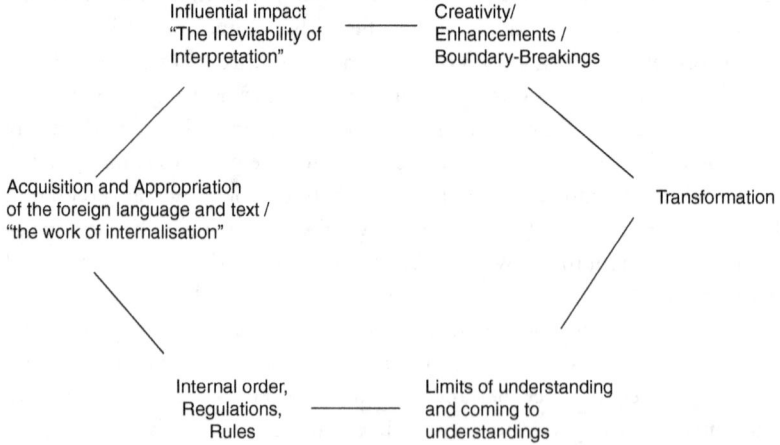

FIGURE 15.1 The translation process as morphological structure

Acquisition and appropriation of the foreign language and text. 'The work of internalisation'

Acquisition and appropriation of the foreign language

Learning a foreign language is a long, arduous task, and so is learning a psychoanalytic approach, interpretative technique, or learning to actually hear what a patient is saying. The fact that the foreign language is not merely a closed system whose acquisition seems to exclude more than it expands often first becomes apparent when the language begins leaving its traces in one's own experience, one's own memory, in the workings of one's own internal world. It involves a sort of mutual coming into being, a gradual disintegration of some brittle, unwieldy, often frightening intransigence. One translator talked about her first visit to Ireland as a child in the 1970s, and how she was completely taken aback and disturbed by the way female sales clerks in all the shops addressed her with terms such as 'my dear', 'my darling', even 'my love'. Her mother had never spoken to her in such unbridled terms of endearment. The knee-jerk desire to recoil in response gradually transitioned into a timorous curiosity; from this sense of awkwardness and trepidation an increasing sense of desire – even a need – emerged in the patient to seek out these little shops in the hope that she would again be spoken to in this manner. Finally, it always felt like a 'heartwarming inner rush'. She was convinced that this experience, which helped to still the profound sense of self-denial she had already absorbed as an infant suckling on a baby bottle – at least for those precious few weeks in Ireland – ultimately contributed substantially to the ease with which she was able to become proficient enough in English to become a translator.

While this may seem an extreme example to illustrate familiarity with a foreign language, it also seems safe to assume that a libidinal anchoring of foreign language is advantageous to every translator. (This might also explain why so many language courses designed to help immigrants to foreign countries with the integration process fail to produce the desired result.) Familiarity with the foreign language need not, however, go so far as to render the foreign language indistinguishable from the native language, in whole or in part. It is equally beneficial to the translator to regard the distance between the foreign and the native language not as a rift, but, rather, as *a linguistic space, a resonant sounding ground, where the material to be translated is able to oscillate between languages, or between the original and the gestures of searching in the mother tongue.*

But imagine the abject loneliness that develops in a child who may be in possession of such an inner linguistic sphere of her own, but which she cannot share with her parents because the child's native language is neither that of her mother, nor that of her father: I learned this from a female patient whose father was Syrian and whose mother was Polish. The only common language between the parents, their only basis for communication, was broken German. This, then, became my patient's 'mother tongue' – to this day, she is not fluent in Polish or in Arabic, and the language she is fluent in, German, she can't share in all its nuances with either her father or her mother. The native language, both on an individual and on a collective level, is replete with associations, images and allusions that can never flow in the same way from the foreign language.

Of course, the closer one's proximity to the foreign language – that is, to the original language of the material one is tasked with translating – the easier it is to appropriate the text to be translated, and yet this also increases the degree of discomfort experienced by the insufficiencies to which every translation is condemned. "The validity of the word can never match the sovereignty of its meaning in the original" (Kinsky, 2013: 22). Esther Kinsky's statements about the literary translator in this regard are almost equally applicable to the analyst:

> The translator is concerned with an original work whose validity rests on the authority of its originator – something the translator must ferry on to a foreign shore without the benefit of laying claim to the same validity. The status of the finished work (…) is not the decisive moment in translation (…) – rather, it is *the manner in which it bears witness to the conflict between, and engagement with, these two fundamental facts of human existence: language and the other.*
>
> *(Kinsky, 2013: 24f translated for this edition, my emphasis)*

(Un)becoming familiar/becoming (un)familiar

Just as a psychoanalyst's own life experiences may have inevitably driven her to reflect on interpersonal human relationships, compelled her to seek to understand the underlying psychic processes behind them, so, too, must the translator – at some point in his life – have been struck and fascinated by the infinite expressive potential of language/s. Similarly, just as every psychic organism is governed by certain fundamental principles[5] while it is, at the same time, endowed with an almost unrecognizable individual uniqueness, so, too, does every language function within the framework of a set of collective rules of governance on the one hand, but, at the same time, maintains its own profoundly individual status as a vehicle of signification. "Once we understand the written text as a world in itself, built upon words, translation then becomes a re-naming of this world" (Kinsky, 2013: 30). The more closely the translation adheres to the frames of reference established in the original, the more likely the translator is able to allow the reader to experience the foreignness of the foreign-language world resonating between the lines of the text—the reader's experience of the text's otherness, its foreignness, is, thus, more authentic than when the translation attempts to transpose the original text's referential framework into the reader's world of association. But what this requires is that the translator has fully appropriated the linguistic universe of the foreign text and is at the same time capable of finding new tonalities in his own language that are equal to the task of lending adequate expression to this other world created in the foreign language; in this sense, he must at once *alienate his own language* in order to construct a space in which the two worlds – that of the source text and that of the target language – can meet.

To break it down into the simplest of terms, one might say that both translators and psychoanalysts work in the interstitial spaces *between* linguistic worlds.

Influential Impact. "The Inevitability of Interpretation" (Geier, 2008: 149)

Coming into the text/penetrating the text

There is obviously a sort of synaesthetic auricular reading that is unique to the translator. All translators consistently iterate: "You have to learn to read!" "You must first consume and digest a text, then it just naturally flies from within into your hands. It involves a particularly intense form of appropriation". One translator, who is not an analyst, stated in an interview: "Developing a sense of empathy for the text is always a challenge. Without it, I would be hard-pressed – on a psychological–intellectual level – to reproduce the text". And yet, at the same time, "It always turns out that the text is in motion. You have done all the work, perhaps even translated it previously, then suddenly something shows up that you've never seen. *You can never completely exhaust a text*".

This inexhaustibility of 'translation' in psychoanalytic work is something Freud (1900) already laid out in *The Interpretation of Dreams*, where he brilliantly identifies the point of connection between the infinite span of the unconscious and the inaccessible or unfathomable as the dream's "navel". And yet, neither translators nor analysts can escape the necessity for making decisions: at some point, whether in verbal or in written communication, we must make a determination concerning the manner in which we convey what we have understood, knowing that it will never be complete, but, we hope, will be fitting enough to suffice.

Responsibility

The debate over translation as a faithful servant to the original or translation as an 'undercover' new text is as old as translation itself. Some of the earliest translations known to Western civilization were from Greek into Latin and the ancient Roman scribes grappled with the Greek texts, often in competition with one another in the effort to produce the most beautiful rendering. In the Middle Ages, attention turned to religious texts, and faithful adherence to the original went so far as to produce word-for-word, interlinear translations that were themselves regarded as sacrosanct. Luther was the first of German translators to apply a less literal, more 'liberal' translation of the Bible. It was Luther who first formulated the principle of translating 'sense for sense' rather than 'word for word', in the Latin *Rem tene, verba sequentur*: 'grasp the subject, and the words will follow' – an axiom which, to this day, remains the guiding principle for many approaches to translation.

'Grasp the subject' – what a fleet-footed expression to describe such a highly complex endeavour. The translator works under the tensions of a whole field of responsibilities: he has a responsibility to the original – perhaps more often than the original text itself, the translation assumes the role of monolithic text because subsequent interpretations/revisions are more likely to be made to the original than to the translation, at least in the case of living authors. In the case of deceased authors, as translator Lillian Banks points out, "the opposite is the case – from the Bible, to Freud, to Einstein, to Kafka, Bachmann … and the translations are more often also shrouded in controversy, heated (even vicious) debate, as each of the above-cited examples clearly illustrates" (2013, personal correspondence).

Though it is but a preliminary punctuation mark, the permanence of the translation exceeds that of its ever-changing readership. But the translator also bears a certain responsibility to the author: when, in the interest of facilitating a more readily accessible rendering of a highly complex original, the translator 'polishes up' the text, this involves introducing revisions to the original version of the text which may be seen as a sort of concealed co-authorship at the hands of the translator. All of the translators I interviewed shared this consensus – the central question must be, "How would this author have expressed himself in my language?"

Indeed, the search for an answer to this question is precisely the segue into the most complex quandaries of translation. Esther Kinsky provides one example worth citing at length here:

> In the Romance languages, the declination of adjectives and participles may identify the narrator [as male or female], but this is not the case in German and English. The narrator's gender is not revealed to the reader unless there is some contextual reference from which the narrator's gender can be deduced, so the text presents a completely different perspective than that of the original. And, on the other hand, in the case of a German, English or Hungarian text, an author may intentionally seek to conceal the gender of a first-person narrator, but this stylistic device is impossible to reproduce in the Slavic languages, where the translator is forced to assign a gender-specific point of view to the narrator. The question is: how, and to what extent, does the translator intervene if there is no potential for consulting the author of the original? And what is the impact of consulting the author on the translation process? Is it presumptuous for a translator to solve these problems independently if the solutions are ones that may be described as alternatives? If they alter the nature of the authorial intent of the text – so, for example, as in the need to decide between a 'gap' and a 'stopgap'. (…) Let's stick with the example of handling the narrator's gender: in one instance, the translator must decide between concealing [in the target text] what is self-evident in the source text, or rendering it apparent, in the other case, the translator would have to reveal [in translation] what

is concealed [in the source text]. And yet, even expressed consent of the author concerning an intervention can do little to remedy the situation because an authorized intervention involves deviation into a function that the translator is not supposed to perform. (...) How is the translator supposed to know whether the author – perhaps years after the text was first completed – is still in agreement with some specific detail in the context of the artwork as it was created at the time.[6]

(Kinsky, 2013: 58–60, translated for this edition)

Esther Kinsky comes to the seemingly radical conclusion that:

the translator's responsibility is to the text, and not to the author; it is to the authorial intent of the author's *text*, not to the author's retrospective opinion of his own text. It is difficult territory. (...) The author (must) 'let go', must simply come to accept that his work will be translated in a specific, subjective fashion that is beyond his reach …

(Kinsky, 2013: 60–61, translated for this edition)

And my translator adds:

My way of summing up this theory/approach: the proof is on the *page*. It is always on the page. It concerns *literary* intent, not authorial intent. And if there is coherence in the literary text, its intent will be revealed. It can be detected from the *text*.

(2013, personal communication)

Reading this, you may have been wondering how much of it is applicable to the translation, or shall we not better say transformation process, in an analytic context. Every analysand takes the risk of having his verbal material interpreted through the lens of our subjectivity (as analysts). However, our position is different, because the analysand is at once author and reader; so we must exercise even greater care and tactful sensitivity in our subjective work with the material entrusted us. On the other hand, we are in the privileged position of being able to experience both the pros and cons of receiving an immediate 'evaluation' of the degree of benevolence we have brought to our interpretation: if we've totally missed the mark, our interpretation falls on deaf ears – then again, if it goes straight to the heart of the matter, it can also be ignored, especially when it shows a lack of tactfulness and sense of timing ('premature interpretations').

So, here, it seems obvious that paralleling the role of a translator and the role of an analyst comes to an end and that some basic differences must be considered (and I thank Dominique Scarfone for opening my mind to these differences): Dominique Scarfone (2015, personal correspondence) reminded me about Freud's famous letter to Fließ (formerly letter 52) where he explains that repression is a failure of translation and of Laplanche's theory of the psyche as a translating apparatus. At first sight, Freud's thesis seems to support the idea of the analyst as translator, since one would think that, if repression is failure of translation, then lifting repression entails translating accurately. But this would omit an important fact: wherever there is a failure of translation, it does not mean that some 'blank' was left behind. As the theory of repression suggests, there is always a substitute formation, therefore *there is a substitute translation that was made by the patient*. Only, the translation was caught in a fixation, a closed loop, creating an impasse: in other words, the translation was not successful because it gave way to a non-evolutionary symbolization, a closed symbolization, hence repetitive and pathogenic. This means that (1) the patient *is himself a translator*, and (2) that he brings to the analyst his entangled defective translations of a lifetime.

As Walter Benjamin, in *The Task of the Translator*, beautifully explains, there cannot be a "translation of a translation". This is because – as one of the interviewees mentioned – there is always a "navel" of the "untranslatable" in every translation, so that in any new attempt at translating (a text), it is vital to always go back to the original. But, in analysis, the only 'text' we have is what the patient brings, so it seems impossible for us to go back to some 'original' – and this is also probably why we do not tend to think of the material as being already a translation. Indeed, the 'original' in psychoanalysis is not necessarily in the form of a text: it may present itself as something different, a 'Thing' (beta elements, thing-presentations, unrepresented states, etc.). And, indeed, we are more often than not confronted with non-symbolized elements that are only 'covered' by ineffective translations, so that under the manifest 'text', there is no well formed 'latent text', but a poorly elaborated, poorly formed, unsymbolized material. Yet, this is what we must try to get at. But how can we do it? We cannot, following Benjamin, do a translation of the patient's translation. So, says Laplanche, the work of the analyst is to help the patient to *de-translate* (reverse translate) his previously formed, fixed and defective translations: *undoing* a translation, writes Laplanche, is exactly the role of *analysis*. From the work of analysis the patient is given a chance to do new and more encompassing translations.

Internal order, rules and regulations

Just as psychoanalysis is governed by certain fundamental principles, so, too, is the field of literary translation subject to its own, and we should be clear about the historical and cultural contingencies behind them. For example, stylistic issues that were once decisively settled by referencing Duden (in German), or perhaps Fowler's (in English) are now handled in ways more commensurate with the individual text at hand; this requires an excellent, highly attentive editor. We have a similar problem in psychoanalysis: is the supervisor (are we as supervisors) one who is able to adequately intuit the unique dynamic and rapport between both parties in the analytic pair, or is it one who insists on imposing his own theoretical convictions on the situation? Svetlana Geier, in the documentary film about her life, *The Woman with the Five Elephants*, provides us with a particularly striking example:

> Several years ago, I translated Tolstoy's later novel *The Devil*. In the decisive moment, the protagonist sees a red skirt coming around the corner. It took quite a bit of effort on my part to insist that it was not a woman in a red skirt, but a red skirt that turned the corner. But that's just Tolstoy, and it was the same way with Gogol.
>
> *(Jendreyka, 2009)*

Reinhard Kaiser speaks in terms of 'deciphering' in this context:

> It would be presumptuous to contend that if the translator would simply exercise enough fidelity to the text in this operation, nothing would get lost. A lot, even a lot of very appealing things, get lost in translation. That is unavoidable. However – if the project is successful – other things come to light, or can be seen in a different light.
>
> *(Kaiser, 2009: translated for this edition)*

And yet, one caveat: most translators find in their 'behind the scenes' position, their inconspicuousness, a pleasurable experience. The opposing position is when the translator is forced to intervene, or becomes aware of a tendency to bring too much of themselves to the text and must develop the degree of self-discipline needed to tame this tendency. So, for example, when the source text is characterized by a dry, monotone tenor, then the translator's task is to reign himself in (if need be) and resist the urge to 'spruce up the text' with a more vivid or diversified language, even though this would be easier or more tempting for the translator.

This might be compared to psychoanalytic approaches predicated on the idea that the patient is helped by cushioning his statements, mitigating their severity, in the attempt to 'calm' or 'reassure' him. This, though, is but an indication of the fact that the analyst is just as frightened by the forces at work in the patient as the patient himself. The analyst who would instead identify the source of the fear, then formulate it into terms that better facilitate conscious awareness of the fear and this naming of that fear, is precisely what allows the patient to overcome it.

Just as every analysis bears the mark of the analyst's character, no translation can ever deny the translator's personal 'signature'. One of the psychoanalysts and experienced translators I interviewed put it in these terms:

> A colleague, who is (...) rather boisterous – I see that boldness reflected in her language, and in the way she translates. Someone who has a markedly substantive style in German will also bring that into his translation. If you know someone well, you can find traces of his personality reflected in his translation style. A colleague who is calm will also translate calmly.

That means the quality of the translation is related to the level of linguistic and emotional development and disposition of the person doing the translating. Whenever I am editing translations for the German Annual of the *International Journal of Psychoanalysis*, reading the original against the translation, the degree of proximity or distance each author has toward the author's position, toward his language, his culture, and his way of thinking almost always jumps out at me from between the lines.

The analyst's personality is also reflected in the way he carries out his transforming function (= Bion's alpha function): again, symptoms must be reverse translated and retranslated, from the symptomatic, often physical level into terms of psychic events: psychic processes that cannot be expressed in verbal terms and, thus, seek alternative ways of making themselves known evoke in the physical constitution of the analyst emotions and thoughts that she must in turn recognize, transform into language (put into words), then communicate them to the analysand, who may now find a new language for what was fixated in an inappropriate 'language' before. We know, not only from the differences in our own day-to-day condition, and from various supervisory and intervisory sessions, that variations in our own physical constitution on any given day may resonate differently, at least in nuances, and, thus, cause us to hear different things on different days.

Creativity/enhancements/boundary-breakings

The creative act

In many cases, though, some concepts do require some sort of creative act. One example is the word 'mind' in English, which, in German, we may variously understand to mean 'Bewusstsein', 'Psyche', 'Inneres', sometimes 'Verstand', or perhaps even 'Zusammenspiel Psyche-Körper', or the old-fashioned 'Gemüt', depending on context.

Translation always entails a deciphering and an analysis of the source text; it is often only through the translation that the full scope of meaning appears on the horizon, only in translation that one gains access to some latent content. It can happen that there is a turn of phrase that works better in the translation than in the source language; a shift in meaning in the sense of a 'post-ripening' may occur (Reichert, 2003).

The translation of a text can lead to transformations that do not lend themselves to reverse translation, as in the example of Freud's concept of 'Nachträglichkeit', rendered in French as 'aprés-coup'. So it is that translation may produce a new concept in the foreign language that, in turn, generates new meaning in its own right and, thus, enriches the vocabulary of psychoanalysis in both languages.

However, this can also result in slight distortions of concepts which then establish themselves to the extent that the distortion can no longer be reversed – there are countless examples of this – perhaps these can be addressed at other times.

The field of psychology is replete with untranslatable terms, or terms that lend themselves only to inadequate translation: container, reverie. And yet, attempts to translate them can hardly be considered wasted time because this can also serve the purpose of defining the concept more precisely. Erika Krejci (our beloved colleague who was the first to translate Bion into German), for example, translated the term 'containment' with 'Behälter'. A considerable amount of thought could be invested in the search for a German term better suited to conveying the character involved in the process of 'containment': Gehäuse, Gefäß...? But you would be hard-pressed to find a more apt term. Nevertheless, the time spent on these deliberations leads to a more precise understanding of the original – it unleashes the manifold meanings contained in the term itself – at least for the translator.

Enhancements and boundary-breaking/s

Every translation requires supplementary research – comparable to studying analytic literature, participate in supervision, intervision, etc. in analytic work. "One must familiarize oneself with the field, the language, the jargon of each individual book" (Geier, 2008: 140).

For most of the translators I interviewed, this sort of "background study" (Geier, 2008: 140), the acquisition/appropriation and development of a new language, a new vocabulary is an enormously rewarding experience. Conducting the research is a pleasant part of their work: one of them stated, "It's sort of like detective work, and I enjoy it". Another professional translator conceded: "Basically, I have this profession to thank for all of the education I have acquired over the past twenty years". Svetlana Geier says: "I have learned so incredibly much— not just for professional purposes. I've learned a lot about life in general!" In the words of another, "It's a sort of feasting, it always leaves me with some sense of nourishment. It's one aspect of the work I particularly enjoy!"

But the fiesta can also backlash into fiasco. The most drastic example of this came from Lillian Banks: while translating my paper on 'Traces of National Socialism in German self-identity' into English (Mauss-Hanke, 2013), she sent me the following email:

> Sigh. I think sometime we'll have to talk about countertransference in translation! You know, a few years ago, I translated about 2,000 pages of original, archival material from the Nazi period—the big, bad brutal Nazis like Hitler, Göring, Goebbels, Krieck, articles from Der Stürmer—all of it, straight from the Nazi-horses' mouths, from photocopies (in Gothic script no less!). I sat there for a good two years—just me, my dead Nazis and George W. Bush on TV; unfortunately, also in office.
>
> I'd been forewarned by the Jewish editors of the volume, who'd compiled these materials from archives in Europe: they said they just had to keep washing their hands while handling the texts. And I had to keep

> *brushing my teeth* because for me – as translator – it wasn't just that I had to dirty my hands with the stuff, I also had to 'put their words in my mouth' … and in fact, four of my teeth died in the process, and had to be treated with root canals … but that couldn't be attributed to the Nazis alone … it seemed to happen every time I had a Hitler speech on my desk while, at the same time, Bush was giving a speech on TV!
>
> OUCH! (That's my inner Jelinek-child screaming), the grown-up Bachmann is just groaning …. and it'll take me a minute to digest your text because all these dead Nazis just surfaced, along with the history that is also my history, even though I'm not "really" a Jew, and not "really" a German, but somehow (based on my personal history and genealogical lineage) both Jew and German.

Banks is not a psychoanalyst herself, but is astute in speaking of "countertransference in translation" in this context: her experience is indeed comparable to the feelings of countertransference we often encounter when treating severely traumatized or perverse patients, or those patients whose symptoms place us in the position of brushing up against the psychic wounds within us that have never completely healed. Without a certain degree of emotional attachment or apprehension, neither the work of translation nor that of analysis would truly bear fruit; and yet, when the effects of countertransference begin having a detrimental impact on the tempered attentiveness required for each of these tasks, when they cause the inner container to burst, this also becomes counterproductive. Here again, the goal is to seek out, and to find, the interstitial space.

Limits of understanding and coming to understandings

Limits of translatability

Just as there are limits to understandings between all individuals, so, too, are there limits to understandings in translatability between languages. We cannot escape the Tower of Babel's shadow. To cite just one example: the examination of different approaches to time in different langages and cultures alone would shed light on, and provide insights into, different collective psychic structures.

Here, too, there are parallels in analytic work with respect to the limits placed on our ability to relate to our patients. This is particularly evident in patients whose cultural background is much different from that of the analyst, but even the ability to relate to a different gender, a different generation, different life circumstances, to an entirely unfamiliar character structure as well as to a different development and world of language has its limits. And yet, precisely these limits allow us to learn from our patients – to learn about new cultures, new ways of drafting our lives and lifestyles, and, not least of all, new aspects of ourselves.

Incompleteness

An untranslatable remnant always remains, resulting from the utopian quest for perfection that is precisely what is so appealing to us as human beings – irresistably so. One of the translators interviewed put it this way:

> When you start translating, the novel has a sort of *poetic resistance* about it. There is a special appeal in getting to the bottom of that. The foreign becomes the familiar. But it never becomes wholly one's own. Everyone runs up against this: it is impossible to bring everything to light. So much ambiguity resides in each gap between two words. Every translation rests upon the conventions of communication and understanding. There is a certain satisfaction in rendering the foreign familiar, but it's still a matter of fluctuating conventions. I never arrive at that point. It is an unending process of searching for meaning and linguistic formulation.

Our position as analysts in this respect is similar: we listen and interpret within the limits of our 'hearing capacities', that is, within the limits set by our personality, development and knowledge, and within the limits of the quality of the contact between ourselves and the patient. The question then becomes one of whether there is any such thing as a 'finished' or 'completed' analysis. And this question leads us to Bion's "O", the "unattainable original" Geier mentioned in the documentary film about her life.

Transformation

Much has been said about the foreignness of the text. This feeling of alienation can morph into one of relative familiarity when the translator is able to transform the text into a gestalt that allows the foreign text, in a sense, to 'find itself' in a strange, unfamiliar language: that is, to produce a translation in which the source text feels well represented in a world that is not its own. As one translator stated: "The bottomless unfathomability is at once brought up from the depths and overcome in that moment of successful transformation". And he immediately added: "That, for example, is a concept that cannot be translated into English or French with only one word, because the German word 'aufheben' means 'to lift or pick up' (here: 'to be brought up from the depths') and 'overcome'". St Jerome, patron saint of translators, advised them "not to translate word for word, but sense for sense" ('Verbum e verbo sed sensum exprimere de sensu'). Along these same lines, Umberto Eco has stated: "So to translate means to understand the internal system of a language and the structure of a text written in this language, then to create a double of that textual system" (2009: 18f., my translation).

The translator must *re-create* the rhythm, the internal structure, the texture of a text. At the same time, the translation must be aware of the fact that it can never become an exact replica of the original. It must accept responsibility for the fact that it is a new version of the original. I believe that, as translators, we should never seek to avoid the tension inherent in the paradoxical mandate to produce a text in our own language that is identical to the original text in the foreign language. This paradoxical mandate inevitably brings a third text into being.

In our psychoanalytical language, we might say: whatever we 'translate' is a transformation – intentionally and unintentionally, *in any case inevitably*. But, again, who in fact is the one in the analytic dyad who is in charge of doing the new translation? Dominique Scarfone says:

> If we want to remain as far as possible away from suggestion, then, *ideally*, the patient should be the sole translator, the analyst working in the opposite direction (de-translating). Obviously, this is the *ideal* situation, and we know it does not happen all the time. But at least, the analyst should as much as possible work in that direction, only supporting the patient's attempts at new translations.
>
> (Scarfone, 2015, personal correspondence)

Conclusions

No psychic production can ever be understood in its entirety, and no text can ever be translated into another language in such a way as to evoke semantic associations that are identical to those which resonate in the original. One might say that a certain structural resistance is inherent to all forms of communication. Were it not for this fundamental resistance, we would have no need to invent language because we would understand one another without having to search for meaning. A profoundly gratifying state we may rarely, if ever, achieve with one or another other – but without doubt a state that always passes by much too fast. It is on this intrinsically human condition of 'coming-to-speech' that both translators and analysts 'knock themselves out' (*abarbeiten* in German).

The basic prerequisite for every translation process is learning the language of the other – the foreign language. While this may be self-evident in the case of literary translation, it is something we sometimes lose sight of in analytical work. Translators often think they make good translators simply because they demonstrate mastery of the foreign language – but if they are not virtuosos of their own language, they may turn out to be sorely mistaken. Analysts, on the other hand, may believe they are well equipped to understand their patients simply because they are well versed in the language of psychoanalysis – and yet, their interpretations often neglect to account for the fact that they are not familiar enough with the conscious and unconscious language of their patients to translate them. I'll come back to the notion of foreign language learning later.

In a successful translation process, both translator and analyst are charged with a certain very special responsibility: each of them is given particularly intimate insights into the material to be translated; in the process, each of them inevitably discovers latent secrets and weaknesses in that material, and, at the same time, each is obligated to resist the urge to assume the role of a ghost writer who 'polishes it up'. The task of the translator and the analyst alike is to continually be confronted with the contradiction involved in conveying material into his own language and his own cultural context while, at the same time, always having to seek out a new tonality in his own language that is equal to the task of acknowledging the difference inherent in the material and bringing this to the fore. Goethe, as early as 1819, pointed out in his meta-theoretical reflections on the translation process that translation always involves the emergence of a "tertium quid". In his commentary to the first edition of the *West–Eastern Divan* in 1819, Goethe first considered the "true art of translating" to be translations that aim "to make a translation identical to the original, not in such a way that the former replaces the latter, but rather occupies the place of the latter".

But, in a footnote he added:

> The latter part of that sentence, which is not particularly felicitous, seeks to express the idea that the translation can never provide a full substitute, only an approximation, it can never be like the original, *pour l'original*, but *au lieu de l'original*.
>
> (DW 61, 476, translated for this edition)

I believe that, as translators, we should always be aware of the *paradoxical mandate* having to produce *a new text in our own language* that is *identical to the original text* in the foreign language. This paradoxical mandate inevitably brings a third text into being. As analysts, we should always be aware that the 'original text', the latent truth, is always hidden under many layers and only exists in multiple distortions and that we, as analysts, need to de-translate the versions that the patient brings to us and help him to find a new language that allows him to create new 'translations' and, by doing so, come closer to his mental richness and freedom.

Notes

1 Translated by Lillian Banks (née Friedberg), who is a professional translator, creative writer and professor with German–Jewish and American–Indian roots and has written and published extensively on the practice of literary translation. Parallel to the process of translating this chapter, we had a fruitful exchange on the ideas it entails and I thank Lillian Banks for the mutual exchange of ideas that deepened my [translator's note: our] understanding of translation processes.
2 On the differences between imitation and incorporation and their coming together to create the process of identification see Eugenio Gaddini, 1970.
3 This case has been extensively described in: Mauss-Hanke 'Psychoanalytic considerations about the *anti-oedipal condition* in Heinrich von Kleists *Penthesilea* and in the analysis of Miss M', *International Journal of Psychoanalysis* 94(3).
4 A first version of this paper was given in Prague, at IPAC 2013.
5 As psychoanalysts, for example, we might say that there are meanings inherent in all forms of psychic expression, but which never present themselves simultaneously, and thus largely function only at the unconscious level at any given time; as analysts, we are able to recognize in these various forms of expression and their meanings certain

regularities that we use to diagnose symptoms, identifying them according to such categories as Oedipal, narcissistic, split, etc.

6 Translator's note: Throughout this Kinsky citation, I have placed brackets around additions I've made to the text for greater clarification: if I wanted to *really* intervene, in order to make Kinsky's language better suit the argument in this paper, I *could* theoretically use the terms 'latent' and 'manifest' – the language used by psychoanalysis to describe dream content. I could use these terms here 'generically', and they would resonate with the whole theory proposed here. That would, however, involve intervening in Kinsky's text in order to render it more supportive of the argument at hand. However, an independent case could be made for using 'latent' (for the German *Verschwiegene*) and 'manifest' (for the German *Offenbare*) here.

References

Benjamin, W. (1972) Die Aufgabe des Übersetzers, in: ders. *Gesammelte Schriften Bd. IV/1*, (pp. 9–21). Frankfurt. www.textlog.de/benjamin-aufgabe-uebersetzers.html

Eco, U. (2003) *Quasi dasselbe mit anderen Worten. Über das Übersetzen*. Munich: DTV, 2009.

Geier, S. (2008) *Ein Leben zwischen den Sprachen. Russisch-deutsche Erinnerungsbilder, aufgezeichnet von Taja Gut*. Dornach: Pforte.

Jendreyka, V. (2009) *Die Frau mit den fünf Elefanten. Dokumentarfilm über und mit Swetlana Geier* (film). www.5elefanten.ch

Kaiser, R. (2009) *Werkstattgespräch: "Mich übersetzen? Ist das Ihr Ernst?"* (Verlagsprospekt) Frankfurt: Eichborn Verlag.

Kinsky, E. (2013) *Fremdsprechen*. Berlin: Matthes & Seitz.

Krejci, E. (2010) Die Vertiefung in die Oberfläche, in: A. Mauss-Hanke (Ed.), *Internationale Psychoanalyse Band 10 – Ausgewählte Beiträge aus dem* International Journal of Psychoanalysis (pp. 67–87). Gießen: Psychosozial-Verlag.

Mauss-Hanke, A. (2013) Psychoanalytic considerations about the *anti-oedipal condition* in Heinrich von Kleists *Penthesilea* and in the analysis of Miss M, *International Journal of Psychoanalysis* 94(3): 477–499. In German (2014) Psychoanalytische Überlegungen zur antiödipalen Verfasstheit, dargestellt anhand Heinrich von Kleists Penthesilea und eines klinischen Behandlungsfalls, in: A. Mauss-Hanke, A. (Ed.), *Internationale Psychoanalyse Band 9: Moderne Pathologien – Ausgewählte Beiträge aus dem* International Journal of Psychoanalysis. Gießen: Psychosozial-Verlag.

Reichert, K. (2003) *Die unendliche Aufgabe. Zum übersetzen*. Munich: Hanser.

Salber, W. (1969) *Wirkungseinheiten*. Cologne: Verlag der Buchhandlung Moll und Hülser, 1981.

16
SAMENESS AND OTHERNESS IN A GROUP SUPERVISION EXPERIENCE

Annarita D'Uva, Loreta Negro, Maria Carmela Schiavone, Alessia Serra and Ludovica Grassi

The origins of supervision, as a fundamental component of psychoanalytical and psychotherapeutic training, are the same as those of psychoanalysis itself, at least since Freud first began to discuss clinical material with his followers: the supervision of Little Hans is the first well-recorded example (Ogden, 2005). Supervision is a form of transmission of knowledge from one generation to the next, which is why it contains a conflictual core due to the unconscious Oedipal dynamics inherent in the master–pupil relationship. Therefore, it brings with it the risk of becoming a traumatic experience as a result of both asymmetry and seduction, which are involved in the supervisor–supervisee relationship, and may sometimes lead to a *confusion-of-tongues*-like situation.

The reasons why therapists look for supervision are indeed feelings of inadequacy, helplessness, stuckness of the therapeutic device, inability to understand, negative feelings towards the patient, or even feelings of triumph and control and the desire to show off, all of which need to be addressed in the supervision (Strømme, 2010, Strømme & Gullestad, 2009). The tendency to regress into inner states, akin to the experience of a helpless child, entails a risk for the supervisee of being emotionally overwhelmed in both the relationship with the patient and with the supervisor. Moreover, both transference and countertransference play a fundamental role in the supervision relationship and processes, and need to be worked through: according to Strømme, supervisees need to find out about, and work through, the feelings that have arisen both in therapy and in supervision in order to achieve a dynamic therapeutic competence (Strømme, 2010).

Ogden (2005) considers the supervisory relationship to be similar to the analytic one, both viewed as forms of *guided dreaming*: the supervisor helps the supervisee to dream elements of his experience with the patient which were either *interrupted dreams*, because of the disturbing potential of thoughts and feelings evoked in the analysis, or *undreamt dreams*, which account for the analyst's unawareness of problems which may lead to psychosomatic or acting-out disorders in the transference–countertransference relationship. A supervisor's *reverie* attitude, even to the point of allowing oneself *time to waste*, enables "dreaming a patient into existence" (Ogden, 2005: 1269) or creating the patient as a fiction, mainly through primary process ties.

As a parallel process is evoked by similar relational dynamics unfolding both in the analytic and supervision relationship, in group supervision, where a complex network of relations between supervisees, supervisors and patient is mobilized, multiple transferences and countertransferences are expected to affect and enrich the group supervision work as well: the group is a powerful activator of resistances, conflicts and regressions but also a strong stimulus for awareness of these dynamics. Moreover, the supervision group is a very large container for all participants, which allows emotions to be expressed and worked out, so that supervision becomes an experiential learning process (Andersson, 2008). Finally, the extension of analytic work, in the form of a reverie and dreaming elaboration, which is made possible by a group mind, enormously expands the potential of evenly suspended attention and free associations that are apt to create new links and to mobilize the clinical material.

According to Ferruta (2010), even when the group members do not have specific analytic training, the clinical group seminar is an analytic experience in all respects: an analytic way of functioning can be set up, particularly when the clinical relationship presented has suffered from a blocking of thought, leading the therapist either to flee into a diagnostic–classificatory attitude or to cling to predefined concepts which are unsuited to modifying the situation. Its well defined setting, as well as its method based on free associations and evenly suspended attention, provide an amplified psychic place that is very well suited for receiving aspects of the patient's mind that are destructured and severely suffering, and which the therapist alone could not tolerate. They also allow for more liberal psychic movement and the unfolding of new psychic reorganizations. Such a group mind can be viewed as a transitional space, where an attitude of playing allows the participants to become elements within the operating dynamics and to undergo a self-changing process (rather than be limited to observing and understanding): that is, a transformative learning. The main source of knowledge is the members' emotional state, by means of their unconscious functioning as split, denied, unrepresented features of the clinical situation or as word- and thought-bearers for its characters. Through a narrative attitude that gives form and meaning to the experience, rather than leading to evacuative discharge, the group takes on a curing and thinking function.

Otherness and strangeness can, therefore, be hosted and metabolized, sometimes for the first time, by virtue of the group narcissistic support. A *gamma function* (Neri, 2004), that is, the group's ability to metabolize sensorial and emotional fragments, allows a new psychic birth to be experienced. The group adopts the patient's subjectivizing and desiring attitudes, only to metabolize and finally return them to her/him.

While in conventional group supervision, the relationship of supervisor and presenter works at a different level from that of the group members' participation; privileging the group dimension over the individual dimension allows Oedipal dynamics to yield ground to fraternal ones. However, at the same time, a state of group illusion (Anzieu, 1975) and a suspension of reality-testing allow a transient diminishing of conflicts, and of envious and paranoid feelings among group members, who enter a specific spatio–temporal psychic dimension of a playing nature. In order to minimize the emergence of malignant group dynamics (basic assumption configurations) that jeopardize the work group asset, Norman and Salomonsson (2005) devised the specific method of *weaving thoughts* for peer supervision groups, based on the members' shared confidence in the validity of learning from experience. The scarcity of information about the patient and his/her context, as well as the implementation of a rule by which the presenter must not answer any questions or comments by the group, serve the purpose of fostering free associations and primary process functioning, with the members of the group functioning as thinkers for unthought thoughts. The moderator does not make any summary, nor does she/he gather and tie together surfacing ideas: she/he is "the watchman of the aesthetic object" (Norman & Salomonsson, 2005: 1289). The group operates as a psychoanalytic mind at work, in close contact with the unconscious way of functioning, which doesn't attempt to solve contradictions or to develop a cogent narrative: it analyses rather than synthetizing.

The birth of the group mind

The experience we are presenting is that of a small group of child and adolescent psychotherapists who went through similar training paths and work in different contexts (as to roles, institutions, and social environment), and have gathered together in order to undergo supervision.

The *weaving thoughts* model, developed by Norman and Salomonsson (2005), needed minor adjustments to address the inescapable necessities of taking decisions and to outline responses to the advice-seeking agencies. It appeared to be the best way to enable exchanges on an equal basis and a dreaming-like attitude, which is the only specific of psychoanalytical thinking.

Whereas, for example, one of the members' initial expectations was to learn further diagnostic skills, this aim soon shifted into the background, as the containing function of the group provided increasingly more freedom to delve into the unrepresentable and most painful experiences of our patients. The plurality of minds appeared to be a facilitating element in the working through of relationships and links: a central issue for the decision of the members to work within a group was indeed the awareness that working with individual patients, particularly children and adolescents, involves a plural dimension that includes parents, families, and inter- and transgenerational links.

However, we cannot proceed without mentioning the paradox of the supervisor being at the same time a member of the group and the one who is appointed by the other members as occupying a different, specific position. This introduced a sort of oscillation between a symmetric and asymmetric structure of the group, harbouring the potential of both limiting the range of the members' associations and destabilizing the group balance towards what is new and unknown (*uncanny*).

The group at work

In previous supervision relationships we experienced quite structured forms of working in asymmetric settings that were aimed specifically at professional growth, and were supposed to take us through a linear movement from a less competent and self-conscious way of working with patients towards a more organized and effective one. By contrast, here we could allow ourselves to let our mental boundaries fade, and to oscillate between past and present, or even to abandon ourselves in a timeless dimension.

Time suspension, as well as silence, have been a specific feature of our group functioning. We start from listening: no information, no details, and no frame. Reading the session report gradually leads us into a dreaming zone and its climax is celebrated by *silence*: at this point we are allowed to breathe before emotions, phantasies, feelings and sounds become actual and possibly materialize through words. Silence takes on different, fresh features compared with previous supervision experiences, when it marked the shift from the therapist's presentation, outlining his/her experience with the patient and its attributed meanings, to his/her own expectation of being fed something good in the form of being provided with meaning by the supervisor, and possibly even directions, suggestions and criticism: two distinct and heterogeneous fields, though involved in a continuous mirroring and imbued with resonances and mutuality. In such a context, by contrast, the group's leader has the role of the representative of the silence. This temporally suspended space allows us to enter the present experience of that particular patient and to be informed by the unfolding of his/her emotions. The group, therefore, works as a choir, letting either similar or contrasting emotions to surface, depending on the psychic layers they express. This is as if a multifocal lens made it possible to view the entire path we walked together with a patient (whether a child, a couple, or a family) until now. Experiencing and freely associating something that affects and moves us, but is unknown to us, entails a ceaseless emotional movement between past and present, the past and the present that belong to each single subject, whether patient, group member or the group as a whole.

This dream-like functioning is always deeply informed by affects, and its mode of expression is made up of fragmented images or other sensorial productions that surface at a somato-psychic level: they sometimes overwhelm the psychic apparatus and appear in the form of somatic sensations or feelings of confusion, heaviness, or saturation. On the other hand, the deconstruction of representations may induce a formal regression (the Botellas' *regredience*) towards sensoriality and somatic states. New images appear to be the result of a work of figuration by the group mind and to replace proto-emotions and proto-sensations, which the patient is still unable to contain and to think.

Sometimes a film sequence is evoked, or a character shows up. During one session, Matteo (7; 6y) introduces Jack, a universal monster who terrifies girls; the group associates this with Jack the Ripper, who hated women, and also with the main character of *Monster and Co.*, who points to the opportunity of overcoming fears through a meaningful relationship. Camilla tells the story of a tiny baby girl who was shipwrecked and remained alone on an island, searched for but not found, raised by zebras, and capable of speaking both human and animal language. In this case, the group associates to the films *Never Never Land*, *Barbie and the Lost Island*, and *Tarzan*.

A member of the group reads from a session report:

> Before coming in, Luca stands as if turned to stone ... absolute emptiness ... his eyes 'light up' and to avoid collapsing he becomes absent and closed ... nothing happens ... I feel his pain ... I know addressing him is useless, he is out of reach. My words are unheard, I feel alone, nobody is with me. My pain is Luca's pain: his words reach only deaf ears, nobody listens or answers ... He has to survive through this nothingness. Luca collapses on the floor.

After this description of Luca as petrified and dissolved, a silence longer than usual falls over the group. Then one member reports a feeling of deep sadness, another says that she disconnected many times. The group agrees that the therapist might have been exceedingly involved, as if caught up. The therapist's emotions begin to be worked out in the group, attention is drawn to the slip about 'lighting up' rather than 'glistening' eyes: the therapist appears to be striving to infuse life into the boy who is lapsing into the catastrophe of dehumanization. Moreover, the figure of Medusa comes up who petrifies everybody looking at her, just as happens with autistic children who block and paralyse us when we dare look in their eyes. Later on, in the same session, Luca asks the therapist for the code word, eventually revealing that it is 'spalato' (shovelled): this word vehemently introduces Luca's mother into the session, who, in the first interview, told the therapist that she "found peace only when I buried my mother". The jellyfish (*medusa* in Italian) also occurs to the group, infamous for the stinging injuries it can inflict on the skin of swimmers: thoughts are raised in the group about boundaries and the sharp psychic pain that, in this family, has been arising from separation, from generation to generation; skin and nervous tissue, indeed, originate from the same ectodermal layer.

The group adopts the function of the word-bearer (Aulagnier), which is what the mother uses to transform plain sensoriality into feelings, and thus helps more words to come to the surface. Those are words that the therapist has difficulties connecting with, but that group members can relate to, such as shovelling, cold, death, loss ... After the therapist was allowed to experience confusion and fragmentation in the group, Luca begins to show new memory and narration abilities that lead him to interconnect sessions in a meaningful sequence. Specifically, he is now able to represent his own birth from the therapist's belly–mind, and the therapist in turn senses that she can offer the boy a good feeding by using the group as a good interiorized object.

Such group function has proved to be crucial in the treatment of disruptive patients, who have the ability to evoke dreadful feelings in the therapist, too: it makes it possible to engineer rapid changes in the emotional climate of the sessions and to allow the disclosure of a transitional space. In this way Alex, an adopted, very aggressive ten-year-old, who particularly frightened his therapist, looked as if he had sensed the presence of the group in the therapist's mind: after a supervision session focused on his case, he asks the therapist whether his space was occupied by other children, and shows a wound caused by a fall some days earlier. For the first time he can use the white space (dream screen) of a sheet of paper to draw broken lines that he asks the therapist to connect and join together. Similarly, in other cases where destructiveness was prevailing, the group carried out the function (Bion's alpha function) of making raw, inchoate elements (Bion's beta elements) thinkable, elements that could have disrupted the therapeutic relationship.

Working with our most damaged patients we must cope with loneliness, blockage and feelings of rejection, when all meanings lose their value and are wasted in the concreteness of sexual and destructive acting. The group houses the therapist's state of paralysis, bewilderment and fear, sometimes inseparable from the patient's condition: often they are therapist's issues that have remained unanalysed and demand a space for being dreamt. In order to effect this, they push their way through, clinging to the most unthinkable aspects of the most 'difficult' patients.

During a supervision session, the group focuses on a sequence from the session in which Giada, an 11-year-old girl who has been in weekly psychotherapy for a year and a half, describes her conflicts with her adoptive mother, which often lead to physical attacks. She adds, whimpering, that her mother speaks ill of her biological family and since her adoptive parents have recently become less sympathetic, she would like to go back to her family of origin. The group emphasizes how this adoptive mother keeps relating everything bad that is happening in their relationship to Giada's pre-adoptive history, and how the transgenerational has become an explosive crossing for her, where the histories of her biological and adoptive families intertwine. At this moment, the group work leads the therapist to recall a story told by Giada a few months before, which her mother returned to in a parents' session. It was an incident dating back to the mother's childhood when, during an excursion to the lake with relatives, some cousins and the uncle fell off the boat and drowned. The group is deeply shocked, together with the therapist, who had set this story aside as if it had no connection with Giada's life: an unelaborated material which the group begins to give meaning to.

We wonder what Giada may represent to her adoptive parents in relation with the maternal cousins who were drowned and whose remains were lost (*devoured by fish*): there is something that cannot be fished out, a hovering ghost that endlessly recalls the deaths that occurred. The narration of a father who drowns with his own children and is the only one to be fished out, though dead, represents for the group the idea of a father who is unable to safeguard his children and even survives them, an original fault that cannot be overcome.

In the group psyche, transgenerational issues come to life that can fish out stories that were lost in the patients' and even the therapists' memory recesses, gaining new meanings that can be brought back into play to stir up painful emotions rather than furtively acting and replicating in the subsequent generations.

Deconstruction in an oneiric state can sometimes induce anxiety, such as when one member realized that, throughout her notes, the name of another member's patient regularly replaced that of a patient of hers. Fading of boundaries, however painful and bewildering, indeed has a creative side, when the group also plays a containing function. The work-group climate of this 'democratic' setting allowed for a productive mutual influence of thoughts, fostering the integration of differences rather than the rejection of otherness, somehow even influencing the course of the therapies and consultations that were presented, as shown in Alex's case.

Conclusions

Fedida (1990) maintains that supervision is not less than a psychoanalysis, but not to be confused either with a personal analysis or an *outside the walls* analysis (Laplanche, 1987). The choice of the case to be brought to supervision is rooted in the analyst's own unconscious and points to a blind spot in his/her own analysis, a request to be reconsidered: it leads to a psychopathologic alliance that informs the countertransference. Supervision is, therefore, also the place and function of figuration for these unrepresentable obstructions: starting from them, the analyst inspires the supervision situation to develop an anticipatory narration that, in turn, amplifies the patient's aptitude for self-representation.

In our specific supervision group, the fact that all members originate from the same psychotherapy training school entrusts the supervision group (just like a fraternal group) with the task of working through the members' transferences and analysing their superegoic identifications with their analysts and teachers, a process never to be completed, but nevertheless inescapable in order to achieve independence.

Our experience of the reverie and transforming functions of the group (from beta to alpha elements) can change the recurrent experience of being skinned alive into a fertile mutual influence of thinking, which results from the conscious and unconscious, intersubjective psychic work of its members. Listening, as a primal way of entering a relationship with the other, is magnified and strengthened in the group mind, and allows for a larger sound envelope to develop.

Suspension of the linear flow of time, together with silence, allows the present time of the group to become a time of transforming experience: it is a second *après-coup* event, in which new meanings are born and a new individual spontaneous rhythm comes to characterize the spontaneous true self of the subject(s). A dynamic field or transitional space is created, where the group psyche can enter a condition of intensified endo-hallucinatory sensitivity (regredience) leading to a figuration work in areas where the psychic weaving appeared to be interrupted or torn out. The plurality of minds at work allowed more flexibility in dealing with individual and intersubjective functioning levels at the same time, as with vertically, transgenerational ones.

To the textile metaphor inherent in the term 'weaving thoughts', which is a spatial one, we may add a temporal–musical one, in order to describe the perception of a different inner resounding of the material within each group member, and at the same time the feeling of being part of an instrumental ensemble that plays a unique melody through dissonances and harmonic complexities. As if in a group painting, from the initial chaos of wandering thoughts something new appears, which is more than the sum of each member's contribution. Moreover, although the group is only allowed to know the age and sex of the patient and the duration and frequency of the therapy, the surprising result is that it always so happens that many features of the story and the situations inherent to the discussed sessions will emerge spontaneously.

References

Anzieu, D. (1975) *The Group and the Unconscious*. London: Routledge, 1984.

Andersson, L. (2008) Psychodynamic supervision in a group setting: Benefits and limitations, *Psychotherapy in Australia* 14(2): 36–41.

Fédida, P. (1990) La contruction du cas, *Novelle Revue de Psychanalyse* 42: 247–260.

Ferruta, A. (2010) Il seminario clinico di gruppo come esperienza analitica, accanto all'analisi e alla supervisione, in: G. Gabriellini (Ed.), *Giovanni Hautman e il pensiero gruppale*. Pisa: Felici.

Laplanche, J. (1987) *Nuovi fondamenti per una psicoanalisi*. Rome: Borla, 1989.

Neri, C. (2004) *Gruppo*. Rome: Borla.

Norman, J. & Salomonsson, B. (2005) 'Weaving thoughts': A method for presenting and commenting psychoanalytic case material in a peer group, *International Journal of Psychoanalysis* 86: 1281–1289.

Ogden, T. (2005) On psychoanalytic supervision, *International Journal of Psychoanalysis* 86: 1265–1280.

Strømme, H. (2010) Confronting helplessness. A study of psychology students' acquisition of dynamic psychotherapeutic competence. Series of dissertations submitted to the Faculty of Social Sciences, University of Oslo No. 205.

Strømme, H. & Gullestad, S. E. (2009) The rise and fall of conflicts in supervision. A contribution to understanding the complexities of student–therapist supervision. Manuscript. Oslo: Department of Psychology, University of Oslo.

17

PSYCHIC DEADNESS IN THE CONSULTING ROOM: THE ROLE OF THE VITALIZING SUPERVISION

From concrete to psychic language

Effie Layiou-Lignos and Vassiliki Vassilopoulou

Bruner (1983) was one of the first to point out that language arose in the context of interactions between infant and mother (carer). Language development is an emotional process. The development from non-verbal communication to psychic language reflects the negotiations of the depressive position and, therefore, the acknowledgement of the other as a separate person. This achievement requires a more articulate communication between self and other, which lays the foundation for symbolic language to develop.

"There are various ways of negating language one of which is concrete language", says Dana Amir, describing concrete and psychic languagein her paper 'From mother-tongue to language' (Amir, 2010: 4). She continues, pointing out that

> [c]oncrete language does not develop via working through loss, but rather swings between an omnipotent pretension of creation and a destructive urge to regress into primordial chaos... Concrete language is a language that cannot create any link. A psychic discourse becomes impossible. ... A person with a concrete language does not view things from afar but is assimilated in them.
> *(Amir, 2010: 4, 3, 9)*

The lack of psychic language – emotional authentic language – is the enactment of an unbearable primary bond.In the case of concrete language, we can imagine a mothertongue willing to name objects but not feelings, shedding light upon the external world but neglecting the internal one. This impairment in the primary relationship leaves the child with "unmentalized experience" (Mitrani, 2001).

Therapy process could compensate for such primary experience. This task is a demanding one, as concreteness attacks any attempt at establishing psychic links. The role of supervision is essential to this process. The psychic language of supervision can function as a substratum for the development of psychic language in the consulting room through dreaming, which gives meaning to experience.

Following Ogden's definition (2005) of the analytic supervisory experience as a form of "guided dreaming", it is the task of the supervisory pair to 'dream up' the patient. That is, to create a 'fiction' that is true to the supervisee's emotional experience with the patient. The supervisor helps the therapist to dream aspects of the analytic relationship that the analyst is unable to dream or is only partially able to dream.

The creation of a fiction refers to the fact that the patient who is presented by the supervisee in the supervisory session is a person created in the medium of words, voice, physical movements and unconscious communications, such as projective identifications. The way the patient is presented in the context of the supervision is connected with various factors related to the patient, the therapist, the supervisor and the patient's parents, in the case of a child patient.

Searles, in 1955, stated that the supervisor's feelings are a reflection of something that is happening in the therapist–patient relationship. The supervisee's uncharacteristic behaviour alerts the supervisor to the presence of an unverbalized conflict that has arisen in the treatment. The therapist does not seem to be aware that she is conveying that impression to the supervisor (Gediman & Wolkenfeld (1980). It is as if the therapist says to the supervisor "I cannot tell you in words what the patient is like, but I can show you and make you feel what the patient is like" (Gediman & Wolkenfeld, 1980: 239). The reverse influence is also observed: analyst and patient re-enact events of the supervisory situation. A state of mind of having 'time to waste', in Ogden's conceptualization of the supervisory process, "may provide an opportunity for a type of freely associative thinking that enhances the range and depth of what can be learned from the supervisory experience" (Ogden, 2005: 1265).

In the clinical illustration presented here, what is acknowledged, thought about and discussed is the importance of the parallel processes that take place in the therapeutic and supervisory sessions and the patient's movement from concrete to psychic language. The clinical material comes from an intensive therapy (three times a week training case under supervision), which lasted three and a half years. The supervisor and the therapist (respectively, the authors of this chapter, EL-L and VV) worked together for this period of time. The therapist, being a trainee, was also concerned about her evaluation with respect to her qualification.

> Nick, as we will call him, was a seven-year-old boy, with a diagnosis of Asperger syndrome, who was referred for intensive psychoanalytic psychotherapy within the Child Psychiatric Clinic of the same children's hospital where he was assessed. The parents turned to the hospital after being prompted to do so by the school, since Nick was behind in class and couldn't mix with the other children. He started refusing to go to school. The parents mentioned that Nick's difficulties started after the birth of his sister, who is three years younger, when his mother became 'depressive' (as she

herself described her mood at that time). Nick was then defiant and aggressive towards his parents, and mainly towards his mother. He gradually became withdrawn, refused to bathe, developed a skin rash, reduced his food intake, masturbated frequently and claimed that he would commit suicide.

Initially, during the therapeutic sessions, Nick does not maintain eye contact with the therapist. Eventually, he makes fleeting eye contact. He often looks as if he wants to speak, but has difficulty finding his words. He expresses himself in a roundabout way, or he says part of the word so his sentences are incomplete. He struggles to express himself and he immediately gives up. Nevertheless, during the first session, when he makes a small shape out of plasticine that resembles a tadpole, he says, "It's a baby rushing to be born. Why did I rush? I thought life would be nice. Why did I come out of there, out of my mother's belly?" He says that he cannot sleep at night, because he is "cold" and because he sees "evil dreams".

During the first six months of therapy, Nick uses plasticine to make snake babies that grow through the process of incorporation, since they eat other snakes in order to gain their strength. During the snake game the mother snake dies after giving birth to the baby snakes. Nick makes fences/graves where he places the snakes. This is where they die, only to be eaten by other animals, so that they in turn can live.

In supervision, the therapist finds it hard to express her countertransference feelings and thoughts. She cannot have associations. The supervisor's (EL-L's) questions, "How do you feel when you are together?" and "What were your thoughts?" are accompanied by embarrassment on the therapist's behalf, by confusion and silence, and by the answer "I do not know". The therapist wonders whether her thinking is suspended in front of this experienced supervisor, whom she admires, while, at the same time, she feels inadequate. During the therapy she feels half asleep and needs to drink coffee before each session, in an effort to stay awake.

Finally, the supervisor's dreaming of the patient in the form of her 'out of the blue' question, "What does Nick look like", startles the therapist as the image of the child comes to her mind. It is as if she notices Nick for the first time: slight and thin, walking mechanically, slowly and carefully as if counting every step. His body is tense, his movement without spontaneity. He sits on the floor to play and when he moves he resembles a reptile. Does this image resemble the child's mental function? A mechanistic function that excludes emotional expression and mental connections? The therapist wonders if she enacts this same function.

The image of a boy slight for his age with a careful, mechanical way of walking was accompanied by the supervisor's phantasy of a body-shell that offers a kind of 'second skin' protection, to use Esther Bick's concept

(1968). Nick seems to live in a world with persecutory phantasies and threatening objects. At this recognition the therapist feels able to breathe, as if something inside her came to life. Up to that point, a sigh of relief was accompanying the end of each session with Nick. The therapist felt able to breathe only when she said time was up. What was it that prevented breathing and vitality in the sessions?

The situation begins to unravel. There is a new dynamic to the therapist's associations. Was drinking coffee a need to stay awake, or a need to reassure herself that she was alive? This realization brought with it a profound shift in her understanding of a great many aspects of her experience with Nick.

The therapist behaved as if under the dominance of the patient's feelings. The language Nick employed was a concrete one: it didn't aim to link, but to withhold linkage or destroy it. The therapist could not think, could not feel and could not dream. Consequently, she could not describe her patient. On the other hand, the supervisor was talking emotionally, 'dreaming up' the patient, keeping alive both the therapist and the patient in her mind and in her speech. In addition to all this, there was also no common language between the therapist and the child's parents. No mentalizing capability. The mother talked about Nick's physical symptoms (rashes, itching, high blood cholesterol), while the father claimed that all this was simply his wife's exaggerations and that there was nothing wrong with the child. The colleague working with the parents also expressed frustration with regard to the inability to communicate with Nick's parents, to build a shared language with them.

The therapist realized that there was a sense of deadness in the transference. As if there were a whirlpool that sucked every trace of life into its centre. This sense could be summarized in Nick's words: he remembers the highbar in the shape of a snail in the playground when he was three years old, that he tried to hold on to that bar, but he felt dizzy and got off. Nick's deadness affected the therapist's capacity to make use of her reverie, leaving her unable to work through what was happening on an unconscious level in the therapeutic relationship. The patient's sense of deadness could not be symbolized and instead was enacted in the lifelessness of the therapeutic experience itself. Deadness had finally become a feeling as opposed to a fact.

The therapist's inability to dream for her patient, being trapped in a shell that deadens, possibly resembles the inability of the mother (the primary object) to dream for her child. Is it possible that the depression of the mother after her daughter's birth, in combination with the family's financial problems, the rejecting attitude of her husband towards her, and her own psychic deficiencies deadened her for that period of time? One wonders if the mother's dreams about this child were not dreams. They were probably projective identifications, where her own deadened self found some space. Associatively, through powerful projective identification, the therapist finds herself in the clothes of the "dead mother". Green (1983) has made a pivotal contribution to the analytic understanding of the experience of deadness as an early internalization of the unconscious state of the depressed mother.

Identifying with the dead mother is probably the only means by which the child establishes reunification with her. He maintains the object in a cannibalistic way. The mother's image remains captive, in order not to disappear and therefore fusion is maintained, while loss is neither acknowledged nor mourned. Separations from the therapist during weekends or during holidays are denied. The next session begins following the exact way that the last session had ended. Any comment regarding the separation was not heard, as if no absence had occurred.

Six months after the beginning of the therapy, as Nick tries to make a fence around a pair of animals (a cow and a bull), he wets himself. This pair seems threatening, as if representing a combined parental figure in a fierce primal scene, which overwhelms him with persecutory phantasies. Nick tries to protect himself from the persecutory object by building fences (like his autistic defences). Under the dominance of extreme persecutory anxiety, he cannot hold his toxic urine in.

Nick's external detachment covered an inner space, inhabited by horror and surrounded by walls. Lacking the capacity to own his feelings and thoughts, he had not developed a coherent experience of selfhood. He dealt with every kind of stress through its physical evacuation, thus leaving himself locked within his own symptomatic language, isolated. The emotional contents were foreclosed, leaving the body to exist as an autistic detached entity whose somatic speech replaced the psychic one.

During the second year of therapy there appears to be a qualitative change in Nick's mental function. Since Oedipal issues are being processed, a three-dimensional vital space opens up. Narrating about his external reality, Nick observes cats and their kittens in his neighbourhood. He wonders about the way kittens are born, if they and their mother survive after birth. He also wonders about how baby cats are placed in their mother's belly, and what is the contribution of male cats in this procedure. As he recognizes more and more the existence of the sexual pair, emotions of jealousy and competitiveness come to the fore. In his play and in his words father is the one who has the mother as a wife and he retaliates against his son for desiring the mother. Nick expresses his anger towards an external threat (trying to have father as an ally). At the same time, Nick displays his skills to the therapist, trying to seek admiration.

Gradually, the therapist's sense that vitality is present in the consulting room is accompanied by the child's request for the window curtains to be opened, "to let the light in, it's better with light", he says. At the same time, his teacher talks about the 'clarity' that Nick has acquired, since he has started to write and read with ease. The path towards symbolization has opened up. The therapist notices that the child has grown taller, his movements are a lot more relaxed. Nick mentions that he is eating more and it seems that he accepts interaction with an object that has survived his attacks.

Meanwhile, the conversation that takes place in the context of supervision has become more creative, with the therapist unravelling her associations. At the same time, in the consulting room, when I ask Nick about his silences, he replies, "I am thinking". Dreaming the existence of the child, the thought that he is alive, allows him to exist, to dream and to develop.

During one of the sessions in the second year, Nick makes a paper aeroplane, directed towards me, that, as he says, must become as big as possible by adding pieces of paper, one on top of another, on the floor (it looks more like a cross). He finally destroys the paper aeroplane after two sessions, saying that it is impossible to make it that big. He immediately then makes a three-dimensional paper aeroplane and a boat, folding over a piece of paper and making all the required moves. He rams the paper aeroplane into the boat and cries out, "I found the letters, a, o..." He starts writing on a piece of paper what he would like to do on his vacation. It appears as if destroying the huge paper aeroplane and replacing it with a different paper aeroplane and a boat signalled the passage to symbolization. Ramming the paper aeroplane into the boat signifies a turning point in his therapy, marking the creative encounter of the two. The creation and destruction of the huge paper aeroplane brings to mind the story of the Babel Tower. After the original fusion, what follows (at a mental level) is separation, individuation and differentiation (Amati-Mehler et al., 1993).

Accordingly, Nick presented, through the construction of the giant paper aeroplane, the ideal state that once existed: an original mythical unity that gives rise to the narcissistic claim of total communication: an ideal state which is actually lost. Both Nick and the therapist were trapped in a narcissistic unity where the capability for symbolizing was impossible. This capability was mobilized in the area of supervision that acted in a 'castrating way', just as the father is called upon to function in the child's symbiotic relationship with the mother, so that the capability for symbolizing can then be put into action in the consulting room.

Nick then tries to build a house out of paper, giving it a three-dimensional viewpoint, placing layers of paper in order to add strength to the walls and roof. The therapist had associations for the interior of this home. The capability for free associating is both comforting and liberating, while the sensation of sleepiness that troubled the therapist is no longer present. At the same time, Nick observes the walls in the consulting room and wonders whether someone has painted them, as he notices their colour for the first time. The pictures on the wall remind him of his favourite places in his village.

Nick is caught up in constructing houses and interior spaces, using bricks this time, while he proceeds to create the first person using Plasticine. He names, as he connects, the different parts of the body. He also incorporates into the game the idea of ownership. On a psychic level, the existence of his internal space becomes evident. He discovers that he has his own ideas and can be creative, having internalized a creative parental couple that allows him to bring things together. Sometimes, when he wonders about the way he can make a construction, the therapist tells him that he can look at the materials provided for him in his therapy box and he will think of a way. He replies, "Thank you, you gave me an idea!" Accordingly, when the therapist asks her supervisor for her opinion about something that took place during the sessions, and she encourages the supervisee to express her own thoughts, she says, "You gave me an idea".

The therapist becomes able to dream of Nick as a person, a boy, a future young man, as an architect, as a sculptor, a carpenter. She thinks of him as an explorer as she observes him busying himself with a number of different constructions. While he used to sit on the floor, playing, resembling a reptile, he now sits in his own chair and makes use of the table. Nick becomes more talkative, his speech is no longer fragmented. He mentions his everyday life, he talks about other children at school, and he calls them "my friends".

Nick remembers how he used to be. He says, "I used to walk slowly; it was a trick, not to fall in the hole. I thought that there were holes on the streets". His movement was rigid, offering him a second skin protection (Bick, 1968). An unthinkable anxiety (Winnicott, 1965) became thinkable and allowed him to feel the ground as solid and safe. He started running and playing.

In one of the last sessions, Nick discovers a piece of plastic wrapping under his chair: "It must have been there since they bought the chair", he says. He pulls it and it sticks on his fingers because of the static electricity. He smiles and he plays with it. "If I throw it, will it fall? No!" He places the piece of plastic wrapping on the tip of one of his finger and it stands upright. "How does this happen?" he wonders… "I am a magician!" and he smiles cleverly. He leaves the room, taking with him this piece of wrapping attached to his finger. He wants to show what he can do with it to his sister. He knows that it is not magic, but at the same time it is magic. The therapist wonders what is it that he takes with him. The ability to play and transform? The transitional space that allows the evolution of play? Does he take with him creativity, curiosity, liveliness? All these functions that are transferred from the supervisor to the therapist and from the therapist to the patient?

Nick's impairment in communication, symbolic capacity, play and language made it difficult for his therapist to have an understanding of *his feelings and his doings* in the way that Anne Alvarez described the "process of reclamation" in her book, *Live Company* (Alvarez, 1992), and be with him "on the right developmental wavelength" (Alvarez, 2012: 167). Nick's language was uncommunicable. His therapist's efforts to convey meaning through her words, to offer him explanatory interpretations of what she thought was his experience, could not be taken in. He was lost for words. His capacity for introjection was limited. Her language could not reach him. His unresponsiveness caused countertransference feelings of frustration and despair and eventually the therapist was sinking into boredom and sleepiness.

Nick projecting into his therapist his identification with a dead mother made the therapist experience the deadness. She found herself unable to achieve reverie for her patient. She could not think for him, let alone with him. No intersubjective analytic space could be generated before the deadness could be fully experienced. Nick's "unmentalized experiences", in the way that Judith Mitrani described the infantile "happenings" (2001), were caught up in a meaningless framework.

This therapy represents a process in which the patient's experience of deadness (identification with the dead mother) was being transformed from a sense of deadness in the therapy into a living, verbally symbolized experience of the patient's (and the therapist's) deadness in the therapy.

The therapist's capacity to house a sense of 'deadening boredom' in being with her patient triggered an awareness of lack of "reverie, transformation and publication", the three components of containment, according to Wilfred Bion (1962). Her containing capacity had to start elsewhere. The supervision became the lively "framework for the imaginary" (Mitrani, 1996), providing a psychic interplay of no intellectual explanations. Images and associations in relation to Nick were first created in the supervisor's mind, then in the therapist's mind, then in his own mind. Nick was able to bring free associations in his sessions only after supervisor and supervisee had a lively exchange of associations about him. No meaningful understanding of Nick could be obtained before this parallel process occurred.

Glenn's phrase encapsulates the essence of what supervision signified for the therapist and, consequently, for the patient: "I subscribe to the belief that the supervisor optimally stirs the student's imagination and curiosity and spurs his creativity" (Glenn, 1987: 583).

References

Alvarez, A. (1992) *Live Company: Psychoanalytic Psychotherapy with Autistic, Borderline, Deprived and Abused Children*. London: Routledge.
Alvarez, A. (2012) *The Thinking Heart: Three Levels of Psychoanalytic Therapy with Disturbed Children*. London: Routledge.

Amati-Mehler, J., Argentieri, S. & Canestri, J. (1993) *The Babel of the Unconscious*. Madison, CT: International Universities Press.
Amir, D. (2010) From mother-tongue to language, in: Amir, D. (2014) *Cleft Tongue: The Language of Psychic Structures*. London: Karnac.
Bick, E. (1968) The experience of skin in early object relationships, in: A. Briggs (Ed.), *Surviving Space: Papers on Infant Observation*. London: Karnac [also in M. Harris Williams (Ed.) (1987) *Collected Papers of Martha Harris and Esther Bick*. Strathtay, Scotland: Clunie Press].
Bion, W. R. (1962) *Learning from Experience*. New York: Basic Books.
Gediman, H. K. & Wolkenfeld, F. (1980) The parallelism phenomenon in psychoanalysis and supervision: Its reconsideration as a triadic system, *Psychoanalytic Quarterly* 49: 234–255.
Glenn, J. (1987) Supervision of child psychoanalyses, *Psychoanalytic Study of the Child*, 42: 575–596.
Green, A. (1983) The dead mother, in: *On Private Madness*. Madison, CT: International Universities Press, 1986 (pp. 142–173).
Mitrani, J. (1996) *A Framework for the Imaginary: Clinical Explorations in Primitive States of Being*. Northvale, NJ: Jason Aronson.
Mitrani, J. (2001) *Ordinary People and Extra-Ordinary Protections*. London: Brunner-Routledge.
Ogden, T. (2005) On psychoanalytic supervision, *International Journal of Psychoanalysis* 86: 1265–1280.
Searles, H. (1955) The informational value of the supervisor's emotional experiences, *Psychiatry* 18: 135–146.
Winnicott, D. W. (1965) *The Maturational Processes and the Facilitating Environment: Studies in the Theory of Emotional Development*. London: Hogarth Press and the Institute of Psychoanalysis.

18

LOST AND GAINED IN TRANSLATION

Language choice, triangulation and transference with bilingual patients

Annette Byford

Introduction

The question regarding the significance of choice of language by bilingual clients and its potentially unconscious dimension has been of interest to psychotherapists and psychoanalysts ever since early case studies by Freud, particularly the case of Anna O (Freud & Breuer, 1895). Following the emigration of many psychoanalysts from Germany and central Europe to non-German speaking countries, conducting psychotherapy with clients who spoke a different language from their therapists became a common situation in the emigrant psychoanalytic community. Today, with the increase in global migration, encounters in therapy where therapist and client have access to more than one language are becoming increasingly common. Such situations present both therapist and client with choices, and those choices are likely to have an impact on the nature of the therapeutic interaction.

This chapter focuses on therapist–client encounters where both participants share access to two languages: their first language (L1), learned and spoken in early childhood, and the second language (L2), learned post childhood. Such a situation gives both participants the choice of conducting the therapy in either or both languages and psychotherapists have been interested in the relevance and impact of such language choices.[1]

In psychoanalytic papers, the use of L2 in psychotherapy, whether by necessity or choice, is generally viewed as a defensive manoeuvre on the part of the client. Ever since Greenson's paper (1950), L2 appears as a language of intellectualizing detachment compared with L1, which is presented as the language of regression and deeper emotional experience. Greenson's statement that the use of L2 renders whole areas of the intrapsychic world unavailable for analysis has been supported by various psychoanalytic case studies (Aragno & Schlachet, 1996; Buxbaum,

1949; Flegenheimer, 1989; Foster, 1992, 1996; Javier, 1989, 1995; Marcos, 1976; Marcos et al., 1977; Mohavedi, 1996; Rozensky & Gomez, 1983; Y del Rio, 1982). There is at times, however, an acknowledgement that L2 may allow a safer start to psychoanalysis by making it possible at least to approach highly charged material that may feel too dangerous in L1. Its use may also be helpful for clients for whom the regression in L1 leads to relapse into symptoms caused by higher anxiety (Altarriba, 2002). L1 is generally seen as the language associated with unconscious or preconscious processes, in Freudian terms the language of the id and early superego, whereas L2 would, in this context, be the language of the ego and its defences (Mohavedi, 1996). Most of these studies agree that L1 affords higher levels of arousal around recall, more detailed recall of early memories, including previously repressed memories, a greater emotional affect associated with those memories and a higher level of regression with associated increase in symptoms. More specifically, clients seem to report a different sense of self when talking about emotionally charged events.

There is evidence supporting this view that L1 and L2 would allow access to different kinds of memories, and a different kind of emotionality associated with them, not just from psychoanalytic case studies, but also from both linguistic and neurophysiological studies. Various experimental studies confirm that autobiographical recall differs depending on whether there is L1–L2 congruity, that is, when the language of encoding is the same as the language of retrieval, thereby making childhood memories accessible in a different way in the language learned and spoken at the time (Altarriba, 2002, 2006, 2010; Marian & Neisser, 2000; Schrauf, 2003, 2006). First, linguistic memories are more likely to be elicited by the language in which the event took place. Second, memories are more detailed and emotionally more intense when told in the language in which they were linguistically encoded (Harris et al., 2006; Marian & Kaushanskaya, 2004; Marian & Neisser, 2000). These studies would support the observations made by therapists.

There seems to be neurophysiological evidence for different parts of the brain being involved in L1–L2 encoding and retrieval. Bilingual patients with stroke or other brain damage have been able to remember and activate one language but not the other. Electrical stimulation of specific areas of the brain has led not only to identification of cortical areas that are specific for each language, but also of areas of dual representation (Oejeman, 1991), suggesting that different parts of the brain are involved in storing and retrieving separate languages. The more relevant research for this chapter, however, is concerned with the question of different degrees of emotionality associated with the two languages. Neuroscientists are particularly interested here in the limbic system. It has been argued that the limbic system, involved in triggering and executing emotions, and also in processing sensory and memory information and in communicative functions, is involved to a lesser extent in the learning of the second, post-childhood language. Particularly classroom learned L2, channelled through explicit memory, will lack the non-verbal sensory representations associated with L1 (Paradis, 1994), leading to a difference between an 'embodied' and 'disembodied' language

(Pavlenko, 2006). Interestingly, this view allows for a stance that leads away from a simple L1–L2 dichotomy and instead puts a greater emphasis on the cultural and individual circumstances of the learning environment for L2 and the emotional experiences processed in it.

Indeed, taking into account the specific autobiographical and cultural context of learning and use of L2 leads to a different view of the *creative* potential of bilingualism and language switching. Far from being a language of detachment only, L2 may allow the approach of emotionally highly charged material which may be taboo in L1, as supported through various linguistic studies: one language may allow both expression and awareness of an emotional state (such as anger) which the other language does not. It may allow for a different blueprint for gender appropriate behaviour where, for example, subservient behaviour is experienced and performed as feminine and appropriate in one language and as weak and unnecessary in the other. One language may allow for a different evaluation of the same state and behaviour as acceptable and perhaps even valued (for example, assertiveness), which may be felt to be selfish or ruthless in the other. One language may be the language of choice for particular relational activities, such as parenting, or parenting of a particular kind, or in particular moments (for example, comforting versus disciplining) or it may allow the speaker to see the funny side of something that they cannot allow themselves to see in the other (Dewaele, 2006, 2010; Harris, 2010; Wierzbicka, 2004).

All this is not just a question of living in a different culture, as in most of these examples, bilingual speakers report these differences as a result of making alternating language choices while living in one culture. Indeed, this difference in the experience of self depending on L1/L2 use is also described by reports in the literature (Hoffmann, 1989; Kellmann, 2003). While in these reports there is again the suggestion that L1 use may be affording a deeper, earlier and more embodied kind of emotionality and memory, many bilingual speakers stress the fact that bilingualism and biculturalism lead to experiencing and presenting themselves as *different* in either language.

Eva Hoffmann traces her own story of learning to inhabit a new linguistic and cultural identity after emigrating to the USA as a young adolescent, and the subtly different rules about what is possible and acceptable to be, feel and say in one language and not the other. "This language is beginning to invent another me" (Hoffmann, 1989, p. 121).[2]

In interviews with bilingual speakers, Charlotte Burck (2005) repeatedly comes across accounts that stress the fact that speaking in either L1 or L2 creates a different voice, allowing the speaker to construct themselves differently, overcoming the constraints of one language in the other and trying out a different identity in the new language.

What runs through all these accounts is the inevitability of experiencing and presenting oneself as ambiguous, having to hold different perspectives simultaneously, a process that Burck refers to as hybridization. In this context, the phrase 'emancipatory detachment' has been used, allowing the speaker to create a new identity narrative with emotional depth and new emotional self-regulation

(Burck, 2011; Hoffmann, 1989; Kellman, 2003; Kinginger, 2010). Burck's notion of "identity as an ongoing project" is of relevance to the bilingual's endeavour to remember and tell their story in two sets of languages that give them access to different linguistic and "culture soaked" sets of associations (Burck, 2011).

This chapter is going to support this latter view of the creative aspect of bilingualism and the use of L2 in therapy. In addition, it suggests that L2 may be the language of an observing ego, but, beyond that, also the language capable of expressing (encoding and retrieving) new superego and id experiences. As such, its use in psychotherapy does allow the bilingual client a range of positions: approaching taboo subjects, processing cross-cultural experiences, not only linguistically, but also, and perhaps mainly, through the experience of the transferential interaction with the transcultural and bilingual therapist. The therapist's bilingualism allows the client to know something about their therapist, just as factors such as age and gender do. At the very least, the bilingual therapist shares with their bilingual client a linguistically mediated access to another culture. In addition to that, both therapist and client have made not just linguistic, but personal and cultural, choices by conducting their work in the country they live in and by choosing the language in which they conduct the therapy. Under these circumstances, the client's at times conscious, at times unconscious, choice of language will not just have a *limiting* impact, but also an *enabling* one as a device *extending* their ability to work through current *and* early conflicts. The following case studies demonstrate how close observation of these language choices and their context and meaning allows the therapist to explore an additional layer of transferential significance.

Case studies

I shall approach this underpinned by my own experience as a client whose training therapy was conducted in her second language, and from my observations as a therapist conducting therapy with clients who came to me because they knew that I spoke their first language, but chose to talk in their second language for long stretches of their therapy.

> I grew up in Germany as a child of German parents, learning English as a second language at school. In my late twenties I moved to the UK and have now lived in this country for more than 30 years. During this time I trained, and then for the past 20 years worked, as a psychodynamic psychotherapist. Most of my private and professional adult life has been conducted in and processed through my second language marriage, motherhood, friendships, bereavements and work. During my training as a psychotherapist, my training therapy also took place in my second language.
>
> While not all psychoanalysts and psychotherapists may support the use of one's own experience in therapy, in a chapter such as this the fact that I

experienced two different therapies conducted in two different languages, one in Germany with a male German psychoanalytic psychotherapist and one in the UK with an English male psychoanalytic psychotherapist some ten years later, alerted me to the role language and culture can play in the transferential field in which a therapy operates. Both therapists were men of the generation of my father, who had been adults during the Second World War. I was born after this war had ended, but the question of intergenerational guilt is a hugely significant one for Germans of my generation and was likely to figure in my therapies.[3]

I think it is interesting that it was the second therapy, conducted in my second language with a British therapist, which allowed me to approach this issue in a way that had not been possible during the first therapy. In my first therapy, in Germany, my father did not figure very highly at all. The issue of having a German father, a father of the generation who were adults under Hitler, remained unexplored. Perhaps I was unable to do that at the time. Did trying to do so in German make it harder?

As it happened (or as my unconscious made it happen), my training therapist a decade later was a British man of the generation of my German father. My English therapist commented on the subjects I read at a German university, namely German literature and history. So, was I interested in the creation of my mother tongue and the history of the fatherland? The history of the German fatherland is a complicated one for the child of a German father who was an adult under Hitler and fought in the war, and now I was to explore that in a language that was not my mother tongue. What had my father done or failed to do in those years? One thing I knew was that my parents' generation had failed to properly process what had happened in Germany under the fascists and what their role in it had been. As an adolescent schoolgirl, I watched reels of footage of concentration camps at school, an educational attempt to make us understand and make sure it would never happen again. But what exactly was my own responsibility for it? With my parents' generation shunting responsibility or not being able to cope with it, it was left to my generation to feel guilty in a rather bewildering way. Something unprocessed leaked into us, something that could only be talked about with our parents' generation in arguments and angry confrontations, adolescent separation soaked in something much more complicated. They had not really thought about it or understood it properly, and we did not understand it either.

How to talk about this in English with an English male therapist? Maybe because that was the only way to do so, at least for me. Here was a man of my father's age, who was not 'branded by guilt', who was capable of reflection, so that I could think, too. My therapist might have fought in the same war, on the 'right' side, but might he have been involved in bombing

German towns, for example? The crucial thing here was that he was capable of bringing up the subject. Through his ability to talk about it and think about it, my own ability to do so grew and, as a result, I could also discover love for a father that had been obstructed by our sharing the same problematic fatherland. Looking back, it seems that this was made possible not only by my therapist's quality, but also by the fact that we did not speak in my mother tongue. The other language allowed me a distance in which the story could be re-told in a safer way. Something might have got lost in that process, but other things could be approached more easily from that distance and opened up. It wasn't so intrinsically linked with the handed down guilt and shame, and that allowed earlier attachments, together with joy and admiration for the father of my early childhood, to surface again.

Of course, many factors not discussed here contributed to this therapy being different from the first. It was my second therapy, I was at a different stage of my life and the quality, personality and skills of my therapists were different. However, my own experience supports the view that the use of L2 was a significant factor. Unlike my own clients discussed later, my therapist and I did not share access to two languages. My therapy was conducted in my second language and I did not have the option of switching languages. However, using L2 throughout somehow lowered the temperature for approaching highly charged emotional taboo subjects, such as the question of transgenerational guilt. I think it is significant that, for me, approaching this was not only to do with the second language, but also to do with the transferential space that was opened up by my therapist's positioning in the other culture. I think, however, that it is too simplistic to think about this mainly in terms of detachment or intellectualizing. Through the medium of the other language and the transferential intercultural space, there was a possibility for me not only to approach questions of intergenerational guilt and denial without feeling overwhelmed, but also to approach earlier infantile aspects of my relationship with my father which had not been available to me in my first language therapy. It seemed the complications of the German mother tongue narrative were one factor blocking access to this.

In my own practice, I offer therapy in English and German, thereby giving my clients the option of using either language. Over the years this has brought me several German clients. While language has played a role in such clients' initial approach to me, their subsequent use of German as a language in therapy varies. Some of my German clients who have not been in the UK that long come with the straightforward wish to conduct their therapy in the language they use to express more complicated emotional or cognitive matters, with English at this stage being very much their weaker language. Other clients choose to use mainly English and some may move between both languages. I always follow their choice.

All clients described in the following clinical examples have been disguised, names and biographical details have been changed, and I sought and gained permission to use the material where I judged it clinically appropriate.

Brigitte

Brigitte is a German woman in her late twenties, married to a German man. They both came to the UK for work. Her English is very good, that of an educated German of her generation. However, she only uses English in either a work context or in social situations. Brigitte is struggling with her feelings regarding bringing up her son in the UK. Her husband likes it here and his career is linked to his post in the UK. Brigitte, however, who had been happy enough here before her child was born, now wants to go back to Germany. We talk throughout in German. I am, during long phases of our work, the person who will 'know what she means' when she describes her feelings about bringing up her child in the UK. Brigitte feels uncomfortable with the English education system, the early school entry age, the early emphasis on formal learning and teaching, the pressure of constant testing compared with what she knows is a more child-orientated system in Germany that allows different choices, certainly in the early years. She does not like what she hears from fellow mothers about a world where children are ferried around in their parents' cars, make arrangements to go and play at other children's houses, but with an absence of public meeting places and playgrounds. She is dismayed by a world where a fellow German mother can be taken aside by the head teacher because she allowed her six-year-old to walk to school on his own. In Germany, her son would be walking together with the other children, cycling to school on safe cycling paths, be allowed to be a child, yet also have more independence. This is an idealized image, yet with some truth in it. Her appeal to me is a constant 'you know what I mean, don't you agree', implied also in the language that we share. I am invited to be an ally, another German woman whose knowledgeable solidarity she seeks.

Transferentially though there is a complication. I am a German woman with cultural and linguistic access to both countries, and I have chosen to live in the UK, and even brought up children here. So maybe I do not agree with her position and that is confusing for her. It opens up another level of our interaction: can she imagine a maternal figure to be happy with her own choice and be happy for the 'daughter' to choose differently? Does she fear that we, therapist/mother and client/daughter, need to be the same or does the difference between us threaten either of us? This is, of course, a common theme for mothers and daughters, but it is my bicultural bilingualism that gives her both information and the potential for phantasies about my choices, which opens up this theme in a particular way.

> ### Ingrid
>
> Ingrid has been in the UK for about a year and seeks therapy for issues initially unrelated to being here. However, her dislike of being in this country is obvious from the beginning and increasingly forms part of our conversations. Ingrid finds the UK and the people who live here strange and a constant source of amusement. She describes her observations to me, inviting me to share some kind of superior joke at their expense. Whether it is health and safety regulations or the way some bathrooms have no mixer taps, it is all a source of mirth and much shaking of the head for Ingrid. While she is clearly lonely and a lot of her posturing is obviously a way of covering up her own difficulties in making social contacts, I find myself struggling to feel for her and my level of anger with her alerts me to something else. While, on one level, there is the invitation for me to join her in laughing at these 'weird' people that we are both supposed to be somehow superior to, there is the fact that, on another level, she knows I have chosen to live here. Indeed, my surname reveals that I am probably married to an Englishman. This allows her to attack mercilessly something that might be dear to me without her having to admit it. I must have liked it here, I must have succeeded here, I must have managed something that eludes her here (and, as we both know, eluded her in Germany, too) and she enviously attacks that. This happens in one language only, in German, so my English language and English identity do not ever need to be acknowledged by her. I have to bring them into the room to open up the conversation around envy and attack.

With both these clients the issue is not only bilingualism, though cross-references between both languages occur. Here, the questions of social, linguistic and emotional access to the culture of both countries are the main focus: the reality of it and the phantasy of it. This gives us a transferential matrix that would not be available if I was a monocultural, monolingual therapist to whom they tell their story. The chance to speak their mother tongue with me may allow them to access a different kind of 'earlier' emotionality, but our bilingual and bicultural experience allows us both to access subtle emotional conflicts regarding their current adult lives, which may then, in turn, lead them to access more infantile and raw emotions. Both Brigitte's fear and confusion around being different from her mother and Ingrid's envy go back to something well before their experience of living in this country, but it becomes visible and active through the transferential reaction to me in the context created by bilingualism and biculturalism.

There is another group of clients, often resident in the UK for longer, who rarely use any German in their therapy with me, although they have chosen me as a therapist knowing that I also speak their first language. They are firmly embedded in an English-speaking social context of friends and family. They do not see themselves as temporary visitors to the UK, but regard the UK as their home. Their English is excellent and often by the time they see me it is their stronger and more active language. Yet they have chosen me as their therapist. There tends to be a stronger identification with me as a German person who, like them, made a decision to stay in this country, and this plus the question of what, if anything, their German identity still means figures highly in these therapies. Here the use of language becomes more complicated.

Barbara

Barbara came to this country in her early twenties, escaping a culturally complicated upbringing in Bavaria. She grew up in a small Catholic village which, every winter, would turn from being a rather narrow and traditional area into a cosmopolitan ski resort. Her father was a mountain guard and, as such, had some rather exotic status with the tourists with whom he would socialize in the winter months, sometimes taking his young daughter with him. Her memories of her childhood paint a picture of parents who were preoccupied with their troubled marriage, and describe a contrasting mixture of narrow Catholic rural values and unbounded sexual behaviour, mirroring the village-to-ski-resort transformation. Barbara's experience of a lack of safe parental care left her with little experience of good parenting and mothering in her mother tongue. She came into therapy having suffered from postnatal depression and was seriously concerned about her capacity to mother her young children. Barbara's husband is English and they speak only English with the children. She has never felt like using her mother tongue for mothering them. She thinks of 'teaching' them German, but the language is not part of her emotional maternal repertoire (or, rather, she does not want it to be). In therapy we talk about this. I also note a slow emergence of German phrases, and there is repeatedly surprised pleasure in her reaction to me using an unprompted German phrase, as if German is newly discovered not only as a language that can touch her adult experience, but also as a language that is associated with a mother/therapist.

Transferentially, I move between this mother/therapist role and that of a role model or potential mirror image of her: the adult who lives in this country, a mother herself, but whose relationship with her language and country of origin is intriguing.

We talk about her ambivalence towards the German language. In one session, she brings me a letter her father has written to her. She recounts whole sections in German but keeps repeating "I don't know what he means by that". Having spent much of her childhood in confusion about what her parents were up to and where she figured for them, their communications now are either bewildering or irritating and the German language is associated with this. Angrily, she declares she does not know what it means. She experiences her father's language as stilted and self-important (*gestelzt*) and both parents are associated with German phrases such as *Hochmut kommt vor dem Fall* (pride comes before the fall), *Zugereiste* (newcomers), *Studierte* (people who went to university); all hostile to any attempt to expand the both narrow and chaotic world of the Bavarian village/ski resort. In one session, she says she needed a new country and a new language to develop a new mind. When she starts using more German language towards the end of her therapy, it feels both like a cautious remembering and an exploration of words that are nearly new. In one of the last sessions, she describes herself as beginning to be at least *grosszuegig in Gedanken* (generous in thoughts) and later she says she has discovered the capacity to be *liebevoll* (loving, literally full of love) towards her children. Feeling *liebevoll* is new, and yet described in the 'old' language. It is less a going back to a mother tongue, but more a remembering and re-exploring of it.

Barbara is, thus, an example of a more complicated relationship with the language of her childhood. In her case, L2 is experienced as liberating, giving her the chance to "develop a new mind", a mind that that has a chance to understand what others and their words and actions 'mean', a mind that knows and can create boundaries. Two points are of particular interest here. First, Barbara already had a strong bicultural experience as a child (Bavarian Catholic village compared with cosmopolitan ski resort), conducted in one language, yet imposing very different values, communication styles and behaviours on her as an observing child. Her 'new' mind allows her a choice that she did not have then. Second, having her own children activates early infantile conflicts. Here, the new mind and the new language seem to offer a safer space, as the original linguistic and emotional messages are frightening and confusing. Barbara uses the second language (and culture) to give herself a chance to re-approach something rather dangerous more safely. To do so together with a bilingual therapist provides something of a bridge between 'old' and 'new' mind through which she can experience being *liebevoll* in a way that was possibly too risky before.

Cornelia

Currently I am working with another German client whose therapy offers me some observations regarding the nature of the 'translation' process and its emotional function.

Cornelia has only lived in this country for two years, her English is excellent, and she chooses to speak in English during her sessions.

On the rare occasions that Cornelia spontaneously uses German, she does something unusual: she will use the German expression or phrase and then immediately translate it into English. That gives me an unusual insight into what she does in the translation and how she may subtly change what she tells me in the process. A powerful example occurred when she tried to describe how her mother, who has a drink problem, and may, when drunk, but also when sober, say something potentially hurtful or upsetting to her daughter without seemingly to consider the impact of what she says. Cornelia has started to confront her mother when that happens. At that point her mother will say: "Never mind, I'll hoover it up". Cornelia then gives me the original German phrase *"ich saug es wieder auf"*.

Both phrases imply the same assumption, which is that you can say something and not bother to worry about the consequences, that you can spill something and it does not matter because you can clean it up again without suffering repercussions. Yet, there is also a cleaning-up process going on in the translation itself from German to English: 'Hoovering' something up is indeed a translation for *aufsaugen*, but *aufsaugen* has a much more powerful additional layer to it. *Aufsaugen* literally means 'sucking something up'. There is a hint in this word of something oral, as if mother's words that need to be sucked back up are like some verbal vomit. There is a dimension of disgust, loss of control, something about body boundaries, that gets lost in the translation into English. Cornelia makes it get lost in her English phrase and then lets me know what she has done in adding the original German phrase, all of it unconsciously, and all of it only possible as a communication to a German therapist who may hear what she actually said.

Cornelia's communication has alerted me to something that also appears in other material: there is a concern about bodily boundaries that may not be able to contain a mess that constantly threatens to spill out. Whether it is actual bodily processes (putting on weight, bodily hair, her own unruly hair, all of them needing to be controlled in a constant grooming process) or her talking about them (what is one allowed to talk about without shocking people) or her generally talking too much. 'Things that come out of my mouth' are expected to put people off or disgust them; they are a subject of constant monitoring followed by worrying about their effect. Can they be cleaned up again or not? Here, the experience of mother and experience of self merge in a way that is disturbing to Cornelia. The degree of its disturbance is most visible to me in the brief moment of translation: it points me in a direction and opens up a line of exploration and conversation for us.

Cornelia, like Barbara, experiences the English language and culture as liberating. She is aware of the subtly different rules regarding self-disclosure and prefers the English rules that allow her different boundaries and a larger register of distancing herself from the intensity of self-disclosure via humour. She feels relief at British approval of this kind of humour, just as she likes social small talk, which she sees as asking participants of an interaction to make an effort to minimize the intensity of dissonance and discomfort when contact between participants is not entirely successful. While she is anxious that she may be 'spilling' when following German rules, she is grateful for experiences of 'containing' distancing devices in English. All this I see as an intercultural–interlingual reactivation of the mother–daughter experience around spilling and containment. The German word *Annaeherungsversuch*, meaning the attempt to come close, being experienced with a tinge of something negative and unpleasant, is used by her both in regard to mother and others' intrusive self-disclosure. The English language, through its perceived potential for distancing, allows her a pause in which she and her mother can have separate minds.

Being judged is always a possibility for Cornelia. Being a linguistically and culturally competent outsider/insider in the host culture carries both the pressure, on the one hand, of having to find out how to fit in, and, on the other hand, having freedom from judgement: when I use the word *Narrenfreiheit* (freedom of the fool) she laughs.

Like Barbara, Cornelia finds that L2 and its culture allow her to approach deep conflicts which were present in her culture of origin, but which are reactivated in a different format in the new bicultural and bilingual situation in which she finds herself. In her childhood, Cornelia travelled between two markedly different social cultures in Germany, with transitions being uncomfortable, offering plenty of potential for confused identity, being judged and ridiculed, and not being clear which social group she belonged to by right. This was already superimposed on a mother–daughter relationship where being the same and being different were complicated states. To have a separate identity that allows for distancing for her is not a question of 'intellectualizing detachment', but rather a question of emotionally intact identity.

So, Cornelia provides the clearest example of the double-edged function of L2 use: it does allow for detachment and an emotional 'cleaning up' and, as such, may limit what she can access or chooses to access in her therapy with me. On the other hand, her use of L2 also allows her a separate space in which to think and process a way of relating in her mother tongue that has been characterized by spilling, lack of boundaries and an unhealthy lack of separateness. Her switching between languages gives a sense of what that state may be like, but the space to approach it emotionally and cognitively is facilitated by the option of the second language.

Summary and discussion

There is evidence from case studies and experimental studies supporting the view that use of L2 in therapy leads to intellectualizing detachment and L1 use leads to deeper emotional recall and re-experience. In the case studies discussed here, there is indeed the dimension of L1 providing access to deep levels of emotional experience and detail of recall, as demonstrated particularly by Cornelia. There is also supporting evidence for the idea suggested in the literature that the use of L2 may allow safer 'entry levels' to therapy, both in my own experience of therapy and the fact that all clients discussed increase their level of L1 use when the therapeutic engagement has deepened towards the later stages of therapy.

However, this alone does not seem to capture the richness of the dynamics involved in the choices made by the clients described above when using either language in therapy. Bilingualism in both therapist and client does more than just provide two different linguistic registers for the therapeutic dialogue. It provides the client with the kind of information about their therapist that can lead to rich layers of phantasies about their therapist and their own relationship with them. Questions such as how much difference can be tolerated and/or is necessary between mothers and daughters, intergenerational trauma, envy, spilling and boundaries are likely to have figured in the therapies described above, with or without the additional factor of bilingualism. However, bilingualism provided a particular kind of access to it. All these clients' choice of language is clearly mapped on to deeper layers of psychic conflict which become visible in the bilingual and bicultural field in which they operate with their therapist, who can take up a number of positions in this dynamic, as demonstrated in the transferential differences and shifts in the case studies. As such, these choices are very much part of the unconscious dynamic, rather than the result of a conscious choice. Paying attention to them in the transference allowed therapist and client to get hold of an additional layer of meaning that enriched the therapeutic process.

For all of these clients, the detachment effect of L2, far from being only *defensive*, allows them a *creative* detachment that makes it possible to *think* about themselves and those inner conflicts. It reminds me of Britton's (1998) use of the idea of internal triangulation, which he sees as the result of a successful working through of the Oedipus conflict. Triangulation refers to the ability to look at ourselves from the outside and for entertaining another point of view while maintaining our own. It allows for a mental 'third position', to be both insider and outsider at the same time. In psychoanalytic language, triangulation interrupts essential egocentricity, allows space for thinking about self, and for the holding of ambiguity. This has intriguing similarities to what bilinguals have reported about their bilingual and bicultural experience (Burck, 2005; Hoffmann, 1989; Pavlenko, 2005), always knowing that their experience of themselves and the world around them is not the only option, but that there are other possible ways of experiencing, interpreting and responding. Hoffman actually uses the word 'triangulation', describing it as a process in which there is an awareness that "I am here… but nothing here has to be the way it is… there is another place – another point at the base of the triangle, which renders this place relative, which locates me within that relativity' (Hoffmann, 1989: 170).

Bilingualism and the linguistically mediated experience of another culture may contribute to an experience of self and the world where "I have learned the relativity of meaning on my skin, [and therefore]… can never take any one set of meanings as final" (Hoffmann, 1989: 275).

From a psychoanalytic point of view, bilingualism and cross-culturalism could, thus, be seen as part of a wider process in which the individual increasingly adopts a position which could be described both in terms of an observing ego, and in terms of Britton's (1998) working through of the Oedipal position as a specific kind of internal triangulation which facilitates the capacity to think and to hold ambiguity. Conceptualized like this, bilingual clients with their access to two different sets of linguistic and emotional ways of processing their experiences make use of this kind of triangulation in therapy. It allows them a distance that can be used defensively, and something will indeed get *lost* in translation. However, this very distance may also allow them to create a space for thought in which they can access internal conflicts through the linguistic and transferential matrix created in their therapy with a bilingual therapist: something valuable is *gained* in translation.

Notes

1 All clinical examples in this paper are of therapist–client encounters where German is L1 and English L2. This brings with it specific cultural and linguistic implications which may not be relevant for speakers of other languages. An exploration of this question was felt to go beyond the scope of this chapter.
2 This raises questions regarding the psychology of exile which, given the scope of this paper, has not been explored further here. For references, see Harlem (2010), Ainshie et al. (2004) and Grinberg and Grinberg (1984).
3 For examples of the growing literature on second-generation Germans' processing of intergenerational issues, see Hardtmann (1998) and Schaumann (2008).

References

Ainshie, R. C., Tummala-Narra, P., Harlem, A., Barbanel, L. & Ruth, R. (2004) Psychoanalytic views on the experience of immigration, *Psychoanalytic Psychology* 30: 663–679.
Altarriba, J. (2002) Bilingualism: Language, memory and applied issues, *Online Readings in Psychology and Culture* 4(2).
Altarriba, J. (2006) Cognitive approaches to the study of emotion-laden and emotion words in monolingual and bilingual memory, in: A, Pavlenko (Ed.), *Bilingual Minds. Emotional Experience, Expression and Representation*. Bristol: Multilingual Matters.
Altarriba, J. (2010) The influence of emotional arousal on affective priming in monolingual and bilingual speakers, *Journal of Multilingual and Multicultural Development* 25: 248–265.
Aragno, A. & Schlachet, P. J. (1996) Accessibility of early experience through the language of origin: A theoretical integration, *Psychoanalytic Psychology* 13: 23–34.
Britton, R. (1998) *Belief and Imagination. Explorations in Psychoanalysis*. London: Routledge.
Burck, C. (2005) *Multilingual Living. Explorations of Language and Subjectivity*. New York: Palgrave Macmillan.
Burck, C. (2011) Living in several languages: Language, gender and identities, *European Journal of Women's Studies* 18: 361–378.

Buxbaum, E. (1949) The role of the second language in the formation of ego and super-ego, *Psychoanalytic Quarterly* 18: 279–289.
Dewaele, J.-M. (2006) Expressing anger in multiple languages, in: A. Pavlenko (Ed.), *Bilingual Minds. Emotional Expression, Experience and Representation*. Bristol: Multilingual Matters.
Dewaele, J.-M. (2010) *Emotions in Multiple Languages*. Basingstoke: Palgrave-Macmillan.
Flegenheimer, F. A. (1989) Languages and psychoanalysis. The polyglot patient and the polyglot analyst, *International Review of Psychoanalysis* 16: 377–383.
Foster, R. P. (1992) Psychoanalysis and the bilingual patient: Some observations on the influence of language choice on the transference, *Psychoanalytic Psychology* 9: 61–76.
Foster, R. P. (1996) The bilingual self: Duet in two voices, *Psychoanalytic Dialogues* 6: 99–121.
Freud, S. & Breuer, J. (1895) Studies on hysteria. *SE:* 2. London: Hogarth Press (1955).
Greenson, R.R. (1950) The mother tongue and the mother, *International Journal of Psychoanalysis* 31: 18–23.
Grinberg, L. & Grinberg, R. (1984) Psychoanalytic perspectives on migration and exile, *Journal of the American Psychoanalytic Association* 32: 13–84.
Hardtmann, G. (1998) Children of the Nazis: A psychodynamic perspective, in: J. Danieli (Ed.), *International Handbook of Multigenerational Legacies of Trauma*. New York: Plenum Press.
Harlem, A. (2010) Exile as a dissociative state: When a self is 'lost in transit', *Psychoanalytic Psychology* 27: 460–474.
Harris, C. L. (2010) Bilingual speakers in the lab: Psychophysiological measures of emotional reactivity, *Journal of Multilingual and Multicultural Development* 25: 223–247.
Harris, C. L., Berko Gleason, J. & Ayçiçeg˘i, A. (2006) When is a first language more emotional? Psychophysiological evidence from bilingual speakers, in: A. Pavlenko (Ed.), *Bilingual Minds. Emotional Experience, Expression and Presentation*. Bristol: Multilingual Matters.
Hoffmann, E. (1989) *Lost in Translation*. London: Vintage Books.
Javier, R. A. (1989) Linguistic considerations in the treatment of bilinguals, *Psychoanalytic Psychology* 6: 87–96.
Javier, R. A. (1995) Vicissitudes of autobiographical memories in a bilingual analysis, *Psychoanalytic Psychology* 12: 429–438.
Kellman, S. (2003) *Switching Languages: Translingual Writers Reflect on their Craft*. Lincoln, NE: University of Nebraska Press.
Kinginger, C. (2010) Bilingualism and emotion in the autobiographical works of Nancy Huston, *Journal of Multilingual and Multicultural Development* 25: 159–178.
Marcos, L. R. (1976) Bilinguals in psychotherapy: Language as emotional barrier, *American Journal of Psychotherapy* 30: 552–560.
Marcos, L. R., Eisma, J. E. & Guimon, J. (1977) Bilingualism and sense of self, *American Journal of Psychoanalysis* 37: 285–290.
Marian, V. & Kaushanskaya, M. (2004) Self-construal and emotion in bicultural bilinguals, *Journal of Memory and Language* 51: 190–201.
Marian, V. & Neisser, U. (2000) Language dependant recall of autobiographical memories, *Journal of Experimental Psychology: General* 129: 361–368.
Mohavedi, S. (1996) Metalinguistic analysis of therapeutic discourse: Flight into a second language when the analyst and the analysand are multilingual, *Journal of the American Psychoanalytic Association* 44: 837–862.
Oejeman, G. A. (1991) Cortical organisation of language, *Journal of Neuroscience* 11: 2281–2287.

Paradis, A. (1994) Neurolinguistic aspects of implicit and explicit memory. Implications for bilingualism and SLA, in: N. Ellis (Ed.), *Implicit and Explicit Learning of Languages*. San Diego, CA: Academic Press.
Pavlenko, A. (2005) *Emotions and Multilingualism*. New York: Cambridge University Press.
Pavlenko, A. (Ed.) (2006) *Bilingual Minds. Emotional Experience, Expression and Presentation*. Bristol: Multilingual Matters.
Rozensky, R. H. & Gomez, M. Y. (1983) Language switching in psychotherapy with bilinguals: Two problems, two models and case examples, *Psychotherapy: Theory, Research and Practice* 20: 152–160.
Schaumann, C. (2008) *Memory Matters: Generational Responses to Germany's Nazi Past in Recent Women's Literature*. Berlin: Walter de Gruyter.
Schrauf, R. W. (2003) A protocol analysis of retrieval in bilingual autobiographical memory, *International Journal of Bilingualism* 7: 235–256.
Schrauf, R. W. (2006) Bilingual autobiographical memory and emotion: Theory and method, in: A. Pavlenko (Ed.), *Bilingual Minds. Emotional Experience, Expression and Representation*. Bristol: Multilingual Matters.
Wierzbicka, A. (2004) Preface: Bilingual lives, bilingual experience, *Journal of Multilingual and Multicultural Development* 25: 94–104.
Y Del Rio, V. B. (1982) Peculiarities of psychoanalytic treatment in a bicultural bilingual situation, *Journal of the American Academy of Psychoanalysis* 10: 173–193.

PART VI
Migration

19

"SO THEY WALKED BEHIND THEIR WORDS"

Language and sense of self in the migration process

Gisela Zeller-Steinbrich

Introduction

In her novel, *Die Brücke vom Goldenen Horn* Emine Sevgi Özdamar describes the experience of a young Turkish immigrant in the Berlin of the 1960s when the first generation of foreign workers, so-called guest workers, came to Germany. Özdamar herself was an immigrant as a young woman and, like her protagonist in this novel, she did not know the language when she came to Germany. In spite of this, she writes in German and she has been awarded many important prizes, such as the Ingeborg-Bachmann-Preis, Heinrich-von-Kleist-Preis, and International Book of the Year by the *London Times Literary Supplement*.

The quote that follows describes how the newly arrived Turkish migrant workers used their native language to create a space in the streets of German-speaking Berlin "as if their way would be cleared by their loud voices, as if they were following their words" (Özdamar, 2011: 44, translated for this edition) and thus ease their walking through cold and snowy Berlin and make the streets more familiar. The words of the native language in a way formed a swathe and a trail in the jungle of the new city and the foreign culture:

> When they crossed a street, they did not cross it to get to another street, but because their loud words in the air preceded them. So they walked behind their words and for people who did not understand these words, they looked as if they went with their donkeys or turkeys through another country. The men came behind their words up to the Turkish Workers' Association; there they smoked and drank tea.
>
> *(Özdamar, 2011: 44, translated for this edition)*

Özdamar intuitively shows how the use of a language creates a verbal world (*Sprachraum*). This can be hermetical, as suggested in her novel where loneliness is only softened by the shelter of the group, which reminds them of a lost familiarity and unreachable homeland: a group formed out of urgent necessity, each member refraining from personal individual identity.[1]

The linguistic space can protect like a shield, can be even hermetical, closed in, as shown by Özdamar with her group of Turkish workers. But I would like to show that it also can be a transitional space and, thus, overcome the trauma of Babel.

The painter Giorgio de Chirico grew up as a child of Italian immigrants to Greece. His father died when he was 17. At 18, de Chirico emigrated, lived in Munich, Paris, New York and finally in Italy. For all of his life, he depicted the famous Italian squares. Krystal (1966) saw this as a symbolic restoration of the Italian homeland: de Chirico would visualise and keep alive the maternal environment, his motherland, in his paintings. Apart from that, in a few of his paintings I noticed a tiny something that could have more to do with de Chirico's father, who worked as a railway engineer: a small or partly hidden steam engine, naïve, as a child would paint it, with proud and phallic clouds of steam, as if a former shared experience with the father of his childhood was symbolized in the little train literally off the rails and sometimes glimpsed from behind the buildings. I would like to understand this artistical 'derailment' as an attempt to come to terms with, and to integrate, his childhood experience and biographical ruptures in his work, turning sadness and loss into a creative act.

Now we can ask whether language in the context of migration can take on a role similar to the squares and the train motif in de Chirico's paintings and what are the psychological conditions for this creative power or the risks of failure. To make this more clear, I have to point out the emotional implications of language development.[2]

Language development, emotional development, identity: we feel according to how we are verbally addressed

In the developmental process, language acquisition and identity construction are deeply connected.

Foundations for the development of semantics, syntax and the use of symbols are formed well before the age of 18 months and prior to the acquisition of two-word sentences. Vocal utterances, intonation, inflection and tone of speech form a first placeholder, a format (Bruner, 1987: 59) that is gradually filled with linguistic meaning. The sound of a sentence, the audio track, so to speak, can be repeated before the comprehension of content. It forms the framework through which the child learns to speak. Along with this, the child's self-image, the perception of who one is and what others intend and think develops (Zeller-Steinbrich, 2011).

Language development, as well as personal development, are based on the interpersonal experiences of early childhood. To point to something is the precursor of naming. Words develop from the pre-verbal, phonetical sounds and pointing gestures, which the child can share with the mother or another person. That means, without shared attention, a foreign language cannot be learned. The crucial point is, psychic and interpersonal experience must be linguistically shared and communicated. Merely sitting in front of a television set cannot achieve that.

Languages differ semantically. Things can be expressed in one language, but not in the other: "I would rather have given birth to a stone", a Turkish mother said, and thus expressed in her metaphorical language her rejection of the child, but, at the same time, also the unconscious reason for this rejection: the almost unbearable liveliness of the child. Speaking may contain the entire relationship and the self-experience of the person addressed: "Please say Betty to me once more", a 17-year-old girl asked me, "you say that in a way…" She felt that everything she was and had become through therapy was contained in her name if spoken by her analyst. And when I met her again 15 years later as a young mother, she said: "The Betty I am did not exist before my psychotherapy as an adolescent".

Language is context- and situation-bound. Contexts are different depending on the culture and the people involved. The ideas are different from one language to another: thinking is sticking to the language, and so do emotions and unconscious content (Zeller-Steinbrich, 2011). The emotional content of speech, prosodic elements, intonation and vocal tone, pre-verbal expression and forms of interaction play a decisive role (Buchholz, 2011). Verbal situations involve speaking and persons acting as well as exchanged affects. The sound itself is saturated with meaning. It carries inescapable affective messages, it shapes our conscious and unconscious experience. The image of ourselves that others have, will be expressed last, but not least, in the tone and melody in which they speak to us.

In his novel *Anna Karenina* Tolstoy describes in a subtle way how the attitude conveyed by the tone of voice can be at odds with the sense of self of the person so addressed and, thus, can lead to a false self through adaptation to an environment which does not satisfy the true feelings and needs.

Little Seryozha is looking forward to a joyful verbal exchange when his father comes home from work. He wants to tell a funny story to him, but first asks whether the father takes pleasure in his new award. The reaction of the father is an agonizingly long sermon.

> Seryozha's eyes lost their sparkle of tenderness and gaiety and shut down under the gaze of the Father. It was that old familiar voice and tone the father always struck with him and Seryozha had already learned to imitate it. Seryozha felt his father would always speak with him as if he had turned into a boy whom father had thought up, a boy like those who were featured in books, but whom Seryozha did not resemble. And with his father, Seryozha always tried to behave as if he were such a boy from a book.
>
> "You understand this, I hope?" said the father.
>
> "Yes, Papa", Seryozha answered, in the tone of the thought-up boy.[3]
>
> *(Tolstoy, 1885, translated for this edition)*

Tolstoy describes masterfully how the tone conveys information about the relationship and tells how the father sees the child and how the child perceives in the tone how he should be, alien to his nature – although he also feels clearly that this is not true: "He was nine years old. He was a child; but he knew his own soul (...)" (Tolstoy, 1885: 795). Seryozha, in his true nature, is a stranger in the father's family and is expected to assimilate.

Language is calming and supporting, an envelope of sound

When babies are born, they already recognize their mother's voice and language and are able to distinguish it from other people's voices. They also distinguish the sound patterns of their native language from that of other languages. In complex perinatal changes there is something which remains the same: the characteristic rhythm, the sound sequence and the intonation in which the primary objects speak. A young father told me about his premature baby in the incubator, separated from the mother. He then anxiously asked if it would be better not to talk to the newborn because the baby began to fidget when the father spoke to her. This baby literally was moved by the voice and the special tone of the father that she recognized.

Agi Mishol, the Hungarian-born Israeli writer, describes the feeling of wellbeing with her native language: "*Pour moi, l'Hongrois c'est comme le lait maternel*"[4] (Aviv, 2004).[5] Similarly, Wormhoudt wrote in 1949 that words would unconsciously be equated with milk (Wormhoudt, 1949, cited in Anzieu, 2003: 13). He is refering to the nurturing, soothing and calming effect speaking can have. But generally, and above all in the first few months before and after birth, it is not the word in its not yet available significance, but the sound of words and sentences and the emotional message transported. Carers who are good enough emotionally talk to their babies long before they develop an understanding of language. They let their infants bathe in sounds for long periods of their time awake. In developing his concept of the *skin-self* (*moi-peau*), Anzieu shows that this "sound envelope of the self" in the first months of life is constitutive for self-development.

> Moreover, as a result of the experience of the 'sound bath' the self emerges as an envelope of sound (...) This bath of sound pre-figures the skin-self with one half of its double face turned to the inside and the other half to the outside.
>
> *(Anzieu, 1979: 29)*

Anzieu completes the interpretation of the fable of Narcissus and its mirror metaphor with the acoustic element of the reflection from this fable: the nymph Echo, who is responding and 'mirroring' by repeating what she hears. According to Anzieu this "sound mirror" of the mother may be insufficient in three ways:

- dissonant when it is not in synchronization with what the child expects, feels or expresses,

- abruptly, that is, either insufficient or excessive, going from one extreme to another, arbitrary and incomprehensible for the child, and ultimately
- impersonal, because there will not be any information about what the child probably feels or how the mother thinks about the child.

The sound mirror and visual mirror, therefore, are only structure-building for the self and the ego if the mother expresses to the child something of herself or of the child in an emotionally coloured way: according to Anzieu, something about pleasure or pain as the primary mental qualities of the early self (Anzieu, 1979: 32). It's all about the emotionally loaded early language in its proximity to the emotions, and, thus, to the bodily functions.[6]

Mother tongue and its sound is experienced as a lasting fascination; this is, as far as I can tell, because of its special capacity to hold and express emotions. We slip into the mother tongue in situations of overwhelming emotion.[7]

The special sound of the mother tongue forms a container for emotional experiences and, as such, is the envelope, the shell, of one's early identity. In the native language, all can be included, which initially, in the course of development, was associated with oneself: self-experience and the perspective of the others speaking in this language with the child. The sound of the mother tongue contains the previous experience of identity, the sum of all experiences of self with others in the processing by the affective particularities and defence needs of the child.

The resistance to talking in the language of the new homeland can, thus, be a self-conserving, protecting refusal to speak 'like parrots' drained of emotion and estranged from oneself (Evgeniya Dodina, in Aviv, 2004).

If the children of immigrants do speak the language of their new homeland, which entails liberation and detachment from parental attributions, then the desire to be at home in the new culture, like all their peers, means slipping into a new skin by means of language. But this linguistic moulting means also a rupture in respect of early emotional experience and relations, a loss and a certain vulnerability. With the new language, in each case a new culture is being filtered down to the migrant. The new language, channelling the way of thinking, can, therefore, be perceived as dictatorial. This includes the risk of self-estrangement.

The Separation function of language

Alienation from one's own experience is immanent to every process of language acquisition, when the all-embracing preverbal contents must be expanded to verbal communication.

> But in fact the language (...) also makes some parts of our experience less shareable with others. It drives a wedge between two simultaneous forms of interpersonal experience: as it is lived and as it is verbally represented.

> Experience in the domains of emerging, core- and intersubjective relatedness, which continue irrespective of language, can be embraced only very partially in the domain of verbal relatedness. And to the extent that events in the domain of verbal relatedness are held to be what has really happened, experiences in these other domains suffer an alienation. (They can become the nether domains of experience.) Language then causes a split in the experience of the self. It also moves relatedness onto the impersonal abstract level intrinsic to language and away from the personal, immediate level intrinsic to the other domains of relatedness.
>
> *(Stern, 1985: 162 f.)*

On the other hand, with the emergence of symbolic language, the space that can be shared with others expands enormously. One can speak of past and future as well as of the absent, not merely of immediate experience. Language is now organizing experience – and experience can be integrated mentally through language and also be constructed through language. Being able to speak means to be independent. But, at the same time, especially when not connected with emotional content, language can be felt as a cold, abstract system of rules.

For migrants, the containing quality of mother tongue can be missing before leaving the native country or else lost through migration: As the poet Aharon Appelfeld says: "J'avais tants de langues, mais ils suffisaient pas à communiquer". He missed the language of the body, "la langue du corps" (Aviv, 2004). As I understand it, he meant the emotionally charged primary language. That is why a person who loses his mother tongue, would be 'disabled' all his life. "The second generation begins at a point of amnesia, if the original language, the language of the heart, is missing" (Haviva Pedaia, in Aviv, 2004).

Adam's mother comes from South America. They live in Germany with his German father. Due to the defence against traumatic experiences, Adam's mother cannot talk about her origins. And she never speaks in her mother tongue to Adam. When his therapist asked him about his multinational origin, Adam only said, depressed, nothing more than: "I'm half".

Together with the language experiences, experiences that took place not only in different times and countries, but also in different language zones are suppressed. The split in the experience of the self (through traumatisation in this case) is reinforced through the change of the language. It leads to an emotional alienation between parent and child. The non-use of the mother tongue by Adam's mother may express her desire to leave experience behind and to assume a new identity, without integrating the old parts into her biographic memory. For Adam, this means that half of his history is missing and cannot be integrated. That is one of the reasons why he is feeling "half".

The transitional function of speaking and of language[8]

As if to compensate for those developmental difficulties, language has important integrating and connecting functions. In early development, as already shown, it helps to build the sound envelope. In the separation–individuation process, the development of language plays an important role in the resolution of the rapprochement phase (Mahler). With the acquisition of language, the child himself forms sounds, later he imitates the speech melody, and finally he produces words and small sentences. These first language productions are like the sensorimotor skills (Piaget). The pre-sleep monologues include word play or parts of nursery songs and rhymes as well as turn-taking question and answer elements. They start at about the age of eighteen months and tend to end close to three.

Here is an example of a half-dream soliloquy by two-year-old Anthony:

> Like it
> Don't like it
> Like it daddy
>
> What colour
> What colour blanket
> What colour mop
> What colour glass

(Weir, 1962, see also Edelheit, 1969: 388)

Before falling asleep, the child is lying in the dark and explores with sounds and noises. In those monologues, in one-word and two-word sentences language is practised and systematized, without any participation of adults. Linguists regard the pre-sleep monologues of the toddler as an opportunity for free practising his developing language capacities. And, indeed, we can find similar sentences in textbooks for foreign language training.

For sure, they are highly functional in terms of language acquisition, but these monologues, situated between inner speech and overt speech, also have an especially calming and self-soothing function. I also regard them as a possible device to manage the separated state, about which the child is concerned. In an earlier publication, I pointed out that language use can be understood in its transitional function (Zeller-Steinbrich, 2011). Vocalizations and words maintain a first acoustic and probably phantasmatic connection to those whom the child is missing. The voluntarily producible sound, whether as a reminiscence of mother's sound bath or as a language symbol or repetition of dialogues that have taken place, has a comforting and bridging function for the child. The spoken language is not an object, nor is the object replaced by the utterances. Talking helps the child to obtain the inner connection in the absence of the object, without denying the separation. The word takes an intermediate position between the subjectivity of the child and the objectivity of the carers, and, therefore, may be regarded as a transitional phenomenon, as Stern, in reference to John Dore, suggested (Stern, 1985: 245).

Multilinguals in the psychotherapeutic process

In a foreign language preconscious, access to further unconscious contents are limited. Associative links may remain blocked. Unconscious scenes can be integrated, most likely when considering the appropriate voice and sound world. In analytic treatments in foreign languages, a certain limit of understanding must be both processed and mourned.[9]

In the work with multilingual patients,[10] we must treat the question of how communication is possible when we do not have an equal command of a common language and, thus, do not have the usual, more immediate, emotional access. In addition, how the patient deals with these different languages in the session is significant. Language competence and language performance and the peculiarities of pronunciation, as ego capacities, are prone to neurotic conflicts[11] and are frequent with migrants.

Changing language in the session might be a key to unconscious material. If we look at the role of language for the development of the ego and superego (Freud, 1923), then we will understand the switch to a language acquired later in the course of therapy primarily as a defensive process and we will assume that the patient wards off anxiety-causing contents, which have to do with early relationships: for example, with a mother experienced as castrating and punitive (Krapf, 1955).

On the other hand, I very often experienced the change of language as an attempt by the patient to approach a subject that is located in a particular linguistic environment.

> One of my adult patients grew up bilingual, her mother tongue was French, later she learned German, during adolescence she had lived in the United States. Now she lived with her children and husband in a German-speaking part of Switzerland where her husband came from. With her family she mostly spoke Swiss-German dialect, her husband's mother tongue. With her husband, and in particular when they touched issues that came from adolescence and adulthood, she liked to talk in English, because in this language she was more at ease. Also, when she came into conflict with her partner, they disputed in English.
>
> In the sessions we mainly spoke German. If she was, however, moved, or when she remembered emotional scenes of her childhood, she changed into French. The French language (which I well understood) focused on the contents of experience from her early days and so far was matching with the subject. On the other hand, as an adolescent in the US, she had lost her father. The English language, as well as the couple conflicts, touched on her fear of loss, which sometimes she tried to ward off by switching into French, her native language. This could be interpreted as resistance by flight into the mother tongue.

A language can represent an important time, important experiences, central feelings that have been formed in this language; it can represent mainly the sense of self of that time. Language forms a safe or hostile, familiar or foreign world, a linguistically mediated cosmos, to which the appropriate language is a key. In speaking this language, these memories are evoked and, through associations, unconscious content of this period becomes accessible. I try to handle this as I would in child analysis, when a change from the talking level to the playing level occurs: analysis continues with the resources that are available.

In the chosen language, interpersonal and emotional experience are included as well as cultural norms, permitted satisfactions as well as expressions of the superego. What is allowed in one linguistic world can be a taboo in the other. There are key words to unconscious fantasies and memories which can only be reached in that specific language.[12]

> An analysand with Turkish roots, speaking perfect German, explained to me, using individual Turkish words which I did not understand, that it would have been so important to accept his gift at the beginning of therapy without talking about it or trying to understand the meaning. He had some psychoanalytic knowledge and explained to himself: "I know it is because of the abstinence". He submitted to the new, the psychoanalytic, 'culture', but nevertheless was very disappointed. Later, he confessed that he had experienced me as similar to his refusing mother, who, as a migrant worker, left him alone and gave him difficult tasks to support her, because she had to make money. He also experienced a *quasi* doctrinaire, highly demanding new environment in which any emotionally saturated experience had to be suppressed, as if I was not willing to get involved with his early satisfactory experience prior to migration. Instead of saying "I know, it is that abstinence", he could have said, "I know, it is now Switzerland". He experienced me as being inaccessible because I did not know and accept the customs or language of his country of origin. Using the Turkish words and stating there was no translation, he put *me* in the position of a stranger in *his* world. It took a long time to understand the irreconcilable differences of culture and to undergo a mourning process: I could not talk to him in his native language or be a gratifying mother to him or understand him completely, even though he, as I mentioned, was perfectly able to speak my language. Occasionally, I encouraged him to speak Turkish when it seemed important to me. He then had to proceed as he did at home with his parents, who were not able to speak the language of the new country and had to rely on their son's translation work.

Svetlana Geier, the translator, once said about her career choice: "I was interested in (...) what happens when you are pouring from one vessel to another and, in fact from the very beginning, what is lost in this process" (Geier, 2009: 135, translated for this edition).

What was lost between Turkish and German, the patient mentioned above tried to reveal with photographs. In this way, the atmosphere which would have opened up by speaking the native language could be partly visually evoked. His language of culture was German, but in the Turkish mother tongue essential identity contents were stored from the first years of childhood, and by no means could be translated thoroughly.

In everyday life my patient exclusively spoke German like a native speaker. Later in his analysis he told me that he had begun to speak Turkish words to his baby daughter and that she would beam and be delighted by her dad whenever he did so. In this way, he told me something of what his native language meant to him.

Transmission from one language to another, from one world to the other, constitutes an ultimate impossibility, "yet is the challenge of life" (Daniel Epstein in Aviv, 2004, translated for this edition).

Identity seeking: too much to handle?

Immigrant children who are not involved in loyalty conflicts with their parents usually tend to learn the language of the new environment as quickly as possible. They are often used by their parents as translators. In addition to being proud of these skills, we can find here also that they are overwhelmed by feelings of insufficiency and have a deep fear of making irreparable mistakes, for example, in contact with the head of a city office. Aris Fioretus, the Swedish writer of Greek and Austrian extraction, was only four or five years old when his father gave him his lectures on medicine for correction.

These apparently excessive demands are rarely overlooked. Less obvious might be that multilingualism from early on is a strain on the synthesizing function of the ego, it might impair self-development and the capacity of affect regulation and mentalization. Effects on the development of integrated self and object representations or a premature individuation may occur; identity conflicts are more likely and require creative solutions. If there is no appropriate symbolization capacity, migrants can even be caught in a pendulum movement, as happened to the writer Hamed Abdel-Samad. As a Muslim Arab, he felt seduced by the freedoms of the Western lifestyle and yet always returned to the Qur'an and the traditional religion of his father. The greater the attractiveness and the desire for the new freedoms, the more fervent the guilt-ridden return to the shelter of the Qur'an. This led to a fundamental split and finally to a mental breakdown.

For multilingual grown-up children, the linguistically mediated subjective experience and the experience of being with others and being seen takes place in different worlds from a very early age. With the linguistic understanding of the world, a number of different cultural contexts must be 'learned'. Without sufficient linguistic continuity, it will be more difficult for them to establish links between different fields of knowledge and identifications. The sense of "self with others" (Stern), the feeling of belonging to a connecting language community and, thus, being bonded with others may be reduced. Decreased transitional functions of language may lead to feelings of cosmic loneliness and to feelings of being forced to submit to an impersonal order.

As early as about three years of age, the autobiographical memory is established (Markowitsch & H.Welzer, 2005). It helps the children to feel homogenous with regard to past, present and future and to position themselves within these temporal zones. If the linguistic offer and the world of intersubjective relationship in which it is embedded is inconsistent, too, it is more likely that the memory of early relationship scenes will be disparate and intersubjective scenes stemming from another linguistic world will be split off, literally excommunicated. In a worst-case scenario, a person with very good language skills in several languages will experience herself as not having an 'own' language, like my patient Dina, who grew up with several languages. Her sense of self resembled the picture of de Chirico with split self- and object representations and the fear of disintegration. Feeling this more clearly through her analysis and feeling desperate, she once shouted at her parents: "You do not know at all how it is, when you cannot speak in your own language!" This meant, for her, having multiple language skills but no language that she experienced as her own, no language by which she had unifying access to her disparate experiences, acquired in different linguistic worlds, no language that contained her early sense of self and which could help with the task of developing a sufficiently integrated identity.

Nowadays, as the social and religious controls are loosened and a liberal civil society multiplies the individual choices, the experience of freedom can turn into feelings of overwork and fundamental uncertainty if a secure basic structure (basic trust, self-esteem) is missing. Children from migrant families are especially forced to choose and design or create their lives because they grow up in two cultures with different loyalty requirements and their corresponding conflicts. Each individual has to attempt a particular work of integration, which no longer is done by society. The risk to all of us is particularly true for them: the possibly excessive demands of endless individual choices and the "expansion of the social fabric" causing "social disembedding" of the psyche, which finds less security in itself and in the social environment (Garland, 2008: 284, cited in Dornes, 2010: 1021, translated for this edition). Their parents' dream of a better life for themselves and for their children can turn into the trauma of failed identity in the second generation (Luhmann, 1995).[13]

Learning the language and customs of the new homeland is crucial for migrants – as is linking back to the roots. Loyalties to the country of origin, to the mother or father tongue is an obstacle for the acquisition of the new language. A feeling of being a stranger in both languages may occur with a change in language at an early age (elementary school age and earlier), like my patient Dina. Children and adolescents then depend more than others on the emotional support of their families. There is emotional neediness and, on the other hand, they are ashamed about being different and speaking differently and about their wish for separation and assimilation to the new environment. Autonomy–dependency conflicts become more critical.

The split linguistic world – emotionally coloured mother tongue and the language of the (new) country and of one's peers – then may lead to sensitivity and to difficulties primarily in the capacity of affect regulation.

The emotionally charged mother tongue also can be felt as a barrier when detaching from the conflicted relations with the parents and building age-appropriate contacts with peers. In order to fully develop their language skills, they must adopt the new country and its language. And it is really like an adoption. Therefore, we should not demand unquestioned assimilation or leave newcomers open to the risk of becoming involved with extreme 'traditional' groups while searching for identification. Instead, it is necessary to become involved and help with their conflicts about keeping faith with the traditions. Those whose origin is despised, or seen as an issue, may try to fill this gap by defiantly identifying with extreme 'traditionalists'. Acknowledgement and esteem of the culture of homeland and roots could help migrants from developing an identity poker, as Abdel Samad (a German–Egyptian political scientist and writer) describes his own severe identity problems, or an intrapsychic, not only social, parallel world. Without this transcultural openness to the linguistically transmitted world of their ancestors, children of migrants can tend to over-identify with the old, and hand down a tradition from which their parents already had detached. This affects not only their social integration, but also the necessary cultural change in societies that adolescents generally stand for.

Only if there is psychic integration can the multilingual and multicultural background of migrants be a source of individual creative achievement and a driver for renewal and enrichment in society. Needless to say, traumatized adolescents and adults need special help with this difficult task.

Conclusion

Freud came as a child from Freiberg to Vienna. He probably missed his native landscape, the Freiberg mountains, in the same way as de Chirico missed his. As far as I know, he did not deal with migration explicitly. Later, in exile in England, after he was forced to flee from the Nazi terror in Austria, he increasingly dealt with his Jewish roots. He is quoted as saying: "Only now I'm really becoming a Jew". For Freud, separation processes were a central theme. In Freud's comments on the *Fort-Da* game of his grandson Ernst, he recognized the role of symbolization, the game *and* the language for the processing of the experience of loss experience (Freud, 1920).

If everything goes well, language can be the transitional space in which losses can be tolerated and processed. Then, language can take on the role of the small train that appears in some of de Chirico's paintings, keeping present what is lost and connecting disparate psychological and cultural worlds.

Notes

1 "Every self was attaching himself to the next self and thus made a plural. Only the material of their <u>trousers</u> or their cardigans were telling their ego-stories (…) only their different dialects were showing that they were born of different mothers" (Özdamar, 2011: 45, translated for this edition).
2 The following sections are based on Zeller-Steinbrich, 2011.
3 Tolstoy, *Anna Karenina*, German translation by R. Tietze, 2009: 792 f. Although there exist several translations of *Anna Karenina* in English, I did not find any that would come close to the highly estimated translation of Tietze, which expresses the aspect of intonation I am referring to.
4 "For me Hungarian is as mother's milk" (translated for this edition).
5 *D'une langue à l'autre*. 55-minute documentary film by Nurith Aviv (2004). Thanks to Andrea Hettlage, Basel, I became familiar with this film.
6 Being touched by the very early experiences of sound might be the key to the disturbing experience of Jews with German mother tongue living in Israel, when they find that they can communicate in a more immediate way and with deeper understanding in German than in Hebrew, although they are very well aware that this is also the language of the perpetrators of the Holocaust (Aviv, 2004).
7 The language of immigrant children sometimes seems very rough. In that respect, we should keep in mind that for all of us it is a lot easier to swear or to break a taboo in a foreign language because the new language is much more distant from our inner experience.
8 This section of the chapter is based on an earlier publication of mine (Zeller-Steinbrich, 2011).
9 When Julia Kristeva was looking for an analyst in Paris, she chose one who spoke French as a foreign language, like Kristeva herself (Kristeva, personal communication, Zagreb, 2014). She wanted to have equal prerequisites, she reported, a level playing field, "spears equally long", as the Swiss say. But how could this be, if both of their spears were shortened?
10 In the first part of the 20th century, analysis with migrants was often conducted in a second language, for example, in Israel or Argentina, where many people lived in exile and very often spoke several languages. Which language was chosen and how this was unconsciously determined was a topic of the analysts of that generation for practical reasons (see also Krapf, 1955).
11 "A person's relation to language is often predominantly governed by superego rules" (Buxbaum, 1949: 286).
12 If a patient speaks, dreams or plays with 'Fenster' in German, the association of 'fensterln' may appear (Buxbaum, 1949: 284). *Fensterln* means getting in through the window to the beloved's room at night. With English 'window(s)', we probably think about the technical and computer meaning and would not necessarily connect them with clandestine romantic and sexual adventures.
13 "Dream and trauma of freedom do unexpectedly blend" (Luhmann, 1995: 132, cited in Dornes, 2010: 1022).

References

Anzieu, D. (1976) Le moi-peau, *Nouvelle Revue de psychanalyse* 9: 195–208.
Anzieu, D. (1979) The sound image of the self, *International Review of Psycho-Analysis* 6: 23–36. [Originally published in French as: L'enveloppe sonore du soi, 1976, in *Nouvelle Revue de psychanalyse* 13: 161–179.]
Anzieu, D. (2003) Pour une psycholinguistique psychoanalytique. Bref bilan et questions préliminaires, in: D. Anzieu, B. Gibello, R. Gori et al. (Eds.), *Psychanalyse et langage. Du corps à la parole*. Paris: Dunod.

Aviv, N. (2004) *D'une langue à l'autre*. Documentary film, 55 minutes.
Bruner, J. (1987) *Wie das Kind sprechen lernt*. Bern: Hans Huber. English edition: *Child's Talk. Learning To Use Language*. New York: Norton, 1983.
Buchholz, M. B. (2011) Körper – Bild – Szene – Geste – Sprechen. Wie alles zwanglos auseinander hervorgeht. Analytische Kinder- und Jugendlichenpsychotherapie. Zeitschrift für Theorie und Praxis der Kinder- und Jugendlichen-Psychoanalyse. Analytical Child and Adolescent Psychotherapy. *Journal for Theory and Practice of Child and Adolescent Psychoanalysis and Psychodynamic Psychotherapy* 42: 7–34.
Buxbaum, E. (1949) The role of a second language in the formation of ego and superego, *Psychoanalytic Quarterly* 18: 279–289.
Dornes, M. (2010) Die Modernisierung der Seele, *Psyche – Z Psychoanalyse* 64: 995–1033.
Edelheit, H. (1969) Speech and psychic structure – the vocal–auditory organization of the ego, *Journal of the American Psychoanalytic Association* 17: 381–412.
Freud, S. (1920) Jenseits des Lustprinzips, *G.W.* Vol. 13, 3–69.
Freud, S. (1923) Das ich und das Es, *G.W.* Vol. 13, 237–289.
Garland, D. (2001) *The Culture of Control. Crime and Social Order in Contemporary Society*. [German edition (2008) *Kultur der Kontrolle*, A. Wirthensohn (Trans.). Frankfurt: Campus Verlag.] New York: Oxford University Press.
Geier, S. (2009) *Ein Leben zwischen den Sprachen. Russisch-deutsche Erinnerungsbilder* (2nd revised edn). Aufgez von T. Gut. Dornach: Pforte.
Krapf, E. E. (1955) The choice of language in polyglot psychoanalysis, *Psychoanalytic Quarterly* 24: 343–357.
Krystal, H. (1966) Giorgio de Chirico. Ego states and artistic production, *American Imago* 23: 210–226.
Luhmann, N. (1995) *Soziologische Aufklärung*. Bd. 6: *Die Soziologie und der Mensch*. Opladen: Westdeutscher Verlag.
Markowitsch, H. J. & Welzer, H. (2005) *Das autobiographische Gedächtnis. Hirnorganische Grundlagen und biosoziale Entwicklung*. Stuttgart: Klett-Cotta.
Özdamar, E. S. (2011) *Die Brücke vom Goldenen Horn*. Cologne: Kiepenheuer & Witsch.
Stern, D. (1985) *The Interpersonal World of the Infant. A View from Psychoanalysis and Developmental Psychology*. New York: Basic Books.
Tolstoy, L. (1885) *Anna Karenina*. Übersetzt und kommentiert von Rosemarie Tietze. Munich: Carl Hanser, 2009.
Weir, Ruth H. (1962) *Language in the Crib*. The Hague, the Netherlands: Mouton.
Zeller-Steinbrich, G. (2011) Mehrsprachigkeit und emotionale Entwicklung zwischen Weltbürgertum und sprachlicher Heimatlosigkeit. Analytische Kinder- und Jugendlichenpsychotherapie, *Zeitschrift für Theorie und Praxis der Kinder- und Jugendlichen-Psychoanalyse*. [English edition: Analytical child and adolescent psychotherapy, *Journal for Theory and Practice of Child and Adolescent Psychoanalysis and Psychodynamic Psychotherapy* 42: 71–92.]

20
QUEST FOR IDENTITY

Borderland adolescents with migration backgrounds[1]

Annette Streeck-Fischer

Although 7.6 million persons from other countries live in Germany and nearly 16.5 million of 80.5 million German inhabitants have a migration background (Federal Statistical Office) – in all, 20% of the population – psychoanalytic literature concerning the psychotherapeutic interaction with migrants is scarce. This is astonishing, especially concerning adolescents for whom identity formation may become a great problem against their bicultural background. Adolescence is a so-called second phase of individuation (Blos, 1962; Mahler et al., 1975), often a time full of crisis and even more unstable in the case of an additional third phase of individuation (Ahktar, 1999), as coping with migration is also called. Generally, adolescents experience role confusions (Erikson, 1950) during their quest for identity. In the case of different cultural conceptions, further disorientation and also culturally determined identity confusion may occur (Jensen et al., 2011).

The Pisa Study (2004)[2] showed that children of migrants in a socially weak environment are insufficiently supported in Germany and mostly have low or even no graduation. Adolescents with migration backgrounds and failure of academic and social integration during their quest for identity become a form of melting pot for dangerous developments – be they antisocial personality, militancy, or drug abuse.

First, the specific characteristics of adolescence and the problem of identity formation of adolescents with migration backgrounds during this phase of life is described.

Adolescence and migration

Adolescence is the time of profound bio-psychosocial restructuring. Epidemiological studies show that this time is characterized by considerable instability. The boundaries between normality and pathology are diverse and it may be difficult to differentiate between healthy and pathological narcissism or between a borderline disorder and borderline-like behaviour (Streeck-Fischer, 2014).

The often risky behaviour of adolescents can be understood against the background of the biological imbalance. Thus, adolescents have only a limited control of their behaviour and tend to seek quick success, variety and immediate satisfaction instead of pursuing long-term goals (Casey et al., 2008). Their capacities for self-regulation are not yet fully developed. The immature ventral prefrontal cortex cannot yet execute sufficient top-down control of affect and reward-promising regions (e.g., amygdala, nucleus accumbens). Many peculiarities of adolescence can be explained by these facts.

Identity contains the individual personality of a human, which arises from relationships to important others during life (Seiffge-Krenke, 2012). Identity is also described as the experience of coherence and continuity (Ermann, 2011). The formation of individual and ethnic identity is complex and a mixture of biological, social, cultural and environmental factors (Mann, 2006). Although identity formation is a lifelong process, the steps during adolescence are groundbreaking for the future. The identity of the adolescent is not just the sum of his childhood identifications but a combination of early and new identifications (Erikson, 1950). This process is full of crises and danger. Now adolescents not only become able to think about themselves as more differentiated, but there are also cognitive changes concerning the handling of relationship experiences. They connect their own pasts with their presents and futures and, at best, develop identity-forming narratives and goals. Thus, identity in adolescence mainly means maturation of self-regulation and complexity of social functioning.

Marcia (1966) describes different levels of identity formation. The *achievement of identity* is the highest level, namely the integration of identity, associated with pronounced self-esteem and mature interpersonal abilities. This level is mainly reached only at the end of adolescence. For the preceding time, the *identity moratorium* is characteristic. It is mainly determined by exploratory behaviour without resulting decisions. In contrast, *identity foreclosure* is characterized by non-exploratory, obedient and conforming behaviour. Identity diffusion is associated with severe psychic and social problems. According to Kernberg (1975) and others, it is the result of a structural pathology. These different levels build a kind of pattern for identity processes, becoming a problem if a desirable *achievement of identity* is not reached at the end of adolescence.

Adolescents are very amenable to foreign cultural conceptions, values and behaviours. Thus, not infrequently, the result is a dissonant acculturation in adolescents in general, but especially in adolescents with migrant backgrounds (Portes, 1997), that is, the adoption of cultural values conflicting with those of the society they live in.

Because of the rapid expansion of the internet all over the world, social networks have developed, meeting the interests of adolescents but also conveying contradictory orientations and values (Jensen, 2011). Thus, during the quest for identity, there may be a rambling between different cultures associated with a feeling of in-between.

The ethnic origin of an adolescent plays an important role concerning the transgenerational transfer of cultural ideals, especially if the migrant adolescent feels rejected by the new society and its culture.

Berry (1997) describes four different patterns of acculturation:

Assimilation as adaption to the new culture with the development of a corresponding cultural identity. In this case, the identity of the country of origin is abandoned. A rift in the family may result if parents do not follow the adaptation of the adolescent.
Integration is a combination of the original cultural identity with elements of the new culture. Such developments are desired but hardly realizable if the values of the cultures are very different.
In the case of *separation*, people refuse the new culture and keep their distance.
In the case of *marginalization*, neither the culture of the country of origin nor that of the new country have importance for identity formation. The resulting problems are usually associated with severe conflicts and may lead to identity diffusion.

If the adolescent does not receive a clear orientation from parents who are having difficulties with their own acculturation or being still little integrated, the third phase of individuation becomes a real challenge. In Germany especially, adolescents from South Europe or Turkey experience severe acculturation stress. Migration as a stress factor is sometimes also considered as a traumatic experience (Grinberg & Grinberg, 1990; Özkan & Hüther, 2012). On the one hand, migration is considered as sequential traumatization (Keilson, 1979), because of persecution and violence in the country of origin and the conditions of the migration process, with periods spent in reception camps, being placed in foreign social environments and lack of occupational integration. On the other hand, the migration process is described as cumulative or tension trauma (Grinberg & Grinberg, 1990) because it is associated with ongoing strain. During the migration process, the adolescents experience uprooting, affecting themselves as well as their parents, and feelings of non-belonging and 'dislocation' (Bhabba, 2000, in German: Entortung) block the development of identity. The resulting encapsulation of adolescence has the function of preventing a loss of self and identity.

There are contradictory data as to whether migrants frequently show more psychic and psychosomatic problems (Glaesmer et al., 2009). While this German study found no difference in frequency, in the US significantly higher rates of depression, suicidality, anxiety, substance abuse and eating disorders were found in adolescent migrants of first and second generation (Pumariega & Cagande, 2013; Pumariega & Rothe, 2010). Results from the German KIGGS Study (2008) suggest that low socio-economic status, as well as the migration background of the family, are risk factors for psychic disorders. Thus, the percentage of borderline abnormal or clearly abnormal values in migrant children (21.3%) is almost as high as in families with low socio-economic status (23.2%) and almost three times higher than in families with high socio-economic status.

Patients with bicultural background often ask for psychiatric or psychotherapeutic treatment. Up to now, the problems arising in psychoanalytic treatment of such patients, especially of adolescents with bicultural backgrounds, have rarely been studied. Other than in the treatment of adolescents with German origin, it is important to additionally offer a transcultural transference space when treating these bicultural patients in order to understand the phenomenon of the foreign culture. Otherwise, therapy might be reduced to a superficial and fragile adaptation to the particular personal and social conditions (Samuels, 2002; Sharabani & Isreali, 2008). In particular, adolescents who are regressing to infantile relationship experiences during their adolescent development need bicultural containers.

Berenstein and Puget (1997) described three spaces of transference:

1. the intra-subjective space, the child creates during its development between itself and the mother,
2. the intersubjective space the individual finds in his environment, his family and society and
3. the trans-subjective or transcultural space between different cultures.

Berenstein and Puget refer to Winnicott (1965), who considers that the transference is an intermediate space of experience with contributions from both inner reality and outer life. To understand the inner reality of the adolescent means also understanding and considering the significance of the deeper and unconscious impact of foreign rituals, symbols and practices (Kohte-Meyer, 2006; Nadig, 2006). Then, the transcultural space of transference may become a space of shelter and identity discovery, where symbolic structures (Özbek & Wohlfahrt, 2006) can be newly developed.

Three cases

The special problems in the psychotherapy of adolescents with migration backgrounds are illustrated with three case reports. Two of the adolescents were in short-term in-patient treatment and activated particular conflicts associated with their migration background in the therapeutic team. The therapists were confronted with helplessness, anxiety, irritation and challenges that were partly dramatized and partly denied. These conflicts could not always be incorporated and contained.

Mainly, three types of problems arose in the therapeutic work with these adolescents:

1. diversion to glorified militant ideologies of the country of origin,
2. offender–victim constellations with reactivation of elements of Nazi past,
3. danger of diagnostic colonization.

All three cases had a common characteristic: the importance of the country of origin which had specially influenced the disorder of the particular adolescent, either as the target of narcissistic self-aggrandizement (Volkan, 1988), or as reactive metaphor for 'deposited' conflict (Volkan, 2013).

"You Germans don't understand us" – nationalistic right-wing ideologies of the country of origin as a target for self-support

C, a 15-year-old adolescent was the son of a Polish–German mother and a Turkish father, who both came to Germany during adolescence, met there, but did not marry. Besides one younger brother, he supposedly had ten half-brothers, nine of them from relationships of the father. C lived with his mother. The father had left her when C was seven years old. C had sporadic contact with his father, who was frequently away on construction jobs. C's outward appearance was a bit strange. He was dressed all in white. His hair was cut close to his head, a bit like Mike Tyson, and he gave the impression of being violently macho or of being affiliated to the extreme right-wing, orientating himself to the rules of a gang milieu.

C said during the first session: "You Germans don't understand us. If someone is poor he just goes to the supermarket and takes what you have". His disorder was characterized by multiple symptoms, such as destructive behaviour against himself and others, transgressing behaviour, increased irritability and deficient impulse and affect regulation. C was at risk of a dissocial development. At the same time, he glamorized the Turkish culture. He had decorated his room with Turkish flags and other Turkish cultural markers. Identification with his father was extremely important for him. He idealized his father, with whom he associated the image of a 'strong guy' and sought to show strength when identifying with his father. The mother remained pale in his descriptions and seemingly did not have any attractive attributes to offer him. However, he emphasized that his family was holy to him.

C lived in a social troublespot where there were street battles between Turkish and Kurdish youth gangs. Integration in school and work as elements of our social expectations held no attraction for him; he had to obey to the rules of the street, where might was right. Because of speech and writing and reading problems, he was on the verge of failure at school. Thus, he searched for orientations in his country of origin to function as props for his distressed self (Streeck-Fischer, 2014) and was attracted by the ideology of the Grey Wolves, a Turkish ultra-national (right-wing) association. As a Turkish nationalist, he could feel he was someone special. This attitude gave him strength, orientation and narcissistic enhancement to counter and survive the discriminations he experienced in his environment. Like his father, who orientated himself to archaic lifestyles of his country, for example, having relationships with several women, C reverted to legitimations allowing him to act beyond the law and order of the country he was living in. Thus he said, "If you are poor you can take what you need". His identity formation resulted in a dangerous para-reality.

The example shows that adolescents with migration backgrounds who are failing at school are easily seducible. Nationalistic ideologies of the country of origin – in Germany these are right-wing fascistic ideologies – are used for super-elevation of the self. The action scene provided by street battles is attractive for adolescents with low academic status and, thus, low future aspirations. Just belonging to a certain group provides narcissistic enhancement. Such adolescents openly seek destructive coping strategies to overcome feelings of paralysis, helplessness and emptiness. Another direction that Turkish adolescents can take is linked to the Islamic religion. There is the danger of developing into a 'holy warrior' if fundamentalist religious leaders become active.

C was in danger of getting into a marginalized situation during his identity development. Attracted by a para-reality promising quick satisfaction and enhancement, he suffered individual, as well as cultural, identity diffusion.

Offender-victim constellations – the Nazi past becomes present

A female adolescent, B, had been having in-patient treatment for only eight weeks. She evoked intense reactions and discussions in the therapeutic team, not only understandable against the background of her severe illness, but also as an expression of a complex process concerning the handling of the transgenerational past in the actual present. B showed multiple boundary distortions. It was curiously unclear whose past was meant and what should be mastered – the fate of the adolescent who was in the process of treatment or the guilt of the Nazi past which was reactivated by the feeling of being an offender during the therapeutic work. A traumatic process was restaged in the transference–countertransference between the adolescent and the therapeutic team (Laub & Auerhahn, 1993).

Sixteen-year-old B was referred for in-patient treatment because of severe anorexia, with vomiting and laxative abuse. She was blonde and had a nice attractive face. She was emaciated, looked bedraggled and evoked much pity and willingness to help her. At the same time she smelled repellent, evoking disgust with her dirty clothes covered with puke. Associations with concentration camps came up, often provoked during the treatment of severe anorexia. However, when the staff of the adolescent ward learned that B came from Russia and was of Jewish origin, multiple anxieties came up, connected to the possibility of her death. Professional distance was no longer possible and it was not clear how many of these anxieties were associated with B personally and how many with the fact that she was Jewish, which evoked pictures of the German past in the staff. The boundary between B's problems and the knowledge of the German past was weirdly blurred.

The family had lived in Moscow until B was 11 years old. Without preparation, B was confronted by her parents, both of whom were graduates with sufficient income, with migration. The parents, who experienced increasing anti-Semitic attitudes in Russia and felt persecuted and excluded, planned to migrate to Israel after the sudden death of B's grandfather. This was not possible and they decided instead to migrate to Germany. The family stayed for one year in a German transit camp. After some months, the father fell in love with another woman and the family broke up. B felt overwhelmed and totally strange in Germany, which she did not choose as her home. She wanted to migrate to Canada to become a model.

B's presence raised many questions: was she a young patient with an ordinary anorexia with typical family background – the breakdown of the family – and high academic demands, or existential familial stress associated with National Socialism, reactivated by migration to Germany, which she, as a member of the third generation, expressed through action? Did she suffer from detachment and separation problems with fixation on a dyadic level of object relations provoked by the leaving of the father? Did she suffer a severe identity crisis concerning her origin and sexuality in this foreign country? Or were there secrets not communicated in this uncommunicative family? For example, it remained unclear if the grandfather died of natural causes. Possibly he had been was followed by some government security people and that was the reason for the family's migration. Moreover, it was unclear whether B had experienced traumatic violence in the camp, for example, sexual abuse. She gave hints that might have indicated this, but eventually the staff was left in uncertainty.

Some members of the therapeutic team felt like torturers and concentration camp guards. To avoid such feelings, they tried to keep B alive – with seemingly sadistic means – but concurrently had to witness her slow decline. Fears were reported that B would demonstrate, through her death, how evil and vicious we Germans are. The discussions in the therapeutic team were very intense, especially on the subject of the establishment of a boundary. From a more abstract position, the establishment of a decentralized viewpoint with an exterritorial position seemed to fail. Some members of the staff refused to tolerate further treatment of B and argued for her transfer. B had exclusive relationships to certain therapists, who seemed to keep her alive by their supporting presence. Thus, B lingered in front of certain doors, sometimes for a long time, and waited – especially for one female therapist – until she was seen and asked to come in. She activated rescue phantasies in this therapist and the feeling of being chosen. The therapist had the ambition to show B that she was not confronted with 'evil Germans' and that her life in Germany could be livable meanwhile. The engagement of the team became more and more polarized – some members full of fear and alarm (e.g., B could die in our care), others full of anger about what B did to us, and yet others who were willing to accompany her through a kind of torture chamber in order to finally find salvation. The female therapist, especially, was accused of trying everything for the treatment of B. Finally, she had to recognize that, due to her rescue phantasies, she was willing to ignore the reality of the possible death of B, even more that she was willing to be entangled in a disastrous process of continued closeness and mutual destruction, as in malign regression to avoid separation, differentness, self-determination or evil, because B's fate and deep pain affected her so much.

While the therapist struggled for her position with B, the team searched with B for tolerable conditions, debated about ingestion and about how she could do something good for herself and her body with our assistance. Finally, she had to be transferred for somatic treatment because her physical state had worsened. In the end, the team was glad about it because B accepted somatic treatment with intragastric feeding, realizing her threatened state without feelings of being overwhelmed. It was this setting of a boundary which she could accept as something not simply evil and against her; moreover, the members of the team hoped that she would come back after being stabilized.

But conditions had changed when B came back three weeks later: B was well fed, perhaps a bit puffy, and her clothes were clean. Now therapy could 'really' have begun. It seemed as if she had arrived freshly in present-day Germany. But B did not want to continue therapy. After her parents had started to speak with her, she wanted to go back to her mother. Thus, many things remained unclear and cryptic. However, it seems as if the team mutually had passed through traumatic events both of B's and our parents' past and the presence of migration – to the point where we got into trouble setting the boundary and became peculiar loving offenders wishing her to 'stay alive for me and my past' (and not for herself), while simultaneously ignoring her possible death. It became possible to overcome this confusing victim–offender constellation by not overwhelming her with measures such as compulsory feeding or compulsory hospitalization, but by accompanying her internally and externally. Until then, we had obviously been caught in the idea that separation means death, as she had experienced in her family, in the world of a concentration camp, which developed between her and us. Perhaps this was the familial tragedy she needed to overcome. You must live for us and our ancestors.

During the first eight weeks, B's family did not give us much insight into their familial conditions. On the contrary, the family reacted with speechlessness, seemingly frozen, and tried to convince us that they would manage everything. They could not admit how frightening and strange the Germans and the foreign culture perhaps were for them.

It can only be speculated if there was also an apparition of the familial past, a past of hunted people who have learned to be unnoticeable. Thus, also in this new country, the family and B appeared unremarkable and adapted. However, B protested, with her embodied message of being deathly sick, against this life in another country.

In the therapeutic team, the deficient boundary between past and present became certainly obvious and the ghosts of the German past (Fraiberg et al., 1975) were activated, the past of the Holocaust, which made professional distance almost impossible. We have no information about B's further identity development but it seemed as if she had accepted being in Germany now.

Danger of diagnostic colonization

Fifteen-and-a-half-year-old A is the daughter of a German mother and a black African father. She was an in-patient because of optical and acoustic hallucinations. She heard voices from three 16-year-old helpers – Caucasian adolescents – commenting on her own behaviour and that of others. Moreover, she was often depressed, had problems falling asleep, showed stagnation and indifferentness and mood fluctuations with hypomanic and depressive states. She was irritable and prone to outbursts of rage. Moreover, she had an obsessive–compulsive symptomatology with ablutomania. Because of her complex symptoms, she had often been absent from school.

A had suffered from hallucinations since she was three-and-a-half years old. When she was 12 years old, she had visited with her father in his African country of origin for three weeks. There she had lived with her father in a separate lodge at the family residence and shared a bedroom with him. She was confronted with impressive mystic rituals. After her return, already suffering from hallucinations, she moved to a boarding school far away from home. At the same time, the life partner of her mother, who had lived separated from A's father for 10 years, moved in. Three months later, A was sexually abused (without penetration) by a black African adolescent, who had been a close friend. The hallucinations became more intense, with imperative characteristics. She heard bullying voices telling her to misbehave.

The question quickly arose as to how to classify her problems. She showed the symptoms of a florid paranoid–hallucinatory psychosis. A herself was afraid of suffering from schizophrenia. However, she was very vital, adequately affective, creative and structured with good cognitive competence and capacities to symbolize. Did she suffer from a dissociative disorder? The sexual traumatization occurred after the hallucinations already existed. Certainly her experiences – being alone with the father in his country of origin, moving to the boarding school, loss of direct contact with parents, sexual abuse – could be seen as cumulative traumatization. Because of her high level of competence, A had no problems integrating in the peer group; she had a rather good standing. The therapeutic team vividly discussed how to diagnose A's symptoms adequately. Was it necessary to quickly treat her with antipsychotics because of her psychotic symptoms? Was it even adequate to classify her with Western diagnostic criteria? There was the apparent danger of making A sicker than she really was. With Western diagnostic instruments and paradigms, A would possibly be deemed to conform to those, as if in Procustes' bed (Pumariega & Cagande, 2013).

For the father and his family of origin, A was the reincarnation of the paternal mother because she was the first child born after the death of his mother. As matriarch of the family, A's grandmother had had a prominent position. Therefore, the father, who had been her most important attachment figure during early childhood, called A 'princess'.

Because her symptoms developed immediately after her visit to Africa, the family had the suspicion that someone could have jinxed her in revenge. When A's symptoms worsened, a relative of the father, a Catholic priest, was asked to build a wooden cross and to worship and bless it for three days. During these three days, A pretended to see a wooden cross on her foot. She tried to remove it but didn't succeed. After a quarter of an hour, the cross disappeared.

As the reincarnation of the grandmother, the matriarch, since her birth, A had been a reservoir of highly important object images representing the father's mother and family traditions (Volkan, 2010). Thus, the dead mother and the traditions associated with her stayed alive for the father. A was a *quasi* replacement child of the dead mother, a totally different kind of replacement than is meant by this term in Western culture, where the characteristics and personality traits of a dead child are deposited into a later-born child. Volkan (2013) consider this depositing to be transgenerational transmission. In this, the generation border is suspended. Apparently, the deficient demarcation between reality and phantasy, past and present – a symptom often found in cases of traumatization – had already been installed and was permanently and intrusively maintained by the special attention of the father for his princess. A might have been jinxed because of her function as growing up matriarchal – either through envy or because she did not at all look like her grandmother – even perhaps because her being considered the reincarnation of the grandmother was an affront to the African relatives. Possibly, also, sexual desires developed during her quest for identity, being inconsistent with the expectations of the African relatives. Perhaps she had experienced something traumatic, for example, too much closeness with her father. Finally, it was imaginable that A internally protested against the familial intrusions and that the jinx was put on the traitorous father and his foreign family.

In the beliefs of the African culture (Maiello, 1999) mental illness is connected with a disturbance in the relationship with the ancestors. Their withdrawal can make the individual and the family vulnerable to deadly witchcraft spells. The essential question does not concern the cause of the disorder, but the bringer. In any case, there is a big difference between ancestors in the African culture and the internal object in Western psychodynamic thinking. Ancestors concretely exist (or have existed) in the external world, whereas in Western culture the concept of the internal objects is a metaphor construed to describe intrapsychic vicissitudes. As long as the ancestor in African culture is believed to give support and advice, he or she has the function of a good internalized object.

Following the beliefs of A's African cultural environment, the ancestors – the grandmother inside of her – have distanced from her. However, disrupting the connection with the ancestors leads to severe splitting processes, attacks on linking or psychotic phenomena (Maiello, 1999). The voices that appeared and bewildered A would then have been an inevitable consequence, the externalizations of coeval companions threatening A's existing self-perception as persecutory objects. Probably, the already deficient boundaries between reality and phantasy were loosened further by the obviously traumatic (presumed) sexual abuse. When the ancestors, especially the grandmother, as the good objects, had withdrawn and A instead was persecuted by dangerous objects, the aim of therapy should be the provision of a new space for the good objects and to re-anchor them at the boundary between the inner and outer world. For example, the grandmother could be present virtually during the therapeutic session and could be asked what she thought about A and how she would stand by her.

Obviously, the African culture supports blurring of the boundaries between reality and phantasy. When this phenomenon is pathologized, the problems of these adolescents during their quest for identity are not adequately addressed. A becomes confused because of different cultural worlds colliding inside her. If only the Western evaluation of A's situation is validated, a superficial assimilation might be accelerated, instead of supporting an integration with both cultures having their place.

Conclusion

All three adolescents spoke more or less good German, so there were no ostensible communication difficulties. The two adolescents with African and Turkish roots grew up in Germany but experienced a (split) world divided in half by their parents from different countries of origin. These different worlds became virulent, especially during adolescence. For both, their origins became both a threat and a temptation during their identity formation. The danger of squeezing adolescent patients with bicultural origins into a metaphorical Procustes' bed is great when applying our usual diagnostic categorizations, particularly because the behaviour of adolescents and young adults may appear quite strange. Therapy then easily may result in the patient's superficial adaptation to our expectations without the basal, cultural and subculturally influenced conflicts really coming into the focus of the therapeutic work. Instead, therapy runs the risk of misdiagnosis, deficient therapeutic alliance, non-adherence (Yilmaz et al., 2013) or dropout.

Under these circumstances, judgemental, sometimes imperial, attitudes may creep into the countertransference reactions of the therapist. Then, sometimes, questions come up as to why the adolescent creates such a parallel world instead of integrating himself, or if he himself is responsible for his condition: after all, his family receives money and he himself is financially supported.

Phenomena like those experienced by C, a young man without orientation, fighting for survival and running the risk of dissocial development and falling into militant marginalization, are dangerous and must not be ignored in the face of Islamic promises of salvation.

All three adolescents showed symptoms that might be considered as the consequences of traumatic stress. In the case of the adolescent with African roots, the boundary between reality and phantasy, between the cultures of mother and father, was blurred with psychotic intrusions resulting in a confusion of values. Blurring of boundaries also emerged in the complex transference–countertransference dynamic between the adolescent with Russian–Jewish origin and the therapeutic team. Having arrived in an 'enemy' country, a mutually initialized offender–victim scene was produced, which finally took a beneficial course. The adolescent with the Turkish background ran the risk of drifting away into a world of phantasy and violence characterized by nationalistic right-wing ideologies. To do justice to these borderland adolescents, it is necessary to provide a transcultural transitional space and to engage in what is culturally strange in order to contain and detect its meaning. That also means overcoming the temptation of quickly applied categorizations and to allow room for ignorance and uncertainty. Finally, that also means having an eye open for the impact of cultural factors on both patient and analyst. As such adolescents often are not able to recognize and denominate the strange, it is helpful to get as much information as possible concerning the foreign culture with its particularities.

When the therapist is able to abstain from attitudes easily conforming to an imperialistic and colonializing character, or, in Winnicott's words, from "strange gestures" (Winnicott, 1971) provoking adaptation, protest or destruction, then dealing with foreign cultures and their immediate consequences for the individual may lead to a fruitful and creative way to achieve the adolescent's identity formation.

Notes

1 First published in the *American Journal of Psychoanalysis*, 2015, Vol. 75, 438–453.
2 The OECD (Organisation for Economic Co-operation and Development), which improves the economic and social well-being of people around the world initiates every three years a PISA study (Programme for International Student Assessment). See www.oecd.org

References

Akhtar, S. (1999) The third individuation. Immigration, identity, and the psychoanalytic process, *Journal of the American Psychoanalytic Association* 49: 1051–1084.
Berenstein, J. & Puget, J. (1997) *Lo vincular*. Buenos Aires: Piados.
Berry, J. W. (1997) Immigration, acculturation, and adaptation, *International Journal of Applied Psychology* 46: 5–34.
Bhabba, H. K. (2000) *Die Verortung der Kultur*. Tübingen: Staufenberg Verlag.
Blos, P. (1962) *On Adolescence*. New York: Free Press.
Casey, B. J., Jones, R. M. & Hare, T. A. (2008) The adolescent brain, *Annals of the New York Academy of Science* 1124: 111–126.
Erikson, E. H. (1950) *Childhood and Society*. New York: Norton.
Ermann, M. (2011) Identität, Identitätsdiffusion, Identitätsstörung, *Psychotherapeut* 56: 135–141.
Fraiberg, S., Adelson, E. & Shapiro, V. (1975) Ghosts in the nursery, *Journal of the American Academy of Child Psychiatry* 14: 387–421.
Glaesmer, H., Wittig, U., Brähler, E., Martin, A., Mewes, R. & Rief, W. (2009) Sind Migranten häufiger von Störungen betroffen? Eine Untersuchung an einer repräsentativen Stichprobe der deutschen Bevölkerung, *Psychiatrische Praxis* 36:16–32.
Grinberg, O. L. & Grinberg, K. (1990) *Psychoanalyse der Migration und des Exils*. Munich: Verlag Internationale Psychoanalyse.
Jensen, L., Arnett, J. J. & McKenzie, J. (2011) Globalisation and cultural identity, in: S. J. Schwartz, K. Luyckx & V. L. Vignoles (Eds.), *Handbook of Identity. Theory and Research*. Springer Science.
Keilson, H. (1979) *Sequentielle Traumatisierung bei Kindern*. Stuttgart: Enke.
Kernberg, O. (1975) *Borderline Conditions and Pathological Narcissism*. New York: Jason Aronson.
KIGGS - Robert Koch-Institut, Bundeszentrale für gesundheitliche Aufklärung (Eds.) (2008) *Erkennen – Bewerten – Handeln: Zur Gesundheit von Kindern und Jugendlichen in Deutschland*. RKI, Berlin Dezember.
Kohte-Meyer, I. (2006) Kindheit und Adoleszenz zwischen verschiedenen Kulturen und Sprachen. Eine kulturelle Perspektive in der Psychoanalyse (pp. 82–94), in: E. Wohlfahrt, M. Zaumseil (Eds.), *Transkulturelle Psychiatrie – Interkulturelle Psychotherapie*. Heidelberg: Springer.
Laub, A. & Auerhahn N. C. (1993) Knowing and not knowing. Massive psychic trauma, *International Journal of Psychoanalysis* 74: 287–302.

Mahler, M. S., Pine, F. & Bergmann, A. (1975) *The Psychological Birth of the Human Infant.* New York: Basic Books.

Maiello, S. (1999) Encounter with an African healer: Thinking about the possibilities and limits of cross-cultural psychotherapy. *Journal of Child Psychotherapy* 28: 217–238.

Mann, M. A. (2006) The formation and development of individual and ethnic identity. Insights from psychiatry and psychoanalytic theory, *American Journal of Psychoanalysis* 66: 211–234.

Marcia, J. E. (1966) Development and validation of ego identity states, *Journal of Personality and Social Psychology* 3: 551–558.

Nadig, M. (2006) Transkulturelle Spannungsfelder in der Migration und ihrer Erforschung (pp. 68–89), in: E. Wohlfahrt & M. Zaumseil (Eds.), *Transkulturelle Psychiatrie – Interkulturelle Psychotherapie.* Heidelberg: Springer.

Özbek, T. & Wohlfahrt, E. (2006) Der transkulturelle Übergangsraum – ein Theorem und seine Funktion in der transkulturellen Psychotherapie im ZIPP (pp. 170–176), in: E. Wohlfahrt & M. Zaumseil (Eds.), *Transkulturelle Psychiatrie – Interkulturelle Psychotherapie.* Heidelberg: Springer.

Özkan, I. & Hüther, G. (2012) Migration: Traum oder Trauma (pp. 173–186), in: I Özkan, U. Sachsse & A. Streeck-Fischer (Eds.), *Zeit heilt nicht alle Wunden.* Göttingen: Vandenhoeck.

Portes, A. (1997) Immigration theory for a new century. Some problems and opportunities, *International Migration Review* 31: 799–825.

Pumariega, A. J. & Cagande, C. (2013) Editorial: Globalization and child and adolescent mental health. *Adolescent Psychiatry* 3: 1–3.

Pumariega, A. J. & Rothe, E. (2010) Leaving no children or families outside: The challenges of immigration, *American Journal of Orthopsychiatry* 80: 506–516.

Samuels, A. (2002) The hidden politics of healing: Foreign dimensions of domestic practice, *American Imago* 59: 459–481.

Seiffge-Krenke, I. (2012) *Therapieziel Identität.* Stuttgart: Klett-Cotta.

Sharabany, R. & Israeli, E. (2008) The dual process of adolescent immigration and relocation: From country to country and from childhood to adolescence – its reflection in psychodynamic psychotherapy, *Psychoanalytic Study of the Child* 63: 137–162.

Streeck-Fischer, A. (2014) *Trauma und Entwicklung –Folgen in der Adoleszenz.* Stuttgart: Schattauer.

Volkan, V. (Ed.) (1988) *The Need To Have Enemies and Allies. From Clinical Practices to International Relationships.* New York: Jason Aronson.

Volkan, V. D. (2010) Psychoanalysis and international relationships: Large-group identity, traumas at the hand of "other," and transgenerational transmission of trauma (pp. 41–62), in: H. Brunning & M. Perini (Eds.), *Psychoanalytic Perspectives on a Turbulent World.* London: Karnac.

Volkan, V. D. (2013) *Enemies on the Couch: A Psychopolitical Journey Through War and Peace.* Durham, NC: Pitchstone.

Winnicott, D. W. (1965) *Maturational Processes and the Facilitating Environment.* London: Hogarth Press.

Winnicott, D. W. (1971) *Playing and Reality.* London: Tavistock.

Yilmaz, H. B., Dalkilic, A., Al-Mateen, C., Sood, A. & Pumariega, A. (2013) Culturally informed care of the Turkish–American child, adolescent and family. *Adolescent Psychiatry* 3: 39–45.

21

AN UNEQUAL MATRIX

Western Germans, Eastern Germans, migrants

Jens Preil

Introduction

I looked forward to writing this chapter as the topic is close to my heart. I was born and raised in the GDR. I was 19 when the Wall came down and the popular uprising forced the SED regime to peacefully transition power. As the son of a father who, early on, devoted himself to communist ideals and also became an ideologue, I had mixed feelings. We wrote each other letters, doubting and determined ones. I remember a silent disappointment and confusion at this change but above all excitement about taking my future into my own hands. This all happened in the long summer of a short democracy between the Wende and German unification. One year later, I went to study in the West. When I returned to Berlin ten years later, there were many things that had been left behind, untouched, encapsulated in time and were now being urged forward. Since then, I've been trying to move closer to the black holes of my memory, cautiously, by asking questions.

Treating these questions academically, I was hoping to dispense with some of them rather quickly to put me at a safe distance from their problematic core. But I got stuck in the middle of my writing. I could find neither a beginning nor an end; there was only a hopeless middle. Today, I think that I tried to put myself on the solid ground of a theory to justify or legitimize my personal experience. In developing the theme, I imagined myself as a defendant and my own defender; and at other times as avenger and victim. And, in between, my story melted away. That's why my chapter will be more personal than I had initially intended, with all the subjective shortcomings and uncertainties inherent to my theses.

I shall begin with East German identity constructions and explore the difficulty in categorizing East and West Germans as two different groups, each with its own identity. In the middle section, I shall examine the interdependence of East and West German self-interpretation and attributions and discuss my theses on the social and political importance of these identity formations and the associated group processes. Finally, I intended to look, albeit briefly, at the increasingly frequent links between East–West discourse and the present migration debate. However, I shall not elaborate on this part, as this gives me more space for the East–West topic and keeps my text more compact. In order to underpin my theses, I shall use psychoanalytic approaches and models from social sciences and cultural studies. Although they are based on different concepts and value systems, I shall try complementing and relating them to each other. This cannot always be done consistently but I do think it is worth examining, as it may provide many different perspectives on this complex subject.

Part of the title of this book, *On Sameness and Otherness*, may suggest that the diverse and complex East–West discourse might be well approached by identity concepts, especially in view of a psychoanalytically educated readership. It is already part of the East–West discourse that there are differences between East Germans and West Germans, which have been investigated over the past 25 years by numerous studies in various areas. The concept of identity seems well suited and popular enough to discover those differences, to describe, to explain and legitimize them in social debates. A thoughtful essay by Christian Meier in his 2010 book, entitled 'Mentality problems of German unification' ironically summarizes what all felt and actually have always known: 40 years of SED rule formed less self-conscious, dependent, and authoritarian characters who were prone to fail in the liberal democracy of the Federal Republic of Germany, or at least would make a lot of trouble. Meier further says:

> On the whole the East Germans became really different from those in the West, who began to live their democracy over time, acquired certain cosmopolitanism, got involved in major debates, honoured economic courage, in a word, became much freer and also more eloquent and had a lot of success reflected in their prosperity.
>
> *(2010: 134–135)*

Exceptions prove the rule. But even if this attribution of stereotypes would not stand up to rational analysis, it remains a perceived subversive uncertainty prompting us: there is a ring of truth about it.

But isn't this 'perceived something' the core of any identity? You can easily deconstruct each identity, but what cannot be taken away is the feeling of being like this and not otherwise: the feeling of familiarity when a person I meet speaks my dialect, when we discover artefacts of a common past, like the nocturnal howling of sirens, when the fathers had to go on battle alert, Zetti chocolate, the smell of burned lignite in cold winter air – when not much needs to be said to understand. Is it our reasoning that decides whether we belong to a certain group or, rather, a sense of belonging and that it has always felt like this?

There are a number of theoretical approaches dealing with the formation of group identities and the passing on of social patterns to individuals. I shall focus on those aspects that may contribute to a deeper understanding of East and West German identity constructions. Especially with respect to the dynamic relation between inner truth and social requirements, I would like to emphasize identity as a process of attribution and self-interpretation. But identity also fosters communitisation. Utilizing group-specific identification objects, identity creates a sense of belonging, which can be experienced by us as security, honesty and personal strength. It is this emotional fabric that connects diverse people who share certain conscious and unconscious fantasies. Thus, the complex phenomenon of identity-belonging can be included in a subject area that can be explored by psychoanalytic meta-theory and critical–hermeneutical method. That's what I want to tell you as a preface to a case study, which is very practically concerned with this topic.

Yet, before I continue with the case study, I would like us to keep the following question in mind while reflecting on identities. Although it is coherent, every theory about an individual, and all the more so with group identity, is confronted with a fact already mentioned by Freud (1921: 144): "Each of us is part of many masses, bound by ties of identification in many directions, and has built up his ego ideal on the most various models". Justifiably, Jureit and Schneider (2010: 69–70) ask,

> how can you speak of a collective identity in post-sovereign, functionally differentiated and mass media societies with an enormously increased complexity. By now it must be clear that competing identities, […] and the immense variety of community structures that are neither related to one collective history nor to collective values, are almost impossible to integrate.

So, what's the story behind identity then?

Case study

Now I would like to present the case study we undertook on the occasion of the 20th anniversary of the fall of the Berlin Wall to investigate our perceived East German identity. 'We' is a working group of psychoanalytically trained fellows, who were born between 1970 and 1976 and raised in the GDR. Is there an East German large-group identity? What would be its essentials? How could this be objectified?

The 'social photo matrix' method (Sievers, 2006) that would bring us closer to these questions, I studied with Burkhard Sievers. In a social photo matrix, people come together with the intention to freely associate, amplify and make connections between the individual photos taken in relation to a specific theme in order to get new insights into their experience and learn more about themselves as a group. In addition, we made the reflection on our interactions and relationships part of the method to enable both a deep hermeneutic and a group-analytic approach to the unconscious, or not yet communicable, dimension of our East German identifications. As the theme of our photo matrix we chose very simply '20 years…', which left plenty of room for a wide range of fantasies. So, one day we went first to Coburg, then to Gotha.

Due to its history, the combination of the two cities seemed ideal for us as a projection screen to reveal our group-related identity constructions. By the end of the German monarchy, both cities had been part of the Duchy of Saxe-Coburg and Gotha. In 1920, the Free State of Gotha merged with the new State of Thuringia and the Free State of Coburg was united with the Free State of Bavaria. Later, post-war order and German division placed Coburg and Gotha into completely different systems on each side of the wall.

In each city we fanned out separately and took photos on the theme '20 years…', following our spontaneous inspirations and, as far as possible, avoided consciously choosing the objects. All photos were collected and anonymized. Random samples of five photos each were taken for three group sessions: one session with pictures from Coburg, another one with pictures taken in Gotha, and a third session with mixed pictures from both cities. During each session we associated on each photo for a given time. The sessions were tape-recorded and later transcribed. In order to generate hypotheses we listened to our tape-recordings one after another at a later time (Büchler et al., 2011). This 'self-listening' and thereby tracing the unfolding scenes worked like a subsequent countertransference analysis and was the moving 'now-moment' of the whole trip. That's what I am going to introduce to you now.

> Our first group session was on the 'mixed matrix', that is, with randomly selected photographs from Gotha and Coburg. There was consternation among us. Tension and silence. "I want to have nothing to do with it". Two pictures of a pulpit were 'fair game'. We understood the massive devaluation of the religious space as fighting our 'GDR downsides', a belief in authority and an ideological dogmatism with which we had identified. Our 'search for consensus' was impressive. Disagreement intensified the fear of speaking openly in assessing the pictures. As if there were an unspoken rule – we have to be the same. Like a picture puzzle, the scenes flipped between two positions: did we just make a statement about 'the West' or were we going to understand something about us as East Germans? 'Tradition as a façade' for example, as an association on the pulpit picture: was it about religion and authority in the Federal Republic, or were the 'East German traditions' we were obviously looking for just a façade? With regard to the GDR's accession to the Federal Republic, I particularly remember the following association: 'the thing feeds on their neighbours' blood'. Again, it was not clear who sucks whom.
>
> During the Gotha matrix (formerly GDR county seat), we saw the demise of the GDR as a loss of something of our own, which triggered shame and defence mechanisms such as idealization and resistance. We sensed our vulnerability. However, it remained unclear whether the shame arose from a GDR reality that we believed remembering, or from the confrontation

with the West German reality which apparently made us feel deprived and guilty under the eyes of the West Germans, in view of the injustices which happened in the GDR. Our analysis of the scenes clearly revealed how we tried to oppose the feeling of shame and loss by imagining an East German identity. But it remained elusive. All that was left were 'feelings like driftwood'. Some quotes from our documentation:

> Two illusions were shattered with the Wende – the past and the future, both turned out to be an illusion. The desire for clear and unbroken walls arises from the double shame of the loser. It is the shame about one's helplessness and naivety.

Identity can only be preserved as a secret. It has been remaining for us as a triumph in secret.

> Something strange happened during our group session on the pictures from Coburg. We experienced ourselves as strangely lifeless while associating on the pictures, whereas most of us remembered our time in Coburg as lively and evocative. We found it difficult to get in touch with the photographs. The associations revolved around *Unorte* (non-place, space off), dullness, uniformity accompanied by a feeling of emptiness, boredom, and sometimes by a silly irritation. We quickly agreed that "the West German Coburg is detached and without any connections; and we wanted it that way". Only through later analysis of the recordings did we understand how we "find in the West what must not be reminded of the East". "These are the 'non-places' (*Unorte*) of our memory – emptiness, parochialism, authority". In the projection on Coburg, we understood what we apparently excluded from our memories of our lives in the GDR. Like the phantasm of an East German group identity in the Gotha matrix, the metaphor of the 'safe place' played an important role in the attempt to create a positive feeling related to our past. However, as in a picture puzzle, the 'safe place' turned into a 'non-place'. Even the meanings of these metaphors reversed. Nothing seemed clear and unambiguous. The 'safe place' became the 'collective hell' from which an outbreak could not even be imagined and where relationship was replaced by massification. In contrast, 'non-places' represented liveliness. By addressing them, we were able to become conscious of the homogenizing phantasm of the collective and found our way back to our diversity. That was liberating and disconcerting at the same time. During the whole period of the existence of our group, we had to go back and work through this process again and again.

Discussion of our findings

Now, what do these findings mean for our questions about an East German group identity and for their critique? At first, they seem to confirm the thesis that East German and West German is not a simple opposition, but a dichotomy that is related to a specific political and historical situation – the revolution in the GDR and the subsequent unification of the two German states as its founding moment. To understand the feelings of guilt and shame, it is important to know that the unification did not take place as equals, but as the GDR's accession to the Federal Republic. This meant the adoption of the West German institutions with a consequent elimination and reorganization of the social, economic and political structures in the acceding territory, including the occupation of the majority of leading positions by West German elites. "We do not want to uncaringly pass over your desires and interests. But this is not the unification of two equal states" (Meier, 2010: 139, translated for this edition). Wolfgang Schäuble left no doubt about the balance of power in negotiating the unification treaty. The 'unification' signified an enormous transformation for the East. Everything had changed except the time, someone found. This period "was marked by the parallel but contradictory process of harmonizing political and economic structures on the one hand and substantiating and elaborating social differences on the other" (Stevenson, 2002: 231). The *Ossi-Wessi* was born. What began as simple generic labels to position oneself in this maelstrom developed in the course of the 1990s into complex social categories. We may hardly remember, but, prior to 1989, *this* dichotomy did not exist, and there were other categories within which we felt and thought.

Jürgen Streek noticed (1995: 434): "As with other ways of classifying people in terms of dichotomies – e.g. Black–White or Occident–Orient – the categorical pair Ossi-Wessi is almost irresistible in its simple but perfect poetic construction. It is too beautiful not to be true" (translated for this edition). Even today, 25 years after the unification, East Germans and West Germans "constitute first-order criteria of identification more significant than occupation, age, or gender. Many Germans' conviction of belonging to discrete social traditions does not appear to have diminished" (Stevenson, 2002: 232). Yet, this dichotomy is not symmetrical. In view of my limited space, I cannot examine the symbols and rituals of (and I refer to Volkan, 2005) the "chosen glories" or "chosen traumata" constructing the split German identities. Rather, I will focus on the narrative introduced by Christian Meier.

Wendl (2010: 113) studied rules of reporting in the weekly newspaper *Die Zeit* since the 1990s and noted:

> The term Wessi is part of a discourse on strangerhood and development aid predominantly signifying individual subjects. The term Ossi is part of a discourse on essentialist features, which is mainly related to the population of East Germans at large.

This reminds me of the analysis of colonial discourses "portraying the Other as an incomprehensible barbarian with the pathological stereotype of the strange but predictable [in this case] Orientale" (Nandy, 2008). A treasure trove of Ossi-stereotypes is Pates and Schochow's anthology *Der Ossi* [The Ossi], from which I shall briefly quote: "They are permanently 'dwarfed', irreversibly 'botched' by their education and upbringing, and largely completely useless" (2013: 7). East Germans were "old fashioned, uptight, naïve, shy away from conflict, opportunistic, lachrymose and immobile" and inclined "to racist and xenophobic acts of violence". At the same time, as demonstrated by Nandis for the colonial discourse in India, "a new discourse has been developed where the basic mode of breaking out of these stereotypes is to reverse them" (Sardar & van Loon, 2010: 86). In the case of the 'Ossi' it is their unique 'transformation competence' which, of course, remains reserved for the younger generation. You may probably know of the 'Dritte Generation Ost' (3rd Generation East), a network of 'Wendekinder' born in the GDR between 1975 and 1985. Being present in the media and courted by politicians, they claim a high integration capability, referring to the current challenges posed by migration, highlight their professional achievements, demonstrating their ability to catch up with West German elites, and emphasize their special civil commitment to an open, democratic and just society (http://netzwerk.dritte-generation-ost.de/): the perfect alternative – capable of integrating and connecting to the future.

Pates and Schochow very nicely show in their anthology, how the East German is made up by specific "engines: censuses (Statistics), normalizing, psychologizing, biologisation, essentialization and last but not least by ethnicising" (2013: 8, translated for this edition). It is noteworthy that the outcome is always what I've just mapped out: a 'civilizational gap' of the East Germans (Engler, 1992: 48). "In a system that privatized the political and politicized the private, where social subservience dominated self-constraints, basic personality structures required in liberal societies could not be acquired" (Pates & Schochow, 2013: 9). My thesis is that this asymmetric categorization has less to do with the different living conditions in East and West Germany, but more to do with the unequal encounter between East and West Germans in the course of unification. Unequal in terms of the political, economic, social and cultural capital, which was, and still is, available to the two groups. Furthermore, I assume that the identity constructions framed by these discourses help to legitimize and to perpetuate this inequality.

What does this mean for the findings in our case study? Looking through the discursive lens, I see the feelings and fantasies about us as East Germans being shaped by the asymmetric frame, within which the real encounters with the West take place. Our memories are not just about Zetti chocolate or homelessness. In a way, every one of us loses the land of his childhood, and also the West Germans have lost *their* BRD, and especially the West Berliners *their* city. Instead, our collective memory is centred on the experience of transformation, the way of the transition to a new society and its inherent economic, social and psychological conflicts that continue to this day. This is the social frame of our memories. Perceived submission produces shame opposed by inverted memories of a 'good GDR'. Guilt about our silence and idleness in the face of the injustice and cynical hypocrisy mingle with anger against stereotyped attributions. Christa Wolf, who often was a spiritual companion to us, asks in her autobiographical novel *City of Angels* (2010: 71, translated for this edition):

> What would have been the right life in the right place if at the end of the war we had succeeded in crossing the Elbe with our refugee trek that we were seeking to reach with the last strength of the carthorses? Would I have become a different person under the other, the proper conditions? Smarter, better, without guilt? But why can I still not wish to swap my life for that lighter, better one?.

Is this the *Unort* which becomes a saving metaphor to us in the struggle for the power of interpretation of our history? As an antithesis to the *Ossi*, which avoids being determined by others and remains open to the variety and diversity of our experience and the images about us, including their conflictual nature, and therefore being alive?

By no means have I denied differences in specific attitudes or behavioural patterns between East and West Germans, conditioned by very different historical experiences. But "where a conflict of interests does exist, it may be rationalized by exaggerating [and re-interpreting] signs of allegedly inherent behavioural contrasts, which then serve as clear boundary markers" (Stevenson, 2002: 232). As an example, studies about linguistic differences between East and West found a communicative dissonance in encounters between East and West Germans: a 'communication without understanding'. However, the authors of one such study warn of interpreting them as different communicative practices: "The economic and social competition between East and West could well lead to an attempt to stabilize differences between ingroup and outgroup by focusing on and over-emphasizing supposed linguistic differences" (Antos & Richter, 2000: 77, translated for this edition). Language can, thus, become, self-attributed or ascribed, a symbol of a group identity associated with political allegiance or social, intellectual or moral worth. Think of Saxon or Kanak, which are spread today by almost every German cabaret artist.

Underpinning this perspective somewhat theoretically, I want to build on the thinking of Maurice Halbwachs (1985). Remembering and memory are always linked to concrete social actors. Outside of social groups, there is no social memory. The interactions of the group members, their mutual knowledge and recognition, form a transpersonal network for which Foulkes (1964) coined the term "matrix". This concept could be extended by means of a cultural science perspective. Thus, each group matrix is embedded in a sociocultural interpretative context which pre-forms experience, but can also be modified by experience. Collective symbolic forms make up social frames that guide our thinking and determine how we experience each other, that is, what we in a group may think, feel and remember. That's a key message of Halbwachs. I would like to add another dimension. Power and dependency are basic human experiences and constitutive for groups. They are also part of the collective symbolic order and are perpetuated by it.

From a group-analytic perspective it could be interesting to approach social framings with the concept of an "exclusionary matrix", a term coined by Mills (2005). It signifies the production of a "dangerous, abject region that circumscribes the identities of ideas, institutions, and selves" (Mills, 2005: 7). In *The World Within the Group* (2014) Martin Weegmann keeps track of the various manifestations of this configuration. As an example, he examined Phillipe Morel's concept of "degeneracy". In the 19th century, it produced an entire conceptual apparatus, and constructed groups, categories, and fears as objects of care and intervention. In addition to the mentally ill, homosexuals, with their promiscuity and sexual instinct, were seen as a threat to the fitness and public health of the emerging nations. In the period of the great social and political changes brought about by the Industrial Revolution, they fulfilled the need for new ideologies: free enterprise, competition, struggle for world markets, colonization. They found their scientific rationalization in Darwinism and their social counterpart in Morel's concept of degeneracy: survival of the fittest, elimination of the unfit (Ellenberger, 2005). These examples show once again the close interaction between identity constructions and their social and political framing.

The uncivilized *Ossi*, who never had to learn how to work and to think independently in the GDR, can only lose in the free market economy. Therefore, productivity in East Germany is "traditionally low", as a reporter recently said, and incomes and pensions considerably lower than in the West: an unequal matrix. The 'mentality problems' diagnosed by Christian Meier is a narrative which helps to make arrangements in a united Germany because it largely conceals or displaces conflicts of interest. Furthermore, it helped to stabilize the newly forming power structures after the *Wende* by making the individual *Ossi* solely responsible for solving his problem and by narrowing the debate about the distribution of income and wealth down to the East–West scheme. For, today, Dortmund and Duisburg are the communities that run the highest poverty risk in Germany.

So, had we better refrain from using the term 'identity' in view of media staging and political instrumentalization? It has rightly been criticized that identity excludes conflict. However, a look at gender and anti-racist theories shows that their advocates emphasize a direct link between identity and political struggle. For example, the Afro-American writer, bell hooks, sees identity not as a constraint, but as a "stage in a process wherein one constructs radical black subjectivity" (Sardar & van Loon, 2010: 128–129). In order for it not to remain a 'fighting identity' and to generate other options besides assimilation, imitation or rebellion, hooks requests broadening the notions of black identity. They must be seen in the true complexity and diversity of 'blackness'. I like this perspective on identity. In this line of thought, 'easterness' would include my conflicting feelings and experiences with regard to the GDR without the need of excluding or denying anything about it. That's perhaps how we experienced ourselves in the photo matrix: we're on shaky ground. We long for a safe place that we know does not exist. If it were there, it would be a prison. In our differences, we come together. These are frightening, but make us alive. There is no turning back, and the future is uncertain. But we know that we are there.

Conclusion and summary

I have tried to provide some preliminary answers. They are not the ultimate truth, but one possible perspective on the "Ossi–Wessi poetry", to use Jürgen Streek's beautiful comparison again. Let me summarize my conclusions as follows.

Imagined or real existential threats, growing social inequality, and the transformation of power structures not only frequently constitute the framework for the re-formation of group identities, and that's where I'd like to position the categorical pair, Ossi–Wessi, but also lead to the homogenization of identity constructions, often creating strong loyalty ties among group members. This has several, partly contradictory, consequences: first the experience of belonging, security and personal strength can effectively allay social and existential fears (for example, fears of loss of identity and social decline during the great transformation). In addition, groups can, thus, legitimize and effectively represent their interests as social actors; the '3rd Generation East' is a good example. On the other hand, conflicts of interest may be concealed or manipulated by identity discourses, which help with stabilizing large groups. Take social distribution conflicts as an example that have nothing to do with East and West Germans.

Referring to identities only makes sense if their essence is replaced by the question of its construction within specific social and political contexts.

References

Antos, G. & Richter, S. (2000) "Sprachlosigkeit" Ost? Anmerkungen aus linguistischer Sicht, in: G. Jackman & I. F. Roe (Eds.), *Finding a Voice: Problems of Language in East German Society and Culture* (pp. 75–96). Amsterdam, the Netherlands: Rodopi.
Büchler, A., Kluge, U., Krüger, R., Preil, J. & Stöbe, M. (2011) Gefühle wie Treibholz. Unpublished manuscript.
Ellenberger, H. F. (2005) Die neuen Lehren: Darwin und Marx, in: *Die Entdeckung des Unbewußten* (pp. 323–341). Zurich: Diogenes.
Engler, W. (1992) *Die zivilisatorische Lücke. Versuche über den Staatssozialismus*. Frankfurt: Suhrkamp.
Foulkes, S. H. (1964) *Therapeutic Group Analysis*. London: George Allen & Unwin.
Freud, S. (1921) *Massenpsychologie und Ich-Analyse*, *GW* XIII. London: Imago.
Halbwachs, M. (1985) *Das Gedächtnis und seine sozialen Bedingungen*. Frankfurt: Suhrkamp.
Jureit, U. & Schneider, C. (2010) *Gefühlte Opfer. Illusionen der Vergangenheitsbewältigung*. Stuttgart: Klett-Cotta.
Meier, C. (2010) Mentalisierungsprobleme der deutschen, in: *Das Gebot zu vergessen und die Unabweisbarkeit des Erinnerns*. Munich: Siedler.

Mills, R. (2005) *Suspended Animation: Pain, Pleasure and Punishment in Medieval Culture.* London: Reaktion.

Nandy, A. (2008) Die Psychologie des Kolonialismus: Geschlecht, Alter und Ideologie in Britisch-Indien, in: *Der Intimfeind.* Nettersheim: Grasworzelrevolution, pp. 86–91.

Pates, R. & Schochow, M. (Eds.) (2013) *Der Ossi. Mikropolitische Studien über einen symbolischen Ausländer.* Berlin: Springer.

Sardar, Z. & van Loon, B. (2010) *Cultural Studies.* London: Icon Books.

Sievers, B. (2006) Vielleicht haben Bilder den Auftrag, einen in Kontakt mit dem Unheimlichen zu bringen. Die Soziale Photo-Matrix als ein Zugang zum Unbewussten in Organisationen, *Freie Assoziation* 9(2): 7–28.

Stevenson, P. (2002) *Language and Disunity. A Sociolinguistic History of East and West in Germany, 1945–2000.* Oxford: Oxford University Press.

Streek, J. (1995) Ethnomethodologische Indifferenz im Ost-West Verhältnis, in: M. Czyzewski, E. Gulich, H. Hausendorf & M. Kastner (Eds.), *Nationale Selbst- und Fremdbilder im Gespräch.* Wiesbaden: Springer, pp. 430–436.

Volkan, V. D. (2005) *Blindes Vertrauen: Großgruppen und ihre Führer in Zeiten der Krise und des Terrors.* Gießen: Psychosoziale-Verlag.

Weegmann, M. (2014) An exclusionary matrix: Degenerates, addicts, homosexuals, in: *The World Within the Group* (pp. 103–118). London: Karnac.

Wendl, J. (2010) Ein Ossi ist ein Ossi ist ein Osi … Regeln der medialen Berichterstattung über "Ossis" und "Wessis" in der Wochenzeitung Die Teit seit Mitte der 1990er Jahre, in: T. Ahbe, R. Gries & W. Schmale (Eds.), *Die Ostdeutschen in den Medien. Das Bild von den Anderen nach 1990.* Bonn: Bundeszentrale für politische Bildung.

Wolf, C. (2010). *Stadt der Engel oder The Overcoat of Dr. Freud.* Berlin: Suhrkamp.

22

ACCEPTING OTHERNESS TO FIND SAMENESS

When a Jewish child realizes that the therapist is an Arab

Caesar Hakim

Individual therapy, notwithstanding therapeutic approach, is based first of all upon the experiential event between two people. In regard to this I will first quote a paragraph from Erri De Luca's gripping book *God's Mountain*. A young boy says the following:

> ... Maria spat at his feet and left ... I've had it with this game, she said ... Now she doesn't want it anymore because *I'm here. I'm here.* It makes me feel important. Till now my being around or not didn't make a bit of difference. Maria says that I'm here. Before you know it, I realize that I'm here, too. I wonder whether I couldn't have realized this by myself. *I guess not. I guess it takes another person to tell you.*
>
> (De Luca, 2002, p. 45, *my italics*)

If I had to say in a few words what is the purpose of individual therapy beyond any particular culture, type of relationship or therapeutic approach, then I would have to say clearly and decisively that the goal of therapy is to let the Other know that he or she is here.

What is behind the sentence, "You are here!"? Well, it is the significance of everything – presence, identity, the feeling of unique existence – the feeling of the existence of a unique being facing the world. It is the recognition of the sameness between this being and other beings that are called humans. At the same time, it is acknowledgement of the uniqueness, the 'one-timeness' of this being – a being that exists on a continuum of past, present and future.

When the patient in our treatment begins to feel that he is someone facing the world, that he is a subject who can think, plan, carry out, feel – a subject who has a past, a present and a future, then it is possible to speak of the beginning of a process that we're moving towards in our treatment of people. When the patient lives in a reality in which he has no control over his life or choices, he senses that he is only an object to which things happen, often unplanned and unexpected. So, he feels the need to be constantly on guard against annihilation. As a result, there is a delay in the forming of the Self, of the subjective. The whole purpose of the therapy is to help him form a firm Self to be able to accept the other.

Case illustration

I'm presenting the case of Almog (pseudonym), whose treatment was undertaken very early in my career; it was in my first year as an intern in clinical psychology. When my identity as an Arab was revealed to Almog at some point in the therapy, it provoked fear in him and his reactions provoked a very hard feeling within myself. Almog couldn't differentiate between Palestinians or other Arab nationalities. The difficulty of being not acknowledged by Almog as Palestinian was similar to my hard experience of living in Israel as a Palestinian citizen and referred to as an Arab, ignoring my identity as a Palestinian.

Almog was 14 years old when we started therapy. At the beginning, he made good contact and quickly brought to our relationship his confused and chaotic world. One saw at first only his drawbacks. He dressed in many shirts and appeared to be a child who lacked understanding and was simple, confused and incoherent. But, slowly, one discovered that under all his shirts there is a hidden child, anxious with a low self-image. He is a child with many unused strengths. The many shirts seem like a wall between himself and others, representing many layers, many parts not connected to each other.

Almog had slight hypotonia, concentration and language problems. He had been followed medically since the age of two and intermittently received speech and physical therapy. At ages four, eight and 12, Almog was sent for psychological testing. The results showed a low level functioning and an overall learning disability in vocabulary and the visual-motoric area. Since nursery school, he hads studied in special programmes and when therapy began he was in a special education, seventh grade class.

Almog's relationships with his parents

Each of his parents saw Almog differently, each seeing only a part of him. It was clear that Almog formed a totally different kind of relationship with each one of them, and, with each, there were particular problems and complexities.

His mother saw him as a small, vulnerable child who needed never-ending help and protection. She had a hard time seeing his healthy and developing parts. As a result, her relationship with him was symbiotic and anxious. His father saw his competent and healthy parts, but had a hard time acknowledging his difficulties. Their relationships are frustrating and disappointing to all three of them.

Course of therapy

First stage (two months): "Your power resides in your shoulder!"

I saw him for the first time in the waiting room. I saw a young person, a little tall for his age, thin and with a delicate facial structure. He looked bizarre, as he was wearing several shirts, one over the other. He smiled easily and immediately established contact. Almog came upstairs with clumsy movements. I thought he might fall and walked after him so I could catch him if he did.

In the therapy room, Almog sits and begins to take off his shirts. I wonder when he would stop. "Hot?" I ask. "It's hot here", he says. He stands, walks around the room and says, "I want to play war [a card game]. Me and Nivah [his prior therapist] played war all the time. I'm really good in war", he adds.

While dealing the cards, I ask him about his prior therapy and how it was to go from one therapist to another when he is alone in the room without parents. Almog answers me, "It's okay". and announces that in the next meeting he wants to mix paints. "When I mix paint, I am smart", he explains. Apparently, Almog doesn't want me to think otherwise.

But at this point I only see what he's lacking. After the meeting I have many questions about the therapy on which I've embarked. How to treat such a child? To play war or to mix paints? Listen to him repeat sentences such as, "What a great move I made", "What a terrific opening move!" It will be a challenge. I should try to relate with his need to show me how good he is, but it would be hard to be enthusiastic.

After several meetings, Almog comes in an irritable mood. When I ask him what's going on, he tells me that the children in school are annoying him. They called him "ugly". "Dirty". When he was describing that, I could not stop thinking how many times I heard "Dirty Arab" in my childhood, and how many times, as a child in the neighbourhood, I heard the other children saying this. "I'll punch them in the face, that's what I'll do" he says. He tells me how he's going to hit them. But, when I ask him, "What did you actually do?", he answers me, "Nothing. I ignored them".

When I try to identify Almog's feelings and reflect them back to him, I don't know if he understands. He doesn't understand what's going on around him, what people think of him and how he feels. He uses my sentences and those of other people to express what he's thinking and feeling. He doesn't know how to react in social situations. The other children's bullying of him stirs something in me. Anger: it's hard for me to hear how the other children are making fun of him and hitting him, and he doesn't react.

In another session, Almog sees some darts. "What are those?" he asked. I perked up when I saw that he was taking an interest in a game other than war and mixing colours. I took a dart and showed him how to throw it. "No, no", he says, looking sad. "It's too hard". I urge him to try. He does but doesn't hit the target. He doesn't even hit the wall.

"See! I couldn't do it", he pouts. I hold the dart and he grabs it, copying how I held it. I throw mine and tell him, "Throw yours harder". He does and this time hits the target, though not in the middle. "I missed", he says again. I say, "You did very well", and I give him another dart. Almog throws and again misses the target. "I didn't get it", he pouts. "You don't have to be a champion", I say.

Now Almog begins to say sentences: "I did very well, not bad, I don't have to be a champion, I won't give up", as he's playing darts. He improves from session to session. I try to get him to focus on process. "There is good and there is better and there is even very good". This is a notion that was unknown in Almog's world. Either you are a champion or you are nothing.

In the session before a Christmas vacation break, Almog comes and says: "When I try to punch, I've got no strength in my hand". I feel Almog is looking for his physical and emotional strength. I tell him, "That strength is in your shoulder. For your hand to take power, you must move the shoulder forward". Almog practises and feels the strength in his hand. I tell him: "You thought you had no strength because you didn't know where it was". "It's in my shoulder", he answers. I find myself wondering where my strength is, as a therapist.

The second stage (8 months): Almog draws a cross

After the Christmas vacation, Almog comes into the therapy room. I heard from his mother that he punched a student in his class; he used the power in his shoulders and reacted to those who insulted him. He enters the room. First, he wants to draw and takes some crayons and draws two intersecting lines on the wall. Then, he wants to play soccer. While I'm trying to figure out if there are meanings to the intersecting lines, Almog jumps around and kicks in the direction of the goalpost. He mostly misses but even when he does, he yells: "What a great goal!" I feel that Almog is nervous about something and I ask him, "What did you draw?"

He stops the game and says, "Caesar, Can I ask you something?" "Of course", I answer. "Do you celebrate Christmas?" He's asking about my identity, I thought. I debate whether to answer directly or perhaps play for some time so that he might forget about it, then, with no conscious volition, I ask him if he wants to know whether I'm a Christian.

A: Yes.
C: What do you think I am?
A: I think you are not a Christian.
C: Why?
A: Because you don't speak Arabic.

I now see a different Almog, one who thinks, asks questions and draws conclusions. Another shirt has been taken off, another part of him is displayed, a part that sees I am different from him. He is not the same simple child who mixes colours and plays war or the only child who uses any intervention concretely, such as when he punched the student at school; he has the courage to ask directly about me.

At this point I don't know if revealing my identity will destroy something or frighten him. Both of us are uncomfortable.

Almog tells of his fear of the Christian neo-Nazis that hurt the Jewish people. At this moment I look at the two intersecting lines on the wall and suddenly I see a cross. I am shocked and try to stay in the moment. What a confusion: Arabs, "neo-nazis?" I thought. Where did he get that from? Is he afraid of me? "They hate Jewish people, Christians killed the Jews", Almog said.

I say in a low voice, choosing simple words, "Almog, you're afraid of all the children who are different from you. And from the Christians, who are different. Maybe you are afraid of me because I'm a Christian. You tried to tell me some of this in your drawing and you've learned that I am in fact different from you … [He said "yes".] You feel that many people are different from you and you don't get along with people different from you".

Almog continues to bring in his awkwardness and fear of me and all Arabs. But he can't seem to put me in a particular group. Who are the Arabs, the Christians, the Muslims? He doesn't know whether I'm a Muslim or a Christian in the next session. In one of his family trips to the Carmel Mountain, he discovers that there is yet another group: the Druze people. He asks me whether the Druze are also Arabs. He is interested in the differences and comparison between the Christian holidays and the Jewish holidays.

Almog makes abrupt turnabouts between excitement about, and fear of, the differences. He is flooded with fear and anxiety about exploring the differences between him and me and it's reflected in his behaviour. He begins to curse everyone: the Arabs, Hizballa, Nusrala, the Lebanese, and the students in his school. He's going to blow up everyone. He throws darts and says that they are 'Kassam' missiles, and that he'll blow up all the children at school, like the air force blew up Lebanon. After expressing his violent feelings, he seems to reverse and tries to get close to me by talking about

Christmas. He ends each session with two sentences: "It's nice at Christmas time, right Caesar? There are presents at Christmas time, right Caesar?"

Almog's need to know how I'm different and how I'm similar was a beginning of a process to accept each other in the therapy room that later helped us to accept more of our own selves. During the sessions, he tried to understand what is going on in the world around him. How things get mixed up and when anxiety appears. How frustrating not to know what's happening and how to behave, with whom one can get close. Who is like him and who is different? Almog goes back and forth from excitement to anxiety. But the movement seems smoother; we are talking about his fear.

In one session, he stops the game, and says, "You're a Christian. Christians aren't Muslims". It was during an election time in Israel. Almog starts to spout all kinds of slogans that we all saw on campaign posters and heard from both good and bad candidates. Almog recently learned to play the game of Taki (a children's card game). When we play, I begin to see that he's a more complex child than I originally thought. He opens a meeting by saying, "Caesar, Lieberman [an ultra-conservative candidate who is very nationalistic and not at all sympathetic to the Arabs] will win". Meanwhile, as we play, I wonder whether what he said was a clever move or simply a mistake – does he really understand what Lieberman ideas about Arabs are. And now I'm sitting across from Almog and the Taki cards get stuck in my hands. Almog yells at me another election slogan, "If there's no loyalty, there is no citizenship". This is one of the worst things that I could think of, except for the Nakba (exile of many Palestinians during the 1948 War), racism, prejudice and war. That a child in my treatment would shout such a sentence, in which my loyalty is challenged and my citizenship is cancelled, was hard for me. I didn't know what to say. I was only thinking that I would not let him win the Taki game today.

I look at Almog and try not to portray anger. I ask him what he thinks I feel when he says things like that. "I guess you don't feel very good". He answers. He goes on and says, "I hate the Arabs. You've got to blow them all up like we did in Gaza. They fired 80 missiles at Sderot [a town in southern Israel]". I stop the game and look at him again. "What?" he asks me, then goes on, "You're a Christian, the Christians aren't Muslims, right Caesar?" I sense I'm confused in looking for the best answer. His confusion washes over me. I'm angry, insulted, too weak to contain his anger or accept him. Maybe because my feelings are similar to his when he must face the children at school who insult him. I understand very well his need to come up with the 'right' answer when facing the children and his fear of their response if he doesn't. I tell him, "You are talking about very hard feelings and mixed thoughts like the colours that you mix every time".

"Yes", he says, "It's scary. You have to hide in a well-defended place, right Caesar?"... A long silence ...Then, Almog asks me: "Caesar, what is citizenship?"

I am looking at the clock and waiting for the session to end; I feel angry, insulted, weak and afraid of being swallowed up in his identity confusion. It isn't clear whether Almog understands what he's saying. But my feeling about being an Arab in Israel is similar to his feelings about the children that insult him, his confusion about how to respond and his fear about the reaction of the Other. I tell him that it's hard for me when I hear all this, but I understand what he's experiencing and can understand that he feels threatened.

Life gets complicated for Almog, and he comes to the room in which he has a growing relationship that is not less complicated than the life outside: a Christian therapist who is also an Arab. This occurs during a period that is equally complex. It's a period of war on Gaza and elections, when the differences between groups are so delineated and so many groups are competing for power. Almog is looking for a defended place where he can get out the confusion inside himself so that he can understand who he is. Talking about him and me helps him work out these issues. Perhaps it also helped me.

The third period (5 months): saving the coral

One day I get a telephone call from Almog's mother, who tells me that Almog is in the hospital. He had got up in the middle of his sleep that night, called his mother and then there was the sound of a loud fall. When his father went into the room, he saw Almog on the floor covered with blood. In the hospital it turned out that the fall and the blow to his head he received were the result of an epileptic fit.

Almog comes to the sessions afterwards bandaged, quiet and hardly gets out of the chair. I feel that Almog is trying to cope with the changes in behaviour, as would any epileptic child trying to take care of himself. He has to do this in addition to his efforts to cope with his other daily difficulties. Now he's got to study, sleep well and be less tired during the day. He can't sit in front of the television screen for more than half an hour so as not to bring on another fit. I experience him as more frustrated and having a hard time accepting his new reality.

"I can't do anything because of the drugs", he tells me resentfully in one of the meetings. "I can't play with the computer like I used to, I can't be like the other children". I tell him: "You can play with the computer but for a shorter time. You want to play longer to be exactly like the other kids. It's hard, isn't it?" I feel sorry for him, and I again find myself being a broker between him and his new and difficult reality.

> We deal with his social survival through discussing the television programme, *Survival*. Before our meeting I hadn't seen the Israeli programme, but I know the American one and also the programme in Arabic. I go home after the meeting and watch most of the earlier episodes from the week's show to bring myself up to date.
>
> In the next session I show him I know a lot about the show's participants, particularly about the show's most manipulative competitor. Almog calls her "the destructive blonde". Through discussing the TV programme, Almog is working out his thoughts about his own social survival. He tries to clarify how he should be in order to acquire immunity to rejection. He learns that it's better for him not to be an Arab. Neither is it good to be handsome and a friend with everyone. It's better to become a manipulator. I try to help him apply most of his conclusions from the TV programme to his daily survival with the other children.
>
> I become his ally. If both of us are rejected, then we should be friends. "You get rejected because you're an Arab. I get rejected because that's what always happens", Almog said. He searches for things we have in common. He tries to talk in Arabic sometimes. He counts the cards in Arabic. For a long time, I had been trying to understand Almog's 'language', and he's now trying to speak in my language. He uses me to understand what is happening to him at home and how he feels that he doesn't belong to his home, parents who see him as a retarded kid, a sister who thinks she is cleverer than him and mostly his father, who keeps telling him he should be more clever at school.

Discussion

In looking back over our treatment, I see that Almog repeatedly revealed a deeper understanding than he showed on the surface. At the start, I experienced him as a simple child, often functioning at an intellectually and socially low level. But, as we became closer, I learned that he had more strengths than I originally thought. He revealed part after part, like the many shirts he would wear one on top of the other.

Some of these parts aroused rejection in the people around him, some aroused their anxiety for him, and some parts aroused their compassion and empathy. The complete picture was hard to see. It took a lot of work to tolerate the confusion. His aggression and his lack of control made it hard to see the whole picture. But, with time and a growing intimacy, he brought to our relationship the many parts of his inner world and his different physical and emotional needs.

Going into Almog's world was a complex experience, like going under water. A coral (Almog's name in English) lives in warm, quiet water and needs a firm foundation to remain alive. But there are different and varied kinds of corals and some live in deeper water. Knowing them all depends on how deep you choose to dive. Knowing the 'other' depends on how deep you dive in yourself.

This unique experience that Almog and I had passed isn't a result of one particular smart intervention or another, but, rather, of the ongoing uniqueness of being the focus of someone else's interest, Telling him "You are here!". This is the significance of an expansive space, whose margins and edges are unclear. The patient experiences a special kind of freedom. He or she can explore freely, not always knowing exactly where they are going. This freedom includes the possibility of delving into the soul and finding things that may be in contrast to outer reality.

I don't mean containment, since the notion of containment includes the possibility of emptying something that we once filled. I mean, rather, integration, inclusion of what belongs to us but what hasn't yet been taken in because of a lack of the presence of an Other, or maybe because of hard feelings that accompanied the experience, or perhaps because there still wasn't a Self that could gather up these kinds of experiences.

It seems that Almog and I were able to get close to the fences and walls that we build to feel secure, keeping away the 'Other' behind the walls. I think we both could hear the voices of similarities that came out from beyond these walls, voices of fear and many other voices of basic needs that all we humans share in common. These voices were an opportunity to re-experience complexity in all its intensity and connect what happened within ourselves to life outside. Perhaps, then, it is possible to face the world and see the 'Other' as a subject, who can experience his desire to be free and not just be an object that knows how to feel distress, to attack and to cry. Or only to be a vulnerable object to which, at any moment, unexpected and unplanned things may happen. Rather, we can begin to advance to a process of self-preparation toward subjectivity. This is the whole purpose of therapy. Children in therapy look for unity with an 'Other', a partnership within which they will grow, within which they can build the foundations of the Self.

I feel that, with a wider subjective space, when we can start to hear and connect to the voices that come from beyond the wall that is built between Palestinians and Jewish people, we can start a process of growing towards acceptance. We can grow up and a compassion for the other can grow within us.

Reference

De Luca, E. (2002) *God's Mountain*. New York: Riverhead Books.

THANK YOU

to the authors who brought this book to life by dedicating a huge part of their time and energy to it;

to Peter von Tresckow for transforming the spirit of the book into his generous gift of the front page illustration;

to Christiane Freudenstein-Arnold for her emotional encouragement and the helpful introduction to the secrets of Excel;

to Michael Buchholz for generously sharing his skills with me whenever I needed it;

to Russell George, Elliott Morsia, and Nick Craggs from Routledge for their never ending professional support, for finding solutions for all sorts of problems and showing friendly patience towards me;

to Yvonne Doney for her most attentive and dedicated editing of the book chapters;

to Stefano Bolognini and Earl Hopper who promoted the project by providing me with encouraging blurbs;

and, last but not least, to Holger Schildt, who shared all the ups and downs I went through while working on this book.

INDEX

Note: *italic* page numbers refer to figures; Page numbers followed by "n" denote endnotes.

Abdel-Samad, Hamed 242
academia *see* educational counsellor training in Israel
academic faculty/profession, psychoanalysis as 160–161
acculturation in adolescence 248–249
acknowledgement 31
Acts 2: 1–13 21–22
Adams, Douglas 20
adolescence/adolescents: acculturation in 248–249; bicultural background, identity formation and 247; clinical vignettes 130–135; cyberspace in 129; Daniele case study 133–134; development 74; digital devices used in clinical settings 129–136; dissonant acculturation in 248; drives during 129; as easily seducible 252; Franco case study 132–133; identity and 129; identity formation in 248; Marco case study 130–132; Marina case study 134–135; migration and 247–258; peculiarities of 247–248; problems arising with migrants 250; psychic representation, cyberspace and 129; social networks 248; transcultural transference space for migrant 250, 258; traumatic experience, migration as 249, 258
affiliation, identity as 145–147, 150–151
Allport, G.W. 46, 53–54
Almog case study 273–280
Alpert, Augusta 105

Alvarez, Anne 212
Amati-Mehler, J. 160–161
Amir, Dana 205
analytic dialects 3, 5–6; constructive and destructive aspects of having different 6–10; Encyclopaedic Dictionary Project 14–15; as enrichment and asset 11–12; gaps in each 11; ideological prejudices 9; passwords, concepts as 8; potentials of Babel 10–12; quarters in city of Babel metaphor 7–8; translation and 12–15
Anderson, Geoffrey 122
Anna Karenina (Tolstoy) 235–236
anorexia nervosa, family therapy of: adolescent development 74; attitudes towards eating and slimness 71, 74; current developments 71–72; development of eating disorders, family influences on 74–75; development of the family, children and 73; individuation-separation difficulties 74–75, 79; 'inner family' 73; Julia case study 76–78; multigenerational 76–79; neurobiological dynamics 72; psychosomatic family model 72–73; regulation of affects 75; stages in 75; vicious circles 75
Anzieu, D. 101, 236–237
Appelfeld, Aharon 238
Arab educational counselling students in Israel *see* educational counsellor training in Israel

Arendt, Hannah 31
Aristophanes 124
art of being natural 156
asymmetry in communicative relationships 27
Attali, J. 123
Auschwitz 145
authority, therapeutic 156
Aviv, N. 238

Babel fish 13, 19n2, 20, 21
Babel metaphor: analytic quarters in 7–8; conflict following 4; constructive and destructive aspects of 6–10; folklore 163; language use as harmful 4; original text 20–21; potentials of Babel 10–12; profession/academic faculty, psychoanalysis as 160–161; psyche between 'inside' and 'beyond Babel' 15–18; religious interpretation of Bible story 3; sameness and otherness and xviii; translation 179; vertical logic 161–164
Babel of the Unconscious, The (Amati-Mehler) 160–161
Banks, Lillian 191–192, 195n1
Barlow, John Perry 116, 120
Bateson, Gregory 167
behavioural contrasts between East/West Germans 268
Benjamin, Walter 143–144, 188
Berenstein, J. 250
Bergson, Henri 10
Berlin, Germany *see* kindergartens
Berry, J. W. 249
bilingual patients: access to culture of countries 221; author's own experience 217–219; case studies 217–225; choice of first/second language 214–215, 217; creative potential of language switching 216–217, 226; creativity of language switching 216–217; emancipatory detachment 216–217; growth in instances of 214; identity 216–217; richness of dynamics 226; triangulation 226–227; *see also* language(s)
Bion, W. R. 5, 8, 10, 14, 88–89, 100, 164, 166, 167, 174, 179, 180, 190, 193, 202, 212
black identity 269
Blumenberg, Hans 144–145
Bolognini, Stefano 11–12, 182
Boston, M. 81
Bouchet, S. 129
boundary-breaking in translation 191–192

Braun, C. 40
Britton, R. 226
Bruner, J. 205
Buchholz, M. B. 161, 167
building of a tower, psychoanalytic work as 170, 171, 172–173, 176
Burck, Charlotte 216, 217, 226
Butler, Judith 99–100

Canham, H. 82, 84
carers in kindergartens 106
Carr, N. 116, 119
Cassirer, Ernst 143
Caterina case study 63–64
chess computer 177
Chiara and Paolo case study 61–63
Chiland, Colette 96
children: choice not to have 60–61, 66; *see also* adolescence/adolescents; kindergartens, educational and therapeutic work in; sibling groups of looked after children
Cierpka, M. 73, 74–75
civilization: mutual transformation with the unconscious 58; new psychic configurations due to 58
Civilization and It's Discontents (Freud) 34, 57
Clarke, Arthur C. 116
clinical psychoanalysis 166
closeness 30–31
cloud metaphor 123–124
Clouds (Aristophanes) 124
coenaesthesia 152–153
collective identity 145–147
communication: behavioural contrasts between East/West Germans 268; coenaesthesia 152–153; information/ performance 153–154
compromise, identity and 149
concrete language 205
Contact Hypothesis 46, 53–54
counsellor training *see* educational counsellor training in Israel
countertransference: group supervision 198; supervision and 197; translation 192
creativity: potential of language switching 216–217; in translation 190–191
cross-cultural training for educational counsellors *see* educational counsellor training in Israel
cultural and social changes: Caterina case study 63–64; Chiara and Paolo case study 61–63; children, choice not to have 66;

families and 58–59; impact of 57; myths 58, 66; new psychic configurations due to 58; professional and family/personal lives of women, reconciliation of 59–66; time for, continuity and 66; Tina and Stefano case study 64–65
cultural identity *see* educational counsellor training in Israel
cultural sensitivity, competence and knowledge 46
cultural thinking, development of 167
culture(s): interrelationship with language 10; psyche and 17
cyberspace *see* teletherapy
Cyberspace Independence Declaration 116, 120

Daniele case study 133–134
Davidson, Donald 22
de Chirico, Giorgio 234
De Luca, Erri 272
de-professionalisation 156
Deep Blue chess computer 177
Defying Hitler (Haffner) 31
degeneracy 269
Deutsch, Helene 98
Deutsches Wesen (Floerke) 143, 145
developmental psychology 166–167
dialects, analytic 3, 5–6; constructive and destructive aspects of having different 6–10; Encyclopaedic Dictionary Project 14–15; as enrichment and asset 11–12; gaps in each 11; ideological prejudices 9; passwords, concepts as 8; potentials of Babel 10–12; quarters in city of Babel metaphor 7–8; translation and 12–15
dialogue work 108
Die Brücke vom Goldenen Horn (Özdamar) 233–234
difference: constructive and destructive aspects of 6–10; Encyclopaedic Dictionary Project 14–15; as enrichment and asset 11–12; gaps in each view of psyche 11; ideological prejudices 9; influence on language 9; passwords, concepts as 8; potentials of Babel 10–12; translation and 12–15
digital era *see* technology; teletherapy
discourses: constructive and destructive aspects of having different 6–10; diversity of 5–6; ideological prejudices 9; tradition of scientific discourse 8
diversity: constructive and destructive aspects of 6–10; Encyclopaedic Dictionary Project 14–15; as enrichment and asset 11–12; gaps in each view of psyche 11; ideological prejudices 9; influence on language 9; of language in psychoanalysis 3–4; passwords, concepts as 8; potentials of Babel 10–12; translation and 12–15
Döring, N. 38
Dornes, M. 166
double novel/identities 141–142
Duncan, B. L. 168

East/West Germany: author's experience 261; behavioural contrasts 268; Dritte Generation Ost 267; East German identity 263–270; exclusionary matrix 269; group matrices 268–269; homogenization of identity constructions 270; identity, use of term 269–270; identity of West and East Germans 261–270; Ossi-Wessi 266–267, 269; social photo matrix method 263–265; unification, impact of 266–267
eating disorders *see* anorexia nervosa, family therapy of
Eco, Umberto 193
Edison, Thomas 120
educational counsellor training in Israel: benefit of Arab/Jewish encounters 54; choice to study together 47–49; Contact Hypothesis 46, 53–54; cultural sensitivity, competence and knowledge 46; explosion of tensions 50–53; guidance for Arab/Jewish students 54; mix of Arab/Jewish students, coping with 52–53; multi-ethnic society 45, 46; past multiculturalism, experience of students 54; philosophy of learning objectives 54; research context 45; research findings 47–53; research population and methodology 46–47; symmetry, Arab/Jewish, creation of 53–54; unspoken tensions 49–50
Eiguer, Alberto 100
emancipatory detachment 216–217
Emanuel, L. 82
emotional development, language and 234–236
Encyclopaedic Dictionary Project 14–15
endogenous determinism of the psyche 58
enhancements in translation 191–192
Erlich, S. 65
Eugenides, J. 145

everyday psychology, psychoanalysis and 175
evocative objects 117–118
exclusionary matrix 269
exile experiences and fantasies 165–166
expert's sovereignty as recognition of dependence 151–152

families, impact on of social and cultural changes 57–59
family therapy of anorexia nervosa: adolescent development 74; attitudes towards eating and slimness 71, 74; current developments 71–72; development of eating disorders, family influences on 74–75; development of the family, children and 73; individuation-separation difficulties 74–75, 79; 'inner family' 73; Julia case study 76–78; multigenerational 76–79; neurobiological dynamics 72; psychosomatic family model 72–73; regulation of affects 75; specificity/non-specificity 72; stages in 75; vicious circles 75
Fédida, P. 203
feminine, the, in psychoanalysis 97–100
feminine myths, transmission of 96–97
Ferenczi, S. 136, 164
Ferguson, N. 147
Ferruta, A. 198
Floerke, H. 143, 145
Folk-Lore in the Old Testament (Frazer) 163
Fonagy, P. 166
foreign language acquisition and appropriation 183–185
Forty-two Lives in Treatment (Wallerstein) 149–150
Foulkes, S. H. 268
Fouqué, Freidrich de la Motte- 142
Franco case study 132–133
Fremdsprechen (Kinsky) 180
Freud, Sigmund 12, 17; analyst as translator 188; communication of interpretations 28, 34; compromise and 149; dark side of people 8; everyday formula of understanding 175; exile fantasy 165; feminine in psychoanalysis 97–98; Fließ, letter to 187, 188; god, man's likeness to 34; identity 263; inexhaustability of translation 185; interpretation of dreams 142–143; as migrant 244; mortality 120; object of the cure 144; pre-language of psychoanalysis, oeuvre as 167; reading and re-reading of 163–164; and Sherlock Holmes 142; social/individual psychology 57–58; translation of concepts 9; uncanny, the 113, 116, 120; vertical logic and 164
Fydrich, T. 160

Geier, Svetlana 178, 188–189, 191, 193, 242
gender identity and the family: definitions 95–96; family psychoanalytic theories 100–101; feminine in psychoanalysis 97–100; links 100–101; sexual identity and 96; transmission of feminine/societal myths 96–97
genealogical tree of psychoanalysis 7–8
Genesis 11: 1–9 20–21
Germany: German-ness 143–144; Second World War, psychoanalysis after 165; *see also* East/West Germany; kindergartens
Gills, Merton 150
Glenn, J. 212
glossolalia 21
Göddes, G. 161
God's Mountain (De Luca) 272
Goethe, J. W. von 31, 195
Goldberg, F. 114
Goldschmit, Georges-Arthur 9, 10, 11
Green, André 9, 13, 166
Greenson, R. R. 214
group supervision: as analytic experience 198; choice of case to bring to 203; conflicts, reduction of 199; containing function 203; disruptive patients 202; emotions, analyst's, working out of 201; examples of 200–203; group mind, birth of 199; as guided dreaming 197–198, 203, 204; images arising from 200–201; origins of supervision 197; otherness and strangeness 198; patient's experience, entering into 200; reasons for wanting supervision 197; risk of supervision 197; silence, use of in 200–203, 204; supervisor as group member 199–200; temporal-musical metaphor 204; time suspension in 200–203, 204; transference and countertransference 197, 198; transgenerational issues 202–203; weaving thoughts method 199
guided dreaming, supervision as 197–198, 203, 204, 206, 211
Gumbrecht, H. 122–123, 125
Gutton, P. 129

Habermas, J. 118
Haffner, Sebastian 31
Halbwachs, Maurice 147, 268
Hegel, G. W. F. 31

Herrmann, Andreas 150
Herrndorf, Wolfgang 145–146
Hindle, D. 81
Hitchhiker's Guide to the Galaxy, The (Adams) 20
Hoffmann, Eva 216, 226
Holmes, Sherlock 142
Holz, Detlef (Walter Benjamin) 143–144
hooks, bell 269
horizontal logic 166–167
Hubble, M. A. 168

'Identität im Wandel' (Seiffge-Krenke) 149
identity: acknowledgement of the other xviii; adolescence and 129, 247, 248; as affiliation 145–147, 150–151; application of concept of 147–148; bicultural background and 247; bilingual patients 216–217; black 269; collective 145–147; crises 141–142; as criticism tool 148; cultural difference 147; double novel/identities 141–142; East German identity 263–270; formation in adolescents 248; historical burden of concept 141–151; homogenization of identity constructions 270; immigrants, language and 242–244; mother tongue 237; original self, concept of 143; paradoxes of psychoanalytical practice 151–156; political context 147; in psychoanalysis 148–151; publications on, amount of 144, 147; search for 142; self as other xviii; sovereignty as recognition of dependence 152; tone of voice addressed with 235–236; transfer to psychological applications 148; violence and 146–147; violent potential of 149–150; of West and East Germans 261–270
ideological prejudices 9
If ... (Anderson) (film) 30
illusion of reality 155–156
immigrants *see* migrants
inanimate objects 119
incompleteness in translation 193
individual/social psychology, link between 57–58
individuation-separation difficulties 74–75, 79
information/performance 153–154
'inner family' 73
inner/outer worlds 155
integrative pluralism, move to 167–168
interactive process, psychoanalytic procedure as 170

interdisciplinary discourses 5–6; translation and 13
International Psychoanalytic Association (IPA) 13–14
internet: case vignette 36–39; impact of 33–34; psychoanalysis applied to use of 41; reality or illusion 34; relationships via 36–41; scepticism/optimism regarding 35; transitional objects, mobile phones as 35–41; virtuality or reality 34; *see also* mobile phones; Society 2.0; technology; teletherapy
interpretation 25–30
Interpretation of Dreams, The (Freud) 142–143, 185
intersubjectivity, links and 100
Israel *see* educational counsellor training in Israel

Jahn, Turnvater 143, 147
James, William 144, 147
Japan 60
Jewish educational counselling students in Israel *see* educational counsellor training in Israel
Jewishness, history of 165
Jones, Ernest 9
Julia case study 76–78
Jureit, U. 263

'K-IPU' 109–110
Kaës, R. 58, 100, 128
Kaiser, Reinhard 189
Katan, Anny 104
Kernberg, Otto 9, 13, 248
kindergartens, educational and therapeutic work in 103–104; carers 106, 108–109; dialogue work 108; goals of project 105; history of therapeutic work in kindergartens 104–105; location of kindergarten 105; low socio-economic circumstances, children in 103; parent-child relationship, strengthening 105–110; participant families 106; psychotherapist's role 106–109; results of pilot phase 109; self-reflection of parents 108; student mentoring project 109–110; support needs of children 106; therapeutic-pedagogical work in 104–105; video work 108; 'Watch, wait and wonder' activity 108
Kinsky, Esther 180, 184, 186–187
Klein, Melanie 166, 167
Koestler, Arthur 4
Krämer, S. 116, 125

Krejci, Erika 182, 191
Kristeva, J. 58, 65
Krystal, H. 234

language(s): behavioural contrasts between East/West Germans 268; as calming and supporting 236–237; concrete language 205; constructive power of 168; as context/situation-bound 235–236; development of 205, 234–236, 239; emotional authentic, lack of 205; emotional development and 234–236; Encyclopaedic Dictionary Project 14–15; harmful use of 4; identity, immigrants and 242–244; interrelationship with culture and the world 10; manifold uses of 4–5; multilingual patients 240–242; potentials of Babel 10–12; psyche and 10–11; scientific worldviews, influence on 9; semantic differences between 235; separation function of 237–238; as sound envelope 236–237; transitional function of speaking and 239; translation and 12–15; understanding as language game 22–23; unity-of-science movement 9–10; universal 168; *see also* bilingual patients; linguistic confusion in the psychoanalytic process; translation
Laplanche, Jean 188, 203
Leikert, Sebastian 153
Lemma, Alessandra 35, 38, 41
Leonhardt, J. 146
Let's Spoil the Party (Polanski) (film) 148
Levine, M. 74
Life-Time and World-Time (Blumenberg) 144–145
Lindsey, R. 46
linguistic confusion in the psychoanalytic process: building of a tower, psychoanalytic work as 170, 171, 172–173, 176; everyday psychology, psychoanalysis and 175; interactive process, psychoanalytic procedure as 170; interpretation of patient's actions 172–174; non-understanding 172, 174; *see also* language(s); translation
links 100–101
Löchel, E. 34–35, 41
looked after children *see* sibling groups of looked after children

Macho, T. 120
Mann, David 27
Marcia, J. E. 248
Marco case study 130–132

Marina case study 134–135
Matahara Net 60
maternity as obstacle to one's life 60–61, 66
McDonough, S. C. 108
McLuhan, Marshall 115–116
Meier, Christian 262, 266
melancholia, overlap with sameness and otherness 81
men, role in families 66
mentalisation 167
'Mentality problems of German unification' (Meier) 262
mentoring project in kindergarten project 109–110
Merton, Robert K. 164
metaphors: cloud, in teletherapy 123–124; temporal-musical metaphor for group supervision 204; use of regarding the psyche 167; *see also* Babel metaphor
micro-interventions 182
Middlesex (Eugenides) 145
migrants: acculturation, in adolescence 248–249; adolescence 247–258; children 242–244; context/situation-bound, language as 235–236; identity 242–244; language 234–236, 242–244; multilingual patients 240–242; problems arising with adolescent 250; psychoanalytic treatment 249–250; resistance to new language 237; risk for psychic disorders 249; semantic differences between languages 235; separation function of language 237–238; sound envelope, language as 236–237; transcultural transference space for 250, 258; transitional function of speaking and language 239; transitional space, linguistic space as 234; traumatic experience, migration as 249, 258; verbal world created by language 233–234
Milgram Experiment 148
Miller, S. D. 168
Minuchin, S. 72
miracle of Pentecost 21
Mishol, Agi 236
Miss May vignette 181–182
misunderstanding 23–24, 26
Mitchell, G. 119
Mitchell, Juliet 99
Mitrani, Judith 212
mobile phones: as erotically charged 35; impact of 33–34; psychoanalysis applied to use of 41; reality or illusion 34; relationships via 36–41; scepticism/optimism regarding 35; as transitional

objects 35–41; virtuality or reality 34; *see also* internet; technology
Monniello, G. 129, 130
Morel, Phillipe 269
Morgenstern, Christian 153
Moser, K. 144
Moses XI 1 162–163
mother tongue 236–237
motherhood as obstacle to one's life 60–61
mourning, overlap with sameness and otherness 81
multiculturalism *see* educational counsellor training in Israel
multigenerational approach in family therapy 76–79
multilingual patients 240–242; *see also* bilingual patients
Musil, Robert 155
myths 58, 66; evolutionary perspective, differentiating from 168; feminine in psychoanalysis 97–100; transmission of feminine/societal myths 96–97

Nach Babel. Aspekte der Sprache und des Übersetzens (Steiner) 168
Neumann, Wilhelm 141–142
neurosciences 16–17
Newitz, A. 118
Niethammer, Lutz 145, 147–148
Nina (case vignette) 36–39
'No kids' movements 60–61
nomadic objects 123
Norman, J. 199
Novolletto, A. 136

Oedipus complex 97–98, 99
Ogden, Thomas 14, 197–198, 206
On the Shoulders of Giants (Merton) 164
online therapy *see* teletherapy
original self, concept of 143
Ossi-Wessi 266–267
otherness: Almog case study 273–280; Babel and xviii; constructive and destructive aspects of 6–10; overlap with mourning and melancholia 81; psychoanalysis as valuing xviii; sameness as linked to xviii
outer/inner worlds 155
Özdamar, Emine Sevgi 233–234

Paolo and Chiara case study 61–63
paradoxes of psychoanalytical practice 151–156
participatory knowledge 153
passwords, concepts as 8
Pates, R. 267

Patient and the Analyst, The (Sandler, Holder and Dare) 13
Paul, Jean 141, 142, 147
Pedaia, Haviva 238
peer supervision *see* group supervision
Pentecost, miracle of 21
Pentecostalism 21
performance/information 153–154
personal encounters in impersonal spaces 154
personal objects 118–119
Philosophical Investigations (Wittgenstein) 22–23
Pierce, C. S. 13
Pisa Study 247
Plato 96
Polanski, Roman 148
politics: closeness and community 31; identity and 147; interpretation in 28–30
Pretorius, Inge 105
prison study, Stamford 148
profession/academic faculty, psychoanalysis as 160–161
professionalisation 156
projection, interpretation or 29
projective identification 5
psyche: culture(s) and 17; definition of, lack of consensus on 5; endogenous determinism of 58; gaps in each view of 11; between 'inside' and 'beyond Babel' 15–18; language and 10–11; metaphors, use of regarding 167; neurosciences and 16–17; potentials of Babel 10–12; self-awareness, limits of 17; as translating apparatus 187–188; vagueness and complexity of 12
psychoanalysis: Almog case study 273–280; clinical 166; diverse voices in, reasons for 5–6; exile fantasy 165–166; feminine in 97–100; identity in 148–151; language diversity in 3–4; modern questions and 41; motivation for change from within 15; paradoxes of practice 151–156; as profession/academic faculty 160–161; purpose of therapy 272–273; as science or not 6
Psychoanalysis Online (Scharff) 114
psychoanalytic identity: historical burden of identity concept 141–151; paradoxes of psychoanalytical practice 151–156
psychoanalytic scenes: cracks and gaps in 172; using 171–172
psychosomatic family model 72–73
Psychotherapy, an Erotic Relationship (Mann) 27
Puget, J. 250

reality of illusion 155–156
Reid, Susan 81–82
remodelling of a tower, psychoanalytic work as 170, 171, 172–173, 176
remote therapies *see* teletherapy
representation, psychic, cyberspace and 129
Richards, A. K. 114
Riederle, Philipp 33
'right to be forgotten' 123
Rimbaud, Arthur xviii
Rivière, Pichon 100
Rolnick, Eran 164
Rorty, Richard 31
Rosenblitt, D. L. 105
Rousseau, Jean-Jacques 97
Russell, Bertrand 25

Salomonsson, B. 199
sameness: Almog case study 273–280; Babel and xviii; otherness as linked to xviii; overlap with mourning and melancholia 81
Sas, Amati 60
Scarfone, Dominique 187, 194
Schaeffer, J. 99
Scharff, J. S. 114
Schäuble, Wolfgang 266
Schmidt, Arno 31
Schneider, C. 263
Schochow, M. 267
science: constructive and destructive aspects of different discourses 6–10; diversity of worldviews 5–6; God's creation plan, search for 3; ideological prejudices 9; tradition of scientific discourse 8; unity-of-science movement 9–10
Searles, H. 206
Second World War, psychoanalysis after 165
Seiffge-Krenke, I. 149
self: bilingual patients 216; original self, concept of 143; as other xviii; publications on, amount of 144
self-awareness, limits of 17
Serres, Michel 35
Sherlock Holmes 142
Shulman, G. 81
sibling groups of looked after children: adults, denial of need for 84–86; assessment of children 82, *82–83*; departure to new families *88*, 88–93, *91*; feelings, management of 84–88; loss, children's sense of 83; loss and departures 88–93; mourning/separation, working through 84–88, *85*, 93; network surrounding 83–84; personalities,

patterns in looked after children 81; referral of children 82; separate foster/adoption placements 83–84; usefulness of groups 81–82
Silverstone, Jennifer 85
Skype, psychotherapy via 113–115, 117–118, 119–125
smartphones *see* mobile phones
Smolak, L. 74
social and cultural changes: Caterina case study 63–64; Chiara and Paolo case study 61–63; children, choice not to have 60–61, 66; families and 58–59; impact of 57; myths 58, 66; new psychic configurations due to 58; professional and family/personal lives of women, reconciliation of 59–66; psychic changes and 128; time for, continuity and 66; Tina and Stefano case study 64–65
social/individual psychology, link between 57–58
social media *see* mobile phones; Society 2.0; technology
social networks, adolescence and 248
social photo matrix method 263–265
societal myths, transmission of 96–97
Society 2.0: adolescence, cyberspace in 129; adolescent patient settings 129–135; analyst's attitude to technology 136; clinical vignettes 130–135; Daniele case study 133–134; digital devices used in clinical settings 129–136; Franco case study 132–133; Marco case study 130–132; Marina case study 134–135; psychic changes, societal changes and 128; reflection on as complex 127
sound envelope, language as 236–237
sovereignty as recognition of dependence 151–152
Spence, D. P. 142
St Jerome 193
Stamford prison study 148
Standard Edition of the Complete Psychological Works of Sigmund Freud - translation of terms in 9
STEEP™ 108
Steiner, G. 168, 177
Steiner, Ricardo 9
Stern, Daniel 152, 237–238, 239
Streek, Jürgen 266
Strober, M. 75
Strømme, H. 197
student mentoring project in kindergarten project 109–110
subsumption, logic of 161

supervision: clinical illustration 206–212; concrete language 205, 208; countertransference 207; deadness in transference 208; emotional authentic language, lack of 205; feelings, supervisor's 206; fiction, creation of in 206; as guided dreaming 197–198, 203, 204, 206, 211; *see also* group supervision
symbolisation 167
synaesthetic auricular reading 185
Szur, R. 81

Target, M. 166
Task of the Translator, The (Benjamin) 188
technology: case vignette 36–39; generational rift 127; impact of 33–34; psychoanalysis applied to use of 41; reality or illusion 34; relationships via 36–41; scepticism/optimism regarding 35; transitional objects, mobile phones as 35–41; virtuality or reality 34; *see also* mobile phones; Society 2.0; teletherapy
teletherapy: attitudes towards 114; cloud metaphor 123–124; disembodiment 120; emotional presence through 121; evocative objects 117–118; extent of use 114; and the future 125; icons, significance of 121; impact on analysts/analysands/analytic process 115–125; inanimate objects 119; interference due to 117; nomadic objects 123; personal objects 118–119; projections and transmissions as easy 122; relationship, change in due to 117; 'right to be forgotten' 123; silence and 122; technical difficulties, impact of 115, 117, 121–122; training of analysts 114; uncanny, the 113, 116, 120, 123; via Skype/Zoom 113–115, 117–118, 119–125
textbooks, translation and 13
therapeutic situations: closeness, understanding as 31; interpretation in 27–28, 30
therapists as always patients 155
Tietze, W. 106
Timaeus (Plato) 96
Tisseron, S. 133, 136
Tolstoy, L. 235–236
Tomasello, M. 167
training of educational counsellors *see* educational counsellor training in Israel
transcultural transference space for adolescent migrants 258
transference: deadness in 208; group supervision 198; supervision and 197; as total situation 5; as used relationship 153–154
transformation in translation 193–194
transgenerational issues: group supervision 202–203; second language use in analysis 217–219
transitional objects/spaces 118; case vignette 36–39; defined 35–36; mobile phones as 35–41
translation: acquisition and appropriation of foreign language 183–185; analyst as translator 187–188; coming into the text/penetrating the text 185; computer programmes 177–178; countertransference 192; creativity 190–191; de-translation of what patients bring 179, 182; earliest representation of 179; Encyclopaedic Dictionary Project 14–15; enhancements and boundary-breaking 191–192; foreign language learning 194; of Freudian concepts 9; incompleteness 193; inexhaustability of 185; influential impact 185–188; internal order, rules and regulations 188–190; limits of translatability 192; micro-interventions 182; Miss May vignette 181–182; morphological structure, process as *182*; need for 12–13; need to be understood 178; as primal human activity 178; responsibility 185–188, 194–195; six dimensions of process of *182*, 182–194; synaesthetic auricular reading 185; textbooks and 13; Tower of Babel 179; transformation 193–194; of translations 188; (un)becoming familiar/becoming (un)familiar 184–185; *see also* bilingual patients; language(s)
triangulation 226–227
Tschick (Wolfgang) 145–146
Turkle, S. 125

uncanny, the 113, 116, 120, 123
unconscious self as other xviii
understanding: *Acts 2: 1–13* 21–22; closeness 30–31; everyday psychology, psychoanalysis and 175; *Genesis 11: 1–9* 20–21; interpretation and 25–30; interpretation of patient's actions 172–174, 176; lack of 23–24; as language game 22–23; misunderstanding 23–24, 26; need to be understood 178; as non-activity 21, 24; non-understanding 172, 174; original text of Babel metaphor 20–21; *Verständnis* 30–31
United States 60

unity-of-science movement 9–10
universal language 168
used relationship, transference as 153–154

Varnhagen, Karl August 141–142
Verständnis 30–31
vertical logic 161–164
video telephony *see* teletherapy
video work 108
violence, identity and 146–147
virtuality: case vignette 36–39; definition problem 34; or reality 34; use of term 34–35

Wallerstein, Robert 9, 149–150
'Watch, wait and wonder' activity 108
Watzlawick, P. 171
weaving thoughts method 199
Wednesday Society 143
Weegmann, Martin 269
West/East Germany: author's experience 261; Dritte Generation Ost 267; East German identity 263–270; exclusionary matrix 269; group matrices 268–269; homogenization of identity constructions 270; identity, use of term 269–270; identity of West and East Germans 261–270; Ossi-Wessi 266–267, 269; social photo matrix method 263–265; unification, impact of 266–267
Winnicott, D. W. 35–36, 36, 40, 118, 250
Wittgenstein, L. 22–24
Wolf, Christa 268
Woman with the Five Elephants, The (Geier) 188–189
women: Caterina case study 63–64; Chiara and Paolo case study 61–63; children, choice not to have 60–61, 66; feminine/societal myths, transmission of 96–97; professional and family/personal lives, reconciliation of 59–66; social and cultural changes, impact of 57; Tina and Stefano case study 64–65
Wood, Beatrice 73
world, the, interrelationship with language 10
World Within the Group, The (Weegmann) 269
worldviews: constructive and destructive aspects of having different 6–10; diversity of 5–6; influence on language 9

Zimbardo, Philipp 148
Zoom, psychotherapy via 113